ABOUT TEACHING
Mathematics

ABOUT TEACHING
Mathematics
A K-8 RESOURCE
MARILYN BURNS

THIRD EDITION

Math Solutions Publications
Sausalito, CA

Math Solutions Publications
A division of
Marilyn Burns Education Associates
150 Gate 5 Road, Suite 101
Sausalito, CA 94965
www.mathsolutions.com

*Acknowledgments for adapted material may be found on page 447, an
extension of the copyright page.*

Library of Congress Cataloging-in-Publication Data
Burns, Marilyn, 1941–
    About teaching mathematics : a K–8 resource / Marilyn Burns. —
3rd ed.
        p. cm.
    Includes bibliographical references and index.
    ISBN-13: 978-0-941355-76-6
    ISBN-10: 0-941355-76-4
    1. Mathematics—Study and teaching (Elementary) I. Title.
    QA135.6.B76847 2007
    372.7—dc22
                                            2007018870

Editor: Toby Gordon
Production: Melissa L. Inglis
Cover & interior design: Catherine Hawkes/Cat & Mouse
Composition: ICC Macmillan Inc.

Printed in the United States of America on acid-free paper
11 10 09 08 ML   2 3 4 5

A Message from Marilyn Burns

We at Math Solutions Professional Development believe that teaching math well calls for increasing our understanding of the math we teach, seeking deeper insights into how children learn mathematics, and refining our lessons to best promote students' learning.

Math Solutions Publications shares classroom-tested lessons and teaching expertise from our faculty of Math Solutions Inservice instructors as well as from other respected math educators. Our publications are part of the nationwide effort we've made since 1984 that now includes

- more than five hundred face-to-face inservice programs each year for teachers and administrators in districts across the country;
- annually publishing professional development books, now totaling more than sixty titles and spanning the teaching of all math topics in kindergarten through grade 8;
- four series of videotapes for teachers, plus a videotape for parents, that show math lessons taught in actual classrooms;
- on-site visits to schools to help refine teaching strategies and assess student learning; and
- free online support, including grade-level lessons, book reviews, inservice information, and district feedback, all in our quarterly *Math Solutions Online Newsletter.*

For information about all of the products and services we have available, please visit our website at *www.mathsolutions.com.* You can also contact us to discuss math professional development needs by calling (800) 868-9092 or by sending an email to *info@mathsolutions.com.*

We're always eager for your feedback and interested in learning about your particular needs. We look forward to hearing from you.

Math Solutions®
PUBLICATIONS

Contents

Preface to the Third Edition   *xiii*
Introduction   *xv*

PART 1   Raising the Issues   1

Introduction   3
You Can't Teach What You Don't Understand   5
A Perspective on Arithmetic   7
Examining Children's Common Arithmetic Errors   10
Using Word Problems to Develop Arithmetic Understanding   13
Beyond Word Problems   16
     What Is and Is Not a Problem?   17
     Problem-Solving Strategies   19
     Pros and Cons of Problem Solving   22
Building Number Sense   24
How Children Learn Mathematics   27
The Role of Manipulative Materials   33
The Importance of Class Discussions   36
Incorporating Writing into Math Instruction   38
     A Variety of Writing Assignments   38
     Strategies for Incorporating Writing   40
Teaching Math Vocabulary   42
Using Children's Literature   45
Linking Assessment and Instruction   47
     Assessment Through Students' Written Work   48
     Assessment Through Classroom Discussion   49
     Improving Mathematics Teaching   50
Managing Classroom Instruction   51
     Organizing for Small-Group Work   52
     Structuring Lessons   54
     A Sample Lesson: The Consecutive Sums Problem   57
     Structuring Independent Work: The Menu   60
     Sample Classroom Management Plans   62
     Organizing the Instructional Program   63
     Getting Started   65

PART 2 Instructional Activities for the Content Standards 67

Introduction 69
Measurement 70
    Overview 70
    A Sample Activity: Body Ratios 72
    A Sample Activity: Introducing the Metric System 74
    Activities 77
Probability and Statistics 85
    Overview 85
    A Sample Activity: Spinner Experiments 87
    Activities 90
    Graphing in the Classroom 103
Geometry and Spatial Sense 107
    Overview 107
    A Sample Activity: Pentominoes 108
    Activities 111
Logical Reasoning 130
    Overview 130
    A Sample Activity: The Game of Poison 131
    Activities 132
Patterns, Functions, and Algebra 144
    Overview 144
    Introducing Patterns 144
    Developing Understanding of Functions 145
    Uses of Variables 147
    A Sample Activity: Painting Towers 148
    Activities 149
Number and Operations 157
    Overview 157
    A Sample Activity at the Primary Level: Number Sums 158
    A Sample Activity at the Intermediate Level: Palindromes 159
    Activities 161

PART 3 Teaching Arithmetic 169

Introduction 171
    Computation 171
    Problem Solving 172
    Number Sense 173
    Putting It Together 173

What Are the Basics in Arithmetic?   174

Results from Classroom Research   175

The Limits of Learning Rules   181

Teaching What to Do versus Teaching What to Do and Why   183

Multiple Strategies for Computing   187

Questions from Teachers   190

Relating Arithmetic to Real Life   192

How Can Arithmetic Understanding Be Developed?   195

Beginning Number Concepts   196

Overview   196

Whole-Class Lessons   196

Independent Activities (Menu)   204

Assessing Understanding of Beginning Number Concepts   207

Place Value   209

Overview   209

Whole-Class Lessons   209

Independent Activities (Menu)   214

Assessing Understanding of Place Value   218

Addition and Subtraction   221

Overview   221

Whole-Class Lessons   221

Independent Activities (Menu)   225

Assessing Understanding of Addition and Subtraction   231

Multiplication   233

Overview   233

Whole-Class Lessons   233

Independent Activities (Menu)   237

Assessing Understanding of Multiplication   243

Division   245

Overview   245

Whole-Class Lessons   245

Independent Activities (Menu)   251

Assessing Understanding of Division   253

Extending Multiplication and Division   255

Overview   255

Whole-Class Lessons   256

Independent Activities (Menu)   263

Assessing Understanding of Multiplication
    and Division with Large Numbers   266

Fractions   267

Overview   267

Whole-Class Lessons   268

Independent Activities (Menu)   279

Assessing Understanding of Fractions   283

Decimals 284
    Overview 284
    Whole-Class Lessons 284
    Independent Activities (Menu) 289
    Assessing Understanding of Decimals 290
Percents 292
    Overview 292
    Whole-Class Lessons 292
    Independent Activities (Menu) 297
    Assessing Understanding of Percents 300

PART 4   Mathematical Discussions   301

Introduction 303
Measurement Problems 304
    Squaring Up (page 79) 304
    Box Measuring (page 81) 305
    Round Things (page 81) 306
    Wraparound (page 81) 307
    Double the Circumference (page 83) 307
    The Area Stays the Same (page 84) 309
Probability and Statistics Problems 310
    Shake and Spill (page 101) 310
    Two-Coin Toss (page 97) 311
    Shake and Spill (page 101) Revisited 312
    Got a Match? (page 97) 314
    The X-O Problem (page 99) 315
    How Many Throws? and How Many Ways?
      (pages 100 and 101) 317
    Fair Game 1 (page 102) 319
    Fair Game 2 (page 102) 321
Geometry and Spatial Sense Problems 322
    The Tangram Puzzle (page 111) 322
    That's Just Half the Story (page 112) 327
    Interior Regions (page 112) 328
    Straight or Curved? (page 112) 328
    No-Lift Letters and More No-Lift Letters
      (page 113) 329
    Square Partitioning (page 117) 330
    The Banquet Table Problem (page 117) 331
    The Four-Triangle Problem (page 122) 332
    Geoboard Line Segments (page 127) 332
    Area on the Geoboard (page 127) 333

Logical Reasoning Problems   335
  King Arthur's Problem (page 132)   335
  The Prison Problem (page 135)   338
  The Three-Sacks Problem (page 136)   340
  The Orange Juice–and–Water Problem and the Two-Color
   Problem (page 139)   341
  Riddles with Color Tiles (page 141)   341
Patterns, Functions, and Algebra Problems   343
  The Handshake Problem (page 156)   343
Number and Operations Problems   348
  Number Sums (page 158)   348
  Making Change (page 162)   350
  How Many Sums? (page 163)   354
  Change from a $10.00 Bill (page 163)   356
  Multiplication Possibilities (page 164)   356
  The Postage Stamp Problem (page 167)   359
  Arrow Arithmetic (page 167)   360

PART 5   Questions Teachers Ask   363

Introduction   365
  Using Fingers for Computing   366
  Math Centers   366
  Patterns   367
  Patterns and Addition   368
  Money   370
  0–99 Chart versus 1–100 Chart   372
  The Language of Math   372
  Addition   374
  Subtraction   374
  Decimals   375
  Interpreting Multiplication   377
  Patterns in Multiples   378
  Multiplication and Division Word Problems   378
  Multidigit Multiplication   379
  Rounding   381
  Assessment in the Classroom   383
  Learning Multiplication and Division Facts   384
  Math Portfolios   386
  Meeting the Needs of All Students   388
  Long Division   390
  Test Prep   391
  Connecting Fractions and Decimals   393

Changing Instruction   395
Order of Operations   397
Homework   398
Supporting Small-Group Work   399

Blackline Masters   403

Centimeter Grid Paper   405
Area and Perimeter Shapes   406
Half-Inch Grid Paper   407
Hexagon Fill-in Puzzle   408
Pattern Block Triangle Paper   409
Toothpick Dot Paper   410
Isometric Dot Paper   411
Large Geoboard Dot Paper   412
Medium Geoboard Dot Paper   413
Small Geoboard Dot Paper   414
Area on the Geoboard   415
Inch Grid Paper   416
Large 0–99 Chart   417
Palindrome Recording Sheet   418
Small 0–99 Charts   419
Addition Chart   420
Ten-Frames Recording Sheet   421
Large 1–100 Chart   422
Small 1–100 Charts   423
Multiplication Table   424
Fractions with Cookies   425
Fractions with Bars   426
Fractions on Grids (4-by-4 Squares)   427
Fractions on Grids (6-by-4 Rectangles)   428
10-by-10 Grids   429
Shake and Spill   430
2-Centimeter Grid Paper   431

References   *433*
List of Activities   *435*
Index   *439*

Preface to the Third Edition

I began teaching in 1962, and *About Teaching Mathematics: A K–8 Resource* has been a work in progress for just about half of my teaching career. The goals of mathematics instruction today are clear—develop children's ability to think and reason mathematically and help them learn the concepts and skills they need to do so. The challenge for teachers is also clear—help all students become successful math learners who can apply their understanding and skills in all of the content areas of mathematics to a range of problem-solving situations. My purpose for writing this book has been to help teachers meet this challenge.

Meeting this challenge for myself has occupied my professional journey of more than forty years. About halfway into my teaching career, in 1981, I wrote the first version of this book, which was available to teachers only as a coursebook for the inservice classes I was teaching. During the years that followed, I spent a good deal of time revising, amplifying, reorganizing, and clarifying my ideas. In 1992, that initial version evolved into *About Teaching Mathematics: A K–8 Resource*, available to all teachers, not just to those enrolled in my classes.

I reviewed the book often after it was published and collected a file of changes that I felt would enhance its usefulness. In 2000, I finally tackled making revisions and published the second edition of *About Teaching Mathematics*. For that edition, I made changes to most of the sections in the book. Also, I added a major section, Part 4, "Mathematical Discussions," where I offered mathematical help in response to the volume of letters I had received from teachers asking for guidance with specific activities and problems in the book.

Now, seven years later, I'm pleased to present the third edition of *About Teaching Mathematics*. Two reasons inspired me to make this revision. One was to overhaul Part 1, "Raising the Issues," the section in which I address concerns that are key to K–8 mathematics teaching. The revised Part 1 includes both changes to the existing text and the addition of other topics, and it represents my current thinking on the issues that I think are important for teachers to reflect on.

Another reason for preparing this third edition was to add Part 5, "Questions Teachers Ask," in which I present responses to questions I've received from teachers over the years. (As I said in my preface to the second edition, I save everything!) For this section, I combed through my correspondence and chose questions that have a broad appeal even though each was raised by an individual teacher. And although the questions were asked from the perspectives of specific grade levels, I suggest that you comb through all of them, as many are appropriate for other grade levels as well.

I hope that this third edition of *About Teaching Mathematics* supports your quest to help students become confident and successful math learners.

Students who understand mathematics can think and reason mathematically and use what they've learned to solve problems, both in and out of school. Teachers who teach for understanding must find ways to engage students actively in their mathematics learning. The goal of *About Teaching Mathematics* is to provide teachers with direction and assistance for implementing instruction that develops students' mathematical confidence and competence. Specifically, the book is designed to help teachers

- deepen their knowledge and appreciation of mathematics;
- understand how children learn mathematics;
- implement effective instructional strategies for teaching mathematics;
- integrate assessment into classroom instruction; and
- establish a classroom environment that supports children's learning of mathematics.

The book is organized into five parts. Part 1, "Raising the Issues," begins with an overview of the K–8 mathematics curriculum and then addresses the role of arithmetic in mathematics instruction, word problems and problem solving, number sense, how children learn mathematics, incorporating writing into math instruction, teaching math vocabulary, linking assessment and instruction, and more. A section on managing the classroom provides information about organizing the instructional program and structuring lessons for cooperative and independent learning.

Part 2, "Instruction Activities for the Content Standards," presents an extensive collection of explorations for the content areas of the mathematics curriculum—measurement; probability and statistics; geometry and spatial sense; logical reasoning; patterns, functions, and algebra; and number and operations. The activities included are models for classroom instruction.

Arithmetic, the topic of uppermost concern for teachers, parents, and administrators, is the focus of Part 3, "Teaching Arithmetic." This section addresses the role of arithmetic in the mathematics curriculum; the three essential aspects of computation, number sense, and problem solving; and strategies for teaching arithmetic to develop both understanding and skills.

It's important that teachers understand the mathematics that underlies the activities with which students are engaged. Part 4, "Mathematical Discussions," addresses the mathematical ideas and skills for about forty of the activities included in the book. Many of the discussions provide solutions to problems, always with guidelines for thinking about the mathematics and explanations about why the solutions make sense.

Part 5, "Questions Teachers Ask," includes questions submitted by teachers over the years and the responses they received. Some of these were general questions about math instruction and others specifically related to *About Teaching Mathematics*. While these questions represent only a portion of the queries actually sent, they reflect the issues that were raised most often by teachers.

Raising the Issues

PART

1

Introduction

Many documents are available to help teachers think about the big picture of the mathematics curriculum. *Principles and Standards for School Mathematics*, published in 2000 by the National Council of Teachers of Mathematics (NCTM), is a useful and comprehensive reference that addresses teaching mathematics in all grades. Frameworks from states and from local school districts define specific expectations about what teachers are to teach and when. Teachers' instructional programs provide yearly road maps for teaching along with instructional strategies and lessons. State and local tests provide additional information that further impacts the curriculum.

Because of the differences among state and local standards, in 2006 NCTM published *Curriculum Focal Points for Prekindergarten Through Grade 8 Mathematics: A Quest for Coherence*. Building on the NCTM 2000 standards document, this guide offers a step toward promoting dialogue about defining a coherent curriculum for the entire country. In contrast to listing goals, standards, objectives, or learning expectations, it describes important mathematical targets for each grade level.

While it's important for teachers to have an overall perspective about teaching mathematics across the grades, the pressing responsibilities of daily teaching leave little time for exploring the many documents in depth. The goal of this section is to present teachers an overview of K–8 mathematics and the issues pertinent to providing effective instruction.

First, a brief guide to the vision presented in NCTM's *Principals and Standards for School Mathematics*. This document is organized into four main parts:

- guiding principles for school mathematics
- overview of the standards for all grades
- descriptions of the standards in four grade bands (preK–2, 3–5, 6–8, 9–12)
- discussion about moving toward the vision

The six guiding principles—equity, curriculum, teaching, learning, assessment, and technology—set the direction and provide the focus for an overall vision of mathematics instruction. They provide perspectives and define assumptions about issues that are crucial to teaching mathematics.

The ten standards address those mathematical understandings and skills that students should acquire as they progress through school. The standards are organized into two groups—content standards and process standards. The five content standards describe the heart of the mathematics, what students should know and be able to do as a result of the math instruction they receive. They address the full range of the math knowledge to be taught.

Content Standards

Standard 1	Number and Operations
Standard 2	Algebra
Standard 3	Geometry
Standard 4	Measurement
Standard 5	Data Analysis and Probability

You may find that the specific organization and terminology used to describe the content of the mathematics curriculum differ from the lists in your state and local frameworks. The important overall messages are that the mathematics students should know blankets a range of mathematical topics, and instruction should address the full breadth of the mathematical topics. Also, although all documents organize the math content into separate areas, it's important to keep in mind that the areas are related to one another. For example, the content of number and operations is used in all areas of the mathematics curriculum. Also, measurement helps students build understanding both of number and of shapes. The NCTM document presents student expectations for each of the content standards in each of the four grade bands.

The five process standards present the vehicles that students use when engaged in doing mathematics. They describe how students acquire and use the content knowledge they are learning. The process standards connect to the content standards by bringing the content of the math curriculum to life and making it accessible. For example, students' competency with numerical understanding and skills relates to their ability to solve problems, and communication and representation are integral to learning in all areas of the content. Interaction between the content and process standards is essential for comprehensive instruction across the grades. This interaction is supported in *Curriculum Focal Points for Prekindergarten Through Grade 8 Mathematics*; the focal points present the content to be emphasized at each grade level, to be addressed in contexts that promote the process standards.

Process Standards

Standard 6	Problem Solving
Standard 7	Reasoning and Proof
Standard 8	Communication
Standard 9	Connections
Standard 10	Representation

You Can't Teach What You Don't Understand

The mathematics curriculum described in NCTM's *Principles and Standards* (2000) and in state and local frameworks is greatly expanded from the notion of arithmetic, the "third R," being the cornerstone of elementary mathematics instruction. While teachers are generally comfortable with the mathematical content included in the area of number and operations, not all teachers feel equally prepared to teach the content of algebra, statistics, or other math topics. A major goal of mathematics instruction is to teach for understanding, so that students build a foundation of mathematical knowledge. But teachers can't teach for understanding if they don't have a firm foundation of understanding themselves.

Even in the area of number and operations, issues about the need for in-depth teacher understanding surface. For example, think about multiplying fractions, a numerical skill that is also important for algebra, probability, measurement, and other topics. Most of us learned the procedure for multiplying fractions—you multiply across the numerators and across the denominators—without understanding why. Frankly, it's easier to teach students the procedure than to help them make sense of why multiplying the numerators and denominators produces a correct answer. But teaching the *why* requires that teachers themselves have thought deeply about multiplying fractions.

There are many other numerical ideas that are the underpinnings of the mathematics we teach to children and that teachers may not have had the chance to think about themselves. For example, why do we always get an odd product when we multiply two odd numbers but an even product when we multiply an odd times an even or two even numbers? What about odd and even sums when we add? Is zero odd or even? What about fractions—can they be odd and even? Why does "canceling" zeros in the fraction $\frac{10}{20}$ produce an equivalent fraction, but not in the fraction $\frac{101}{201}$? It's important for teachers to think about questions like these in order to teach effectively.

Glenda Lappan, past president of NCTM, addressed the importance of teacher knowledge in her article "Knowing What We Teach and Teaching What We Know" (n.d.). She states:

> Our own content knowledge affects how we interpret the content goals we are expected to reach with our students. It affects the way we hear and respond to our students and their questions. It affects our ability to explain clearly and to ask good questions. It affects our ability to approach a mathematical idea flexibly with our students and

to make connections. It affects our ability to push each student at that special moment when he or she is ready or curious. And it affects our ability to make those moments happen more often for our students.

When teachers are asked to think deeply about how to multiply one fraction by another fraction, they may wonder, "What's the point of understanding that when students are tested only on the answer to the problem?" Being able to compute answers without also understanding the underlying mathematics is an insufficient and shallow goal for students' mathematics education. All instruction must foster students' ability to think, reason, and solve problems.

There are opportunities throughout this book to help you deepen your own mathematical knowledge. It's important to bring a sense of curiosity to these opportunities and pursue making sense of ideas that are new for you. The payoff will be not only for you but for your students as well.

A Perspective on Arithmetic

Even though the mathematics curriculum has expanded far beyond arithmetic, the content area of number and operations remains central to elementary mathematics and receives the greatest emphasis in elementary mathematics instruction. Standard 1 in NCTM's *Principles and Standards* (2000) addresses the importance of giving attention to this area of the elementary mathematics curriculum area: "In these Standards, understanding number and operations, developing number sense, and gaining fluency in arithmetic computation form the core of mathematics education for the elementary grades" (32).

Arithmetic instruction has traditionally focused on developing students' proficiency with paper-and-pencil computation. Implied, however, in the renaming to number and operations, is a call for a broader view of arithmetic instruction. Computation is still important, of course, and students must learn how to compute accurately and efficiently. But instruction must also help students learn to apply computational skills to problem-solving situations. When facing problems that call for numerical calculations, students need to know how to choose the operations needed, decide on the numbers to use, do the necessary calculations, and then appropriately interpret the results. Also, arithmetic instruction must help students develop number sense so that they are able to make reasonable estimates, think and reason flexibly with numbers, make sound numerical judgments, and see numbers as useful. Computation, problem solving, and number sense are essential aspects of instruction that addresses the content standard of number and operations.

In order to examine instructional decisions, it's helpful to consider the role of arithmetic in real-life situations. When teachers are asked to list occasions outside of their classroom when they use arithmetic—that is, when they have to add, subtract, multiply, and/or divide—most responses include the following types of situations: when I calculate my checkbook balance, when I'm in the supermarket figuring how much I'm spending or doing price comparisons, when I need to know how much wallpaper or floor covering I need, when I'm deciding on the tip in a restaurant, when I want to know the mileage I'm getting on my car, when I'm figuring how long a roast or turkey needs to cook, when I'm deciding what time to leave to arrive at the movies on time. When they review their list to see how they typically do the arithmetic required, teachers report that they most often either use a calculator or figure mentally; relying on paper and pencil is less common. When teachers evaluate their lists to decide when being accurate is necessary and when an estimate does fine, or is even more appropriate, teachers generally find a fifty-fifty split between the two. Complete the questionnaire that follows to analyze your own use of arithmetic.

At the same time, teachers admit to spending the bulk of their instructional time for number and operations on paper-and-pencil drill, with students practicing arithmetic skills in isolation from problem-solving situations. The arithmetic exercises are usually provided on worksheets or textbook pages, neatly arranged and ready for children to apply computation procedures for figuring answers. Yet in all of the real-life needs for arithmetic, problems do not present themselves ready for calculation. Deciding what to do is the important first step before doing any calculation.

---

1. List all the situations outside of school responsibilities during the past month for which you've used arithmetic—that is, you've had to add, subtract, multiply, and/or divide.

   _____   _____
   _____   _____
   _____   _____
   _____   _____
   _____   _____
   _____   _____
   _____   _____
   _____   _____

2. There are three methods people generally use when doing arithmetic:
   (1) calculator,
   (2) paper and pencil, or
   (3) mental arithmetic.
   Number each item on your list to indicate the method you usually use in that situation. Which method do you use
   most often? _____
   Least often? _____

3. Review your list once more and mark each item with *estimate* or *accurate* to show which is usually required for that situation.
   What percentage of your items did you mark *estimate*? _____
   Accurate? _____

Learning to do paper-and-pencil arithmetic on isolated examples does not ensure that children will truly understand the algorithms or develop the ability to use them when needed. This fact is obvious to teachers when they assign addition practice and a student asks, "Do I have to carry on this page?" It's obvious when they assign word problems and a student asks, "Do I need to add or subtract?" It's clear when a child makes a division error, omitting a zero in the quotient so the answer is ten times too small, and the student doesn't even notice. All of these examples indicate students' lack of understanding and are substantiated by research findings.

This does not mean that children do not need to learn arithmetic. Doing arithmetic mentally demands mastery of basic facts along with the ability to estimate. Using a calculator successfully requires understanding of the arithmetic processes called for in a variety of situations. It is inappropriate when teaching arithmetic to focus on computation in isolation from the problem situations that require those skills.

Can students determine whether it's cheaper to buy things two for a nickel or three for a dime? Can they name a fraction that is larger than one-third yet smaller than one-half? Can they figure out what to do when halving a recipe that calls for $\frac{3}{4}$ cup of sugar? (What would you do?) Merely learning paper-and-pencil arithmetic algorithms is not sufficient preparation for solving problems that demand reasoning ability, not just computation ability. Arithmetic instruction must be accompanied by instruction in problem solving and number sense.

Examining Children's Common Arithmetic Errors

Examining the errors children make when practicing arithmetic can provide additional insights into their thinking and our instructional problems. For each of the arithmetic exercises below, purposely record incorrect answers that reflect errors that you've seen students commonly make.

1. $3 + \boxed{} = 7$	2. $\begin{array}{r} 35 \\ + 67 \\ \hline \end{array}$
3. $\begin{array}{r} 42 \\ -17 \\ \hline \end{array}$	4. $\begin{array}{r} 300 \\ -136 \\ \hline \end{array}$
5. $12\overline{)3840}$	6. $\dfrac{1}{2} + \dfrac{2}{3} =$
7. $2.06 + 1.3 + 0.38 =$	8. $\begin{array}{r} \$5.40 \\ \times 0.15 \\ \hline \end{array}$

With the exception of errors that result from carelessness with basic facts, the errors that students make are not random. They are remarkably consistent. Teachers see the same mistakes over and over, year after year. In most instances, children's errors are rule bound, the result of applying an incorrect procedure in place of a correct algorithm. This incorrect procedure, however, may have some logic for the child, even though that logic is incorrect. Often, the child has been taught the rule by a teacher but applies the rule in an inappropriate situation. The following errors and explanations describe the kinds of incorrect thinking children typically apply.

1. $3 + \boxed{10} = 7$ A plus sign means to add.

2. $\begin{array}{r} 35 \\ + 67 \\ \hline 912 \end{array}$ Add the numbers in each column and write the sums under the line.

3. $\begin{array}{r} 42 \\ -17 \\ \hline 35 \end{array}$ When you subtract, you take the smaller number from the larger.

4. $\begin{array}{r} 2\,9\,9 \\ \cancel{3\,0\,0} \\ -136 \\ \hline 163 \end{array}$ You can't subtract a number from zero, so you change the zeros into nines.

or

$$\begin{array}{r} \cancel{3}^{\,2}\!\!\stackrel{\prime}{0}\stackrel{\prime}{0} \\ -136 \\ \hline 174 \end{array}$$

or

You can't subtract from zero, so you borrow from the three and the zeros become tens.

5. $12\overline{)3840}$ with 32 above

You can drop the zero at the end of the problem.

6. $\dfrac{1}{2} + \dfrac{2}{3} = \dfrac{3}{5}$

When you add fractions, you add across the top and across the bottom.

7. $$\begin{array}{r} 2.06 \\ 1.3 \\ .38 \\ \hline 2.57 \end{array}$$

Line up the numbers and add.

8. $$\begin{array}{r} \$5.40 \\ \times 0.15 \\ \hline \$81.00 \end{array}$$

After you figure the problem, bring down the decimal point.

It's valuable to think about possible causes for these examples of erroneous reasoning. When learning arithmetic processes, children focus on the symbols and tend to see arithmetic as doing something to those symbols to get the right answers. They typically learn that a plus sign means to add, but a problem like $3 + \square = 7$ calls for figuring how many more, not finding a sum. The same children who incorrectly put 10 in the box in the first example most likely know that $3 + 10$ is not equal to 7. When tackling a missing-addend problem, children who make the common error are not focusing on the meaning of the problem but on the symbols in the example. However, the error doesn't typically occur when children think about the same numerical problem set in a context: *You have three birthday candles, but you need ten altogether. How many more birthday candles do you need?* When given this problem, children generally interpret the situation and correctly figure how many birthday candles they need; they don't make the error they commonly do when dealing with the same problem presented only numerically.

The implication from the examples of arithmetic errors is that children rely on recipes rather than reasoning. Following recipes results from learning arithmetic as a collection of specific methods used to arrive at answers, rather than thinking about what makes sense. Many teachers express concern when students come to class and want to know if they can do the division using the method someone at home showed them. (What would you do in that situation?) It's not uncommon for a teacher to respond that children must learn to do it the way the book says. The implication is that the specific algorithm is important, not that children should understand that different algorithms are possible and they should make sense of whatever method they use.

When making errors, children rarely notice or even seem to care when they arrive at an absurd answer. Though teachers urge children to estimate or check their answers, generally children are concerned primarily with finishing. Their goal seems to be to get the problem or page done, not to evaluate their answers. They figure 15 percent of $5.40, produce a result of $81.00 (as shown on the previous page), and accept the answer without question, even though $81.00 is fifteen times greater than $5.40. The problem springs from an educational issue larger than mathematics instruction. If children believe that getting quick, right answers is what is valued in school, then this response is an obvious result. Instruction should aim not toward an answer-oriented curriculum but toward one that values reasoning processes and calls for evaluating answers as an essential part of any assignment.

Not only is the mastery of algorithms presented as the most important goal in elementary mathematics instruction, but the algorithms taught are often presented as if they are the only way to perform a calculation. In this light, the following exercise is revealing:

> Mentally double 38. Then analyze the method you used in order to arrive at the answer.

When teachers are asked to double thirty-eight mentally and then describe how they accomplished this, methods vary. Some visualize the problem symbolically and perform the algorithm mentally, seeing two 38s lined up on their mental chalkboards, adding the 8s, carrying the 1, and so on. Some use this approach, but mentally multiply thirty-eight by two instead of adding. Some add the thirty and thirty-first and then add on sixteen. (And we know that children are discouraged from ever adding the numbers in the tens place before those in the ones place.) Some double forty and subtract four. Some double thirty-five and then add six. Invariably, such a range of methods is offered. Why, in school, is the implication that there is one right way to do arithmetic? And why is the symbolic method used to produce arithmetic results so often separated from the meaning in the situation?

Using Word Problems to Develop Arithmetic Understanding

I f teaching computation skills by starting with numerical symbols is a backward approach, the traditional sequence of teaching computation first and then applying those skills to problem situations is just as backward. It doesn't make sense to teach arithmetic skills in isolation from contextual situations for which those skills are needed. Research findings have shown that this pedagogical version of putting the cart before the horse doesn't work.

When research studies examined why children's ability to solve word problems falls far below their ability to compute, they found certain common myths to be untrue. For example, children's difficulties are not caused primarily by poor computation skills or insufficient reading ability. When given a word problem, children simply do not know how to choose the correct operation to apply to the problem. In order to solve word problems, children have to connect the suitable arithmetic processes to the contexts presented in the stories. Although children can perform the computations adequately, they do not understand the meaning of the arithmetic operations in ways that enable them to make those connections to the word problems.

Try the *Dealing in Horses* problem on the next page. It will help you experience the sort of difficulty children encounter with story problems. (It's also an interesting problem to discuss with friends or present to a class, if the children can deal comfortably with the numbers.)

Generally, people offer different solutions and reasoning for the *Dealing in Horses* problem. It's not typical of the word problems children face. Although it can be translated into an arithmetic problem and solved by computation, it involves more than the usual word-problem demands. However, the difficulty adults have deciding on the solution is similar to the difficulty many children have when applying their arithmetic knowledge to common word-problem situations.

Understanding the situation is not the difficulty with *Dealing in Horses*; the scenario is clear. Adding and subtracting the numbers in the problem also is not difficult; the numbers are easy to handle mentally. Yet deciding precisely what to do isn't obvious to everyone. The difficulty lies in knowing the correct way to connect the arithmetic operations to the situation in order to arrive at a solution. The confusion that adults experience with this situation is similar to the confusion that children experience when presented with a page of mixed word problems that leads them to ask: "Do I need to add or subtract?"

Dealing in Horses

A man bought a horse for $50 and sold it for $60. He then bought the horse back for $70 and sold it again for $80. What do you think was the financial outcome of these transactions?

☐ Lost $20 ☐ Earned $10

☐ Lost $10 ☐ Earned $20

☐ Came out even ☐ Earned $30

☐ _____ Other (describe) _____

Explain your reasoning: _____

_____

_____

_____

_____

Facility with computation does not ensure children's ability to know when to use those skills in problem situations. Problem situations should be the starting place for developing understanding of each of the four basic operations of arithmetic—addition, subtraction, multiplication, and division—thereby establishing the need and context for computation skills. Children need to see that learning to compute serves a purpose—for solving problems. Too often, the message is reversed, and children see word problems as a way of providing computation practice, and a mysterious way at that.

This suggestion does not mean that teachers should begin arithmetic instruction by assigning the word problems in the textbook. Assigning word problems accomplishes no more than testing students' abilities to solve those problems. It's teaching that is needed, not testing. Teachers should present word problems for children to discuss and find solutions to, without the distraction of numerical symbols. This needs to be done frequently, several times a week throughout the entire year, at all grade levels. The goal is for the children to generalize for themselves—from many, many experiences—how the arithmetic operations are described in the language of the real world. Also, students should be encouraged to figure their own ways to arrive at solutions and make sense of situations numerically.

A caution: Teachers often resort to helping children solve textbook problems by providing word cues: when it says "altogether," you are supposed to add; "how many more" means to subtract. Teachers provide these cues to help children be more successful with word problems. However, instruction of this type does little more than offer children tricks to find answers. Even worse, the implication is that getting the answer is most important and that relying on tricks is an effective strategy for finding those answers. This message often results in children looking for tricks, rather than trying to make sense out of problems.

Beyond Word Problems

The mathematical problem-solving situations that children encounter in the elementary grades should include problems that require thinking beyond what traditional word problems demand. Word problems require children to focus on the meaning of the arithmetic operations. To solve a word problem, a child needs to translate the situation into an arithmetic problem (or sometimes more than one problem) and then perform the computation called for. There is usually one right way to get the answer; there is always one right answer.

Making traditional word problems the only or main emphasis of the problems children encounter is not sufficient for the elementary curriculum. Doing so gives an unrealistic message to children about the way mathematics will serve them as adults. Most daily problems adults face that require mathematical reasoning and skills are not solved by translating the available information into arithmetic sentences and then performing the needed calculations.

In real-life problems, you're rarely given all the information you need in one tidy package; you often have to collect the data and often from a variety of sources. There's rarely only one possible method or strategy that emerges from real-life problems; usually you choose one from several viable possibilities. You don't always know for sure if the solution you choose is the right or best one; you decide on one plausible solution and it may be only later that you can evaluate your choice. Sometimes you never are sure about a solution; life has no answer book.

When solving problems in real life, you call upon all the resources you've developed in other situations, including knowledge, previous experience, intuition. You need to analyze, predict, make decisions, and evaluate. In order to function in our complex and ever changing society, people need to be able to solve a wide variety of problems. The elementary math curriculum must prepare children to become effective problem solvers.

Teaching children to be problem solvers does not minimize the importance of arithmetic. Arithmetic is necessary for solving many problems in life. Also, not all the problems children deal with in school need be real-life problems. Although many situations that arise daily in classrooms afford opportunities for the application of math skills—collecting lunch money, deciding on how many cars are needed for a field trip, taking attendance, and so on—children also benefit from word-problem situations that build their problem-solving abilities. After all, school is the place where children can safely develop and practice problem-solving skills. The challenge for curriculum choices is to pose problems that motivate students, spark their natural curiosity, and allow them to use, in a safe and supportive environment, the skills they'll need later. The following exercise provides a classroom application for these ideas:

---

1. If A = $0.01, B = $0.02, C = $0.03, and so on, what is the value of your first name? _____
2. Using this alphabet system, one of the days of the week is worth exactly $1.00. Which one is it? _____
3. Find other words that are worth exactly $1.00.

How did you go about figuring the value of your name? Did you write the alphabet and list the value of each letter? Did you separately figure out the value of each letter in your name? (Did you use your fingers for this?) Did your method for figuring out the value of your name help you find the day of the week worth exactly $1.00? How did you go about finding which day of the week is the $1.00 word? These are the kinds of questions that are valuable to discuss with students. It gives them the opportunity to see that there are different ways to approach a problem. Also, not providing a list of the alphabet letters and their values gives students a chance to decide how they'll collect the data they need.

Finding $1.00 words opens up addition practice to a multitude of possibilities. More than one thousand $1.00 words have been discovered by students and teachers across the United States. Some teachers have organized class or school $1.00 word contests. Some have simplified the problem for young children to one of finding the most expensive and least expensive three-letter or four-letter words. Students develop different strategies for searching for $1.00 words, and these are useful to discuss in class. This type of problem provides both arithmetic practice and a broader problem-solving experience. Also, the riddles in *The $1.00 Word Riddle Book* (Burns 1990) give clues that direct students to finding $1.00 words.

What Is and Is Not a Problem?

What is the definition of a problem? A problem is a situation in which a person is seeking some goal and for which a suitable course of action is not immediately apparent. In the context of the mathematics curriculum, a problem is a situation requiring that mathematical skills, concepts, or processes be used to arrive at the goal.

Whether a situation is a problem is an individual matter, depending on an individual's reaction or relationship to that situation. The individual must understand the situation and be interested in resolving it, yet there must be some block preventing immediate resolution. If these conditions do not exist, then a situation is not a problem for that individual. What may be a problem for one student may not be a problem for another. Analyzing the definition produces four criteria that define mathematical problems for students:

Criteria for Mathematical Problems

1. There is a perplexing situation that the student understands.
2. The student is interested in finding a solution.
3. The student is unable to proceed directly toward a solution.
4. The solution requires use of mathematical ideas.

Refer to these four criteria in answering these questions:

---

1. Was the *Dealing in Horses* problem a problem for you? Why or why not? Answer in terms of the four criteria.

2. Was finding the value of your first name a problem for you? Why or why not?

3. Was finding $1.00 words a problem for you? Why or why not?

4. Would these be problems for your students?
   Solving *Dealing in Horses*: Yes ☐   No ☐
   Finding the value of your first name: Yes ☐   No ☐
   Finding $1.00 words: Yes ☐   No ☐
   Why?

Do not confuse arithmetic exercises with problems. If a student meets a situation that calls for two-place multiplication and has not been taught an algorithm for this process, then this might be a problem for that student. Generally though, arithmetic exercises are used to provide students practice with using standard mathematical procedures. Although a child may have difficulty arriving at a correct arithmetic answer, deciding on the method for getting the answer is not usually part of the child's task. Executing specific procedures—the algorithms—is the child's task.

Textbooks often present word problems so that all those on the same page are solved with the same operation. The first one on the page may be a problem for a student. But if the student realizes that the same procedure can be used for all the others (and students are quick to notice this), the rest are not problems. They are merely exercises that do not require thinking or reasoning but rather repetitive application of the same algorithms.

Problem-solving situations, on the other hand, each demand that the child develop a plan for solution as well as execute the plan. Problem-solving techniques do exist, but they are general approaches, not algorithms that can be routinely applied to specific problems. Although arithmetic is essential for solving many problems in life, it is not the only mathematical skill generally needed. Figuring how much floor covering is needed for a room requires applying both geometry and measurement skills. Deciding on the best place to put savings involves ideas in the areas of probability and statistics. Assembling a bicycle that arrives in a crate calls for the application of logical thinking skills.

At each of the grade levels, mathematics instruction should provide children problem-solving experiences in all of the content areas of the elementary math curriculum. While the content areas are organized differently in state and district frameworks, they generally include number and operations; measurement; probability and statistics; geometry; patterns, functions, and algebra; and logical reasoning. Although arithmetic is primarily part of number and operations, arithmetic skills are needed to understand ideas and to solve problems in each of the other areas as well.

Problem-Solving Strategies

Students benefit from learning about problem-solving strategies that are useful for analyzing and solving problems. Strategies are not specific to particular problems or to particular areas of the mathematics curriculum but can be applied alone or in combination with other strategies to solve a wide variety of problems. Students use many strategies intuitively when they solve problems. However, gaining familiarity with a collection of strategies by seeing them modeled, and then by trying to apply them, provides students with useful tools for tackling problems and broadens their problem-solving abilities. The following is a list of useful problem-solving strategies.

Problem-Solving Strategies

Look for a pattern.
Construct a table.

Make an organized list.
Act it out.
Draw a picture.
Use objects.
Guess and check.
Work backward.
Write an equation.
Solve a simpler (or similar) problem.
Make a model.

It's important to discuss with students both the specific strategies they used to solve problems and why those strategies were effective choices. Class discussions are useful because they provide opportunities for students to hear others' points of view. Having the list of problem-solving strategies posted in the room is also helpful. That way, when a problem is summarized in class, the list serves as a reference for helping students label their methods. As students become familiar with the various strategies, they can refer to the list as a source for approaches.

Usually, it's possible to solve a particular problem using different strategies or a combination of strategies. The following exercise focuses on this issue. For each of the three problems provided, decide which strategies are possible or reasonable to use. After making a list of these strategies, choose one or a combination of strategies to try first in solving each problem. Then solve the problem. Record for each of the problems as indicated.

Problem 1: Show all the ways that fifteen objects can be put into four piles so that each pile has a different number of objects in it.

Possible or reasonable strategies:

_____

_____

_____

Which strategy or combination of strategies will you try first to solve the problem?

_____

Solution: _____

_____

Did you change strategies or use others as well? Describe. _____

_____

Problem 2: Lisa and David are playing a game. At the end of each round, the loser gives the winner a penny. After a while, David has won three games, and Lisa has three more pennies than she did when she began. How many rounds did they play?

Possible or reasonable strategies:

_____

_____

_____

Which strategy or combination of strategies will you try first to solve the problem?

_____

_____

Solution: _____

_____

Did you change strategies or use others as well? Describe. _____

_____

Problem 3: If you spend $1.85 and pay with a $10.00 bill, you get $8.15 in change. Notice that the digits in your change are the same as the digits in what you spent. There are four other amounts you could spend so that the change has the same digits. Find them.

Possible or reasonable strategies:

_____

_____

_____

Which strategy or combination of strategies will you try first to solve the problem?

_____

Solution: _____

_____

Did you change strategies or use others as well? Describe. _____

_____

Pros and Cons of Problem Solving

Some teachers think that much of problem solving is too demanding or unrealistic. Several arguments have been raised: There isn't enough time; parents expect us to teach arithmetic; problem solving is too hard for the struggling students who need work in basic skills; I was never very good in math myself and I don't feel comfortable teaching what I don't understand. It's important to examine each of these issues.

Argument 1. There isn't enough time.

The reality of classroom instruction is that teaching the basic skills of arithmetic is time-consuming. There is just so much time in the school day and, over the years, more and more curriculum responsibilities have been added. A focus on problem solving is too much to expect and isn't realistic. Besides, the major complaint of secondary math teachers is that the students aren't well enough prepared with basic arithmetic skills.

There's no quarrel with the reality of how difficult and time-consuming teaching is. It has never been easy. But that's no excuse for not taking a serious and critical look at how the math instructional time, no matter how limited, is being spent. Research has shown that spending the bulk of mathematics instructional time to teach arithmetic skills does not prepare students to solve problems. Teachers are well aware of this when they assign even the most rudimentary of word problems and find that students are unable to solve them. Continuing to emphasize arithmetic in isolation rather than in the context of problem solving makes little sense, especially when this choice is considered in the perspective of what children need to function in our complex world.

Argument 2. Parents expect the school to teach arithmetic.

Parents are concerned about their children's arithmetic skills. They want their children to bring home papers that show the arithmetic work they are doing in school. They don't want another rerun of the "new math" fiasco. Parents argue that they learned arithmetic when they were in school without all this fuss about problem solving, and that should be good enough for their children.

Teachers need to explain the full scope of math instructional goals to parents, stated in the context of what children require for success in higher education and in our changing society. The world differs greatly today from when parents were in elementary school; the technological explosion has affected all areas of everyone's life. To cling to what was suitable when parents were in school is clinging to nostalgia rather than examining what is currently essential. Professional educators have the job of reeducating parents, not just complying with demands that are obsolete.

Argument 3. Problem solving is too hard for students who have difficulty with the basic skills.

For many students, mastering basic computation requires both more instructional time and more practice. Without this, they are not able to perform arithmetic calculations. It's better for students who learn more slowly to concentrate on the skills rather than attempt to do even more complicated problem solving.

Instead of merely considering how to give struggling students more instructional time for arithmetic, why not examine what is really basic for those students? Skills are tools. The value of a tool is its usefulness. Being able to do paper-and-pencil computation will not serve students without the ability to interpret a problem, analyze what needs to be done, and evaluate the solution. What's needed is a redefinition of what is really basic to mathematics instruction.

Argument 4. Some teachers are not very good in math and do not feel comfortable teaching problem solving.

Some teachers studied mathematics only as long as it was a requirement, and for some this means that their last math course was high school geometry. To be afraid of mathematics, to feel inadequate, and even to dislike it are not uncommon reactions from people, professional educators included. All teachers can do arithmetic; not all have that same facility in the other strands of mathematics. It's not fair to expect teachers to teach what they don't understand themselves.

Indeed, there are professional educators who are not comfortable with mathematics. Too often, it is taken for granted that teachers have a firm grasp of the content of grades K–12 mathematics when they leave high school. This isn't always the case. Many teachers have taken only two years of high school mathematics, and many who have taken additional courses still have not developed a full understanding of the ideas and relationships in the high school mathematics curriculum. It is a myth that some people do not have a mathematical mind and therefore cannot learn mathematics. All teachers responsible for teaching mathematics face the challenge of introducing children to important mathematics concepts and motivating them to enjoy and appreciate mathematics. Teachers who have never been at all interested in mathematics or who have a limited background in it can continue their learning of mathematics through mathematics courses, conferences, inservice workshops, and other professional development activities.

Building Number Sense

Developing students' number sense is a generally recognized goal of the K–8 mathematics curriculum. Along with computation and problem solving, number sense is an essential ingredient of what's basic to students' learning about number and operations. It relates to the ability to make sense of numerical concepts and procedures. Rather than search for a concise definition of number sense, it's helpful to consider characteristics that are indicators that a student has number sense.

Students with good number sense can think and reason flexibly with numbers, use numbers to solve problems, spot unreasonable answers, understand how numbers can be taken apart and put together in different ways, see connections among the operations, figure mentally, and make reasonable estimates. These students seem to have good intuition about numbers and see numbers as useful. This isn't a definitive list, nor is it meant to be a checklist. Rather, it's a start for thinking about those qualities that we want to foster in students when helping develop their number sense.

In contrast, students with poor number sense tend to rely on procedures rather than reason, often do not notice when answers or estimates are unreasonable, and have limited numerical common sense.

Third graders were asked to figure out, in their heads, how many chopsticks were needed for their Chinese New Year celebration for everyone in the class to have two. Including their teacher, there were twenty-eight people in all. (How many chopsticks did they need?) Eddie guessed seventy-five chopsticks. Rosa thought maybe eighty. Jayden said, "Those are too big because if there were thirty people, we'd only need sixty."

Josh chimed in, "It's can't be seventy-five because the answer has to be even."

Meanwhile, Rebecca had been counting by twos and reported that she got fifty-six. Carla agreed and explained, "I know that twenty-five plus twenty-five is fifty, and we have three more people, so we need six more chopsticks." (How would you judge these children's number sense?)

Here are teaching strategies that can help you build students' number sense.

Model different methods for computing. When children think that there is one right way to compute, they focus on learning and applying it, rather than on thinking about what makes sense for the numbers at hand. A one-way approach does not help students learn to think flexibly, which is essential to developing number sense. For example, for the chopstick problem, you could record Rebecca's thinking by writing the 2s on the board—*2, 4, 6, 8, 10*, and so on, up to *56*. You could record Carla's method by writing:

$$25 + 25 = 50$$
$$50 + 6 = 56$$

Similarly, you could record other children's methods, or introduce a method of your own. For example, you might elaborate on Jayden's suggestion about thirty people requiring sixty chopsticks by subtracting four chopsticks for the two extra people:

$$60 - 4 = 36$$

Ask students regularly to calculate mentally. Examining our everyday uses of arithmetic reveals that we most often rely on mental computation when we use arithmetic—to get to the movies on time, figure the tip in restaurants, double or halve a recipe, and so on. In the classroom, try hands-on-the-table math. Asking students to put their hands on the table means that they have no other materials available to help them—no paper, no pencils, no manipulative materials, no books. You present a problem and the students solve it by relying only on their ability to reason.

For example, for younger students, have them each put two cubes in a jar and then, in pairs, figure out the number of cubes in the jar altogether. To verify, count the cubes by twos, fives, and tens. (Not all young children know that you'll get the same result no matter how you count.) For older students, have students count scoopfuls as you fill a jar by scooping beans with a coffee scoop. Then give each pair of students a scoop of beans to count. After discussing with the class what might be the average number of beans in a scoop, have students mentally calculate how many beans are the jar.

Have class discussions about strategies for computing. When students report results for hands-on-the-table math, be sure to ask them to explain how they reasoned. Then ask, "Who else can explain?" When others report, don't worry if they give the same reason—explaining in their own words supports students' learning. Also, as you guide the discussion, keep track of students' ideas on the board. This helps model for students how to numerically represent different ways to figure.

Make estimation an integral part of computing. Ask students for an "about number" when posing a problem. For example, a multidigit multiplication problem, such as 148×21, isn't an appropriate mental computation problem if the goal is to find the exact answer. However, asking fourth or fifth graders to decide if the answer is closer to 1,000, 2,000, 3,000, 4,000, or 5,000 is a good challenge that gives students important practice with estimating.

Question students about how they reason numerically. Probe students' thinking by saying: "Why do you think that?" "Explain why that makes sense," and "Tell more about how you reasoned." Ask students regularly, not just when they make errors. This gives students the message that thinking numerically is about reasoning, not just memorizing.

Pose numerical problems that have more than one possible answer. For example, tell children that you have $1.00 and pose one of these problems: *How could I spend exactly $1.00 by buying two things with different prices? How could I spend exactly $1.00 by buying three things with different prices?* or *How could I spend exactly $1.00 by buying three things with different prices if one of them costs $0.39?* There are multiple answers to each of these problems, so each one is useful for giving students a good deal of practice figuring mentally.

Number sense rests on the premise that there are multiple ways to reason numerically, and the selection of a particular approach depends on the numbers at hand. Number sense develops over time and from many experiences with reasoning numerically. Number sense is enhanced by knowing the basic facts so that students can calculate more efficiently. Most importantly, in the classroom, teachers need to provide students with many opportunities to reason numerically, talk with others about their ideas, and see different ways of thinking about numbers.

How Children Learn Mathematics

Not only is it important to consider the content of the elementary math curriculum, but it's also important to make use of what is known about how children learn mathematics. Children need to learn mathematical concepts and to see relationships among these concepts. Mathematical concepts and relationships are abstract ideas that people learn through the process of sense making and constructing understanding. The same is true for children.

In much of math instruction, children are expected to accept an entirely organized intellectual discipline, usually presented symbolically. They may learn to deal with symbols well enough to perform arithmetic operations. However, having mastered arithmetic procedures is not a sufficient indicator that children truly understand the concepts that symbolic manipulations represent. It does not guarantee that they will be able to use those concepts to solve problems.

Learning mathematics requires that children create and re-create mathematical relationships in their own minds. Therefore, when providing appropriate instruction, teachers cannot be seduced by the symbolism of mathematics. Children need direct and concrete interaction with mathematical ideas. Continual interaction between a child's mind and concrete experiences with mathematics in the real world is necessary. The following exercises are designed to help you experience this process of interaction.

The Ratio of Your Height to Your Head
How many times do you think a piece of yarn or string equal to your height would wrap around your head as a headband? _____

Unless you've tried this before, your initial response most likely was based purely on your perceptions. You have some mental picture of your body, and you rely on that perception to make a guess. Adults' answers to this question usually range between two and ten. (Ask at least five others this same question to verify this for yourself.) Few make an accurate estimate based on their perceptions.

Perceptions are not always based in reality. We see this with young children who are shown five objects and claim that there are more when the objects are spread out. This is what they perceive. Their response is not based on logical reasoning but on their perception. If you've never explored the ratio between your height and your head, there is no reason to assume you have learned that relationship. You need to do the measurement to find out the ratio. To learn concepts, experience in the real world is needed.

Height/Circumference

Imagine a soft drink can. Suppose you take a piece of yarn and wrap it around the can to measure its circumference. Do you think the circumference is *longer*, *shorter*, or about the *same* as the height of the can? Indicate on the drawing how high you think the circumference measure will reach.

As with the previous experience, many people guess incorrectly. The common misperception is that the yarn will be about the same length as the height of the can. There's an element of surprise when that perception is proved to be incorrect. More than surprise, there is often a feeling of consternation, of being puzzled about what has been shown, often of uncomfortableness. It's as if you thought you had more understanding about the relationship between the height and circumference of a soft drink can.

The realization of a misperception produces mental confusion. You now have a problem—you've been faced with a contradiction. This state of confusion is what Piaget calls *disequilibrium*. At this moment, you have the greatest potential to learn, to gain new understanding about a relationship. To develop the understanding that takes you beyond your misperception to what really is so requires that you reorganize your mental construct (in this instance, about the relationship between the circumference and height of a soft drink can) that led you to the erroneous conclusion in the first place.

Only you can accomplish this reorganization, in your own mind. The source of this understanding is inside you. Then, when you come to new understanding—based in reality rather than on how you perceive reality—you no longer are confused. You are in what Piaget terms the state of *equilibrium*. Your intellectual balance is restored, and you no longer experience discomfort or confusion.

To follow up the experiment of measuring the soft drink can, you would benefit from additional experiences with cylinders that had different proportions. One experience is not generally sufficient to cement understanding of a relationship that is new to a learner.

Repeat the experiment with the soft drink can using at least six other cylindrical containers. Use glasses, jars, paper cups, wastepaper baskets—whatever is available. For each, make a drawing of the object and predict before measuring. Record your prediction (longer, shorter, or same) and the actual result for each.

What conclusion can you now make about the relationship of the circumference and the height of a cylindrical container? If it's not possible for you to make a conclusion, what more might you do?

_____

_____

_____

The process of resolving disequilibrium is called *equilibration*. This process is benefited by ample concrete experience by the learner. It's generally not sufficient to be taught a concept abstractly. Actually, when you studied geometry in high school, you probably were "taught" this concept. You were taught that the circumference of a circle is equal to pi times the diameter ($c = \pi d$ or $c = 2\pi r$) and that pi is equal to $3\frac{1}{7}$ or 3.14. You may have learned the formula and also may have been successful applying it in textbook situations. But you did not learn about the formula or about pi in a way that made it accessible for you to apply in a new situation; that is, that the circumference is about three times the diameter and that using this information enables you to make better estimates in measurement situations.

For many people, there is little relationship between the abstractions of mathematics and the concepts those abstractions represent. The mathematics instruction we provide to children should emphasize meaning, relationships, and connections, and we should be mindful of what our students understand, not merely what they can do. There's an old joke about a used-car salesman who reported to his boss: "I sold the car, but the customer didn't buy it." It's not enough to teach without careful attention to what is learned.

Learning often begins with the recognition of a problem. The process of equilibration is one in which there is continuous interaction between your mental conceptual structures and your environment. It's a repeated cycle of going from confusion to new understanding. Confusion is essential to the process. Yet in school, confusion is often seen negatively, as a hindrance rather than an opportunity for learning. It's as if the goal for a child is to be right all the time, to complete papers correctly, to be successful continually. This makes no sense when the process of learning implies that some concepts have not yet been learned.

Try the following experiment with cylindrical containers. Take two 5-by-8-inch cards and roll each into a tube, rolling one the short way and the other the long way. Tape them. As in the previous experiments, predict whether the circumference is *longer*, *shorter*, or about the *same* as the height. Also predict *how much* longer or shorter the height is. Then measure.

Prediction: _____   Prediction: _____
How much: _____   How much: _____
Result: _____   Result: _____

Suppose you filled each tube with rice or beans to compare how much each holds. Do you think each holds the same? If not, which one do you think holds more than the other? Why?

_____

_____

Follow the procedure shown and record the results.

_____

For learning to occur, three conditions are necessary: maturity, physical experience, and social interaction. The process of equilibration coordinates these three conditions.

Maturity

The older children are, the more likely their mental structures will act in coordinated ways. Young children shown a group of objects frequently claim there are a greater number when the objects are spread out, but older children no longer make this error. Younger children report what they perceive; older children have reached a level of mental maturity that allows them to understand that the number of objects does not change when the objects are repositioned. A child who does not see the contradiction between perception and reality is not in a state of disequilibrium.

Physical experience

The more experiences children have with physical objects in the environment, the more likely related understanding will develop. Firsthand experimentation is needed. Merely looking at a soft drink can does not reveal the relationship between its height and its circumference. Testing an idea with physical materials provides valuable feedback for understanding relationships.

Social interaction

The more opportunities children have to interact with peers, parents, and teachers, the more they hear other viewpoints that help them gain perspective on their own ideas. Social interaction stimulates children to think through their own ideas and to approach objectivity. This type of interaction is also an important source of information about social customs and conventions.

What are the teaching implications of these conditions for learning? Essential to making instructional decisions is to consider the source of the learning of any new concept or skill. Mathematics relies on logical structures, and learning mathematics calls for making sense of these structures, for thinking, reasoning, and searching to uncover meaning. Learning mathematical ideas is all about sense making, and the source of the knowledge is internal; that is, it lies *inside* the learner.

Social knowledge, however, is also an aspect of mathematics. The symbolism that we use to represent ideas—the numerals we write to represent quantities and the symbols that we use to describe relationships—are social conventions that help us communicate about mathematical ideas. Because of this, the source of knowledge for vocabulary and symbols is external; that is, it lies *outside* the learner. It is not possible to figure out through reasoning or through searching to uncover meaning that the numbers we multiply are called *factors* and the answer to a multiplication problem is called a *product*, or that we use a symbol that looks like a period when expressing decimal numerals, for example, 5.76. These are arbitrary, agreed-upon conventions. The sources for learning social knowledge can be other people, books, TV shows, movies, or other sources outside the child.

For both types of knowledge—social and logical—explicit instruction is essential. However, the character of the instruction vastly differs. For teaching social knowledge, the correct, and really only, pedagogical choice is to provide the information to the learner, that is, to teach by telling or to give the learner access to the information from another resource—a book, a magazine, a video—always drawing from a source of knowledge that is external to the learner. There's no way to figure out, for example, that numbers that aren't divisible by two are called *odd* numbers—we have to acquire knowledge of the terminology from an outside source. However, knowing if a specific number is or isn't divisible by two calls for understanding the characteristics of numbers that do and don't have a remainder of one when divided by two—we have to acquire this mathematical knowledge by making sense, synthesizing what we know about division, and connecting this understanding with what we know about patterns of numbers. For teaching logical knowledge, the appropriate pedagogical choice is to provide the learner with opportunities to interact with the ideas with the goal of bringing meaning to them—the source of the knowledge and the process of developing understanding are internal to the learner.

It's long been held as a true notion that you know something best when you teach it. Teaching in this context is typically thought of as explaining, with the goal of making concepts clear. In order to be able to explain an idea, you have to think it through for yourself first, understand it, and come up with some sort of sequence for presenting it. The process of preparing to teach in this way calls for sense making on the part of the teacher. While teachers always need to make sense of the mathematics they teach, the challenge is then to find ways for the students to make sense for themselves so that they can connect new ideas to existing mental constructs in order to develop understanding of new ideas.

A teacher, another child, or a book can set a child in a direction for learning, offer some useful information, or explain an idea, but children have to construct understanding for themselves in order to make sense of mathematics. Rather than teaching by telling, teachers must structure learning activities that make use of physical materials, allow for social interaction, and provide opportunities for children to think, reason, and make sense of mathematics. You cannot talk a child into learning or tell a child to understand.

The Role of Manipulative Materials

Supplies of manipulative materials for teaching mathematics exist in most classrooms—tiles, cubes, pattern blocks, Cuisenaire rods, geoboards, tangrams, counters, and more. Manipulative materials have long been staples for math instruction, and for good reasons.

One reason is that manipulative materials help students make sense of abstract ideas. Just as we say that a picture is worth a thousand words, there is no substitute for firsthand concrete experiences. Materials provide children physical models with which they can interact and which help them form mental models that they can then connect to abstract symbolic representations. For example, young children learn about even and odd numbers, that even numbers can be split into two equal numbers. But instead of teaching this idea simply numerically (for example, since 12 = 6 + 6, 12 is an even number), use manipulative materials: Have the children take a handful of objects and see if the objects can be split into two equal groups or arranged into two equal lines. If they can, the number is even; if they can't, then it's odd. Matching up counters in groups or lines for many quantities helps children build mental models that they can then translate to the abstract idea. Learning in this way is natural and effortless. And when they organize and examine the numbers that turn out to be even, the numerical pattern (2, 4, 6, 8, 10, and so on) emerges. For older students, for example, learning about square numbers is greatly enhanced when they actually arrange tiles into squares and see how the square numbers grow—2 by 2, 3 by 3, and so on. (Yes, square numbers are actually square!) Students can then connect their concrete experience to multiplication (2×2, 3×2, and so on) and think about the pattern of square numbers (1, 4, 9, 16, 25, and so on) both numerically and visually.

Another reason for using manipulative materials is that they provide students ways to test and verify ideas. We know that partial understanding and confusion are natural to children's learning, and manipulative materials can provide the support students need to cement or extend their understanding. For example, when young children are first learning about even and odd numbers, their understanding is typically fragile. They may not be sure if a particular number, say seventeen or twenty-six, is even or odd. But they can always check to find out by counting out that many counters and seeing if they can arrange them into two equal lines. Or when older students studying square numbers are expected to understand the pattern of how they relate to sums of odd numbers ($4 = 1 + 3, 9 = 1 + 3 + 5, 16 = 1 + 3 + 5 + 7$, and so on), they can actually build understanding as they build a pattern with tiles. They start with one tile, add tiles to surround it on two sides to build the next square number, then surround this new square on two sides to build the next, and so on. The pattern of adding consecutive odd numbers emerges visually from the students' interaction with the physical materials.

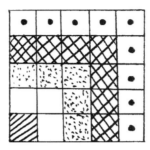

Also, manipulative materials are useful tools for solving problems. For example, think about the formulas we learned for calculating areas of geometric shapes. Textbooks provide ample practice for applying the formula for the area of a triangle—$A = \frac{1}{2}b \times h$. Manipulative materials add the dimension of helping students understand the why, not just the how, of the formula. Students can rely on geoboards and rubber bands, cut squared paper, or engage in some other concrete experience to help them build understanding. For problems that involve three-dimensional shapes, such as finding the volume and surface area of cubes, actually using cubes to construct larger cubes and then figuring their volumes and surface areas are valuable and effective first steps. Concrete materials help students get their hands as well as their minds around many of the mysteries of mathematics.

A fourth reason is that manipulative materials make mathematics learning more engaging and interesting by lifting mathematics off textbook and workbook pages. They involve students as active learners. They motivate students to understand concepts and skills that they then learn to represent abstractly.

It's important to make manipulative materials part of the regular classroom supplies, available to students as needed. This calls for organization, ground rules, and discussion. Here are suggestions for supporting appropriate classroom use of manipulative materials:

- Talk with students about how manipulative materials can help them learn. These discussions are essential for first-time users and useful refreshers to refocus students from time to time.

- From day one, set ground rules for using materials. Explain that with toys or games, children make up their own rules. With classroom manipulative materials, however, they will have specific problems to solve and activities to do. Encourage students to stay on task as they make their own discoveries and explore new ideas.
- Set up a system for storing manipulative materials and familiarize students with it. It's important that students know where and how to store the materials they use.
- Time for free exploration is essential for allowing students to satisfy their curiosity so they don't later become distracted from assigned tasks. After children explore a material, ask what they discovered. Record their observations so students can learn from one another's ideas. Then assign a specific task.
- For easy reference, post charts in your classroom listing the names of the manipulative materials the students will use. The charts let students know that you value manipulative materials and help students learn the materials' names and how to spell them.
- Send home a letter that lets parents know why their children are using these materials. Explain that even if parents did not learn math with materials like these, current research and classroom results show that they are solid learning tools. You might have students take home materials and activities to do with their families.

The Importance of Class Discussions

Classroom discussions are integral to classroom instruction and are important vehicles for supporting students' mathematics learning. Through classroom discussions, students share what they know, explain how they reason, ask questions, try out new ideas, and get feedback on their thinking, both from the teacher and from other students in the class. Discussions give students access to mathematical ideas and give teachers access to what students understand.

NCTM's *Principles and Standards* (2000) calls for incorporating communication into mathematics instruction to help students organize and consolidate their thinking, communicate coherently and clearly, analyze and evaluate the thinking and strategies of others, and use the language of mathematics. However, talking about mathematical ideas may not come naturally to children. Teachers need to provide students specific support for learning to talk about their mathematical ideas.

First of all, it's important that the classroom atmosphere supports students in participating in discussions, and teachers must be deliberate about establishing that atmosphere. Part of this involves the teacher modeling by giving students time to collect their thoughts, listening attentively when they talk, being curious about their ideas, and allowing them ample time to finish their thoughts. But it also involves the teacher being clear to the class about expectations. Tell students that it's OK for them to change their minds at any time, as long as they can explain why. Establish that it's OK to make mistakes, that errors are opportunities for learning. Also tell students that you expect them to listen to each other with respect, show patience when someone is searching for a thought, and never, never ridicule anyone for his or her ideas.

These ideas will be useful only if they are consistently put into practice. Post a chart of general guidelines for classroom discussions:

> Share your ideas.
> Explain how you reason.
> Listen, with your hand down, when someone else is talking.
> Ask questions.
> Offer your comments about others' ideas.

These guidelines will mean more to students after they've experienced how you lead discussions. Also, it's good to review them from time to time and add to them with additional suggestions that come up during the course of lessons.

It is also helpful for students to become familiar with the kinds of questions that you will ask. It may help to post a general list of questions that you will be asking during class discussions:

How did you figure out the answer?
Why do you think the answer is reasonable?
Who has another way to explain? (Or Who has a different answer?)
Who can explain what _____ said in your own words?

It often helps students collect their thoughts for a class discussion by first talking with a partner or in a small group. Some teachers refer to this as *turn and talk* and others refer to it as *think, pair, share*. Explain to students that talking in this way helps them try out ideas and prepare to present their ideas to the whole class.

In their valuable and important book, *Classroom Discussions: Using Math Talk to Help Students Learn*, Suzanne H. Chapin, Catherine O'Connor, and Nancy Canavan Anderson (2003) explicitly describe specific tools that teachers can use to support productive classroom conversation. Specifically, they present five "talk moves" that provide a solid base for teachers to rely on when leading discussions, and they provide many examples of actual classroom discussions. One talk move is revoicing, in which the teacher tries to repeat what a student has said and then asks the student to verify whether the revoicing is correct. This is especially helpful when you understand what a student has said but aren't sure that others have. Another talk move is to call on a student to revoice by asking, "Can you say what _____ just said?" This gives the rest of the students another version of an idea. A third is to ask: "Do you agree or disagree, and why?" This encourages students to apply their thinking to others' ideas. A fourth is to ask for additional input by asking, "What can you add on?" And the fifth is to use wait time, being explicit when a student is struggling by saying, "Take your time . . . we'll wait."

Students should know that participating in class discussions is part of their responsibility as members of your class. Acknowledge that you know that speaking to the whole class is more difficult for some, but that it's important for everyone to contribute. Then provide the support to help all students become better communicators. (For more information about using classroom discussions for assessment, see the section "Linking Assessment and Instruction," on page 47.)

Incorporating Writing into Math Instruction

For many people, math and writing seem like oil and water, subjects with little in common. This is an unfortunate viewpoint. Teaching math can be greatly enhanced by making writing an integral aspect of students' learning. As William Zinsser says in his book *Writing to Learn*, "Writing is a way to work yourself into a subject and make it your own" (1988, 16).

Writing in math class supports learning because it requires students to organize, clarify, and reflect on their ideas—all useful processes for making sense of mathematics. In addition, when students write, their papers can be useful for assessment, providing a window into their understandings and misconceptions about the content they are studying. NCTM's *Principles and Standards* states that "written communication should be nurtured" (2000, 62) and that math instruction should enable all students to

- organize and consolidate their mathematical thinking through communication
- communicate their mathematical thinking coherently and clearly to peers, teachers, and others
- analyze and evaluate the mathematical thinking and strategies of others
- use the language of mathematics to express mathematical ideas precisely (60)

The writing that you ask students to do in math class generally differs from the writing they do in language arts. Writing in math class isn't meant to produce a polished product, but rather to provide a way for students to reflect on their own learning and to explore, extend, and cement their ideas about the mathematics they study. Aside from the students themselves, you as the teacher are the primary audience for their writing. Pay attention to what that writing shows about their math understanding—*what* they write, not *how* they write it.

A Variety of Writing Assignments

Writing assignments can fall into four categories: keeping journals or logs, solving math problems, explaining mathematical ideas, and writing about learning processes. Each of these categories focuses the students on their math learning in a different way, and each provides useful information for assessing their progress. It's beneficial to make writing a regular feature of math class with a variety of assignments.

Keeping journals or logs. When students create ongoing records about what they're doing and learning in math class, they have a chronological record of their learning experiences. It's helpful, especially for assignments at the beginning of the year, to post suggestions that help students focus their journal writing:

> Write about what you did in class.
> What did you learn?
> What are you unsure about, confused by, or wondering about?
> Describe what was easy and what was difficult for you.

At times, give guidelines that relate to a specific lesson. For example, "Explain why Raul's answer made sense," or "Write about why Kaisha and Robert disagreed."

You can create students' journals in various ways. You can staple sheets of paper into booklets with construction-paper covers, giving students a new booklet—and thus a fresh start—several times a year. (Remember the pleasant school ritual of having new notebooks for courses at the start of each semester?) Or you can ask students to write on loose paper and then file their work in folders. This makes reading a class set of papers easier than rummaging through individual journals or logs. Or consider providing each student with a notebook. (A notebook with grid paper is especially helpful for students.) Whatever the approach, keeping the students' journals or logs in the classroom, except when you take them home to read, ensures that they will be available for students to use during class.

Solving math problems. Use writing to engage students in applying a variety of strategies for solving problems and also for teaching them to monitor and reflect on their problem-solving processes. Writing enhances both of these skills. Even when students work cooperatively on a problem-solving situation, it's beneficial to have each student write his or her own paper. Group work gives students access to other ideas, while writing requires them to clarify and express their own thinking.

Explaining mathematical ideas. From time to time, you might ask students to write what they think about an idea or a math concept. Their responses often provide useful information for assessing what they understand. For example, at the end of a unit on division, ask the students to write about how multiplication and division are alike and different. Or, in the middle of a unit, ask students to write on the topic "What I Know About _____ So Far." (This title conveys to students that you don't expect them to know everything yet.)

Writing about learning processes. Instead of focusing on a math problem or concept, a writing assignment can be used to have students address a general aspect of the their learning during math class. For example, ask students to write about their favorite and least favorite activities in a unit or about the qualities of a good problem-solving partner in math class. Sometimes they can write directions for an activity or a game so they can teach it to someone at home. Or consider asking students to write letters describing the activities you do in class, to be used as an introduction for visitors who come to class to observe.

Strategies for Incorporating Writing

Following are classroom strategies that are useful for incorporating writing into your math instruction

Establish the purpose for writing in math class. Make sure students understand the two basic reasons that writing is an important part of math: to support their learning and to help you assess their progress.

Establish yourself as the audience. Let students know that their writing will help you teach them better by providing valuable insights into their understandings, misconceptions, and confusions.

Ask students to include details and to explain their thinking as thoroughly as possible. Encourage them to use words, numbers, and, if they like, pictures to provide as much information as possible.

Have students discuss their ideas before writing. Most students find talking easier than writing, and opportunities to talk about their thinking can help students formulate ideas that they will then try to explain in writing. Class discussions are useful, but having students talk in small groups enables more students to express their ideas. After a discussion, remind students that they can write about any idea they heard, as long as it makes sense to them and they can explain it.

Post useful mathematics vocabulary. Maintain a class chart showing pertinent mathematics vocabulary that comes up in class discussions. Before students begin work on an assignment, ask if there are other terms they might use that they'd like to see on the chart. Keep this list posted and add to it during the year.

Write a prompt on the board to get students started on a writing assignment. Sometimes a general prompt is appropriate: *I think that the answer is _____. I think that because _____.* Sometimes you'll want to use a prompt that relates more specifically to the assignment. For example, for third graders solving the problem of how many chopsticks are needed for the twenty-eight people in the room, you might write on the board: *We need _____ chopsticks. I figured it out by _____.*

Give individual assistance as needed. No matter how thoroughly you prepare students for a writing assignment, some will need additional assistance to get started. Talk with these students first to ascertain that they understand the assignment. Then encourage them to verbalize their thinking by asking them such questions as, "What do you think?" "What's one idea that you have?" and "What do you remember about what others said?" After students offer an idea, ask them to repeat it aloud. Then suggest that they repeat it silently to themselves. Finally, tell them to write those exact words on their paper. This process often helps jump-start students' writing. If it doesn't, try refocusing the assignment and asking students to write about what they find confusing.

Have students share their writing in pairs or small groups. Before handing in an assignment, students may benefit from reading their papers to another student or to a small group for feedback. This exercise not only serves the writer but also enables students to hear other points of view.

Use students' writing in subsequent instruction. Student papers can provide useful springboards for extending lessons, and using them in this way reinforces the idea that you value students' writing.

Use student papers to create class inventories. Reading a set of papers from an assignment can provide a useful overview of how the class responded to particular lessons. Was the experience accessible to all? Did it interest or challenge the more capable students? What additional instruction do students need?

Teaching Math Vocabulary

Mathematics is sometimes described as its own language and the teaching of math as the teaching of a second language. There is a good deal of truth in thinking of math in this way. While many of the words that we use to describe mathematical ideas are familiar to us, their meanings in general usage are often very different from their mathematical meanings.

For example, think about the terminology of *even* and *odd*. In common usage we talk about shares being *even* when each person has the same amount, or knitting stitches being *even* when they are consistently the same size. We *even* talk about having to *even* up the piles. In mathematics, however, we use *even* very specifically to describe a number that's divisible by two; that is, it can be divided (shared, if you like) into two equal groups with nothing remaining. While in common usage, *odd* describes something unusual, in mathematics, *odd* describes a number that isn't even; that is, it's not divisible by two, or can't be divided into two equal groups without having a remainder.

In common usage, when we talk about things that *multiply*, such as animals or plants, we mean that they increase in number. When we *multiply* numbers in mathematics, however, we specifically mean that we are combining a certain number of equal-size groups, which we often describe as repeated addition. And while the numbers always increase in real-world contexts when things multiply, in the world of mathematics, sometimes the answer to a multiplication problem is less that one or both of the numbers we multiplied—for example, $6 \times \frac{1}{2}$, which we can think of in one way as $\frac{1}{2} + \frac{1}{2} + \frac{1}{2} + \frac{1}{2} + \frac{1}{2} + \frac{1}{2}$, produces an answer of 3, which is less than than 6.

Many examples exist of words whose unique meanings when used as mathematical terminology differ from their common meanings—*difference, product, factor, power, face, remainder, dividend, times, compass, expression, positive, negative, improper, rational, irrational, real*, and on and on. Even the word *half* has a common nonmathematical colloquial use when a child says, "Your half is bigger than my half." In mathematics, the important idea about halves of the same whole is that they are exactly the same!

Read the paragraph below. Think about the meanings of the italicized words in common usage and then about their mathematical meanings. How might you teach the common usage of these words in a language arts lesson? How might you teach the mathematical meanings of these same words?

Even if it rains tomorrow, our football team will *face* the opponent. The two teams are pretty *even*. One *difference* is that their team was last year's state champion. We think that the weather will be an important *factor* in the game's outcome.

However, learning mathematics as a second language isn't exactly analogous to learning a second language. When studying a new language, you learn how to use it to serve your purposes of naming things, asking questions, and describing your thoughts. You already have knowledge about the ideas you want to express, and learning the new language is all about learning a new way to communicate these ideas.

The purpose of learning the language of mathematics, however, is for communicating about mathematical ideas, and first it's necessary to acquire knowledge about those mathematical ideas. Only then is there a reason for learning the correct mathematical language. Teaching knowledge of the mathematical ideas and relationships must precede teaching vocabulary— there is no purpose or value for learning mathematical vocabulary without understanding the mathematics it describes.

The vocabulary of mathematics is an example of social knowledge, socially agreed-upon conventions for labeling mathematical ideas. (See the section "How Children Learn Mathematics," on page 27.) For vocabulary instruction in mathematics, it's essential that the mathematical concepts that the vocabulary describes are understood prior to the vocabulary being introduced. The vocabulary by itself will not reveal the meaning of the concept, nor will it serve any useful purpose without the prerequisite mathematical understanding. Once a learner has made sense of a mathematical concept, then it's appropriate, and essential, to connect the learner's knowledge to the standard mathematical language. And this calls for explicit and systematic teaching.

Teaching strategies that are effective for teaching mathematics vocabulary can draw on practices that have been found helpful for teaching vocabulary as part of students' literacy instruction. Also, it's important for vocabulary instruction to focus both on vocabulary that specifically describes mathematical content, such as *equation*, *multiply*, and *decimal numeral*, and on words that describe processes that students engage in when interacting with mathematical ideas, such as *compare*, *explain*, and *represent*. And, while teaching mathematical vocabulary is important to mathematics instruction, it's essential that knowledge of mathematical vocabulary is neither the end goal of mathematics instruction nor the primary indicator of students' mathematical success. That said, following are instructional strategies that address vocabulary instruction in the context of mathematics lessons:

- *Identify the vocabulary to be taught.* It's important to determine the relevant terminology for each unit of study and for daily lessons.
- *Introduce vocabulary after developing understanding of the related mathematical ideas.* Vocabulary instruction must always follow students making sense of the ideas being taught.
- *Explain the vocabulary by connecting its meaning to the students' learning experiences.* Keep explanations brief and directly connected to students' firsthand experiences. When vocabulary relates to mathematical symbols, point to the symbols when saying the words.
- *Have the students pronounce the words.* It's valuable to have all of the students say a new word together several times when it is first introduced.
- *Write new vocabulary on a class "Math Words" chart.* Seeing words written is supportive for all students and essential for some students to be able to learn them.
- *Have students keep their own lists of math words.* Copying words from the chart provides students a first experience with writing them down. For use on their own assignments, students can refer to the math words either on the class chart or on their own lists.
- *Use the vocabulary repeatedly.* Be consistent and use new terminology as often as possible. Again, when vocabulary relates to mathematical symbols, point to the symbols as you say the words.
- *Encourage students to use the vocabulary in discussions and on assignments.* Prompt students to use new terminology when they present ideas or complete assignments.

For more on this topic, see "The Language of Math" on page 372.

Using Children's Literature

For many teachers, the storybook shelf isn't the first place to look when planning a math lesson. But children's books are effective tools for teaching mathematics. Children's books can spark students' imaginations in ways that exercises in textbooks or workbooks often don't. Connecting math to literature can boost confidence for children who love books but are wary of math. And students who already love math can learn to appreciate stories in a whole new way.

Key to the value of incorporating children's books into instruction is making good choices about the books to use. Consider these three questions when identifying a book to use as a springboard for a math lesson:

Is it of high quality from a literary perspective?

Does it present content that is mathematically sound and grade-level appropriate?

Is it effective for helping students learn to think and reason mathematically?

While the goal after reading a book aloud is to launch a math lesson, it's important first to provide time for students to enjoy the book, savor the text, and examine the illustrations. Also, as for any read-aloud experience, it's important to provide the opportunity for class discussion about the book. Then it's appropriate to make the math connection and shift the students' attention to the math goal of the lesson. After the lesson, it's a good idea to make the children's book available for students to revisit on their own and encourage students to check out books to take home and enjoy with their families.

Here's a general lesson design to follow for structuring math instruction around a children's book:

1. Read the book aloud. (At times, reread the book if it's appropriate to do so.)
2. Allow time for class discussion of the book.
3. Introduce the math connection to the class and assign the math work to be done in class, typically an activity, a problem, an exploration, or a game.
4. After students have had time to complete the assignment, lead a class discussion for students to present their work and listen and respond to one another's ideas.
5. If appropriate, assign homework based on the lesson.

The "Beginning Number Concepts" section in Part 3 (page 196) presents some examples for using children's books. For additional suggestions, not only for young children but also for older students, see the Math, Literature, and Nonfiction series published by Math Solutions Publications (www.mathsolutions.com).

Linking Assessment and Instruction

Making assessment an integral part of instruction is essential for improving the effectiveness of classroom math instruction. When learning math in school, we all experienced doing assignments and taking quizzes to give our teachers information about how we were doing. Typically, these assignments and quizzes called for performing calculations and solving problems with the focus on getting right answers. And while assignments and quizzes are useful vehicles for measuring students' progress, and correct answers are important, merely checking whether or not answers are correct is insufficient. Assessments must also uncover what students understand and provide insights into how they think and reason. Key to assessing students' math learning is to delve into how students arrive at answers.

To accomplish this, assessment must play an integral role in classroom instruction, not only to monitor individual students' progress but also to reflect on our teaching to maximize the effectiveness of our lessons. After teaching a lesson, it's helpful to ask: What did the students learn? If I teach the same grade level next year, should I repeat this lesson? Should I make changes to it? If I decide not to repeat the lesson, how might I rethink what I was trying to accomplish? This continual evaluation of instructional choices is at the heart of both monitoring student progress and improving our teaching practice.

Posing questions is an effective instructional tool for stimulating students' thinking. It is also an essential assessment tool for uncovering what students understand. It's important to consider the kinds of questions, both oral and written, that serve to provide insights into how students think. When we ask a question that calls for a correct response, we need to broaden our listening focus so that we don't listen merely for the correct answer (that we hope to hear) but also push further to listen to the reasoning behind the answer. And while it's typical to probe students when they give an incorrect answer, it's just as important to probe them when their answer is correct. Correct answers can mask confusion.

Here's an example. Fourth graders were asked to write five fractions in order from least to greatest—$\frac{1}{4}, \frac{11}{16}, \frac{3}{8}, \frac{1}{16}$, and $\frac{3}{4}$. They were also asked to write about their reasons for ordering the fractions. After they had time to solve the problem, they participated in a whole-class discussion. Robert reported first. He said with confidence, and correctly, "The smallest fraction is one-sixteenth." When asked to explain how he knew that $\frac{1}{16}$ was the smallest fraction, Robert read from his paper, again with confidence, "Because one-sixteenth is the lowest number in fractions."

The students had previously cut and labeled strips of construction paper to make fraction kits, and $\frac{1}{16}$ happened to be the smallest piece in their kits (see page 271). The fraction kit—a standard and effective instructional tool—had led Robert to an incorrect generalization. Requiring that Robert give more than the answer, but also the reasoning behind it, unveiled his misconception. This experience called for not only dealing with Robert but also rethinking how to use the fraction kit so that students would understand that we could cut smaller and smaller fraction pieces and find fraction names for even the tiniest sliver.

Incorporating students' reasoning into both written assignments and classroom discussions is a crucial step toward making assessment an integral and ongoing aspect of classroom instruction. It should be a staple of math teaching.

Assessment Through Students' Written Work

One main strategy for assessing students' learning is to incorporate writing into math assignments. There are many ways to present writing assignments that yield information about how students are thinking (see my book *Writing in Math Class* (1995) and also the section "Incorporating Writing into Math Instruction" [page 38]). Here are four strategies.

Ask for more than one strategy. Solving math problems often requires making false starts and searching for new approaches. Students need to develop multiple strategies so that they become flexible in their mathematical thinking and are able to look at mathematical situations from different perspectives. Even when students are performing routine computations, asking them to demonstrate more than one way to arrive at an answer provides insight into their thinking.

Let students set parameters. A good technique for assessing students' understanding as well as differentiating instruction is to make an assignment adjustable in some way, so that it is accessible and appropriate for a wide range of students. For example, asking students to write their own word problems—and solve them—can give you information about their numerical comfort as well as their computational skill.

Assess the same concept or skill in different ways. Students' beginning understanding, although fragile, can provide useful building blocks or connections to more robust learning. Sometimes a familiar context can help a student think about a numerically challenging problem. Using flexible assessment approaches enables us to build on students' strengths and interests and help them move on from there.

Take occasional class inventories. Compiling an inventory from a set of papers can provide a sense of the class's progress and thus inform decisions about how to differentiate instruction. For example, after students complete an assignment that includes having them explain their reasoning, review their papers and list the strategies they used. Use this information to inform future lessons and for providing intervention for the struggling students.

Assessment Through Classroom Discussion

Incorporating assessment into classroom discussion serves two goals: it provides insights into students' thinking, and it ensures that no student is invisible in the class, that all are participating and working to understand and learn. Try the following strategies. (And for more information about getting the most out of class discussions, see the section "The Importance of Class Discussions," on page 36.)

Ask students to explain their answers, whether or not the answers are correct. Follow up on both correct and incorrect answers by asking students to explain their reasoning. While you know the correct answer, avoid having a preconceived response about how a student should have reasoned. Students can arrive at correct answers in unexpected ways. For example, Brandon, a fifth grader, when comparing $\frac{4}{5}$ and $\frac{3}{4}$, changed the fractions so that they had common numerators—$\frac{12}{15}$ and $\frac{12}{16}$. He knew that sixteenths were smaller than fifteenths, so $\frac{12}{15}$, or $\frac{4}{5}$, had to be larger!

Ask students to share their solution strategies with the class. After a student responds to a question and explains his or her reasoning, ask, "Who has a different way to solve the problem?" or "Who has another way to think about this?" Provide sufficient wait time to encourage students to collect their thoughts. In addition to providing insights into students' thinking and understanding, this method also reinforces the idea that there are different ways to think about problems and lets the students know that you value their individual approaches.

Call on students who don't volunteer. Let your students know that it's important for you to learn about how each of them thinks and, for that reason, to hear from all of them. Reassure them, however, that if you call on them and they don't know the answer, they should just let you know, because that is valuable information that will help you think about the support they need.

Use small-group work. This technique is especially useful for drawing out students who are reticent about talking in front of the whole class. After posing a problem, say, "Turn and talk with your partner," or "Talk with your group about this." Then eavesdrop, paying especially close attention to the students who don't typically talk in class discussions.

Improving Mathematics Teaching

As stated in NCTM's *Principles and Standards* "To ensure deep, high-quality learning for all students, assessment and instruction must be integrated so that assessment becomes a routine part of the ongoing classroom activity rather than an interruption. Such assessment also provides the information teachers need to make appropriate instructional decisions" (2000, 23).

Making assessment an integral part of daily mathematics instruction is a challenge. It requires planning specific ways to use assignments and discussions to discover what students do and do not understand. It also requires teachers to be prepared to deal with students' responses. Merely spotting when students are incorrect is relatively easy compared with understanding the reasons behind their errors. The latter demands careful attention and a deep knowledge of the mathematics concepts that students are learning.

The benefits are worth the effort. By building and using a wide repertoire of assessment strategies, we can get to know more about our students than we ever thought possible. The insights we gain by making assessment a regular part of instruction enable us to meet the needs of the students who are eager for more challenges and to provide intervention for those who are struggling.

Managing Classroom Instruction

Providing effective mathematics instruction calls for thinking about what's required to support and facilitate student learning—organizing the physical classroom, establishing a safe environment for learning, helping students establish productive learning habits, structuring effective lessons, and more. This section offers suggestions and specific examples.

One essential aspect of supporting learning is helping students develop the attitudes and skills they need to engage with learning mathematics effectively. In order to become successful learners of mathematics, students must develop the following characteristics:

- interest in finding solutions to problems
- confidence to try various strategies
- willingness to risk being wrong at times
- ability to accept frustrations that come from not knowing
- willingness to persevere when solutions are not immediate
- understanding of the difference between not knowing the answer and not having found it *yet*

This is a substantial list of qualities, and the amount of time and effort needed to establish them depends on the students themselves and their previous learning experiences. In order to help students develop these characteristics, it's essential for teachers to model them. Only then will students feel that their teacher values their thinking and has established a safe environment for them to be willing to participate openly and fully.

One aspect of modeling is for teachers to be willing to tackle problems or initiate investigations without always knowing the answers or what the outcomes will be. This willingness can help students develop the attitudes of "let's try" and "we can." To support this, it's helpful for teachers to address the issue of making mistakes. Students need to see errors not as unfortunate occurrences, but rather as opportunities for learning. They must feel that it's OK to offer an idea that might be incorrect and that they will have the support of their teacher and classmates to resolve incorrect thinking. One aspect of this is to emphasize, when asking students to think about an idea or solve a problem, that you value persistence, not speed. Putting the value on quick right responses does not help establish a classroom environment that supports students' learning.

It's also valuable for teachers to encourage students to find ways to verify solutions for themselves. Having students think about problems in more than one way—by talking with a partner or hearing others' ideas in a class discussion—can provide alternate views on solutions. Not only does this make sense for classroom instruction, but it also is a helpful skill in real-life situations. For many problems we face, there is not necessarily one correct solution but several possibilities. Often, an exact solution isn't required and being close enough is sufficient. Most important, in real life, it's often up to the problem solver to decide when a solution is right or best. (Life has no answer book!) In light of those issues, it's good classroom practice to urge students to evaluate their own solutions and to provide them support for doing so.

Along with not providing answers, teachers need to encourage students to explain their approaches and results, even when they are totally correct. Often, teachers nod and affirm a child's correct response and question the child when there's an error. If teachers question children only when their responses are wrong, they soon catch on. Instruction should be structured so students describe their methods and solutions not only to the teacher but to their classmates as well. Time for discussions is needed, and students should be encouraged to listen, question, and learn from each other.

Organizing for Small-Group Work

One way to organize the classroom to establish an environment that is safe and supportive for problem solving is to have students work in pairs or small groups. A small-group structure has the potential to maximize the active participation of each student and to reduce individuals' isolation. It provides a setting that values social interaction, a necessary element of children's learning. When children are organized into pairs or small groups, more students have the opportunity to offer their ideas for reaction and to receive immediate feedback. Organizing a class into small groups may require reorganizing the classroom physically, redefining the students' responsibilities, and shifting the teacher's role.

Let's consider the physical reorganization first. The classroom needs to be organized so that groups of two to five students can talk together. Getting the students into small groups is easy enough. Desks can be moved into clusters, or, if tables are available, each group can be seated at a table or pairs can share a table.

It's beneficial for students to have the opportunity to work with all of their classmates over the course of time. To this end, consider changing groups from time to time. Some teachers like to form groups randomly. Playing cards work well to accomplish this. Label the clusters of desk or tables— *ace, 2, 3, 4,* and so on—and then pull out the corresponding cards from a deck of playing cards (two, three, or four of each, depending on the size of the groups). By shuffling the cards, distributing them, and asking students to sit at the cluster or table that matches their card, you can quickly organize the students into groups. Using cards in this way is a fair system that mixes groups with each reshuffle. It removes the responsibility from the teacher of deciding who works with whom and communicates the message that students need to learn to work with all their classmates. Other teachers, however, prefer to make decisions about the composition of groups depending on the particular activities and interests of the students.

Whatever the system, it helps to prepare students to work together by establishing guidelines. The following three are an effective blend of rules:

1. You are responsible for your own work and behavior.
2. You must be willing to help any group member who asks.
3. You may ask the teacher for help only when everyone in your group has the same question.

These rules are only as useful as they are understood and practiced in actual operation. After explaining them to the class, it's valuable to discuss them for at least the first half dozen times students work in groups. The first rule is not new for any student. Even so, it helps to clarify it with further explanation: "You have responsibilities in this class and your job is to meet them. If you don't understand something, your first option is to ask your group for help. On the other hand, if you do understand, don't take over and give answers; listening to others' ideas is also a part of your individual responsibility. Sometimes, although you are sitting with your group, you will have an individual assignment to complete. Other times, your group will have an assignment to complete jointly, and then your responsibility is to contribute to the group effort."

Two comments help clarify the second rule: "Notice that the benefit of this rule is that you have willing helpers at your disposal at all times, with no waiting for help. Also, remember that you are to give help *when asked*." Caution students not to be pushy or overbearing, to wait for group members to ask, and to help not merely by giving answers, but by trying to ask questions that would help someone focus on the problem at hand.

Rule 3 eliminates many procedural concerns, such as "What are we supposed to do?" "When is this due?" and "Can we take this home?" This rule directs students to seek help from each other first, relieving the teacher of the tedium of having to give the same directions or information over and over again. When a teacher talks to the entire class, it's rare to have everyone listen attentively; chances are better that at least one out of each group is listening at any one time.

Staying true to Rule 3 may seem uncomfortable at first. It's typical during initial small-group experiences for individual students to ask questions or to make requests. When this occurs, direct them first to check with their group and remind them that when all hands are raised, you will come and discuss their problem or request. Responding in this way is not contrary to being a responsive, sensitive, helpful teacher; rather, it motivates children to rely more on themselves. As teachers watch children become more confident and independent, they become convinced that this is an invaluable learning experience.

One benefit students gain from working collaboratively in groups is that they have more opportunity to voice their thinking and to respond to others' ideas. This system also provides students with an organized way to get support from one another, rather than depending solely on the teacher's feedback. It builds students' independence, which, in turn, can free teachers to provide attention to individuals.

The benefits of small-group work will be realized only if you give enough time and attention to implementing guidelines for students. There is no guarantee of instant success from seating students in pairs or small groups and explaining the rules. Students need practice, encouragement, and discussion to learn to work together productively. Although students may have heard much about cooperation, functioning cooperatively is not a skill they've necessarily put into practice. And although they've always been told they're responsible for their own work and behavior, meeting that responsibility independently doesn't come naturally. In order for the system to best serve teachers and students, it's important to carefully plan instruction that utilizes this organization.

Structuring Lessons

While small-group work can maximize student involvement, it's best to begin lessons by presenting information to the whole class about the nature and expectations for their small-group work. It's helpful to think of lessons in three phases:

> introducing
> exploring
> summarizing

Introducing

In this part of the lesson, it's most effective to address the whole class with the goal of helping the students understand what they are to investigate, explore, or solve. Also, you may want to present guidelines for how they should record results. When introducing a lesson, it helps to think about these teaching steps:

1. Present or review concepts.
2. Pose an accessible example for the students to try. (This can provide an initial small-group opportunity for the students.)
3. Present the problem to be solved. (Writing directions on the board is supportive, especially for students who more easily process information when they see as well as hear it.)
4. Discuss the task to make sure students understand what they are to do. (Having students restate the directions helps.)

Exploring

Once the students understand what to do, the exploring part of the lesson begins. While the students are working in groups, the teacher has three responsibilities:

1. Observe the interaction, listening to groups' ideas, strategies, and work procedures, which you may want to bring up later in a whole-class discussion.
2. Offer assistance when needed, either when all members of a group raise their hands or if a group is not working.
3. Provide an extension for groups that finish more quickly than others.

When offering assistance, your goal is to help the group work productively and independently. Determine the nature of the problem, offer assistance, and move on once the group gets going. There are two types of problems that occur with groups, each calling for a different type of assistance.

One problem is difficulty with the activity itself. The group either is stuck or is pursuing an incorrect line of thought. If students are stuck, the teacher can assist by helping students restate what they know so far, posing a simpler example for them to solve, and explaining concepts again if needed. Once they can do an example successfully and can restate the problem, they should return to work. If students are pursuing an erroneous idea or have made an error, it helps to point out a contradiction that illustrates their erroneous thinking or to ask them how they arrived at a certain conclusion. Teachers should avoid telling correct answers and should leave a group when the students are aware of their mistake.

However, the difficulty may be with the group rather than with the problem. Groups bog down for different reasons. For instance, the group may lack the needed impetus to get started. This may be obvious because of lack of materials—paper, pencil, blocks, whatever. If this is the problem, it helps for the teacher to join the group for a short time, to suggest that someone do what's necessary to get started, and, when a student in the group accepts that responsibility, to leave. Groups may also need help with focusing. You may hear questions like "What are we supposed to do?" or "Didn't the teacher say to do it this way?" Offer the needed clarification.

Other problems may arise. Sometimes, one person takes over and ignores the others' ideas. At times, a member of the group does not contribute or does not understand what the group is doing. In these kinds of situations, teachers should point out to the group what they observe and should restate that the group's job is to work together. In these instances, it is helpful to give the group more specific guidelines. Following are some examples:

- To make sure that everyone has an equal chance to speak, after you've spoken, wait until everyone else has offered a thought before you speak again.
- Find a way that everyone can contribute some part to the solution of the problem.
- We all need encouragement, so tell each other when someone offers an idea that is helpful.

Remember that when groups are working well, it's best not to interrupt or intervene but rather to listen and to observe as students work. This is helpful for assessing how students are thinking and learning.

During the exploration stage, it's necessary to have some extensions of the problem to offer groups who complete their work early. Extensions may be given verbally and/or with written directions.

The exploring stage should continue until most groups have completed their solutions to the problem. It's helpful to structure the class so that groups move on independently to other work after they have checked with the teacher for completeness. That way, groups have the maximum time possible to finish their work.

Summarizing

Three goals are important when summarizing for the whole class:

1. Have groups report their processes, both group procedures and strategies used.
2. Have groups present solutions.
3. Generalize from the solutions.

The following questions are useful for helping groups report about their experiences: "How did you organize the work in your group? What problems did you encounter? Was your method effective, or can you think of a better way to have worked?" For a discussion of groups' problem-solving strategies, ask: "What strategy did your group use? Did any group use a different strategy?" Allow enough time for all groups to present their methods.

When presenting solutions, groups should state their findings and, whenever possible, display their work. Ask: "How did you decide if your findings make sense? How can you check your solution?"

Generalizing a solution involves extending it to other situations not necessarily dependent on the specific limitations of the problem. The following questions are effective in eliciting generalizations: "Are there patterns or relationships you can see from your solution? Can you think of another problem you've solved that this reminds you of? How are the two problems alike and different?" It's also helpful to give the students an altered version of the problem and ask how their solution or methods of solution would change.

Before they summarize, all the students should have ended their explorations and should have prepared for a class discussion. Having children come together in a gathering place helps them focus. Other classroom hints: Have students speak one at a time; direct groups to choose a spokesperson to report to the entire class; encourage students to respond to each other's comments; record data on the board as it's presented.

Do not summarize any extension activities at this time unless all groups have had a chance to tackle them. They can be discussed later with the appropriate groups. Posing additional challenges at this time is one way to extend the problem for the more interested or able students.

About timing: At times, a class will complete all three stages within one math period. But keep in mind that teaching a lesson should not necessarily imply a one-day experience. Investigations can extend for two, three, or more days so that all groups have adequate time to explore and can contribute to the summarizing. Also, summarizing is extremely important and should not be skipped or shortened for lack of time. It's valuable for students to reflect on their learning, to hear from others, and to connect others' experience to their ideas. Don't let the clock push the curriculum; rather, stay attuned to the learning needs of the students.

A Sample Lesson: The Consecutive Sums Problem

A good beginning small-group investigation is *The Consecutive Sums Problem*. It reinforces a skill students have practiced—addition with sums to twenty-five—and extends this skill in a way that promotes cooperative small-group work. Following are directions for teaching this lesson.

Introducing

1. Present or review concepts.

Consecutive numbers are numbers that go in order, such as 1, 2, 3, 4 or 11, 12, 13. Each comes right after the other without skipping. Ask students for sequences of three or four consecutive numbers. Ask them to explain why 15, 16, 18, for example, are not consecutive.

2. Pose a part of the problem or a similar but smaller problem.

Ask: "Who can tell me a way to write the number nine as the sum of consecutive numbers?" The usual response is $4 + 5$. Record this on the chalkboard. Underneath this, write $9 = 2 + 3 + 4$. Ask them to verify if this is true. Tell the class that this shows that it's possible to write nine as the sum of consecutive numbers in at least two different ways. Try another example if you think it's needed.

3. Present the problem to be solved.

Ask the students, in their groups, to find all the ways to write the numbers from one to twenty-five as the sum of consecutive numbers. (For younger children, finding the sums for the numbers from one to fifteen may be sufficient.) Tell them that some of the numbers are impossible; challenge them to see if they can find the pattern of those numbers. Direct them to search for other patterns as well, such as how many different sums there are for different numbers. Provide groups with large paper for recording, and ask them to put their group label on their recording sheet (ace, 2, 3, etc.) as well as their group members' names. On their recording sheet, they should also write statements that describe the patterns they find.

4. Discuss the task.

Ask for questions. Review the guidelines for group work if you think that's necessary.

Exploring

1. Observe the interaction.

Notice work procedures. Some groups divide up the numbers so that one person does one to six, the next does seven through twelve, and so on. In other groups, individuals work on whichever numbers they choose and add their findings to a group chart. Some groups have one person do all the recording;

others share that job among the members. Recording formats differ as well. Some groups list the numbers from *1* to *25* and write the sums next to each. Other groups organize the numbers by how many different sums they found for each, so all those that could be written in only one way are in one column, those that could be written in two ways are in another, and so on.

2. Offer assistance when needed.

Sometimes a group will summon you to ask a procedural question, such as whether they should orient the paper the long way or the short way. Let them make those decisions for themselves; tell them they'll see later what other groups decided. Keep in mind that although it may seem like a minor decision to you, it isn't so for children. Organizing work on paper is a skill students need to acquire; group decisions can help them do so.

Groups sometimes make erroneous generalizations. For example, when they find it's impossible to write 2 and 4 as the sums of consecutive numbers, they may conclude that 6 would fit the pattern and also be impossible. In such a situation, confront them with a contradiction. Ask the group to consider $1 + 2 + 3$. When they realize that the sum of those numbers is 6, leave them to rethink their hasty generalization.

You may notice a group bogged down in a way related not to the problem itself but to some procedural issue. For example, the group isn't keeping a group record. Join that group and ask: "How are you supposed to record your results?" (This way you find out if they understood your instructions about which paper to use.) Then ask: "Who will get the paper for your group?" (This may prompt someone to do so.) Or ask: "What do you need to do in order to get started?"

Sometimes, a group has written all the sums it can find and calls you over to announce it has finished. However, when you look at the recording, you see that the students haven't written any statements about patterns they've found. The usual response is that they can't think of any. Ask probing questions to kindle their thinking: "Can you see a pattern to the numbers that are impossible? How could you describe that pattern in a summary statement? What do you notice about all the numbers that had three possible sums? Which numbers had only one possible sum?" When the students have begun to consider some of your questions, leave them to write statements. Help them word one if you feel they need more support.

3. Provide an extension.

If a group has completed work to your satisfaction, offer a challenge: "Can you find a way to predict how many ways thirty-six can be written as the sum of consecutive numbers? Can you predict for any number?"

Summarizing

1. Have groups share their processes, both group procedures and strategies used.

Ask groups to report how they divided up the work. Ask if they thought their method was a good one or how they would change it if they had to extend this exploration to include the numbers up to fifty.

Discuss strategies the groups used. Usually, some took a number, such as twelve, and used the *guess-and-check* strategy to find sums that worked. Others worked the other way, using the *work backward* strategy, starting with the sums and then writing them under the appropriate total. Younger children may have used counters to help—the *use objects* strategy. Most groups use the *look for a pattern* and *make an organized list* strategies. The different methods are important to discuss so students become aware that there are a variety of ways to approach problems. Also, such discussions can provide valuable insights into students' approaches to learning.

2. Have groups present solutions.

If possible, have groups post their recording sheets for the others to see. Discuss any differences and similarities in solutions. Ask groups how they were sure they had found all the possible ways to write any particular number.

3. Generalize from the solutions.

Review the summary statements, being sure that when incorrect generalizations appear, you provide counterexamples to help students reconsider their ideas. Ask about the impossible numbers, drawing out as many different descriptions as possible. Encourage children to explain in their own words: "Start with one, and multiply by two." "They're doubles." "They're powers of two." Ask for the patterns for numbers that were written two ways, three ways, and so on. Ask older children to examine the primes and describe what they notice. Present the challenge of finding a way to predict how many ways any given number could be written.

Structuring Independent Work: The Menu

Another way to organize the classroom for instruction is to provide a menu of learning activities that can include problems, games, and investigations that students work on independently. All students do not have to be working on the same task at the same time.

A menu may provide class work for several days, a week, or an even longer period of time. The number of tasks on a menu can vary according to the topic and the age of the children. In general, the tasks on a menu are not hierarchical and do not conceptually build upon each other. Rather, menu activities pose problems, set up investigations, and suggest games that help students interact with one or more mathematical ideas that relate to the content being studied.

Teachers report different ways for managing the use of menu activities. Some write directions for each task on a 12-by-18-inch sheet of tagboard or construction paper. They post the tasks and orally introduce them to the class, discussing the directions. When students need clarification, they refer to the posted directions. Students take the materials they need from a general supply and return them when they finish their work or at the end of the class.

Rather than post tasks, other teachers duplicate about half a dozen of each, mount them on tagboard, and make them available for students to use. Children take copies of the tasks to their seats along with the materials they need. Some teachers prefer to set up stations, assigning different locations in the classroom for tasks and putting at each location the directions and materials needed.

Each of these systems encourages children to be independent and responsible for their learning. They are allowed to spend the amount of time needed on any one task and to make choices about the sequence in which they work on tasks.

A posted list of the menu tasks provides a class assignment pad for all the students to see. Some teachers also post a class list and label a column for each task so that children can indicate when they complete each activity. Others have students copy the list of menu activities and use it to keep track of tasks they've completed. Whatever the system, it's important that it be clear to the students and provide information about their progress.

Introducing a new menu requires explaining the activities to the entire class, making any special materials available, and clearly establishing due dates. It may take as long as one class period to introduce a menu. Or teachers may prefer to introduce a few tasks, have the students begin work, and then introduce the others a few days later.

Summarizing needs to be done for each activity. However, it's not advisable to do all the summarizing at one time. Stagger it, making sure that all students have had the opportunity to complete an activity before you begin a class discussion.

Using menus has several advantages for students. It provides them with the opportunity to make choices, to learn to manage their own time, and to work on learning activities at their own pace. Although they have to complete their menu work in a specified time, there are no rigid time limitations for any particular task. Within a menu, students are able to make choices, both about the order in which they tackle the tasks and about which of the optional tasks, if any, they choose to do.

The menu has advantages for you as well. When students are working, you can have discussions that provide you valuable insights into their understanding. Also, it's possible to work with individuals or a small group to meet their specific needs. And if you are absent, the children have ongoing work that they can do with the supervision of a substitute teacher.

Sample Classroom Management Plans

The following descriptions present ways that teachers at different grade levels use the menu in their math programs. None of these solutions may fit all teachers' needs. That's not their purpose. They're meant to provide alternatives for consideration and to give a sense of the range of possibilities.

Carol teaches fifth and sixth graders. Her program is structured so that children do a weeklong menu of problem-solving activities for three out of four weeks. Children are randomly placed into groups of four and change groups weekly. Each week's menu presents problems from each of the strands and includes both cooperative and individual work. During the fourth week, Carol specifically focuses on arithmetic and uses manipulative materials as the primary instructional tools for whole numbers, fractions, and decimals.

In Donna's sixth-grade class, the menu serves as the overall curriculum organizer for all subjects. Each Monday, she posts a clean piece of chart paper and lists assignments. Some assignments are new for the week and some are carried over from the previous week. Also, additional work may be added to a menu during the week and some assignments will be crossed off as due dates pass. For math, students keep a "math lab" book that they create using construction paper for the cover and newsprint for the inside. Their books are kept in a class mailbox. Donna works with small groups while the other students work on menu tasks; she schedules whole-group instruction as needed, to introduce new concepts or to discuss completed work.

Bonnie uses a similar system with her third graders. However, she uses the menu just for math. She introduces a new menu on Mondays and often spends that math time in whole-group instruction, teaching any skills that the children will need in order to do the tasks. For example, if the children are to do a spinner experiment, she'll teach how to make a spinner. If she plans to have them make 0–99 number puzzles, she'll introduce coloring patterns on the 0–99 chart. During menu time, children may work alone or with others, but they must ask three other people for help before asking the teacher. Bonnie varies instruction by intermittently providing cooperative problem-solving lessons.

Doris teaches eighth and ninth graders, five classes a day, each for a fifty-minute period. She organizes all her classes into groups of four and changes groups every two weeks. She uses this organization for both her general math classes and her algebra classes and has students correct homework assignments and quizzes in their groups. Doris varies the instructional time among cooperative problem-solving activities, menus, and whole-group instruction. Working on menus allows Doris to maintain ongoing work in the classroom; although work is interrupted by the end-of-the-period bell, the next day students pick up where they left off.

Barbara teaches first grade. She devotes about three times a week to menu time, which is structured without written tasks. Barbara has established eight work areas in the room and has a box designated for each area into which she puts the materials needed for an activity. She introduces each activity to the entire class. On a given day, there may be one or two new activities, with the rest familiar ones. The children learn to distribute the materials, carrying the boxes designated to each space and returning them to storage at the end of the work period. Each area is set up to accommodate a fixed number of children, and children are free to go to an area as long as space is available. Whole-group instruction for various purposes (such as introducing a new activity or teaching word problems or doing a graph) occurs for short periods of time, two to four times weekly. These instructional periods may precede menu time on a given day or may use the entire math time. Barbara does small-group instruction during the menu time when a classroom aide is available to supervise the rest of the children. Barbara also structures cooperative problem-solving activities intermittently, about once every few weeks, usually for twenty to thirty minutes.

Organizing the Instructional Program

Organizing the math curriculum into units of instruction is one way of structuring the yearlong content. A unit is a collection of activities that deals with mathematics that is important for children to study and appropriate for their grade level. A unit can have one main content but should also include activities that engage students with ideas from other content standards so that students can see connections among the different areas of mathematics.

For example, as well as providing experience with number and operations, a unit on fractions can involve students with ideas from geometry, measurement, and statistics. In this way, a topic that is usually relegated to the number strand with a focus on arithmetic skills can be taught in a way that more fully integrates mathematical ideas.

Although topics for units may be similar to chapter titles in traditional textbooks, the format of instruction is much different. Rather than providing a sequence of experiences that guide students toward mastery of a concept or skill, a unit is a collection of experiences that offer students a variety of ways to think about an idea. A unit of instruction can last from two weeks to five or six weeks. All activities in a unit should require and encourage children to think, reason, and solve problems.

Components of Units

When thinking about the organization of a unit, teachers will find it helpful to consider the following components:

Unit of Study

    I. *Introductory Lessons*
        Present concepts and language.
        Introduce procedures and materials.
    II. *Independent Explorations (Menu)*
        Present learning activities.
        Integrate math ideas and language.
        Make activities nonsequential and nonhierarchical.
        Use individual and cooperative activities.
    III. *Whole-Class Discussions*
        Summarize and interpret results.
        Have children share thinking.
        Focus on relationships and connections.
    IV. *Assessment*
        Do before, as part of, and after instruction.
        Focus on understanding, skills, and reactions to learning.
        Use children's writing.

Introductory Lessons

These serve to introduce the mathematical ideas in the unit to the whole class. Activities in these whole-class lessons introduce the procedures, materials, and language that the children need for menu tasks they will pursue independently. (See "Structuring Lessons," on page 54, for additional information.)

Independent Explorations (Menu)

Independent explorations offer the children a collection of activities, all of which provide experience with the mathematical focus of the unit. Through these explorations, children have opportunities to use the mathematical ideas and language introduced in the whole-class lessons. The activities may be for children to work on alone, with partners, or in small groups, and students in a class can work on different activities during the same math class. All tasks are problem-solving activities that promote mathematical thinking and reasoning, involve the children with various manipulative materials, incorporate writing, and encourage communication. (See "Structuring Independent Work: The Menu," on page 60, for additional information.)

Whole-Class Discussions

Whole-class discussions are held after the children have had time to explore a particular activity or idea. Teachers use these discussions to summarize and interpret results from explorations, have children share their thinking and ideas, focus children on mathematical relationships, and help children make connections between and among the activities.

Assessment

Assessment should be an integral part of instruction, before, during, and after the unit. Assessments should focus on children's understanding of ideas, problem-solving abilities, and reactions to their learning. A teacher can assess from listening in whole-class discussions, observing during small-group work, and reading students' writing. (See "Linking Assessment and Instruction," on page 47, for additional information.)

It's important to note that the separation of the components of a unit does not imply a sequence for instruction. For example, all the introductory lessons are not meant necessarily to precede the independent explorations, nor do whole-class summarizing discussions need to wait until the children have completed all the independent explorations. It's possible, for example, to teach one or two of the introductory lessons and then introduce several independent explorations. The children might then work with the independent explorations for several days before you do another whole-class introductory lesson or introduce more of the menu activities. Also, it might be advisable on a particular day—because of the weather or a school event that disrupts the schedule or causes excitement—to take time out, change the pace, and switch to a different activity.

Getting Started

A note to teachers: It makes sense to start slowly, beginning with the current system and trying new ideas and ways of organizing the curriculum and the students within the structure of what you usually do. Rather than jump into a massive restructuring, ease into changes with moderation. Think about instituting changes as your own professional research project. Decide to do something, try it, and then evaluate it. Try something new several times before making a decision. (Remember, the larger the statistical sample, the more valid your decisions based on that sample will be.) Things rarely work as smoothly the first time as they do the second. The third time will be even more comfortable. The more you work with a new idea, the more opportunity you have to internalize parts of it, which frees you to consider other aspects. This is how learning occurs best, for teachers as well as for students.

Instructional Activities for the Content Standards

Introduction

In this section, mathematics activities are presented for each of the following areas:

measurement
probability and statistics
geometry and spatial sense
logical reasoning
patterns, functions, and algebra
number and operations

The ideas presented are not meant to be comprehensive. They are meant to serve as examples of the kinds of activities recommended for students' problem-solving experiences. Grade levels are not indicated. Teachers should read through each section and choose activities that are suitable for students.

The sections are organized in the following way:

1. *Overview.* Background information about the strand is presented to explain its importance to the elementary math program.
2. *A Sample Activity.* For each of the strands, except for patterns, functions, and algebra, a cooperative problem-solving experience is outlined in detail. The patterns, functions, and algebra strand describes a sequence of activities for introducing patterns instead of presenting one model lesson. Activities for all strands are suitable for a wide span of grade levels. Two sample activities are included for number and operations—one for primary children and one for the intermediate grades.
3. *Activities.* Most of the activities are suitable for independent explorations and are well suited for students to work on cooperatively in small groups; the directions for these activities are written for students. Some activities are marked "WHOLE CLASS" because they are more appropriate for whole-class investigations, and the directions are written to the teacher. Whole-class activities often prepare students for similar and related independent explorations.

Measurement

Overview

Concepts and skills in the measurement strand of the math curriculum all deal with making comparisons between what is being measured and some suitable standard of measure. Key to the development of skills in measurement is ample experience with measuring activities. Children acquire measuring skills through firsthand practice. Also important is the reality that measurement is never exact, that even the most careful measurements are approximations. Children need to learn to evaluate when their measurements are "close enough." Children also need practice making estimates in measurement.

Why teach measurement?

Measurement tools and skills have a variety of uses in everyday adult life. Being able to measure connects mathematics to the environment. The abilities to use measuring tools—rulers, thermometers, measuring cups, scales, and the like—and to estimate with these tools are necessary skills for children to develop.

Instruction in measurement intersects with other strands of the elementary math curriculum. Measuring gives children practical applications for the computation skills they are learning. It also provides a way to tie basic geometric concepts to number concepts. In addition, measurement offers opportunities for interdisciplinary learning in subjects such as social studies, geography, science, industrial arts, home economics, art, and music.

What concepts in measurement should be taught?

In the organization of classroom measurement activities, four successive stages in learning need to be considered:

1. *Making comparisons between objects by matching.* Children compare objects by matching, without the use of other tools of measurement. They order things by this method of comparison.

2. *Comparing objects with nonstandard units.* Children use a variety of objects for measuring—parts of the body, straws, cubes, books, and whatever else is readily available.

3. *Comparing objects with standard units.* Standard units should emerge as a convenient extension of nonstandard units, useful for the purpose of communication. It makes sense that children become comfortable with both the metric and English systems. We live in a "bilingual" measurement world, and children need to be familiar with both ways of measuring.

4. *Choosing suitable units for specific measurements.* Children learn to select the appropriate standard units of measurement needed for specific applications.

Instruction should progress through these four stages in each of the areas of measurement: length, time, weight/mass, volume/capacity, temperature, and area. Within each of these areas, students need to learn to use standard units and tools of measurement and to develop the ability to estimate. Also, underlying all areas of measurement is the idea that the physical act of measuring produces, at best, an approximate measure. The concept of rounding off becomes meaningful when applied to measuring procedures.

It's not possible to say precisely when children are ready to function in each of the stages. However, a general guideline is that before third grade, children spend their time most profitably using direct comparisons and nonstandard units to make comparisons. After the third grade, more emphasis can be placed on using selected standards of measure. It's also important to check children's abilities to conserve in each of the different measurement areas.

A Sample Activity: Body Ratios

This is an activity that uses nonstandard measurements to explore body ratios. In addition to the measuring experience, it provides a way to introduce the concept and symbolic notation of ratios. For younger children, however, the ratio notation is inappropriate. A more suitable activity would be to cut a string equal to one body measure and to use that string to find things in the room that are longer, shorter, or the about the same length.

Materials

string, enough for each student and the teacher to cut off a piece equal to his or her height

Introducing

1. *Present or review concepts.* Ask the students to estimate how many times a piece of string equal to their height would wrap around their head as a headband. When they've done this, have a student assist you in cutting a piece of string equal to your height. Wrap the string around your head. Your height is equal to about three times your head measurement. Show students how to record that as a ratio, using either or both of the two symbols shown:

$$head : height = 1 : 3 \qquad \frac{head}{height} = \frac{1}{3}$$

(**Note:** There is often confusion about whether to write this ratio as 1:3 or 3:1. Substituting the actual measurement values for head and height into the ratio shows where the smaller and larger numbers belong.)

2. *Pose a part of the problem or a similar but smaller problem.* Ask: "What do you think the ratio is between the length of my foot and my height? How could I find out?" Demonstrate this for them. Your height should be about six or seven times your foot length. Record: *foot/height* $= \frac{1}{6}$. Also show with your string that your foot and your forearm are just about the same length. Record that as well: *foot/forearm* $= \frac{1}{1}$.

3. *Present the problem to be solved.* Tell the class: "First cut a piece of string equal in length to your height. Help each other do this. Individually, with your height string, explore ratios on your body. Record at least ten ratios using the notation shown. Then, in your groups, compare all the ratios you individually found, and see how many you can find that are true for all of you. Be prepared to report group ratios back to the class."

4. *Discuss the results.* Ask for questions. It might be a good idea to reinforce the notation, helping the students see how to decide which number goes where in a ratio. This notation is totally arbitrary, as is all mathematical notation, but is the conventional way to record ratios.

Exploring

There shouldn't be much for you to do. Circulate, encouraging groups to stop and compare their individual ratios when a reasonable time period has elapsed. No extension is needed; students can find more ratios.

Summarizing

Discuss the group processes. Ask students to compare working individually and working cooperatively in their groups—which was easier, more enjoyable, and so on. Ask groups to report what they did if they found they hadn't explored the same ratios individually when they compared ratios in their groups.

List the groups' common ratios on the board. See if any were the same for everyone (or almost everyone).

Ask: "Which ratios would be different for babies and why?" If any of your students have infant brothers or sisters, send a note home asking their parents to help the students measure the baby's height and head circumference.

Extensions

Are You a Square?

Have students compare their heights with their reaches, both arms outstretched. Post a graph for them to record their names in the proper place. Squares have equal heights and reaches. Tall rectangles have heights that are longer than reaches. Wide rectangles have longer reaches than heights.

A Half-Size Me

Tell students: "Fold your height string in half and cut a length of butcher paper that is equal to that measurement. This is the height of a half-size you. Measure the height of your head with your string. Fold it in half, and measure down from the top of the paper. That shows where your chin will be. Continue measuring this way, using string to find half the width of your face, half the height of your neck, half the width of your shoulders, and so forth. The more measurements you take, the more accurate your drawing will be. When you've drawn yourself, color the drawing to show how you're dressed today. Post your portrait."

Index Card Portrait

Follow the procedure for the previous activity, but this time you have to fit your drawing on a 5-by-8-inch index card. Calculate how many times you'd have to reduce your dimensions so your drawing will fit. Then do it.

The Statue of Liberty Problem

(This activity is suitable for older or more able students.) The Statue of Liberty's nose, from bridge to tip, measures 4 feet, 6 inches. This information is available in an almanac or encyclopedia. How could you use your string and your own body to figure out how long her right arm is, from shoulder to fingertip? (The Statue of Liberty's right arm actually measures 42 feet.) If students' answers are far off, ask them to surmise why.

A Sample Activity: Introducing the Metric System

This sequence of activities is a plan for introducing children to the metric system, focusing mainly on length. Give children a 12-by-18-inch piece of construction paper to make a folder in which they will keep their recordings.

Have children title the booklet: *My Metric Length Book*. At the end of the unit, children take the booklets home to share with members of their family.

Materials

white and orange Cuisenaire rods, 1 of each per student
train of 10 orange Cuisenaire rods taped on a table
string, enough for each student to cut off a 1-meter piece
5-by-25-centimeter tagboard strips, 1 per student
12-by-18-inch construction paper for folders, 1 piece per student

Initial Concrete Experience

Each student needs a white rod, an orange rod, and a piece of string equal in length to ten orange rods. Set out a train of ten orange rods on a table for students each to measure and cut their own string. Their task is to find at least five things that are the same length as each of these three measures. They record on three sheets of paper as shown. Draw facsimiles of the measures on the board for them to use as models.

You may need to discuss a procedure with your students for cutting the string so they all don't bunch up around the table. Also, discuss the fact that measurement is never exact, and give examples of objects that are close enough in measurement for their lists.

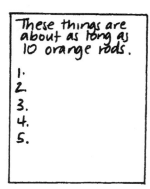

Connecting to the Metric Labels

Tell the students that there are other names for the measuring tools they've been calling the white rod, the orange rod, and the string. They're also called 1 centimeter, 1 decimeter or 10 centimeters, and 1 meter or 10 decimeters or 100 centimeters. It helps some students to relate this to the fact that they may call their parents Mom and Dad, but some people call them by their first names or by Mr. and Mrs. These are all labels for the same people.

When a new concept is taught, it's important to connect the correct mathematical language and symbolic notation to the students' concrete experience with the concept. For this reason, have the students first measure without introducing the names for the metric measures. Then write the following sentences on the board and have the students record them at the bottom of the appropriate sheets.

The white rod is 1 centimeter long. (1 cm)
The orange rod is 10 centimeters or 1 decimeter long. (10 cm = 1 dm)
The string is 1 meter or 10 decimeters or 100 centimeters long. (1 m = 10 dm = 100 cm)

Relating to Body Measures

Have students find some measures on their bodies that match the three lengths so they'll always have a reminder of those measurements with them. Record on a page like this:

Making a Metric Ruler

Give each student a 5-by-25-centimeter strip of tagboard to make their own centimeter ruler. They use their white and orange rods to make the marks. It helps to tell them to think of making the strip into a metric number line with one edge being zero. You may wish to explain that if they divided each of the centimeters into ten equal parts, each part would be called 1 millimeter (mm).

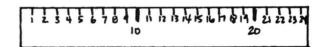

Practicing Measuring

Draw the chart on page 77 on the board for the students to copy on a piece of paper. Advise them to measure after each estimate rather than making all the estimates first. Then each example can help them with the next. They are to use the ruler they made and their string.

	Estimate	Measurement	How Far Off ?
Length of Hand			
Length of Foot			
Around your wrist			
Around your head			
Length of arm			

An Extension into Language

Have students write a story titled "If I Were 1 Centimeter Tall."

An Extension into Volume and Capacity

Have each student construct a 10-centimeter cube from heavy paper or tagboard. Bring in empty milk cartons in quart and half-gallon sizes. Have students compare their cubes with the cartons to see that the cubes are about half of the half-gallon carton. This means a cube would hold about 1 quart. If you have a plastic 10-centimeter cubic container, you can demonstrate this.

Tell the students the metric measure for the cubes they made. One cube holds 1 liter by metric measure. If filled with cubic centimeters, it would hold a thousand of them. Also, if you filled this liter container with water, that much water would weigh 1 kilogram. Metric measures are all related to each other in a tidy fashion. If you have balances and containers, students can benefit from exploring weights and capacities. There is no substitute for firsthand experience.

Activities

Foot Cutout

You need: construction paper, 1 sheet

Trace your left foot (with your shoe off) on construction paper. Cut it out. Record your name, shoe size, and the length of your foot in centimeters. Compare your shoe size and foot length with those of others. Do longer feet always have larger shoe sizes?

Foot Figuring

You need: a partner
your cutout foot

Make two guesses:

1. How many of your feet equal your height?
2. How many of your feet equal your standing broad jump?

Then find out. Record the information on the back of your cutout foot as shown.

	Guess	Measure
Height		
Broad jump		

Foot Area and Perimeter

You need: your cutout foot
string
centimeter grid paper, 1 sheet (see Blackline Masters)

Trace around your cutout foot on centimeter grid paper. Figure the area of your foot in square centimeters and record. Cut a piece of string equal to the perimeter of your foot. Measure it in centimeters. Can you find someone with the same length perimeter? Are your foot areas the same?

Extension
Cut a piece of string half as long as the perimeter of your foot. Use it to make a foot shape on centimeter grid paper. Compare this area with the area of your foot.

Squaring Up

You need: string and foot area (from *Foot Area and Perimeter*)
centimeter grid paper, 1 sheet (see Blackline Masters)

Tape the string that is equal to the perimeter of your foot to a piece of centimeter grid paper in the shape of a square. Answer these questions:

1. What is the area of the square?
2. How does this compare with the area of your foot?
3. Why do you think the areas are different?

Extension
Giant Foot. Draw a giant foot that is about twice the size of yours. Compare the length and perimeter of this giant foot with the length and perimeter of your cutout foot.

Book Measuring

You need: books, 5
measuring tape or string
scale

Choose five books and label them *A*, *B*, *C*, *D*, and *E*. Order them from largest to smallest in the ways listed below. For each, predict first before measuring.

	1st	2nd	3rd	4th	5th
weight					
thickness					
height					
width					
size of cover					

The Perimeter Stays the Same

You need: centimeter grid paper, 1 sheet (see Blackline Masters)

Draw three different shapes on centimeter grid paper following three rules. Record the area inside each shape.

1. Stay on the lines when you draw.
2. You must be able to cut your shape out and have it stay all in one piece.
3. Each shape must have a perimeter of 30 centimeters.

Record the area on each shape. Cut out the one that has the greatest area and the one with the least. Tape them on the class chart.

Your Height in Money

You need: nickels, at least 20
               quarters, at least 20
               measuring stick or tape

Which would you rather have: your height made of quarters laid end-to-end or your height made as a stack of nickels? How much is each worth? Estimate first. Then figure.

How Thick Is Paper?

How thick is a sheet of paper in this book? Devise a way to find out and then do it. Compare your result with others' results.

Extension
Try the same investigation for paper in other books.

Box Measuring

You need: centimeter grid paper, several sheets (see Blackline Masters)

If you had a piece of 20-by-20-centimeter grid paper, you could cut a square the same size from each corner and fold up what's left to make a box.

1. How many different-size boxes could you make using this method, making each from a different piece of 20-by-20-centimeter squared paper? Do it.
2. Which of these boxes holds the most? Figure the volume of each to find out.

Round Things

You need: ruler or other measuring stick or tape
                 string for measuring circumferences (optional)

Look for circular shapes in the class and around school. For each one, measure its diameter and its circumference. Record your results on a chart. Do this for at least ten objects. What pattern can you find when you examine the relationship between the diameter and circumference of each?

Wraparound

Make a measuring tape that, when wrapped around a tree or pole or other circular object, tells you the diameter of that object.

How Long Is a Minute?

You need: a partner
way to time 1 minute

How many times can you do each of the things listed in the chart below in 1 minute? Make a guess for each and then have your partner time you. Record on a chart as shown. Take turns timing each other.

	Guess	Count
Bounce a ball.		
Write your name.		
Say "six sick sheep."		
Count by three's to 30		

Ratio with Cuisenaire Rods

You need: Cuisenaire rods, 1 individual set

Measure across your desk using only light green rods. Then figure out how many rods it would take to measure the same distance if you used only red, only white, or only blue rods. Explain your answer; then test by measuring with the rods.

Extension
Do the same for the other color rods as well.

Yarn Shapes

You need: yarn or string
color tiles, about 100

Cut a piece of yarn or string 50 centimeters long and tie the ends together so you have a loop. Make a shape with your loop. Predict how many color tiles will fit inside your shape. Then fill it. Use ten tiles of each color to make counting easier. You may want to tape your loop in several places to hold it while you fill it. Make a sketch of your shape and record how many tiles filled it.

Repeat for four more shapes, making them as different from one another as you can. Examine the shapes that held the *most* and *least* numbers of tiles. Write what you notice about these shapes.

Double the Circumference

You need: small circular object to trace (jar lid, cup, etc.)
string
centimeter grid paper, 1 sheet (see Blackline Masters)

Trace around the circular object onto the centimeter grid paper. Figure the area in square centimeters and record it inside the circle.

Use string to measure the circumference of this circle. Cut a piece of string double the circumference of the circle and use it to form a new circle on the paper. Tape it in place. What is the area inside the new circle? Predict first and then figure. Write a sentence that describes the relationship between the circumferences and areas of the two circles.

What will the area be for a circle with a circumference equal to half that of the original circle? Predict first and then find out.

Extension
When the circumference of a pizza pan doubles, should the price double? Explain your reasoning.

Perimeter with Cuisenaire Rods

You need: Cuisenaire rods, 1 red, 2 light green, and 1 purple
centimeter grid paper, 1 sheet (see Blackline Masters)

Use one red rod, two light green rods, and one purple rod. Arrange the rods into a shape on centimeter grid paper in such a way that when you trace around it, you draw only on the lines of the grid paper. Also, you must be able to cut out the outlined shape and have it remain in one piece. (Corners touching are not allowed.) Make several different shapes in this way. Trace each and record its perimeter. Experiment to find how to arrange the rods to get the longest perimeter and the shortest perimeter.

The Area Stays the Same

You need: 5-by-8-inch index cards, 2
centimeter grid paper, 1 sheet (see Blackline Masters)

Cut a square that measures 5 centimeters on each side from a corner of one of the index cards. Use the centimeter grid paper to help you. Use this shape to make other different shapes. You can do this by cutting the square on the diagonal into two triangles and putting them together in various ways or by cutting the square in other ways and arranging the pieces together.

Trace around the different shapes you make, cutting each from the index cards. You will need at least five shapes, including the 5-centimeter square. All of your shapes will have the same area.

On plain paper, draw a line segment equal in length to the perimeter of each shape. (You can use the actual shapes and trace around each edge.) Label each line segment with the shape.

How do the perimeters compare? Record and make a statement about your findings.

Probability and Statistics

Overview

Statistics is the science or study of data. Statistical studies require collecting, sorting, representing, analyzing, and interpreting information. The information is then used for predicting, drawing inferences, and making decisions. There is always some degree of uncertainty with data that are collected. This means that statistics is most often concerned with using information in the face of uncertainty. Probability gives a way to measure uncertainty and is therefore essential to understanding statistical methods.

Why teach probability and statistics?

Recent technological advances have made more statistical information available to us than ever before. In conversation, on television, and in newspapers, we are flooded with data that demand an increasing understanding of statistics for us to understand their use. What is the effectiveness of seat belts and should you wear them? What can you do to protect yourself against the rising cost of living? Is there a justifiable connection between smoking and disease? Which money market or retirement fund makes the most sense? What does a particular advertising claim really mean? Is the death penalty a deterrent to crimes of murder? How do you weigh the benefits of birth control pills against their dangers? Should a certain food dye be banned because it has caused cancer in rats under some conditions? What effect will the rate of population growth have on our lives? How should the increased number of older people in our society affect social decisions? For all of these questions, and many others, probability and statistics concepts are integral for making decisions.

Statistics has never enjoyed a terrific reputation. It's been said that you can prove anything with statistics. To some, statistics and lies are often synonymous. Many people have been hardened against statistics by claims of politicians and advertisers. However, our society is increasingly making use of ideas found in statistics and probability. Students need to develop skills that enable them to live in this statistical society so they will not be misled or blinded by statistics. Without these skills, they will have an incomplete understanding of the world they live in.

Learning probability and statistics provides real applications of arithmetic. When basic computational skills are used in a context, students have the opportunity to see the advantages and limitations of their calculations.

Most everyday applications of arithmetic are statistical, done with variability in mind and with some degree of uncertainty—estimating costs, calculating the amount of wallpaper or floor covering needed, figuring time for trips or cooking. The simple arithmetic done is valuable only in the context of its application. To understand those applications, we need probability and statistics, and therefore, they are essential elements of students' basic number skills.

Studying probability and statistics also helps students develop critical thinking skills. In carrying out experiments in probability and statistics, students develop ways to cope with uncertainty as they search for the truth in a situation and learn to report it faithfully. Approaching situations statistically can make students face up to prejudices, think more consistently about arguments, and justify their thinking with numerical information. This approach has applications in all areas of life—social, political, and scientific.

What concepts in probability and statistics should be taught?

The teaching of probability and statistics should stem from real problems. A theoretical or abstract approach is not appropriate for the elementary grades. The approach should be based on experiments that draw on children's experience and interests. Children's intuition needs to be challenged first. Once they sense what "should happen" in a situation, then it's timely for them to carry out an experiment to test their predictions. Not only will such experiments provide firsthand experience in collecting, organizing, and interpreting data, but they will also reinforce computational skills. Basic to probability and statistics are the following ideas:

1. *Collecting Data.* Students need experience gathering both factual data and data that involve opinions. The latter require that students consider how to collect data in a way that avoids biased responses.
2. *Sampling.* In real life, even though information is often needed about an entire population, it may be possible to sample only a part of the population. That information from the sample is then used to infer characteristics about the total population. Students need to learn the difference between random and nonrandom samples and the importance this difference makes in statistical studies. For example, to determine the percentage of people in the general population who are left-handed, you would not poll professional baseball players as a random sample. (Why?)
3. *Organizing and Representing Data.* Students need experience organizing data and representing them graphically in a variety of graphs, tables, and charts.

4. *Interpreting Data.* Students should learn to read graphs, making quick visual summaries as well as further interpretations and comparisons of data through finding means, medians, and modes.

5. *Assigning Probabilities.* Initial experiences with measuring uncertainty should be informal and should include discussion of whether a result is possible or likely, or whether outcomes are equally or not equally likely. Assigning probabilities gives further information for making a decision in the face of uncertainty. The probability of an event can be represented by a number from 0 to 1. For example, the probability of rolling a 4 when rolling a die is $\frac{1}{6}$. The probability of rolling an even number when rolling a die is $\frac{3}{6}$. The numerator of the fraction represents the number of outcomes you're interested in; the denominator represents the total number of possible outcomes.

6. *Making Inferences.* Students need to draw conclusions based on their interpretation of data. They should learn to justify their thinking using numerical information they've collected and analyzed.

A Sample Activity: Spinner Experiments

Spinner experiments provide a good beginning probability and statistics experience for children of all ages. They give students the opportunity to make individual predictions, to collect data using a graph, and to compare their individual results with a larger class sample. Younger children benefit from the practice of writing numerals; older students can be challenged to extend the experiment into a more formal analysis of the probability involved. Making the spinners gives all students practice in following directions. (Young children may need more assistance with this part of the task.)

Materials

5-by-8-inch cards, 1 per student
paper clips, 1 per student
plastic straws, $1\frac{1}{4}$-inch length per student
half-inch grid paper for graphing, 1 sheet per group
   (see Blackline Masters)

Introducing

1. *Present or review concepts.* Describe and show how to make a spinner, following the directions on the next page. (You may choose to give students who prefer to make them from the directions themselves the opportunity to do so.)

How to Make a Spinner that Really Spins

1. Cut a 5-by-8-inch index card in half. Cut a circle, about 3 inches in diameter, from one half of the card. Divide and label it as shown.

2. Mark a dot in the center of the other piece of card. Draw a line from the dot to one corner of the card.

3. Bend up the outside of a paper clip. This part should point straight up when the paper clip is lying flat on the desk.

4. Poke a hole in the center of the circle (be exact) and another hole in the dot on the card.

5. Push the bent end of the paper clip through the hole in the card. Tape the rest of the paper clip to the bottom of the card. Make sure the side of the card with the line is facing up.

6. Put the $\frac{1}{4}$-inch length of plastic straw and then the spinner face on the paper clip.

7. Cover the tip of the paper clip with a piece of tape.

2. *Pose a part of the problem or a similar but smaller problem.* Ask: "When you spin the spinner, is any number more likely to come up than any other number? Why do you think so?" Explain: "You can keep track of spins on a graph recording sheet that is three squares by twelve squares." Demonstrate for the class how to cut a 3-by-12 recording sheet from half-inch grid paper, spin, and record by writing 1s, 2s, and 3s in the correct columns as they come up on the graph. After

three or four spins, ask: "What do you think the entire graph will look like when one number reaches the top of the paper?"

3. *Present the problem to be solved.* Explain: "Each of you needs to make a spinner and a graph recording sheet and try the experiment. When one of the numbers reaches the top, you've completed the experiment. Then post the paper to show which number 'won.' [You should provide bulletin board or wall space with sections labeled 1, 2, and 3.] When everyone in your group has finished the experiment, let me know and I'll start you on another."

4. *Discuss the results.* Ask for questions.

Exploring

Circulate and clarify as needed for groups whose members all have the same confusion. Usually, there are no major problems.

Extension: Two-Person Spin

Students work in pairs. If they spin their spinners and add the numbers that come up on each, there are five possible sums: 2, 3, 4, 5, and 6. Each pair of students makes a graph recording sheet that is five squares wide. First, partners should predict which sum they think will come up most often. Then they spin their spinners and take turns recording the sum of the two numbers that appear. When one sum reaches the top of their graph recording sheet, they post their results.

Summarizing

Discuss the class results. Most likely, 3 was the winning number on most of the graph recording sheets, but there will be instances of 1 or 2 as winner. Ask the students how they might find out if the number 3 actually came up in half of all the spins. Ask for volunteers to add up the total number of spins for each number and report back to the class later.

Although the number 3 is twice as likely to come up as either 1 or 2, there is no guarantee that 3 will come up twice as often when you do the experiment. Very few of the graph recording sheets (if any) will actually reflect that result. The mathematical theory of probability says that the more times you spin a spinner, the closer the results will match the theoretical distribution.

If enough of the class has completed *Two-Person Spin*, summarize it. If not, wait until more of the students have posted results. Also, refer to the additional spinner activities in this section for more investigations.

Activities

WHOLE CLASS: Tiles in the Bag (Version 1)

You need: small paper bag
color tiles in two colors, 10

This is an introductory activity for all grade levels. Place ten tiles in a bag, some of two different colors. Tell the students what you've done (without telling them how many of each). Go around the class, asking individual students to draw out a tile without looking, to note its color, and then to replace it. (This is called taking a sample with replacement.) Have a student record the colors on the board.

Do this for ten draws, and then ask groups to look at the information and decide whether they are willing to predict what is in the bag, or if they need more information. Have groups share their opinions.

Then do ten more draws, and again have groups discuss and share. Repeat as many times as needed for most of the students to feel they're willing to predict what is in the bag. (For younger children, the question might be which color do you think there's more of in the bag?)

Suggestions for recording:

Extensions

1. Change the colors and the quantity of the tiles.
2. Choose a group to decide on the tiles to put in the bag. The group must tell the rest of the class the total number of tiles in the sack before they start the activity.

For some children, this experiment is an exercise in guessing, with a smattering of some intuition and a lot of hopeful predicting. For others, some notions of ratio and proportion are useful for predicting. Taking fifty or one hundred draws (if the students are interested) makes predicting easier and more valid.

WHOLE CLASS: Tiles in the Bag (Version 2)

You need: 3 small paper bags filled with color tiles in this way:

        25 red, 5 blue
        20 red, 10 blue
        10 red, 20 blue

Write this information on the board. Have a student choose one bag at random so that even you do not know which it is. Then, in the procedure described in *Version 1*, make 25 random samples with replacement. Record each to have a list of the samples in order. Compute the percentage of red tiles for each of these: the first 5 samples, the first 10 samples, the first 15 samples, the first 20 samples, all 25 samples.

    Have groups answer these questions:

1. Which bag do you think you used?
2. Which bag would you have chosen if you had based your decision on five samples? Ten? Fifteen? Twenty? How many samples do you think you needed?

Design Your Own Spinner

You need: spinner
        half-inch grid paper, 1 sheet (see Blackline Masters)

In this activity, you design your own spinner and test what happens. Follow the directions:

1. Design and make a spinner.
2. Cut out a graph recording sheet from grid paper and paste it to a blank sheet of $8\frac{1}{2}$-by-11-inch paper (see illustration) (**Note:** The graph recording sheet should be twelve squares high and as many squares wide as numbers on your spinner.)
3. Make a prediction and record it.
4. Do the experiment, recording the numbers that come up on your graph recording sheet.
5. Write about the results.
6. Post your work.

WHOLE CLASS: Sampling Bean Populations

You need: white beans, 1 package
brown beans, 3 packages
(Choose beans that are about the same size.)

Mix all beans together. Have each student take a small handful of beans and sort them. Then ask the children in each group to pool their samples and to organize them into rows.

Ask each group to predict which of the following they think they would most likely get if they were to take four beans from the bag with their eyes closed:

3 white and 1 brown
2 white and 2 brown
1 white and 3 brown
4 white
4 brown

Have groups present their predictions and their reasoning.

Return all the beans to the bag. Then have each student pick out, without looking, four beans. Have students record on a class graph the number of each color bean they picked. Discuss the results.

Divide the beans among the groups and have the students actually count the number of brown and white beans. Compare these totals with the samples of handfuls and the samples of four beans.

WHOLE CLASS: The 1-2-3-4 Activity

You need: slips of paper, about 3-by-3 inches, labeled with the numbers 1 2 3 4, 1 per student

In the *San Francisco Chronicle* on November 30, 1980, the following item appeared: "Write the numbers 1, 2, 3, and 4 on a piece of paper. Ask somebody to circle any one of these numbers. Four out of five so asked will circle the 3." Try an experiment to test this.

1. Distribute slips with 1 2 3 4 on them. Ask each child to circle a number and turn the slip facedown, with no discussion.
2. Have each child write his or her answer, individually, to these questions: Do you think any one number will be circled lots more than any other and, if so, which one? Why do you think that?
3. In their groups, ask students to come to consensus about the questions and choose one person to report back to the class.
4. List the numbers *1, 2, 3,* and *4* on the board. Have students tape their papers next to the number they circled to graph the class data.
5. Analyze the results. Do they match the newspaper prediction? Would the results change with a larger sample?

Extensions

1. Have each student take home three additional slips for others to circle a number. Have them predict how these additional samples will affect the graph.
2. What if the numbers had been in a different order? What if the slips had a b c d on them instead? What about other letters or shapes? Have interested students devise and carry out their own investigations.

WHOLE CLASS: Alphabetical Probability

This investigation uses probability and statistics techniques to analyze the frequency of letters in the English language.

1. Have students decide, individually, what they think are the five most commonly used letters in the English language. They should list their predictions, starring the letter they think is the most common.
2. Ask students to share their individual predictions in their groups and to arrive at one group prediction.
3. Then have each student pick a sentence from a book and tally how many times each letter appears in the sentence. Have groups compile their individual results and put their results on a class chart. Analyze the class chart and list the letters of the alphabet in the order of frequency according to the students' findings.
4. Compare the class results with students' predictions and with the actual order of frequency in the English language:

    E T A O [N I] S R H L D C U [P F] M W Y [B G] V K [Q X] [J Z]
    (Those bracketed have the same frequency of occurrence.)

Extensions

1. Would this be the same for other languages? Find out.
2. What is so strange about these three sentences?—*This is odd. Do you know why? Try and find out.*
3. A language exercise: Have students write, or talk, without using one of the common letters.
4. Each letter in the cryptogram below stands for another letter in the alphabet. Can you figure out what it says?

    AB CD EDDF AG FXD HIJY,
    A CAKK LMN NZM IG AWD WJDIE WZGD.

    Here's another clue to help you: The most frequently used words in the English language are *the*, *an*, *a*, and *and*.
5. Examine the games of Scrabble, Boggle, and so forth to see how they used the information about frequency of letters.
6. Buy some transfer lettering from a stationery or art store. Analyze the frequency of the letters provided.

(continued)

7. When Christopher L. Sholes invented the typewriter in 1867, he purposely scrambled the letters so typists couldn't type too quickly and jam the keyboard. (Your two most agile fingers rest on rarely used J and K, while your left pinky is used for A.) Have students design a keyboard that makes use of this mathematical investigation. Then compare their keyboard with the one pictured. This was designed by August Dvorak in 1930 to make better use of the frequency of letters.

The Left-Handed Experiment

By taking a sample of some people in your school, can you determine approximately how many right-handed people there are for every left-handed person? Follow this procedure:

1. Find out how many people there are in the school.
2. Decide how many people you'll sample. Pick a place to ask this number of people whether they're right-handed or left-handed.
3. From this sample, figure out how many right-handed people there are for each left-handed person.
4. Now take a census to find out how many right-handed and left-handed people there actually are in the school. Visit each class and take a poll. Compile your results. How many right-handed people are there for each left-handed person in the entire school?
5. Compare the results of your sample with the census. Are they similar? Were you satisfied with your sampling procedure? If not, how would you improve the way you sampled? Write a report.

Extension

The procedure outlined in *The Left-Handed Experiment* can be used by individuals or small groups of students to investigate a variety of topics:

By sampling, determine approximately how many red-, blond-, brown-, and black-haired people there are in your school.
By sampling, decide how many people there are with each eye color.
Use sampling to learn about students' weekly allowances.
Use sampling to determine the favorite TV show of students in your school.

Tile Trading

You need: 2 paper bags, labeled A and B
color tiles, 15 red and 15 blue (or any two colors)

Place fifteen red tiles in Bag A and fifteen blue tiles in Bag B. Without peeking, put one tile from A into B. Shake B. Then put one from B into A. Shake A. Then move one from A into B. Continue until you have moved thirty tiles, but first predict how many of each you'll have in each bag after doing this:

A _____ red _____ blue
B _____ red _____ blue

Now do it. What was the outcome?

A _____ red _____ blue
B _____ red _____ blue

Try the experiment several more times. Discuss with others what you think "should happen." **Note:** You may want to move fewer tiles or more tiles.

The Two-Dice Sum Game

You need: a partner or small group
counters, 11 per player
pair of dice

This is a game for two or more players. Each player makes a number line from 2 to 12, with spaces large enough for the counters to fit on the numbers. Place your eleven counters on your number line in any arrangement. (You may put more than one counter on some numbers and none on others.) Take turns rolling the dice. On each roll, every player removes one counter that is on the number that matches the sum on the dice. (If players have more than one counter on a number, they may remove only one.) The winner is the first player to remove all eleven counters.

Decide on the best winning arrangement of counters on the number line. Explain your thinking.

Two-Coin Toss

You need: coins of two different denominations, 1 of each

Toss two coins together twenty-five times. After each toss, record what comes up—two heads, two tails, or one head and one tail. What do you think will result?

    Prediction: two heads _____ two tails _____ one head/one tail _____

    Outcome: two heads _____ two tails _____ one head/one tail _____

Note: If you toss just one coin, there are two possibilities: heads and tails. If you toss two coins, there are four equally likely possibilities.

The Birthday Twins

If you asked people to tell you their birthdays (the month and the day), how many people do you think you'd have to ask before you found two that were birthday twins?

    Prediction: _____ people

    Now try it and see. Take a poll. List each person's birthday. Stop when you get a match.

    Outcome: _____ people

Note: Mathematicians say that in a group of thirty people, there is a better than 50 percent chance there will be a pair of birthday twins. In a group of one hundred, there is a 97 percent chance! How do your results relate to this theory?

Got a Match?

You need: a partner
                 identical spinners, 2

You and your partner are to spin your spinners twenty-four times. Each time, compare to see if you have a match. Predict on how many spins you think your results will match. Then do the experiment, recording what comes up each time. Figure out how many matches you had. Record the outcome.

How Many Rolls to Get a 1?

You need: die

Roll a die until a 1 comes up. Record how many rolls it took. Do this five times. Put your five results on the class chart, such as the one shown.

HOW MANY ROLLS TO GET A 1 ?
Use tally marks to show your results.

1	11	21
2	12	22
3	13	23
4	14	24
5	15	25
6	16	26
7	17	27
8	18	28
9	19	29
10	20	more

Extension

How many rolls to get a 6? Would the results be similar or different? How could you find out?

Shake and Peek

You need: a partner
               shake-and-peek box (a small box containing 10 beads or
               marbles of two colors, taped shut, with a corner cut out
               for viewing)

Shake the box, peek through the open corner, and record the color you see. Repeat many times. Stop when you and your partner feel you have a sufficient number of samples to predict what's in the box. (Hint: The box has ten beads.)

The X-O Problem

You need: 3 cards the same size, marked as follows:

        1 with an X on both sides
        1 with an O on both sides
        1 with an X on one side and an O on the other
    paper sack

Play the following game with the materials: Draw one of the three cards at random from the sack and look at what is marked on just one side. Predict what you think is on the other side. Check your prediction. Score a point each time you predict correctly.

Decide what would be a good strategy for predicting so that you would score the most points possible. Then test your strategy by playing the game thirty times, recording your prediction and outcome each time. How many points did you score? Are you satisfied with your prediction? Try another strategy if you like.

What's the Record?

You need: pair of dice
        a small group

Who can set a record for the most rolls of two dice without getting doubles? Try the challenge. Roll two dice and tally the number of rolls you make before getting doubles. Who set the record in your group? On the class chart, record how many rolls the winner made.

The Game of Pig

You need: pair of dice
        a partner or small group

This is a game for two or more players. The goal of the game is to be the first to reach 100. On your turn, roll the dice as many times as you like, mentally keeping a running total of the sum. When you decide to stop rolling, record the total for that turn and add it to the total from previous turns.

The catch: If a 1 comes up on one of the dice, the player's turn automatically ends and 0 is scored for that round. If 1s come up on both dice, not only does the turn end, but the total accumulated so far returns to 0.

After becoming familiar with the game, write a strategy for winning.

How Many Throws?

You need: a partner

dice of two different colors, 1 of each

charts as shown, 1 of each

RED

	1	2	3	4	5	6
1						
2						
3						
4						
5						
6						

WHITE

How Many Throws?

Here are the jobs for each partner: One rolls the dice and makes a tally mark on the "How Many Throws?" chart for each roll. The other enters the sum that comes up on each roll on the "White-Red" chart (unless it was already entered before). The colors are important. For example, red 3 and white 2 gives 5; red 2 and white 3 also gives 5; *but* they go in different boxes. So there are thirty-six possible sums.

Discuss with your partner how many throws you think it will take to complete the chart of sums. Then roll and record until all the sums have been entered. **Note:** When there are only five blanks left on the chart, write in the missing sums.

Extension

On class charts, post the number of throws it took to roll all sums and the last five sums you entered. Discuss what the information posted reveals about two-dice sums.

How Many Throws?
Write the number.

Last Five Sums
Make tally marks.

2
3
4
5
6
7
8
9
10
11
12

How Many Ways?

You need: chart as shown

Complete the chart of possible outcomes when rolling two dice. As in *How Many Throws?* 3, 1 is a different outcome from 1, 3. After you complete the chart, answer the questions.

Possible Totals	2	3	4	5	6	7	8	9	10	11	12
			2,2 3,1 1,3								
Total Ways			3								

1. Add across the Total Ways row on the bottom. Did you get thirty-six? If not, there's a goof somewhere.
2. List the possible totals in order, from the ones with most possibilities to the ones with least.
3. The probability of rolling a 7 is six chances out of the thirty-six possible outcomes. Mathematicians write this as $\frac{6}{36}$ or $\frac{1}{6}$. Why?
4. What is the probability of rolling each of the other sums?
5. Add up the probabilities for all the sums. What is the total? Explain why this total makes sense.

Shake and Spill

You need: two-color counters, 6

If you spill the counters and record how many red sides and yellow sides come up each time, do you think you'll get one result more often than the others? If so, what will it be? Why do you think that? Try it, spilling the counters at least twenty-five times. Record your prediction and your actual results.

Extension
Try the experiment with other numbers of counters.

Fair Game 1

You need: group of four

Play the paper, scissors, rock game with three players and one recorder. All players make a fist and on the count of four, each player shows either:

paper (by showing four fingers)
scissors (by showing two fingers)
rock (by showing a fist)

Decide who is Player A, Player B, and Player C and play twenty times with these rules:

Player A gets a point if all players show the same sign.
Player B gets a point if only two players show the same sign.
Player C gets a point if all players show different signs.

Tally the winning points:

Player	Tally	Total
A		
B		
C		

Is this game fair? Which player would you rather be? How could you make the game more fair?

Fair Game 2

You need: a partner
pair of dice

Take turns rolling the two dice. Player A scores a point if the sum is even. Player B scores a point if the sum is odd. Is the game fair? If not, how could you make the game fair? Explain your reasoning.

Play the game again, this time figuring the product. Player A scores a point if the product is even. Player B scores a point if the product is odd. Is the game fair? If not, how could you make the game fair? Explain your reasoning.

The Popcorn Problem

You need: cubes, 1 each of six colors
paper sack

A popcorn company found that sales improved when prizes were put in the popcorn boxes. They decided to include a felt-tip pen in every box and to use pens in six different colors. The company bought equal numbers of pens in each color and were careful when shipping popcorn to stores to send boxes with the same number of each color pen. When you buy a box, you have an equal chance of finding any one of the six colors of pens inside.

About how many boxes of popcorn do you need to buy to have a good chance of getting a complete set of six different-colored pens? Explain your reasoning.

Try the following experiment to simulate the situation: Put six different-colored cubes in a sack to represent the pens. Reach into the sack and, without looking, draw a cube. Note its color and replace it. Continue until you have drawn out one of each color, keeping track of the number of draws you make. (How many draws do you think will be needed?)

Repeat the experiment. Then compile results from other class members.

Discuss the popcorn problem in light of the information gathered from the simulations.

Extension
Repeat the simulation, this time putting sixty cubes in the sack, ten each of six colors. Compare the results with the first simulation.

Graphing in the Classroom

Graphing is a way to present data in a concise and visual way that makes it possible to see relationships in the data more easily. In order to learn to interpret graphs and use them as a problem-solving tool, children need to make their own first. Making graphs requires collecting and then sorting and classifying data. Such experiences can be provided at all grade levels.

Introducing Graphs to Young Children

For younger children, graphing experiences best begin concretely. For example, have everybody take off one shoe, then sort all the shoes into two rows: with laces, without laces. This creates a concrete graph. A pictorial representation of that relationship can be introduced at a later stage; still later, a symbolic graph could be made. The possibilities for things to graph should be taken from the interests of the children and experiences that occur in the classroom.

REAL GRAPH

PICTURE GRAPH

SYMBOLIC GRAPH

- *Real graphs* use actual objects to compare and build on children's understanding of more and less. Some examples include: Is your pencil dull or sharp? Which paste jars need filling and which don't? Are the bottoms of your shoes smooth or bumpy?
- *Picture graphs* use pictures or models to stand for real things. Children can draw pictures to represent objects, or they can cut pictures from magazines. Some examples include a rubbing of the bottom of their shoes, a picture of the cookie they like best, and a picture of a pet.
- *Symbolic graphs* are the most abstract because they use symbols, such as a colored square or tally mark, to represent real things.

An important aspect of a graphing activity is the discussion and interpretation of the information. Progress made by students is directly related to the time spent on discussion. The following are the kinds of questions that can be asked about graphs, whether they are real, pictorial, or symbolic.

Which column has the least?
Which column has the most?
Are there more _____ or more _____ ?
Are there fewer _____ or fewer _____ ?
How many more _____ are there than _____ ?
How many fewer _____ are there than _____ ?
How many _____ are there altogether?

After children become more familiar with graphs, they should be able to draw conclusions from the information without being prompted with questions.

Attendance Graphs

Using a daily attendance graph is one way to provide regular graphing experience. When the children enter the room in the morning, they mark themselves on the graph. The graph can be concrete, pictorial, or symbolic.

There are three categories of graphs: graphs that ask for opinions, graphs that require factual reporting of information, and graphs that require some processing before the information needed can be recorded.

OPINION

FACT

PROCESSING

Process the graphs in the following ways:

- Use the graphs to write arithmetic equations that show the relationships reported. In the "What age would you like to be?" graph, you can write an addition sentence to show the number of children who would like to be a different age than they are now: $17 + 4 = 21$.

- Write generalizations from graphs. For example: *Most students in our class wish they were older. Less than one-fourth of the students are content with their present age.*

- Write questions that can be answered from the graph. Children can answer them individually or in groups. In this way, graphs give a ready supply of word problems that relate to information from the students. For example: *What percent of our class has brown eyes? What fraction of the class would like to be older?*

- Have groups take responsibility for writing the questions for everyone to answer.

Eventually, have pairs or groups of children prepare attendance graphs.

Ideas for Graphs

1. Do you have a library card?
2. Is your Halloween costume scary or not scary?
3. How many scoops of rice do you think will fill the jar?
4. How much allowance do you get?
5. What time did you go to sleep last night?
6. At what age do you think you'll be a grown-up?
7. How many glasses of milk do you drink each day?
8. What's your favorite TV show?
9. How many pencils are there in your desk?
10. Which do you think there are more of on the U.S. flag—long red stripes, long white stripes, short red stripes, or short white stripes?

11. How many letters are there in your first name?
12. Is your last name longer, shorter, or the same length as your first name?
13. Are your earlobes hanging or attached?
14. On what day of the week were you born?
15. Who decides when you get your hair cut?
16. How many doors are there in your house?
17. Do you have a middle name?
18. What's your favorite ice-cream flavor?
19. Do you have a younger brother or sister?
20. How much do you think this costs? (a can of juice, a bag of peas in the pod, a bowl of apples, etc.)
21. Are you left-handed or right-handed?
22. Do you have moons on any of your fingernails?
23. What color are your eyes?
24. How many sections do you think are in this orange?
25. Are you a square, a tall rectangle, or a wide rectangle?
26. How many times do you think a string equal to your height would wrap around your head?
27. What do you like to have on your hamburger?
28. Which hamburgers do you like better—McDonald's or Jack in the Box?
29. What do you call your mother—Mother, Mom, Mommy, something else?
30. Do you like spinach?
31. Will you buy your lunch today?
32. How many cubes can you hold in one hand?
33. Have you ever visited another country?
34. How many of your feet equal your height?
35. Does your last name begin with a letter in the first half of the alphabet or the last half?
36. How do you like to eat eggs—scrambled, hard-boiled, soft-boiled, fried, other, not at all?
37. What is your birthday month?
38. If A = $0.01, B = $0.02, C = $0.03, and so on, how much is your first name worth?
39. Is your hair straight, curly, or wavy?
40. Which holiday do you like best—Thanksgiving, Halloween, or April Fool's Day?
41. How many glasses of milk do you drink on average each day?
42. How many televisions are there in your house?
43. Do you think children should have to earn their allowances?
44. Do you like to roller-skate?
45. Should children choose their own bedtime?

Geometry and Spatial Sense

Overview

In the elementary grades, experiences in geometry should provide for the development of the concepts of shape, size, symmetry, congruence, and similarity in both two-dimensional and three-dimensional space. Experiences should begin with familiar objects and should utilize a wide variety of concrete materials to develop appropriate vocabulary and to build understanding. In middle school instruction, more formal generalizations in geometric relationships can be stressed. The activities provided in this section are designed to provide problem-solving experiences in geometry that help students develop understanding of geometric properties and relationships.

Why teach geometry?

Young children have considerable experience with geometry before entering school. They spend a great deal of time exploring, playing, and building with shapes. In their play experiences, children encounter relationships among shapes naturally. They sort and resort objects, make discoveries about how different blocks fit together, and learn about shapes that roll, slide, or do neither.

These initial investigations should be nurtured and extended in children's school learning of mathematics. In their classroom experiences, children should have opportunities to explore shapes and the relationships among them. They benefit from problem-solving situations that lead them to investigate patterns and structures in shapes and to develop reasoning processes in spatial contexts. They need experiences that relate geometry to ideas in measurement, number, and patterns. Through these kinds of activities, students grasp how mathematics adds to their understanding of the world.

Although elementary mathematics textbooks include sections on geometry, it's not uncommon for teachers to treat these sections as optional and to skip them or to present them to the children as if they were less important. There are several explanations for this. Because the major emphasis in elementary mathematics has been on the teaching of arithmetic skills, some teachers think that geometry in math instruction is not as significant for elementary students. Also, many teachers remember geometry as a high school subject that dealt mainly with formal proofs and complicated terminology. However, geometry is a significant branch of mathematics, the one most visible in the physical world.

Developing spatial ability has applications in everyday life, a fact that any adult encounters when having to figure quantities for wallpaper, floor covering, paint, fabric, lawn needs, or a myriad of other home projects. Geometric concepts and relationships are also essential to many branches of industry, the building trades, interior design, architecture, as well as other work situations. Geometry should be included as an integral part of the mathematics program.

A Sample Activity: Pentominoes

The emphasis in this geometry activity is on informal, concrete experience, not on the symbolism and formal definitions that are the focus in many textbooks. *Pentominoes* calls on a different kind of reasoning than is needed for numerical tasks. In the classroom, children who are not generally considered to be good math students often enjoy success in these kinds of spatial experiences.

There are two aspects to this activity. One is searching for possible arrangements of squares, a geometric visualization task. The other is deciding when all possible arrangements have been found, which requires the use of logical reasoning.

Materials

square tiles (about 1 inch on a side), 5 per student
paper ruled into squares the same size as the tiles, 2 sheets per small
 group of students

Introducing

1. *Present or review concepts.* Three points need to be presented here. First, demonstrate the rule for making shapes in which one whole side of each square touches at least one whole side of another. Draw the following examples on the board or overhead:

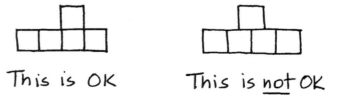

   Second, explain how to decide if two shapes are the same or different. Cut the two shapes in question out of paper and move them about to see if one fits exactly on the other. You might have to flip one over, or rotate one, but if they can be made to fit, they are called *congruent* and are considered to be the same.

Finally, discuss the derivation of the word *pentomino*. Draw a picture of a domino on the board or overhead. It's made of two squares. A pentomino is a five-square version. A three-square version is a triomino; a tetromino is made from four squares.

2. *Pose a part of the problem or a similar but smaller problem.* Ask: "Suppose you were trying to find all the different arrangements of three squares. What shapes could you make?" Have students try this. There are only two triominoes: ▭▭ and ⌐⊔. Have them try the same with four squares. (There are five possible tetrominoes.)

3. *Present the problem to be solved.* Ask groups to investigate different ways to arrange five squares. Direct them to cut each of the pentominoes they find out of the graph paper provided.

4. *Discuss the results.* Ask for questions.

Exploring

Two situations typically arise during the exploration. Some groups cut out two shapes that are the same but believe they are different. In that case, comment that you notice that two of their shapes are the same, and leave them to find the congruent shapes.

The second situation arises when a group has found all it can. Usually the students will ask you if they have them all. Tell them that is for them to decide and encourage them to find some way to analyze their arrangements to see if they think their collection includes all that are possible. Also tell them this issue will be discussed after all the groups in the class have finished the activity.

Extension

Direct the group to sort the shapes into two sets, those that will fold into a box and those that will not. Demonstrate with the shape that looks like the Red Cross symbol: ⌐⊔. Ask: "Can you see how you could fold up the sides of this shape so that it would be a box without a lid? Which side do you think would be the bottom of the box, opposite the open side? Mark that with an X. Now try folding it to check your prediction. With each of the other shapes, predict whether or not you think it will fold into a box, marking with an X the side that will be the bottom."

Summarizing

Discuss their group processes. Ask students to report how they found different shapes and decided who would cut out the pieces.

Discuss how they knew when they had found all the pieces possible. This is a good opportunity to discuss the issue of answers. If you had told them in advance that there were twelve shapes, you would have limited their opportunity for problem solving. Students benefit from hearing you reinforce the importance of problem solving. The goal in this activity is not just to find all the shapes; it is also to know when you've found them.

In classrooms, children often learn to depend on the quicker thinkers to provide answers. They also learn to depend on the teacher for finding out if they are right or wrong. It's valuable for children to learn to become self-reliant in their thinking processes. You can support this by keeping the emphasis on the problem-solving process and by not providing answers.

Discuss the challenge if all groups have had a chance to explore it. If not, discuss it at a later time, after students have had sufficient time to tackle it.

More Extensions

The Pentomino Game

Students each make a set of pieces from sturdy paper and a game board that is a 5-by-12-squared sheet, with squares matching the size of the squares they used for the pentominoes. As an individual puzzle, they try to fit all twelve pieces onto the board. As a two-person game, players take turns placing pieces on the board. The object is to be the last player to play a piece, making it impossible for the opponent to fit in another. In this second version, all the pieces do not have to be used.

The Factory Box Problem

Someone in a factory bought lots of cardboard that measured 5 squares by 4 squares. He figured that each sheet of cardboard could be cut into four pieces so each piece would fold into a topless box. How could the sheet be cut?

Milk Carton Geometry

Save school milk cartons. (Rinse them well!) When you've got enough so each student can have several, let them cut the tops off so all are topless boxes. Then students try to cut them so they lie flat in the different pentomino shapes.

Pentomino One-Difference Loop

Arrange the pentomino pieces into a loop, so that only one square needs to be moved to change a shape into the one next to it.

Activities

WHOLE CLASS: The Tangram Puzzle

You need: 6-inch squares of construction paper, 1 per student

The tangram is cut from a square. Having children each cut their own is a good lesson in following directions. Also, children are then convinced that the pieces truly go back together to make a square. The directions below show how to cut the square into the seven pieces: two pairs of congruent triangles, one middle-size triangle, one square, and one parallelogram.

Using just the three smallest triangles, make a square. Then use those same pieces to make a triangle, a rectangle, a trapezoid, and a parallelogram. Then use the five smaller pieces (all but the two large triangles) to make the same shapes. Repeat with all seven pieces. Record on a chart as shown.

Extensions

1. *Tangram Areas and Perimeters.* Compare the areas of the square, the parallelogram, and the middle-size triangle. Then compare their perimeters.

2. *Tangram Puzzle Cards.* Have children explore making shapes using all seven pieces. When they find one that pleases them, have them draw around the outline of the shape on drawing paper. They then name it, sign it, and put it in a class tangram box so others can try to fit their pieces into that shape. Students sign their names on the backs of each other's puzzles as they solve them.

3. *Using All Seven.* There are thirteen different convex shapes you can make with the seven pieces of the tangram. Find them.

4. *Making Squares.* You can show a square with just one piece of the tangram or by using all seven. What about using two, three, four, five, or six? One of those is impossible. Which is it, and why isn't it possible?

That's Just Half the Story

You need: small rectangular mirror

Some letters have mirror symmetry. That means when you place the mirror on them, you can see the whole letter—half on your paper and half in the mirror. Which letters work this way? Which work more than one way? Record the uppercase letters on a chart. Put in dotted lines to show where you placed the mirror.

These work one way.	These work more than one way.	These do not have mirror symmetry.
A	X	F

Interior Regions

Which uppercase letters have interior regions? That means if you built a fence in the shape of that letter, it would keep your dog inside. Record on a chart as shown.

YES	NO
P	E

Straight or Curved?

Which uppercase letters have only straight line segments? Which have only curves? Which have both? Record like this:

STRAIGHT	CURVED	BOTH
A	C	B

Then put your results on a Venn diagram, like this:

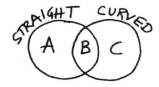

No-Lift Letters

It's possible to draw this shape ⬆ without lifting your pencil and without retracing any line. Try it. Then investigate the alphabet. Which uppercase letters can you write without lifting your pencil and without retracing any line? Record.

More No-Lift Letters

You can tell if a letter will work by looking at the points where line segments meet or end (the vertices) and by seeing how many of these points have an odd number of line segments meeting there (odd vertices).

Count the odd vertices for all the letters than can be written without lifting your pencil or retracing. What's the pattern?

LETTER	B	C	D		
ODD VERTICES	2	2	0		

Extensions

1. Try all the activities with lowercase letters.
2. Some letters have rotational symmetry. That means they are the same when turned upside down. Make a list of these.

Geometry Building

You need: a partner or small group
identical sets of materials (blocks, toothpicks, squares, etc.), 1 set per student
walls (from books or binders) so each person has a working space that no one else can see

One person builds a structure using some or all of the materials and then describes it so the others can build it. The others can ask questions at any time. Finally, lift your walls to see if the structures you built are the same. Try it again so all students have a chance to be the describer. Discuss the language used, focusing on what was useful and what was not.

Pool Hall Math

You need: centimeter grid paper, 1 sheet (see Blackline Masters)

A pool table is a rectangle or square of any dimensions. The ball always starts at the lower left corner. It moves by going to the opposite corner of each square it enters and keeps moving until it reaches a corner. Examples:

If the ball goes through *every* square on the table, then that pool table is *interesting*. If the ball doesn't go through every square, the table is *boring*. Find ten interesting and ten boring pool tables. Record. Can you find a pattern for predicting whether a pool table is interesting or boring before you test it?

Extensions

1. *Exit Corners*. Examine where the ball leaves each pool table. Some go out at A; others at B or C. Find ten different pool tables for each exit corner. Can you find a way to predict the exit corner?

2. *Paths*. The ball takes different paths on different tables. Find all the different patterns for the paths the balls take.

Area and Perimeter

You need: a partner or small group
Area and Perimeter shapes, duplicated on tagboard
  (see Blackline Masters)
large piece of chart paper

Cut out the shapes on the *Area and Perimeter* sheet. Use these pieces to do the following:

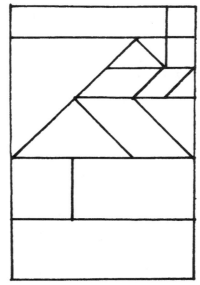

1. Order the pieces according to their areas.
2. Then compare the perimeters of the pieces.
3. Display results to show the relationships between the areas and perimeters.
4. Write statements that describe what you discovered.

Extensions

1. *Sorting by Shape.* Compare the areas and perimeters of each of the triangles, then the squares, then the rectangles, and finally the parallelograms. Write statements that describe what you discovered.
2. *Similar Shapes.* Similar shapes have the same shape but are different sizes. You can informally test to see if two shapes are similar by "sighting" with one. Here's how. Place the large square on the table. Stand up so you're looking down on it. Hold the small square in one hand, close one eye, and move the square up and down until it exactly covers the larger square. Because it can cover it exactly, they are similar. Will all squares be similar? Test the triangles, parallelograms, and rectangles the same way. Which are similar and which are not?
3. *Arrangements.* All of the pieces on the sheet fit perfectly into a rectangle. Could all of them be arranged into a triangle? A square? A parallelogram? Find ways to arrange them into other shapes.

Mirror Cards

You need: 3-by-5-inch index cards, 3
small piece of yarn or string
marker
small mirror
hole punch

Follow the directions to make mirror cards:

1. Cut two of the index cards in half.
2. Punch holes in the same corner of the four half cards and in the card that wasn't cut. Put the stack of cut cards on top and tie all five cards together with a piece of yarn. Write your name on the back of each card.
3. On the bottom half of the uncut card, make a design.
4. Put a mirror anywhere on the design, and draw on the first half card what you see both on your design and in the mirror.

5. Flip that half card up. Move the mirror and draw what you see now on the second half card.
6. Continue until you've drawn five designs in addition to your original one.
7. Try to solve others' cards, using the mirror to figure out where the creator placed it to get the design drawn. Write your name on the back of the uncut card to show you've solved the set.
   If you have trouble solving one, talk with the person who drew it.

The Fold-and-Cut Investigation

Fold a piece of paper in half. Cut out a small shape on the fold. Try to draw what the paper will look like when you unfold it. Then unfold and compare. Do this at least five times. **Note:** Try deciding on a shape first and then cutting to see if you get it.

Try the same activity, but fold the paper twice before cutting.

Square Partitioning

Draw nine squares on a sheet of paper. Number them as shown. Then divide each square into the number of smaller square regions written beside it. Examples:

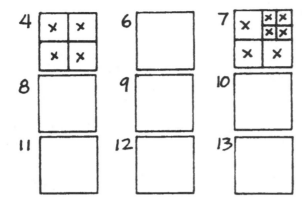

Extensions

1. *There's More Than One Way to Cut a Square.* Find all the different ways you can partition a square into a given number of smaller squares.
2. *What's Wrong with Five?* Notice that five was omitted. How come?
3. *Going Further.* Continue the activity for larger numbers.

The Banquet Table Problem

You need: color tiles, 24
            centimeter or half-inch grid paper (see Blackline Masters)

A banquet hall has a huge collection of small square tables that fit together to make larger, rectangular tables. Arrange tiles to find the different numbers of people that can be seated if twelve small tables are used. Do the same if twenty-four are used. Record on squared paper.

Extensions

1. *The 100-Table Problem.* If one hundred small square tables are arranged into a large rectangular table, find the most and least numbers of people that can be seated.
2. *Banquet Cost.* If the banquet hall charges by the number of square tables used, what's the least expensive way to seat sixteen people? Fifty people? Sixty? One hundred? Any number?

Introductory Explorations with Pattern Blocks

You need: pattern blocks, 1 set
9-by-12-inch construction paper, 1 piece
marker

Try the following introductory explorations to become familiar with pattern blocks.

1. Make a floor, covering as large an area as you'd like. Try this using blocks that are different kinds. Then see if you can do it using only one kind of block. Will all blocks work?
2. Make a straight road using only one kind of block. Can you do this with each different block? Which of your roads can you make turn a corner?
3. Make a design with the pattern blocks on a piece of construction paper. Trace around the outside of your design with a marker. List how many of each block you used. Exchange papers with classmates to see if you can fit the proper pieces into each other's designs.
4. Try building a larger triangle using only green triangles. Try building a larger square using only orange squares. Try the same with each of the other pieces. Which work and which do not?
5. Try building a shape exactly the same as (congruent to) the yellow hexagon using only green triangles. Try this with each of the other pieces. Which work and which do not?
6. If the area of the green triangle has the value of 1 unit, find the value of the area of the blue, red, and yellow pieces. Do the same with the area of the blue diamond as 1 unit, and then again with the red and yellow pieces as 1 unit.
7. Compare the areas of the orange and white pieces. Convince a friend of your comparison.

Hexagon Fill-in Puzzle

You need: pattern blocks, 1 set
Hexagon Fill-in Puzzle worksheet (see Blackline Masters)

You need six blocks to fill the hexagon shape with as few pieces as possible—three yellow hexagons and three blue parallelograms. (Try it.) To fill it with as many blocks as possible, you would use twenty-four green triangles. Explore the following:

1. Can you find ways to fill the hexagon shape with each number of blocks from 6 to 24 (7, 8, 9, 10, etc.)? Record.
2. For each of the numbers possible, find different ways to fill the shape. Record. (A different way means a different collection of blocks, not a different arrangement of the same blocks.)

Extension

In how many different ways can the hexagon shape be filled using pattern blocks?

Hexiamonds

You need: green triangles from the pattern blocks, 6
pattern block triangle paper, 1 sheet (see Blackline Masters)

Hexiamonds are shapes made from six equilateral triangles arranged so that each triangle touches at least one other. Whole sides must touch. Use the green triangles to find all the different (noncongruent) hexiamonds. Cut them out of the triangle paper to verify that they are different. Record your solutions. Explain how you know you have found them all.

Angles with Pattern Blocks and Hinged Mirrors

You need: pattern blocks, 1 set
pair of rectangular hinged mirrors
5-by-8-inch index card with a dot and line on it, as shown below

The size of an angle is a measure of rotation, and degrees are used to measure angles.

Part 1. Figure out how many degrees there are in the angles formed by the corners of each pattern block. Use the following procedure:

1. Place a corner of a block in the hinged mirrors.
2. Close the mirrors so the corner nestles snugly.
3. Use pattern blocks to build the design.
4. Sketch or trace it.
5. Figure the degrees in the nestled corner by dividing 360 degrees by the number of blocks in the design. Label your drawing to show the number of degrees in each angle.

Part 2. Construct other-size angles using the pattern blocks, hinged mirrors, and the index card. Experiment with the following procedures:

1. Use combinations of pattern blocks. For example, the orange square and blue parallelogram can be put together to make an angle that is 90 degrees plus 60 degrees.
2. Use the hinged mirrors and the index card. For example, place the hinged mirrors so you see five dots and a pentagon. Trace along the base of the hinged mirrors to draw the angle created. Divide 360 degrees by 5 to figure the size of the angle traced. Label the angle.

Extension
What size angles cannot be constructed using pattern blocks and hinged mirrors?

Explorations with Four Toothpicks

You need: a partner or small group
                 flat toothpicks, about 80
                 toothpick dot paper, 1 sheet (see Blackline Masters)

Investigate all the different ways to arrange four toothpicks by following two rules:

1. Each toothpick must touch the end of at least one other toothpick.
2. Toothpicks must be placed either end-to-end or to make square corners.

These are OK.   These are not OK.

| L | V = X

If a shape can be rotated or flipped to look like another shape, both shapes are the same. It's helpful to draw the shape in question on a piece of paper, flip it, and hold it up to a window to see if it's the same as another shape.

These are the same.

Record your shapes on the dot paper. When you find all sixteen shapes, cut your dot paper to make a set of cards.

Play a game. You need your cards and four toothpicks. Choose a starting card and make the pattern with the toothpicks. Deal the remaining cards to each player. (Discard extras so each player has the same number of cards.) Players place their cards faceup so all are visible. In turn, each plays a card that shows a pattern that can be made from changing the position of exactly one toothpick on the pattern shown. Players help each other with moves and discuss patterns. Players pass if they can't play. The player who uses all his or her cards first is the winner for that round.

Extension

The Put-in-Order Problem. Arrange the cards so that each pattern can be made from the previous pattern by changing the position of just one toothpick. Can the cards be arranged in a continuous loop? Can they be arranged in more than one way?

WHOLE CLASS: The Four-Triangle Problem

You need: 3-inch squares of construction paper in two colors,
            about 150 of each color
            18-by-24-inch newsprint, 1 sheet per pair of students

In this investigation, children explore shapes made from construction-paper triangles. Begin by showing children how to cut a square in half on the diagonal to make two triangles. Have them explore the different ways to put the triangles together, following the rule that two edges the same size must be matched. Discuss the possibilities with the class. (There are three—square, triangle, and parallelogram.) Then continue with the following explorations:

1. Have children, in pairs, investigate the different shapes they can make using four triangles. They should tape the triangles together or paste them on newsprint. Have many squares available for their exploration.
2. On a class chart titled "Polygons," organize the shapes the children found. To introduce the standard vocabulary, label columns: *Triangle*, *Quadrilateral*, *Pentagon*, and *Hexagon*. Have children post their shapes.
3. Have children choose one four-triangle shape. Using two triangles of each color, they make the shape with different arrangements of the colors.

Extension
Rotating Shapes. Children choose a four-triangle shape, trace it on tagboard, and cut it out. They draw a dot near the middle of a 12-by-18-inch sheet of drawing paper. They place a corner of their shape on the dot and trace. Then they rotate the shape and trace again. They continue rotating and tracing.

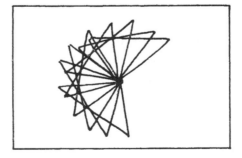

Penticubes

You need: interlocking cubes (Snap or Multilink cubes), about
                50 per student

This activity extends the pentomino exploration (see page 108) into three dimensions. Penticubes are three-dimensional shapes made from five cubes each. See how many you can construct.

Extensions

1. *Penticube Jackets.* Using paper ruled into squares the same size as the faces of the cubes, cut a jacket to fit a penticube. (Jackets are nets that fold to cover exactly all faces of the penticube.)
2. *More Penticube Jackets.* Take one penticube and find different possible jackets. (Is the number of possible jackets the same for each penticube?)
3. *Surface Area.* Compare the surface area of different penticubes. What do you notice about the shapes of penticubes with different surface areas?
4. *Penticube Riddles.* On grid paper, draw three views of a penticube—top, bottom, and side. Staple the drawings to a paper bag that holds the actual penticube. Others try to build the shape from the drawings and check their construction with the structure in the bag.
5. *Perspective Drawing.* Use isometric dot paper to draw penticubes.
6. *Building Rectangular Solids.* Put together several of the same or different penticubes to make rectangular solids. Investigate which dimensions of rectangular solids are possible to build.

WHOLE CLASS: Explorations Using the Geoboard

You need: geoboards, 1 per student
              rubber bands, about 6 per student

The following ideas are useful for beginning investigations.

1. Have children make numerals on the geoboard.
2. Have children make their initials. Ask them to make other letters.
3. Ask children to make something that can fly. Have students show what they made. Discuss. For example: "Joe made a rocket. Did anyone else make a rocket? How are the rockets alike? How are they different?"
4. Ask children to use just one rubber band and to make a shape that touches four pegs with one peg inside. It helps to describe this as making a fence that has four fenceposts and one tree inside the fence. Have children check with their neighbors to see that everyone has done it correctly and if there are different solutions. Continue: make a shape that touches five pegs with zero inside; make a fence with five fenceposts and two trees inside, and so on.
5. Ask children to use one rubber band to make a shape that is not a square and looks the same no matter which side the geoboard rests on. Ask: "How many different shapes did we make in the class?"

More Explorations Using the Geoboard

You need: a partner or small group
geoboard
rubber bands, 2 per student

Each student finds a solution for the first direction. In your group, check each other's solutions, compare results, and discuss similarities and differences. Then continue with the next direction.

1. Make a shape that touches five pegs. (Think of the rubber band as a fence, and the pegs it touches as fenceposts.) Then try shapes that touch six and four pegs.
2. Make a shape that has three pegs inside. (That means if the shape is a fence, the pegs inside are trees inside the fence.)
3. Make a shape that has ten pegs outside it, not touching the rubber band. (Think of them as trees growing outside the fence.)
4. Make a shape that has five fenceposts with three trees inside. Then try six fenceposts with two trees inside and three fenceposts with two trees inside. A challenge: Are there any combinations of fenceposts and trees that are not possible?
5. Use two rubber bands. Use each to make a line segment so the two line segments touch a total of nine pegs.
6. Repeat Step 5 again, this time finding different ways to make the line segments (a) parallel, (b) intersecting, (c) perpendicular, and (d) the same length.

a line segment

7. Make a triangle with one square corner and no two sides the same length.
8. Make a four-sided polygon with no parallel sides.
9. Make a four-sided polygon with all sides different lengths.
10. Make a four-sided polygon with no square corners but with opposite sides parallel. (What is this polygon called?)
11. Make a four-sided polygon that is not a square, not a rectangle, not a parallelogram, and not a trapezoid.
12. Make two shapes that have the same shape but are different sizes and are not squares.

WHOLE CLASS: Sorting Shapes on the Geoboard

You need: geoboards, 1 per student

               rubber bands, 1 per student

Each student makes a shape using one rubber band. Have eight to twelve students prop their geoboards on the chalkboard tray. Sort them in some way, separating groups by moving them on the tray. Have the students discuss in small groups how you sorted them. When groups think they know, they bring up a different shape and add it to the category it fits. After a while, have someone describe how the shapes were sorted. Repeat.

    Some ways to sort shapes include:

do or do not have at least one right angle

touch a corner peg or not

have zero, one, two, . . . pegs inside

have three, four, five, . . . sides

are or are not symmetrical

Extension

Have groups brainstorm different ways to sort shapes and choose one to try on the class. The group sorts the shapes and the rest of the class, teacher included, try to guess.

Square Up

You need: a partner

               geoboard

               rubber band

               Unifix cubes or game markers with holes in them, 12 each

                 of two colors

This game is for two players. Each takes twelve cubes in one color. Take turns putting one cube of your color on an empty peg on the geoboard. When you think four of your cubes mark the corners of a square, say, "Square up." Then your partner says, "Prove it." Prove it by stretching a rubber band around the pegs you've marked.

Geoboard Line Segments

You need: geoboard
              rubber band

Find the next-to-the-longest line segment you can make on the geoboard. Explain why you are sure your answer is correct.

Extension
How many different-length line segments are there on the geoboard? Find a way to record them and order them from shortest to longest.

Areas of Four on the Geoboard

You need: geoboard
              rubber band
              small geoboard dot paper, several sheets (see Blackline Masters)
              large geoboard dot paper, 1 sheet (see Blackline Masters)

The square made by stretching a rubber band around four pegs with no pegs inside has an area of 1 square unit. Find other shapes with an area of 4 square units. Record them on small geoboard dot paper. Choose one shape, copy it on large geoboard dot paper, cut it out, and post it. (**Note:** Post a shape that is different from those already posted.)

Area on the Geoboard

You need: geoboard
              rubber bands, at least 6
              Area on the Geoboard Recording Sheet (see Blackline Masters)

Find the area of each shape.

Shape Construction on the Geoboard

You need: geoboard
rubber band
small geoboard dot paper, several sheets (see Blackline Masters)

Construct shapes that fit each of the following. Record on geoboard dot paper. Can you find more than one solution for any of these?

  1. a rectangle with area of 2 square units
  2. a triangle with area of 2 square units
  3. a triangle with area of 3 square units
  4. a parallelogram with area of 3 square units
  5. a hexagon with area of 4 square units
  6. a rectangle and square with the same area (Which has the smaller perimeter?)

Geoboard Square Search

You need: geoboard
rubber bands, at least 7
small geoboard dot paper, several sheets (see Blackline Masters)

Find all the different-size squares you can make on the geoboard.
(Hint: There are more than four.) Record on geoboard dot paper.

Geoboard Triangle Search

You need: geoboard
rubber band
small geoboard dot paper, 1 sheet (see Blackline Masters)

Find triangles with areas of 5 and 7 square units. Record on geoboard dot paper.

Pick's Theorem

There is a function called Pick's theorem (named after the mathematician who discovered it) that enables you to find the area of any shape on the geoboard from the number of pegs on the perimeter of the shape (P) and the number of pegs inside the shape (I). The following sequence of activities suggests a way to find this theorem.

1. The square with an area of 1 has four pegs on its perimeter and zero pegs inside. Investigate other shapes with four pegs on the perimeter and zero pegs inside. Compare their areas. What about shapes with four pegs on the perimeter and one peg inside? Two pegs inside? Three? Four? Five? Any number? Write a formula that describes the relationship.

   Remember: P = pegs on the perimeter
                I = pegs inside
              A = area of the shape

P	I	A
4	0	1
4	1	
4	2	
4	3	
4	4	
⋮	⋮	

2. Do the same investigation for shapes with other numbers of pegs on the perimeter.

P	I	A
3	0	
3	1	
3	2	
3	3	
⋮	⋮	

P	I	A
5	0	
5	1	
5	2	
5	3	
⋮	⋮	

P	I	A
6	0	
6	1	
6	2	
6	3	
⋮	⋮	

3. Now investigate patterns for the areas of shapes when the number of inside pegs stays constant and the number of pegs on the perimeter varies. For example:

P	I	A
3	0	
4	0	
5	0	
6	0	
7	0	
⋮	⋮	

P	I	A
3	1	
4	1	
5	1	
6	1	
7	1	
⋮	⋮	

P	I	A
3	2	
4	2	
5	2	
6	2	
7	2	
⋮	⋮	

etc.

4. Finally, can you find a master formula that allows you to figure the area (A) for any combination of pegs on the perimeter (P) and pegs inside (I)? That's Pick's theorem.

   Just to check your formula:

P=8 I=2 A=?

P=6 I=1 A=?

P=9 I=5 A=?

P=4 I=1 A=?

Logical Reasoning

Overview

The development of logical reasoning is closely tied to children's language development. Elementary mathematics instruction should help students learn to organize ideas, understand what they're studying, and explain their thinking. Math lessons should encourage students to make conjectures, generalizations, and conclusions; to justify them with logical arguments; and to communicate them to others.

Logical reasoning is usually categorized as a process standard rather than as one of the mathematics topics included as a content standard. However, it is included here to provide specific instructional suggestions for fostering students' reasoning that draw from ideas in several of the content areas.

Why teach logical reasoning?

The process of reasoning is basic to all mathematics. Mathematics is first and foremost a way of thinking, rather than a body of facts. This is an important distinction for children to understand. At all grade levels, children benefit from experiences that help them gain clarity and precision in their thought processes. This is not only essential for learning mathematics but also has applications in all curriculum subjects and in ordinary life situations.

What concepts in logical reasoning should be taught?

The approach to logical thinking from kindergarten through grade 3 should be informal. At these grades, there should be many opportunities for children to explore and manipulate concrete objects, to identify likenesses and differences, to classify and categorize objects by their characteristic features, and to state generalizations. Verbal experiences must be provided that use terms integral to logical thinking, including *all, some, and, or, if . . . then*, and *not*. Using these terms helps children gain familiarity with the language of logic.

At the upper-elementary levels, students should have problem-solving experiences with both deductive and inductive reasoning. Deductive reasoning requires moving from assumptions to conclusions. Students use this type of reasoning regularly in daily living situations: *It is raining, so I need to wear my raincoat. My grandparents are coming to visit, so I can't go visit my friend.* Problems that utilize this kind of reasoning at the elementary level will enhance students' abilities as well as help prepare them for later formal study of the basic principles of deduction.

Inductive reasoning is usually informal and intuitive and involves examining particular instances to come to some general assumption. When thinking inductively, students make hypotheses, extend thought patterns, use analogies, and make reasonable conclusions from examining what appears to be a large enough body of evidence. Again, students do this regularly in ordinary life situations: *Mom never lets me go to the movies during the week, so she probably won't let me go this time, either. If I get good grades on the next two quizzes, I think I'll get an A in the class.* Students benefit from problem-solving activities that require the use of these thinking skills.

A Sample Activity: The Game of Poison

Poison is a version of the game of nim. It provides an opportunity for logical reasoning at several levels, so it can be used beneficially at all grade levels.

Materials

small objects, 13 per pair of students

Introducing

1. *Present or review concepts. Poison* is a game for two people. For a first game, use thirteen objects. Players take turns removing one object or two objects. Play until all objects have been taken. The last object to be removed is considered to be the poison. Whoever gets stuck taking it loses.
2. *Pose a part of the problem or a similar but smaller problem.* Play the game once with a volunteer. To enable the class to observe the game, use objects on an overhead or draw marks on the board.
3. *Present the problem to be solved.* Give these directions: "You need to play five games with each member of your group. After you've done this, as a group, discuss what you noticed about the game. Your group task is to try to find a winning strategy for avoiding the poison. Write down statements that describe your thinking. If your group thinks you have a winning strategy, raise your hands so you can try to poison me."
4. *Discuss the results.* Ask for questions. It is useful to reinforce the idea that the group's task is to cooperate in finding a winning strategy, not to focus on competitive play.

Exploring

Circulate and observe. Encourage groups to stop playing and to discuss strategies if they seem to be lagging. If you're called over by a group to "be poisoned," be sure that the entire group is involved and that all members understand the strategy being used. If you suspect that one person is doing all the thinking and has not communicated with the others in the group, ask one of the others to play. This helps focus students in a group on sharing their thinking. For a group that has a winning strategy and is able to poison you, offer the first extension and, if there is additional time later, the others.

Extensions

1. *Changing the Number of Objects.* Add one more object to the pile and play again. Try playing with other numbers of objects.
2. *Changing the Number You Can Remove.* Change the rules so it's possible to remove one, two, three, or some other number of objects on a turn.
3. *Making the Poison a Treat.* Play the game so the person who removes the last object wins. How does this affect your strategies?

Summarizing

Explain that the game of *Poison* has a winning strategy. This means the game will never end in a draw, as tic-tac-toe can. Someone will always win, and figuring out how requires logical thinking. Encourage students not to reveal the winning strategy if they know it so that others have a chance to continue their thinking. Encourage them, however, to test their thinking by varying the number of objects used in the game or the number a player can take on a turn. **Note:** It's possible to find a master strategy for playing with any number of objects and being allowed to remove any number of them on a turn.

Activities

King Arthur's Problem

This is a fictionalized historical problem. King Arthur wanted to decide who was most fit to marry his daughter. He chose the following method. When all his knights were seated at the Round Table, he entered the room, pointed to one knight, and said, "You live." The next knight wasn't so fortunate. "You die," said King Arthur, chopping off his head. To the third knight, he said, "You live," and to the fourth, he said, "You die," chopping off his head. He continued doing this around the circle, chopping off the head of every other knight, until just one was left. The remaining knight got to marry the daughter, but, as the legend goes, he was never quite the same again.

The problem is to figure out where you should sit in order to live. Do this for different numbers of knights. Find a pattern so you can predict where to sit no matter how many people are seated in the circle.

WHOLE CLASS: Junk Sorting

You need: collection of objects for each group (keys, jar lids, fabric swatches, buttons, nuts and bolts, postcards, shells, polished rocks, etc.)
string cut into 2-foot pieces, 4 pieces per group

Give the groups a chance to inspect their collections. Then ask them to sort their materials into two sets. Have them do this several different ways. Have them sort their collections into three sets. Then have them decide on one way to sort their collection for other groups to analyze. Have them follow these directions:

1. Groups sort materials into two, three, or four sets, making loops of string to keep the sets separate.
2. On a piece of paper, groups write down the attributes of each set and place the paper facedown on the table.
3. Groups rotate to a different table, where they try to figure out how another group has sorted its materials. When they think they know, they turn over the paper to check their predictions. Then they sort the materials in a different way, writing the new attributes under the old ones, and move to another table.
4. Groups continue to rotate as long as there is interest. Then they return to their original tables and examine the different ways their materials were sorted as listed on the papers.

Note: For young children, give a small group a collection of similar materials to explore. After they have had time to explore the collection freely, ask for a volunteer to tell one thing he or she noticed about the objects. For jar lids, for example, a child may offer, "Some are white." Then the group can sort them into two piles—the lids that are white and the lids that are not white. Then ask for something else someone may have noticed, and sort again. Continue until the children have exhausted all possibilities.

Difference Trains

You need: a partner or small group

attribute blocks or Attrilinks, 1 set

Start with one block or link. Arrange the blocks or links into a train so each piece is next to another that is different from it in just one way. Try to use all the pieces. (This may take some rearranging.) Then try to join the ends of the train to make a continuous loop. (This most likely will necessitate more rearranging.)

Difference Puzzle

You need: puzzle cards

attribute blocks or Attrilinks, 1 set

To make puzzle cards, first decide how many blocks or links you'd like to use and draw that many circles. Put a block in each circle and then draw lines connecting circles to show the number of differences between the shapes in the joined circles. For example, if the pieces are both large and red, but one is a square and the other is a triangle, they differ in only one way—shape. If the pieces have different shapes and sizes but are the same color, they have two differences. Remove the pieces. You now have a puzzle with at least one solution.

Then have others place pieces in the circles so that they have the number of differences as described by the lines.

——————————————————— one difference

═══════════════════ two differences

≡≡≡≡≡≡≡≡≡≡≡≡≡≡≡≡≡ three differences

Record as shown in the example.

RECORDING SYSTEM

L: Large   R: Red   C: Circle
S: Small   Y: Yellow   D: Diamond
            B: Blue   S: Square
            G: Green   T: Triangle

LYT: Large Yellow Triangle

SAMPLE

The Prison Problem

There was a jail with one hundred cells in it, all in a long row. The warden was feeling very jolly one night and told his assistant that he wanted to give all the prisoners a wonderful surprise. While they were sleeping, he wanted the assistant to unlock all the cells. This should be done, he told the assistant, by putting the key in each lock and turning it once.

Following the order, the assistant unlocked all the cells and then came back to report that the job was done. Meanwhile, however, the warden had second thoughts. "Maybe I shouldn't let all the prisoners go free," he said. "Go back and leave the first cell open, but lock the second one, by putting the key in and turning it once. Then leave the third open, but lock the fourth, and continue in this way for the entire row."

The assistant wasn't very surprised at this request. The warden often changed his mind. After finishing this task, the assistant returned, and again the warden had other thoughts. "Here's what I really want you to do," he said. "Go back down the row. Leave the first two cells as they are, and put your key in the third cell and turn it once. Then leave the fourth and fifth cells alone and turn the key in the sixth. Continue down the row this way."

The assistant again did as instructed. Fortunately, the prisoners were still asleep. As a matter of fact, the assistant was getting pretty sleepy, but there was no chance for rest yet. The warden changed his mind again, and the assistant had to go back again and turn the lock in the fourth cell and in every fourth cell down the row.

This continued all through the night, next turning the lock in every fifth cell, and then in every sixth, and on and on, until on the last trip, the assistant just had to turn the key in the hundredth cell.

When the prisoners finally woke up, which ones could walk out of their cells?

The Three-Sacks Problem

You need: 3 sacks with cubes as described below:
   1 with all red cubes
   1 with all blue cubes
   1 with red and blue cubes

There are three sacks with red and blue cubes in them. One is labeled All Red, one is labeled All Blue, and the third is labeled Red and Blue. There's one thing you know for sure—each of the three sacks is mislabeled. The problem is to figure out which sack really is which. You can't look into any of them, but you can reach into any one sack and remove one cube at random. Which sack would you reach into?

WHOLE CLASS: Decision Making

You need: die

Teach the game by asking each student to set up a blank addition problem as shown. Roll the die five times. Each time, call out the number that comes up. Students have to write the number in one of the five boxes. Once they write the number down, they cannot change its position. The goal is to place the numbers to produce the largest sum possible. Play the game several times until you're sure all the students understand it.

Then assign the group task. Groups are to write one procedure that the entire group will follow in playing the game as a team. They may write this decision-making strategy any way they like, as long as it is clear to all group members and accounts for all possible rolls.

When groups have completed their procedures, play five rounds of the game. See if any group's strategy produces more wins than any other.

Have groups post their procedures to compare the different ways the procedures were written and the different strategies the groups used.

Sally and the Peanuts

On the way home from school, Sally McCrackin likes to eat peanuts. One day, just as she was reaching into her sack, a hideous, laughing creature jumped into her path, identified itself as a pig eyes, and grabbed her sack. It stole half of her peanuts plus two more. A bit shaken, Sally continued toward home. Before she had a chance to eat even one peanut, another horrid creature jumped into her path and also stole half of her peanuts plus two more. Upset, she continued on. (What else could she do?) But before she had a chance to eat even one peanut, another of these tricksters jumped out and did the very same thing—took half her peanuts plus two more.

Now there were only two peanuts left in Sally's sack. She was so despairing that she sat down and began to sob. The three little pig eyes reappeared, feeling some sense of remorse, and told her they would return all her peanuts to her if she told them how many she had altogether when she started.

How many peanuts had been in Sally's sack?

Extension

Suppose Sally had been left with three peanuts? Or there had been four nasty pig eyes that left her with just two peanuts? Can you find a way to predict how many peanuts Sally had in her sack to start with regardless of how many she was left with or regardless of how many pig eyes stole peanuts from her?

Your Choice Tic-Tac-Toe

You need: a partner

Play on a regular tic-tac-toe board. On your turn you can put down either an X or an O, changing your mind on each turn if you wish. The winner is the one who finishes a row with either all Xs or all Os in it.

Number Sorting

You need: 30 cards or slips of paper, numbered 1 to 30

Sort the numbers in these ways:

1. into two groups
2. into three groups
3. into four groups

Record how you did this as shown in the example. Trade your paper with a classmate. Each of you tries to figure the rule the other used for sorting.

EXAMPLE :

Can you guess how this was done?

Latin Squares

You need: 16 color tiles, 4 of each color
one-inch grid paper, 2 sheets (see Blackline Masters)
crayons or markers, 1 each of four colors

Try each of the following:

1. Start with nine tiles, three each of three different colors. Arrange them into a square with one of each color in each row and each column. Record on squared paper.
2. Use all sixteen tiles and build a 4-by-4 square following the same rules. Record.
3. Repeat each, making the long diagonals contain one of each color also.

The Orange Juice–and-Water Problem

Suppose you have two glasses that are the same size and shape. One has water in it. The other has orange juice in it. The glasses have the same amount of water and juice.

Now suppose you take a spoonful from the glass of orange juice and put it in the glass of water. Mix it up. Then you take a spoonful from the glass of water (with the orange juice in it) and put it in the glass of orange juice. Mix it well. Once again, put a spoonful from the orange juice glass into the water glass and then a spoonful from the water glass back into the orange juice glass.

Now for the problem: Is there more orange juice in the water glass than there is water in the orange juice glass? Or the same of each in each?

The Two-Color Problem

You need: set of 20 objects, 10 each of two colors (10 red and 10 black playing cards, 10 tiles of each of two colors, etc.)
paper bags, 2

Separate the objects by color and put each set of ten in a paper bag. Reach into one bag and remove three objects. Put them in the other bag. Mix the contents of the second bag, and then reach in and remove three objects (at random) and put them in the first bag. Repeat this process three more times. Now examine the contents of each bag.

Consider the following questions:

How is this problem like *The Orange Juice–and-Water Problem*?
How is it different?
How would the activity change if you moved five objects each time or some other number?
What if you kept changing the number of objects you moved on each turn, rather than keeping it the same for the entire process?

The Card Problem

You need: 10 cards, numbered 1 to 10

Figure out how to arrange the cards so that the following can happen: Turn over the top card, which should be a 1 and place it faceup on the table; move the next card to the bottom of the deck. Turn over the third card, which should be a 2, and place it faceup on the table; move the next card to the bottom of the deck. Continue this way, turning over a card, placing it faceup on the table, and moving the next card to the bottom of the deck. When you are done all the cards should be faceup in order on the tabletop.

Logical Breakfast

Steven, Doreen, and Jay each ate something different for breakfast. One had granola, one had scrambled eggs and toast, and one had a banana split. (The last one was allowed because the parents were away on vacation and there was a very lenient baby-sitter.)

Jay did not have scrambled eggs and toast or a banana split. Doreen did not have scrambled eggs and toast.

Whose parents were on vacation?

Guess My Word

You need: a partner

One player thinks of a three-letter word for the other to guess. Whenever the person guesses, the player who thought of the word tells whether the guess comes before or after the word in the dictionary.

WHOLE CLASS: Riddles with Color Tiles

You need: color tiles, about 20 per student

                     small paper bags, 2 per pair of students

Students use clues to figure out the color tiles in a bag. For the first riddle each bag should have four yellow, four green, and four blue color tiles. It's helpful to present each clue separately, giving the students a chance to use their color tiles to make a combination that might be in the bag. For the second riddle, each bag should have four blue and two yellow color tiles. The second riddle can be done in the same way as the first riddle, or you can give students the first three clues to analyze together. After students are comfortable solving riddles, they work in pairs to make up their own riddles for others to solve.

Riddle 1
Clue 1:   I have twelve tiles.
Clue 2:   I used three colors.
Clue 3:   There are no red tiles.
Clue 4:   There are the same number of green and blue tiles.
Clue 5:   I have four yellow tiles.

Riddle 2
Clue 1:   There are fewer than ten tiles.
Clue 2:   I used two colors.
Clue 3:   I have no green or red tiles.
Clue 4:   I have twice as many blue tiles as yellow tiles.
Clue 5:   I have two yellow tiles.

Race for 20

You need: a partner

Take turns. On your turn, you may count one or two numbers. So the first person says: "One," or "One, two." And the second continues with one or two more numbers. The player who says "twenty" wins.

A Mathematical Tug-of-War

The problem is to use the information given to figure out who will win the third round in a tug-of-war.

Round 1: On one side are four acrobats, each of equal strength. On the other side are five neighborhood grandmas, each of equal strength. The result is dead even.

Round 2: On one side is Ivan, a dog. Ivan is pitted against two of the grandmas and one acrobat. Again, it's a draw.

Round 3: Ivan and three of the grandmas are on one side and the four acrobats are on the other.
  Who will win the third round? Write an explanation of your reasoning.

Digit Place

You need: a partner

Each person picks a three-digit number with no two digits the same. Partners take turns guessing each other's numbers. Each time someone guesses, the other person tells how many digits in the guess are correct and how many of the correct digits are in the correct place. A chart (see right) is useful for keeping track of the information.

Guess	D	P
293	0	0
356	1	1
296	0	0
⋮	⋮	⋮

  Do not tell *which* digits are correct or in the correct place, just *how many*. Whoever guesses the other player's number first wins that round.

Four in a Row

You need: a partner or small group
                 1-inch grid paper (see Blackline Masters)
                 color tiles, 15 of 1 color per student

This game can be played by two to four players. The grid paper is the playing board. Each player chooses a different color and uses the tiles of that color. On each turn, a player places a tile on a square. The first to get four in a row—horizontally, vertically, or diagonally—wins.

After students are familiar with the game, have them discuss and write about their strategies. **Note:** Unlike the game of *Poison* (see page 131), it is possible for this game to end in a draw.

Color In

You need: a partner
                 playing board (as shown)
                 crayons or markers, 1 each of
                     two colors

Each player, in turn, colors one square or two squares with a common side. Whoever colors in the last square wins.

Odd Number Wins

You need: a partner
                 counters, 15

Take turns. On your turn, you can pick up one, two, or three counters. Whoever has an odd number of counters when all have been picked up is the winner.

Patterns, Functions, and Algebra

Overview

Patterns are key factors in understanding mathematical concepts. The ability to create, recognize, and extend patterns is essential for making generalizations, seeing relationships, and understanding the order and logic of mathematics. Functions evolve from the investigation of patterns and make it possible to predict results beyond the information at hand. Functions are useful for solving problems in mathematics and in many other fields of study—including science and economics. Algebra makes it possible to represent patterns and functions and study and understand them further.

What's important about patterns, functions, and algebra?

Studying patterns, functions, and algebra involves students in investigating numerical and geometric patterns; describing them verbally; representing them symbolically in several ways, including in tables, with symbols, and graphically; using them to make predictions and generalizations; and exploring properties of our number system. By studying patterns, functions, and algebra, students learn about the various uses of variables and how to solve equations.

Introducing Patterns

Looking for patterns is natural for young children, and early experiences should focus on recognizing regularity, identifying the same pattern in different forms, and using patterns to make predictions. For example, introduce a repeating pattern like *clap, snap, clap, snap, clap, snap, . . .* and have children join in. Give them materials with which they can represent the pattern—by making a train of interlocking red-blue-red-blue-red-blue cubes, for example. Represent the pattern with letters, in this case *ababab* . . . . Also, ask children to predict what comes later in the sequence. In this pattern, for example, the twelfth element will be *snap*, *blue*, or *b*. Mix easy patterns with more complicated ones:

clap, clap, snap, clap, clap, snap, clap, clap, snap, . . .

□ □ △ □ □ △ □ □ △ □ □ △ . . .

a a b a a b a a b a a b . . .

Number sequences, like *2, 4, 6, 8, . . .* and *1, 2, 4, 8, 16, . . .*, also provide patterns for children to investigate. Growth patterns like these are *recursive patterns;* that is, each number is found from the previous number by repeating some process. Students benefit from examining such sequences and figuring out how to determine subsequent terms—for example, *adding 2* or *doubling.*

What comes next ?
1, 4, 7, 10, 13, 16, . . .
0, 2, 6, 14, 30, 62, . . .
2, 12, 22, 32, 42, 52, . . .

Developing Understanding of Functions

Looking for patterns in the relationships between two sets of numbers is a key way to develop students' understanding of functions. For example, we know that one tricycle has three wheels and two tricycles have six wheels. How many wheels do three tricycles have? Four tricycles? How about *n* tricycles? The number of wheels is a function of the number of tricycles. This means that since each tricycle has three wheels, we can use the rule of multiplying the number of tricycles by three to determine the number of wheels for any number of tricycles. One way to describe this relationship between tricycles and their wheels is as a set of pairs of numbers: (1, 3), (2, 6), (3, 9), (. . . , . . .) (one tricycle and three wheels, two tricycles and six wheels, and so on). This set of pairs of numbers form what is called a *function.*

Younger children can have beginning experiences with functions by exploring number patterns that describe relationships that exist in the real world. For example, have children come to the front of the room and count their eyes. One child has two eyes, two children have four eyes, three children have six eyes, and so on. The number of eyes depends on the number of children, and therefore the number of eyes is a function of the number of children. Children can record the eyes pattern as shown on the next page. Then have them predict beyond the information they have recorded.

Other patterns to investigate with young children in this same way include fingers, thumbs, toes, noses, the number of points on any number of five-pointed stars, the amount of money for any number of nickels or dimes, the number of children needed to turn any number of jump ropes, and so on.

Older students should be introduced more formally to the concept and standard notation of functions. A function is defined as a set of ordered pairs, such as in the tricycle-and-wheels example of (1, 3), (2, 6), (3, 9), (. . . , . . .), in which no two pairs have the same first number. Note that the order of the numbers in each pair is significant: (3, 1) would mean that for three tricycles there is one wheel, and that's not true. Also, for any number of tricycles, there is only one correct number of wheels; it's not possible to have a different pair of numbers beginning with 1, 2, 3, or any other number.

An important first step for students is to describe patterns like these verbally. An important goal of mathematics instruction is for students to learn to represent functions in the following three forms:

1. table
2. formula
3. graph

Table

For the tricycle example, using T to represent tricycles and W for wheels, you can represent the function in a table. You can think of T as the *input* and W as the *output*.

Formula

The relationship between tricycles and wheels can also be represented in an algebraic equation using T and W as variables: $T \times 3 = W$
Because the number of wheels depends on the number of tricycles, mathematicians often refer to W, the quantity of wheels, as the dependent variable, determined by a rule that is applied to T, the independent variable.

Graph

Coordinate geometry makes it possible to represent functions graphically. Graphing a function calls for using the ordered pairs to place points on a co-ordinate graph. The standard way to do this is to start where the two heavy lines (the *axes*) meet. This point is called the *origin*. Use the first number in each pair to count over from the origin, use the second number to count up, and place a dot. Young children can learn this system of placing points without much difficulty. Notice that the dots for the tricycles-and-wheels function are in a straight line, indicating that it is a linear function.

Uses of Variables

Representing functions algebraically calls for the use of variables, as T and W were used to represent the function about tricycles and wheels. However, variables serve other purposes as well. Young children typically first learn about using variables as placeholders for unknown numbers; for example, $\square + 3 = 10$ or $5 + n = 12$. In these situations, variables represent answers—specific, nonvarying numbers that can be determined by solving the equation.

Later, students learn that variables can be used not only for specific unknown quantities but also for a wide range of values. Equations that use variables in this way can generalize arithmetic properties. For example, $\square + 0 = \square$ is true for any value of $\square$ because we know that adding zero to a quantity results in the same quantity. Zero is called the *additive identity*. Similarly, $n \times 1 = n$ for any value of n; the number one is the *multiplicative identity*. Other examples of using variables to describe arithmetic properties include $a + a = 2a$, $\square \times 0 = 0$, and $x + y = y + x$. Each of these equations is true for any values of a, $\square$, x, or y.

Variables are also used in formulas; for example, $A = lw$, with A, l, and w representing varying quantities of area, length, and width.

A Sample Activity: Painting Towers

Suppose you build a tower of interlocking cubes that is ninety-nine cubes tall. And suppose you paint every square on all four sides of the tower, as well as the top. (You don't have to paint the base of the tower.) How many squares do you have to paint? What is the relationship between the height of the tower and the number of squares to paint?

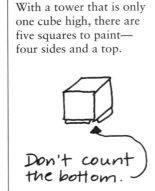

With a tower that is only one cube high, there are five squares to paint—four sides and a top.

Don't count the bottom.

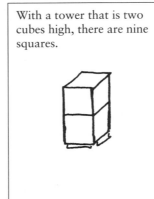

With a tower that is two cubes high, there are nine squares.

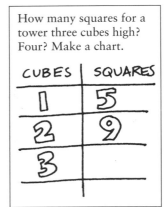

How many squares for a tower three cubes high? Four? Make a chart.

CUBES	SQUARES
1	5
2	9
3	

Painting Towers is a sample of the kinds of problems that follow. Each problem presents a situation that you can investigate geometrically, numerically, and algebraically. For each, continue the table started until you can identify a pattern. Then think about how to solve the problem without continuing the pattern, but by looking for the functional relationship. Represent the function with a formula and graph enough of the pairs of numbers to describe the pattern made by the points.

Activities

Paper Folding

Suppose you fold a piece of paper in half, and then in half again, and again, until you make six folds. When you open it up, how many sections will there be?

With one fold, you will have two sections.	With two folds, you will have four sections.	Make a chart. Continue the folding. Look for a pattern.

More Painting Towers

You Need: interlocking cubes (Snap or Multilink), about 125

Suppose you build a cubical tower that is ninety-nine cubes tall. And suppose, as you did for *Painting Towers* on page 148, you have to paint every square on the four sides and the top of the tower. (You don't have to paint the base of the tower.) How many squares do you have to paint?

With a cubical tower that is only one cube high, there are five squares to paint—four sides and a top.	With a cubical tower that is two cubes high, there are twenty squares.	How many squares for a cubical tower three cubes high? Four? Make a chart.
		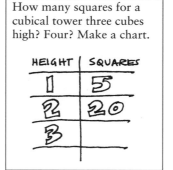

Dot Connecting

Suppose you draw ten dots on a circle. If you draw lines connecting every dot to every other dot, how many lines will you draw?

With just one dot, there will be zero lines.	With two dots, you can draw one line.	How many lines will you draw for three dots? Four? Make a chart.
		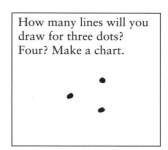

Paper Tearing

Suppose you tear a piece of paper in half and give half to someone else. Then each of you tears your piece in half and passes half on to someone else. How many people will have a piece of paper after ten rounds of tearing like this?

With one tear, there will be pieces for two people.	After the second round of tears, there will be pieces for four people.	Continue tearing the paper. Record on a chart. Look for patterns.

  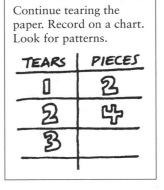

The Diagonal Problem

If you have a twelve-sided polygon (a dodecagon), how many diagonals can you draw? Remember that diagonals connect the corners of shapes.

A triangle has three sides and no diagonals.	A four-sided figure (a quadrilateral) has two diagonals.	What about a pentagon? A hexagon? And so on?

  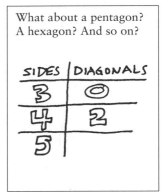

Points Dividing a Line

If you put twenty points on a line segment, how many sections can you count?

With one point, you will have two sections.	With two points, there will be three sections.	Continue making points and counting sections.

The Ice-Cream-Cone Problem

If an ice-cream shop sells thirty-one different flavors of ice cream, how many different double-dip cones can they make? Hint: Use different-colored interlocking cubes for flavors and build the cones.

If the shop has only one flavor, there will be only one possible double-dip cone. 	With two flavors, there are three combinations for double-dip cones. 	How many double dips are possible with three flavors? Four? Make a chart and look for patterns.

Extensions

1. If you count vanilla on top and pistachio on the bottom as different from pistachio on the top and vanilla on the bottom, how will your result change?
2. Try the same problem for triple-dip cones.

Squares from Squares

If you build larger and larger squares from small squares, how many squares will you need to build one that measures 12 on a side?

For a square with sides of 1 unit, you need one square. 	For a square with sides of 2 units, you need four squares.	For a square with sides of 3 units, you need nine squares.	Continue the pattern.

More Squares from Squares

If you build squares as in *Squares from Squares*, what will be the length of the perimeter of a square that is 12 on a side?

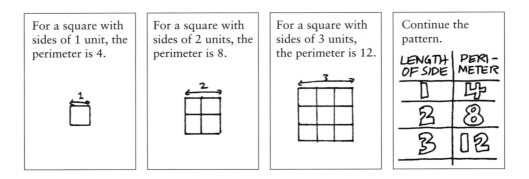

For a square with sides of 1 unit, the perimeter is 4.	For a square with sides of 2 units, the perimeter is 8.	For a square with sides of 3 units, the perimeter is 12.	Continue the pattern.
			LENGTH OF SIDE / PERI-METER 1 / 4 2 / 8 3 / 12

Rod Stamping

Imagine the white Cuisenaire rod is a rubber stamp that stamps 1-centimeter squares. How many stamps would it take to cover each of the other rods? What is the pattern?

The white rod takes six stamps.	The red rod takes ten stamps.	Continue the pattern.
 (DON'T FORGET THE BOTTOM)	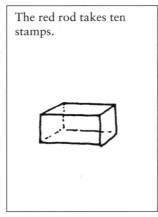	ROD / STAMPS 1 white — 6 2 red — 10 3 green 4 purple 5 yellow 6 dark gr. 7 black 8 brown 9 blue 10 orange

More Rod Stamping

Suppose you take rods of one color and pretend to glue them together as the picture shows. Figure out how many stamps are needed for each and look for the pattern.

The purple rod (as a sample) takes eighteen stamps.	Two purple rods glued take twenty-eight stamps.	Continue the pattern.
	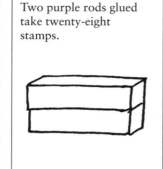	RODS | STAMPS 1 | 18 2 | 28 3 |

Extension

Suppose you glue the rods together, offsetting each 1 centimeter, as the picture shows. Make a chart of the stamps needed and look for the pattern.

A Row of Triangles

If you line up one hundred equilateral triangles (like the green triangles from the pattern blocks) in a row, what will the perimeter measure? (You may think of this as a long banquet table made from individual triangular tables. How many people can be seated?)

With one triangle, the perimeter is 3 units.	With two triangles, the perimeter is 4 units.	With three triangles, the perimeter is 5 units.	Continue the pattern.
		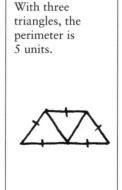	TRI-ANGLES | PERI-METER 1 | 3 2 | 4 3 | 5

A Row of Squares

If you line up one hundred squares in a row, what will the perimeter measure? (As in *A Row of Triangles*, you may think of this as a long banquet table made from individual square tables. How many people can be seated?)

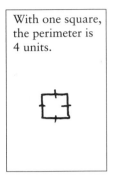

With one square, the perimeter is 4 units.

With two squares, the perimeter is 6 units.

With three squares, the perimeter is 8 units.

Continue the pattern.

SQUARES	PERI-METER
1	4
2	6
3	8
4	

A Row of Pentagons

If you line up one hundred regular pentagons in a row, what will the perimeter measure?

With one pentagon, the perimeter is 5 units.

With two pentagons, the perimeter is 8 units.

With three pentagons, the perimeter is 11 units.

Continue the pattern.

PENTA-GONS	PERI-METER
1	5
2	8
3	11
4	

A Row of Hexagons

If you line up one hundred regular hexagons in a row, what will the perimeter measure?

With one hexagon, the perimeter is 6 units.

With two hexagons, the perimeter is 10 units.

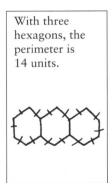

With three hexagons, the perimeter is 14 units.

Continue the pattern.

HEXA-GONS	PERI-METER
1	6
2	10
3	14
4	

Note: There is a way to figure out the pattern for a row of any regular polygon. Try it if you're interested.

Interlocking Trains

If you make trains ten cubes long using two colors of interlocking cubes, how many different arrangements can you make? (**Note:** The order of the colors matters. For example, for a train that is three cubes long, red-red-blue and red-blue-red each count as a different arrangement.)

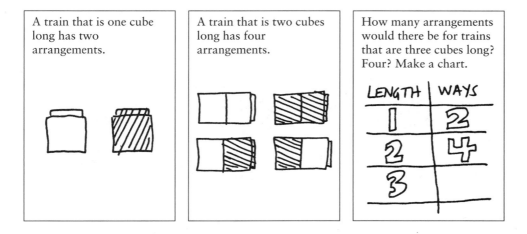

A train that is one cube long has two arrangements.	A train that is two cubes long has four arrangements.

How many arrangements would there be for trains that are three cubes long? Four? Make a chart.

LENGTH	WAYS
1	2
2	4
3	

Toothpick Building

If you continue the pattern shown to build a row of one hundred triangles, how many toothpicks will you need?

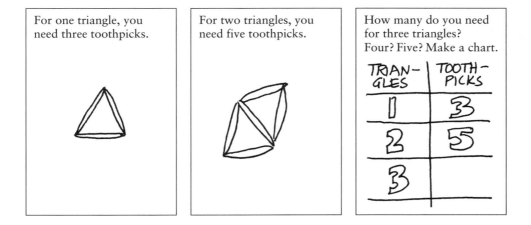

For one triangle, you need three toothpicks.	For two triangles, you need five toothpicks.

How many do you need for three triangles? Four? Five? Make a chart.

TRIANGLES	TOOTHPICKS
1	3
2	5
3	

Extension

Try the problem for rows of squares, pentagons, and hexagons.

The Handshake Problem

Suppose everyone in this room shakes hands with every other person in the room. How many handshakes will that be?

With only one person in the room, there will be no handshake.

PEOPLE | HAND-SHAKES

1 | 0

With two people, there will be one handshake.

PEOPLE | HAND-SHAKES

1 | 0
2 | 1

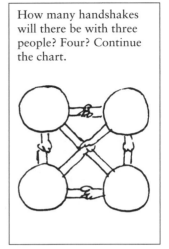

How many handshakes will there be with three people? Four? Continue the chart.

Number and Operations

Overview

Numbers are used to describe quantities, to compare quantities, to identify specific objects in collections, and to measure. Children must be able to make sense of the various ways numbers are used. They need to develop a sense of number that enables them to recognize relationships between quantities; to use the operations of addition, subtraction, multiplication, and division to obtain numerical information; to understand how the operations are related to one another; to be able to approximate and estimate when appropriate; and to be able to apply their understandings to problem situations.

What concepts in number should be taught?

Children's math learning should emphasize the development of number sense, should help them see relationships among numbers, and should encourage them to examine the properties of numbers. Children should investigate the use of numbers in many situations so that they develop the confidence and flexibility to apply their understanding in new situations.

The study of patterns is valuable for helping children discover and develop generalizations about number. Investigating patterns in numerical relationships needs to be an ongoing part of the elementary mathematics program.

The nature of numbers includes such ideas as whether numbers are prime or composite, whether they are even or odd, what their factors and multiples are, and how numbers relate to other numbers. Experiences with these ideas help students develop understanding of our number system.

Students need to develop an intuitive understanding of the *commutative*, *associative*, and *distributive* properties of the basic operations. Instruction should introduce these concepts in problem-solving settings rather than present their definitions abstractly.

The activities in this section require that students apply numbers in problem situations. These problem situations differ from traditional word problems for which specific skills are used to get single answers. The focus here is on the use of numbers in problems for which there are often a variety of solutions or a variety of possible ways to arrive at a solution. It is assumed that students have calculators available for their use at all times.

A Sample Activity at the Primary Level: Number Sums

This activity requires that children can write sums for numbers less than ten. Although practice of basic addition facts is provided, the emphasis of the problem is to use the facts to find all the possible ways to represent sums.

Introducing

1. *Present or review concepts.* Review with the children the fact that there are different ways to write sums of numbers. Use the number three as an example, showing the children the three ways to write three as a sum using addends greater than or equal to one. Record on the board:

$$1 + 1 + 1$$
$$2 + 1$$
$$1 + 2$$

2. *Pose a part of the problem or a similar but smaller problem.* Ask the children to help you find all the ways to write four as a sum. Remind them that if the addends are in a different order, the sum will be counted as a different way. Record the seven ways on the board:

$$1 + 1 + 1 + 1$$
$$1 + 1 + 2$$
$$1 + 2 + 1$$
$$2 + 1 + 1$$
$$1 + 3$$
$$3 + 1$$
$$2 + 2$$

3. *Present the problem to be solved.* The groups' task is to find all the ways to write sums of the number five.
4. *Discuss the results.* Ask for questions.

Exploring

Circulate and observe. If a group calls you over to announce that it is finished, look at the sums. If you notice the children have repeated any, tell them, but leave them the task of finding the repeats. If you know there are more ways to be found, ask them to continue to think about the problem. If they've found all fifteen different ways, suggest that they try the investigation for the number six.

Summarizing

Discuss the group processes. Ask how they organized themselves to work together. Ask how they decided when they had found all the sums. Have children report their findings.

Look at the pattern in the number of ways there are to write the sums for three, four, and five. Ask the children to predict how many ways there are to write six. Assign the problem of finding the different ways to write sums of six to groups that did not get started on it during the exploration. Have the other children continue trying to figure out the pattern so they can predict how many sums there are for seven and eight.

Number	How many sums?
3	3
4	7
5	15
6	:
:	:

A Sample Activity at the Intermediate Level: Palindromes

This activity engages students in looking for number patterns, both visually and numerically.

Materials

large 0–99 chart, 1 per student (see Blackline Masters)
Palindrome Recording Sheet, 1 per student (see Blackline Masters)
crayons or markers

Introducing

1. *Present or review concepts.* A palindrome is a number that reads the same forward and backward, such as 44, 252, or 8,008. A number that is not a palindrome, such as 13, can be changed into a palindrome by using a particular procedure: You reverse the digits and add. Demonstrate on the board how to do this. Since it takes one addition, 13 is a one-step palindrome.

$$\begin{array}{r} 13 \\ +31 \\ \hline 44 \end{array}$$

Some numbers take more than one addition. Demonstrate with 68.

$$\begin{array}{r} 68 \\ +86 \\ \hline 154 \\ +451 \\ \hline 605 \\ +506 \\ \hline 1111 \end{array}$$

2. *Pose a part of the problem or a similar but smaller problem.* Have the students try to change forty-eight into a palindrome. As they work, do it on the board so they can check their work. Then show the class how to record the results for thirteen, sixty-eight, and forty-eight on the *Palindromes* recording sheet.

3. *Present the problem to be solved.* Each group is to investigate all the numbers from zero to ninety-nine. First they should decide how to divide the work. Everyone is to keep individual records on the chart as demonstrated. Also, each person is to record on a 0–99 chart, coloring the numbers that are already palindromes with one color, coloring in one-step palindromes with another color, two-step palindromes with another color, and so on. As a group, they should agree on the colors to use. Direct them to look for patterns on both charts. Also, tell them not to tackle ninety-eight and eighty-nine unless they are ready for a serious bout with addition. (Each number takes twenty-four steps with a resulting palindrome of 8,813,200,023,188.)

4. *Discuss the results.* Ask for questions.

Exploring

Problems do not generally arise during this exploration. Several class periods may be required for all groups to finish their work. Before beginning work on the second day, it may be useful to have a brief discussion about their progress so that students can hear from others about organizational tips, problems, and so on.

Summarizing

Discuss the group processes. Ask groups: "How did you divide the work? Was your system a good one? Did you change your system during the activity? What do you think would be the best way for a group to do this activity?"

Ask about patterns that emerged on charts. Start a chart of the students' discoveries. Some groups, for example, notice that when the sum of the digits of a number is less than ten, the number is always a one-step palindrome. Others notice that all resulting palindromes are multiples of eleven. Have the class look for other patterns such as these.

Ask how they colored one-digit numbers. There is no right answer to this, but groups should be able to explain their ideas.

Activities

WHOLE CLASS: Investigations with Raisins

You need: $\frac{1}{2}$-oz. boxes of raisins, 1 per student

$1\frac{1}{2}$-oz. boxes of raisins, 1 per small group of students

Lesson 1

1. Show a $\frac{1}{2}$-oz. box. Have the students guess how many raisins it contains.
2. Distribute the boxes. Each student opens a box, counts the raisins that are visible, and makes an estimate of how many raisins are in the entire box. (Be sure to remind them not to remove any raisins yet.) They then discuss their estimates in their groups, decide on a group estimate, and report it in writing, explaining their reasoning.
3. Each student counts the raisins in his or her box, arranging them on paper so it's easy to see how many there are. Record the counts on the board.
4. Based on the information recorded on the board, students predict what one number might be a good guess for how many raisins typically are in a box. Have them record individually and explain their reasoning, discuss their ideas in their groups, and finally report to the class.
5. Students figure how many raisins there are altogether in their group's boxes. They record and explain how they figured. Finally, they can eat their raisins if they wish, but have them save the boxes for the next lesson. Also, save the information you recorded about their actual counts.

Lesson 2

1. Give each group a $1\frac{1}{2}$-oz. box of raisins. Have them estimate how many raisins are in it and explain in writing how they did it. Have groups report to the class.
2. Have groups count the raisins in the box and then figure out how to share them equally. They write about how they solved this problem.

WHOLE CLASS: Coin Riddles

You need: dimes, 4
        pennies, 2

With the coins hidden from view, present the clues to the class in the sequence given. After each clue, have groups discuss what they know for sure. Ask if they have sufficient information to guess the coins you have or if they need another clue. The coins can be guessed from the following clues.

> Clue 1: I have six coins.
> Clue 2: I have only dimes and pennies.
> Clue 3: I have at least two pennies.
> Clue 4: I have more dimes than pennies.

Simpler riddles are more suitable for younger children. Be sure to provide children with coins to use for figuring.

> **Riddle 1.** I have two coins worth eleven cents.
> **Riddle 2.** I have three coins worth twenty-seven cents.
> **Riddle 3.** I have four coins worth twenty-two cents.

Making Change

Find all the ways to make change for $0.50.
Easier version: Find all the ways to make change for a quarter.
Harder version: Do the same for $1.00.

Number Bracelets

Choose any two numbers from 0 to 9 and follow this rule: Add the two numbers and record just the digit that appears in the ones place in the sum. For example, if you start with 8 and 9, then the next number would be 7. Then add the last two numbers (the 9 and the 7) and record *6*, the ones place of their sum. Continue until you get back to where you started: 8, 9, 7, 6, 3, 9, 2, . . . How many numbers in your series until you get a repeat?

Answer these questions:

1. How many different possible pairs of numbers can you use to start?
2. What's the shortest bracelet you can find?
3. What's the longest bracelet?
4. Investigate the odd and even patterns in all your bracelets.

The 0–99 Chart

You need: small 0–99 charts, 1 sheet (see Blackline Masters)
crayon or marker

Follow these directions to color each of the 0–99 charts:

1. Color all the even numbers.
2. Color all the numbers with digits that add to eight.
3. Color the numbers with digits that differ by one.
4. Color all the numbers with a 4 in them.
5. Color the multiples of three.
6. Color the numbers with both digits the same.

(For more, see "0–99 Chart versus 1–100 Chart" on page 372.)

How Many Sums?

If you add two or more of these numbers, find all the different possible sums you can get.

19   21   15   17   13

Pascal's Triangle

Figure out how to extend this pattern to include additional rows. Look for patterns in rows and diagonals.
    Find out who Pascal was.

1

1 1

1 2 1

1 3 3 1

1 4 6 4 1

1 5 10 10 5 1

Change from a $10.00 Bill

If you spend $1.85 and pay with a $10.00 bill, you get $8.15 in change. Notice that the digits in your change are the same as the digits in the amount you spent. Try to find all the other amounts you could spend and get change with the same digits. Explain why you think you have found all of the possibilities.

Addition Table Explorations

You need: addition chart (see below; see also Blackline Masters)

+	1	2	3	4	5	6	7	8	9	10
1	2	3	4	5	6	7	8	9	10	11
2	3	4	5	6	7	8	9	10	11	12
3	4	5	6	7	8	9	10	11	12	13
4	5	6	7	8	9	10	11	12	13	14
5	6	7	8	9	10	11	12	13	14	15
6	7	8	9	10	11	12	13	14	15	16
7	8	9	10	11	12	13	14	15	16	17
8	9	10	11	12	13	14	15	16	17	18
9	10	11	12	13	14	15	16	17	18	19
10	11	12	13	14	15	16	17	18	19	20

Describe general rules or shortcut methods to find the following:

1. The sum of any three horizontally adjacent numbers.
2. The sum of any three vertically adjacent numbers.
3. The sum of any 2-by-2 array of numbers.
4. The sum of any 3-by-3 array of numbers.
5. The sum of any 10-by-10 array of numbers.
6. The sum of any cross of five numbers.
7. The sum of any three diagonally adjacent numbers.
8. The sum of any four diagonally adjacent numbers.
9. The sum of any five diagonally adjacent numbers.

Invent at least three other problems like these and describe rules for them.

Multiplication Possibilities

Find as many ways as you can to fill in this problem so the arithmetic is correct:

$$\begin{array}{r} \square\ \square\ \square \\ \times\ \square \\ \hline 9\ 6\ 6 \end{array}$$

Where Does 100 Land?

If you write the counting numbers in rows of seven numbers each, in which column will 100 land? In which row?

```
1 2 3 4 5 6 7
8 9 10 11 12 13 14
15 16 17 · · ·
```

Write the counting numbers in rows of six numbers each. What's the location of 100 in this array?

```
1 2 3 4 5 6
7 8 9 10 11 12
13 14 15 16 · · ·
```

Write arrays with other length rows. Find a way to predict in which row and column 100 will land for any array of numbers.

Extension
From Column to Column. For each array, if you add a number from the second column to a number from the third column, in which column will the sum land?

WHOLE CLASS: The Border Problem

You need: 10-by-10 squares cut from centimeter grid paper, 1 per student (see Blackline Masters)
5-by-5 squares cut from centimeter grid paper, 1 per student

Ask students to figure out how many squares there are in the border of a 10-by-10 grid. Record all the different ways reported by translating their verbal explanations to arithmetic notation. Then have students test their methods on a 5-by-5 grid.

Show the class a larger square grid, one for which they do not know the number of squares on a side. Ask them to describe how they would go about figuring the number of squares in its border. Show how to translate one of their methods into an algebraic formula. Have them work together to translate all their methods into formulas.

On Which Day of the Week Were You Born?

Follow these directions to find out on what day of the week you were born:

1. Write down the last two digits of the year in which you were born. Call this number *A*.
2. Divide that number (*A*) by four, and drop the remainder if there is one. This answer, without the remainder, is *B*.
3. Find the number of the month in which you were born from the Month Table below. This number is *C*.
4. On what day of the month were you born? This number is *D*.
5. Add the numbers from the first four steps: *A* + *B* + *C* + *D*.
6. Divide the sum you got in Step 5 by the number seven. What is the remainder from that division? (It should be a number from zero to six.) Find this remainder in the Day Table. That tells you what day of the week you were born on. (This method works for any day in the twentieth century.)

Month Table

		Day Table
January 1 (leap year is 0)	July 0	Sunday 1
February 4 (leap year is 3)	August 3	Monday 2
March 4	September 6	Tuesday 3
April 0	October 1	Wednesday 4
May 2	November 4	Thursday 5
June 5	December 6	Friday 6
		Saturday 0

The Postage Stamp Problem

You can combine different denominations of stamps to get the proper postage for a letter or package. In this problem, you investigate the postage amounts that can be made when you are restricted to using only certain stamps.

To begin, if stamps came only in 3¢ and 5¢ denominations, what amounts of postage would be impossible to make? Is there a largest impossible amount? Explain your answers.

Do the same investigation if there were only 5¢ and 8¢ stamps. Then continue with other combinations of two denominations of stamps. For each, investigate the following:

1. How many impossible amounts are there?
2. Is there a largest impossible amount and, if so, what is it?

Write an explanation for each of your answers.

Arrow Arithmetic

You need: large 0–99 chart (see Blackline Masters)

Look at the starter hints, using the 0–99 chart for reference. Then solve the others.

Starter hints: 18 $\rightarrow$ = 19 18 $\leftarrow$ = 17 18 $\uparrow$ = 8 18 $\downarrow$ = 28

How about these? 18 $\nearrow$ = ? 18 $\nwarrow$ = ? 14 $\swarrow \rightarrow \rightarrow$ = ?
                76 $\searrow \uparrow \uparrow$ = ?

True or false? 16 $\downarrow \downarrow \rightarrow \rightarrow$ = 38
              24 $\rightarrow \swarrow \nearrow \downarrow$ = 34
              61 $\uparrow \nearrow \rightarrow$ = 42
              24 $\searrow \searrow \searrow$ = 67
              83 $\uparrow \uparrow \uparrow \uparrow \nwarrow$ = 22

Make up problems for others to solve.

Extension
How would you solve these? 9 $\rightarrow$ = ? 7 $\uparrow$ = ? 70 $\leftarrow$ = ?
(For more info, see "0–99 Chart versus 0–100 Chart" on page 372.)

Teaching Arithmetic

Introduction

Arithmetic, as one of the time-honored "three Rs," receives the largest share of attention and concern of all the topics in the elementary mathematics curriculum. It still reigns as the high-stakes math topic, addressed in the first content standard of number and operations. The rationale for this is obvious—arithmetic skills are necessary life tools that people use regularly every day. A person who is not able to do arithmetic is handicapped in many situations.

However, while the importance of arithmetic has not diminished over time, the criteria for evaluating students' proficiency with arithmetic and the methods for teaching arithmetic have shifted and broadened. Computation is only one aspect of arithmetic competence. Instruction in arithmetic must also develop students' number sense and help them develop the ability to use numbers to solve problems. Computation, problem solving, and number sense are the three essential aspects of arithmetic instruction, like the three legs needed for a stool to be sturdy and balanced. The goal of arithmetic instruction is for students to demonstrate competence and confidence with each.

Computation

Students with computational proficiency can calculate accurately and efficiently. Accuracy and efficiency do not necessarily mean that all students use the same procedure for all problems—different methods are suitable for different numbers. Students should learn various ways to reason numerically.

For example, computing mentally is an important computational skill, often shortchanged in school. This may be, in part, because figuring in their heads doesn't produce written evidence or lead to homework assignments that students can take home. Also, students' ability to calculate in their heads isn't measured on standardized tests, and these tests have an enormous effect on what's taught. However, to be proficient with computation, students should be able to do a good deal of computing in their heads without resorting to paper and pencil. (See the opening section in Part 1, "A Perspective on Arithmetic," page 7, for a further development of this idea.) When asked to figure 50 percent of a number, or to multiply a number by ten or one hundred, for example, students' first impulse should not be to reach for pencil and paper but, rather, to think about the problem mentally.

When problems are too complex or unwieldy to solve mentally, it's appropriate for students to figure answers with the help of paper and pencil. This does not imply, however, that students must necessarily use one specific procedure. Conforming to one particular method does not indicate proficiency. Rather, students should use paper and pencil as tools to keep track of how they reason and to provide a record of their thinking.

Memorization has an important role in computation. Calculating mentally and with paper and pencil requires having basic number facts committed to memory. However, memorization should follow, not lead, instruction that builds children's understanding. The emphasis of learning in mathematics must always be on thinking, reasoning, and making sense.

Problem Solving

While being able to compute accurately and efficiently is essential, it's also essential that students learn to apply computation skills to problem-solving situations. Word problems have long been traditional in mathematics instruction. They present situations for students to translate into arithmetic operations and then figure the answers.

However, students should also have experience solving nonroutine problems other than word problems. These require reasoning beyond translating situations to arithmetic operations. They may have more than one solution and/or more than one way to arrive at a solution. (See "Beyond Word Problems" in Part 1, page 16.)

For example, a routine word problem might be *The center region on a dart board is worth 100 points; the next ring is worth 50 points; the next,*

25 points; and the outermost, 10 points. Betty throws three darts in the outermost ring, one in the next ring, and two in the ring next to the center. What is her score?

A nonroutine problem about the same dart board might be *Betty throws six darts and earns a score of 150. Where might her darts have landed?* Or *Betty throws six darts and each lands in a ring. What are the possible scores Betty can earn?*

Number Sense

Number sense encompasses a wide range of abilities, including being able to make reasonable estimates, think and reason flexibly, make sound numerical judgments, and see numbers as useful. Students with number sense have good numerical intuition. When applying computation skills to solve problems, they can judge if solutions are reasonable. Should they forget a procedure or part of a procedure, students with number sense can reason their way to a solution. They see numbers as tools, not barriers. They're curious about numbers and comfortable with them.

Students with number sense can solve the routine dart board problem mentioned in the previous section by calculating mentally. They might jot down the number of points that Betty earned in each of the rings—30 in the outermost ring, 25 in the next one, and 100 in the ring next to the center. But they wouldn't need to line up the numbers and add the standard way; they'd add 30 and 25 mentally to get 55 and then add on 100 for an answer of 155.

Putting It Together

It's possible that a given arithmetic lesson might focus on just one or two legs of the stool, but it's important to keep in mind that computation, problem solving, and number sense are not discrete and separate topics. Developing number sense depends on learning to compute. Solving problems also depends on computation. Deciding whether an answer makes sense, an important aspect of problem solving, draws on a student's number sense. The legs of a stool stand up because they're bound together by the seat of the stool and, perhaps, with additional bracing as well. A plan for arithmetic instruction must incorporate attention to each leg so that students have a firm and well-balanced base on which to rest their understanding of number and operations.

What Are the Basics in Arithmetic?

The real-life situations people face that call for using arithmetic generally require that they do the following:

1. choose the operation (or operations) needed
2. choose the numbers to use
3. perform the calculation, either using a calculator, using paper and pencil, or figuring mentally
4. evaluate the reasonableness of the answer and decide what to do as a result

Why has pencil-and-paper arithmetic computation, which is just one aspect of Step 3 above, become the mainstay of the elementary curriculum? It seems clear enough to understand. The ability to do calculations has long been seen as essential for the successful use of arithmetic. This practice was in place and well entrenched long before calculators and computers removed the drudgery from computation. There was no way to arrive at arithmetic answers other than doing calculations by hand. Because of the present availability of calculators and computers, however, the challenge is even greater to teach students to think and reason, not to rely on results without being able to evaluate their accuracy and appropriateness.

With or without calculators and computers, however, learning to do paper-and-pencil arithmetic and practicing on isolated examples have never ensured that children learned to use these skills when needed. This deficiency is obvious to teachers when word problems are assigned and children repeatedly ask, "Do I need to add or subtract?" Arithmetic practice in isolation does not lead children to notice when they make a division error, such as omitting a zero in the quotient and thus producing an answer that is ten times too small.

This does not mean that children do not need to learn any procedures for arithmetic. Arithmetic skills are necessary life tools. Doing arithmetic mentally demands mastery of basic facts along with the ability to estimate. Using calculators and computers successfully, and evaluating the answers, requires an understanding of the necessary arithmetic processes and the ability to identify if solutions are reasonable. Being able to use paper and pencil for arithmetic problems too complex to solve mentally is important.

The very definition of teaching arithmetic needs to be revised. Arithmetic competence cannot be measured solely by evaluating students' mastery of computational algorithms. Mastery of arithmetic must include, as basic and integral, knowing which operations are appropriate to particular situations, which numbers are most reasonable to use, and what decisions can be made once the needed calculations have been done. It makes no sense to say that a child can do arithmetic but cannot apply it to situations. The basics of doing arithmetic must include being able to apply arithmetic operations to situations, as well as being able to calculate answers.

You would never say that a person who can play only scales on the piano knows how to make music. You would not assume that a person who can catch a football knows how to play the game. You would not make the judgment that a person who can saw a board knows how to build a bookcase. The rudiments are necessary, but they would be senseless to learn as ends in themselves.

The motivation for learning skills in life is their eventual use. Children who practice scales have heard music. Children who practice catching and throwing a football have seen football games. In school, however, children are expected to practice their arithmetic skills without any sort of mathematical bookcase to build. No wonder so many are not motivated to develop their proficiency. What sense does it make? Instead of seeing arithmetic skills as useful tools that save work, children often see them as making work, with a sole purpose of completing pages of exercises.

If a child were able to read a story aloud but couldn't tell what the story was about, his reading teacher would not say that the child was a proficient reader. Comprehension is essential. Similarly, a child who can perform addition, subtraction, multiplication, or division calculations but neither explain why the procedures work nor apply them to problems has not demonstrated proficiency. Our definition of proficiency must include being able to apply skills to problem-solving contexts, calculate mentally, use numbers comfortably to come to reasonable estimates, and understand relationships among the numbers and the arithmetic operations. Also, students should develop confidence and competence in their number understanding along with an appreciation and fascination for numbers.

Results from Classroom Research

Sandra Nye, a teacher in West Babylon, New York, asked her fourth graders to find the answer to 19×21. This was early in December. Sandra had not yet focused instruction on multiplication that year but knew her students had had some experience with multiplication in the third grade. She put them into small groups of four or five students and asked each group to choose a recorder to write down everything the group did. As the children worked, Sandra circulated, reading what they were producing and making notes on their papers to have them go further or to clarify their thoughts. Her goal was to get insights into the children's thinking, rather than merely to test their ability to do the computation. Following are the actual written dialogues between Sandra and each group.

The Red Group

Children: *First we ×'s one times nine. Next we ×'s the one by the one. Then we go down a line and put a zero under the nine. Next we ×'s the two by the nine and the two by the one. Now that we have two answers (one on top and one on bottom) we add them and get an answer of 399.*

$$
\begin{array}{r}
19 \\
\times\,21 \\
\hline
19 \\
380 \\
\hline
399
\end{array}
$$

Sandra: *Why did you go down a line? What do the two answers mean? Why did you add them?*

Children: *We changed lines because the rules are to change lines and the rules are also to put a zero in the beginning of the second line. The rules are that way because there is no way to get 399 with 380 on the same line as 19. We found this out in third grade. We added them because that's the way we were taught and it gives a sensible answer.*

Sandra: *Now, can you explain each of the numbers in your answer?*

Children: *The 19 means that one times 19 equals 19. The 38 means that two times 19 equals 38. (Remember it's a rule to put a zero on the second line.) The 399 means 19 plus 380 equals 399. That's how we did this problem.*

Sandra: *Why is it a rule to put a zero on the second line? What's the purpose of the rule?*

Children: *Nobody in our group can remember why we put the zero on the second line. We told you above that it is a rule to put the zero on the second line.*

The Blue Group

Children: *This is how we solved our problem. First we times 19 × 21 and we got 389 and we found out it was wrong. The teacher put some answers on the board and told us they were wrong. The answers were 57; 3,819; and 389. Then about 5 minutes later we found out the real answer is 399. We added 21 19 times. We proved it by making a 21 × 19 rectangle. The way you set it up is:*

$$
\begin{array}{r}
19 \\
\times\,21 \\
\hline
19 \\
380 \\
\hline
399
\end{array}
$$

That is the way you set it up because any time you're timesing two digit numbers, first you put down the first answer and then you put down a 0 on the next line before you multiply.

Sandra: *How do you get the first answer? What does it mean?*

Children: *You get the first answer by timesing 1 × 19. It means that you have the first part done.*

Sandra: *Why do you "put down a 0" on the next line? What does the number on that line show?*

Children: *So it makes the number bigger. That line should be the larger number.*

Sandra: *Why should that line be bigger?*

Children: *So you get a reasonable answer.*

Sandra: *What does 380 show? What numbers do you multiply to get 380?*

Children: *It shows 38 with a 0 on the end. You multiply 19 × 20 to get 380.*

Sandra: *Where is the 20?*

Children: *The 20 is the 21 without the one because you times the one already.*

The Purple Group

Children: *We wrote it this way:*

$$
\begin{array}{r}
19 \\
\times 21 \\
\hline
19 \\
38 \\
\hline
57
\end{array}
$$

Then we found out that we left out the zero in the second number.

Sandra: *How do you know there should have been a zero in the answer? And how did you realize that your first answer was wrong?*

Children: *There should be a zero in the second number because when you multiply with tens you put a zero in the ones place because you are not working with the ones. We realized that the answer should be much bigger than 57 because if you put 21 down 19 times it wouldn't add up to 57. It would be much bigger.*

Next we wrote down 19 21 times. Then we crossed off two 19s at a time, and put down 38. Then we crossed off two 38s at a time, and put down 76. Next we crossed off two 76s at a time, and we put down 152. It looked like this when we finished.

$$\begin{array}{r} 152 \\ 152 \\ +95 \\ \hline 399 \end{array}$$

Finally we put it like this and it was right.

$$\begin{array}{r} 19 \\ \times 21 \\ \hline 19 \\ 380 \\ \hline 399 \end{array}$$

Sandra: *How did you decide to write it this way?*

Children: *We figured out the answer with addition and then we figured it out this way.*

If merely given a quiz on which they were asked to do the computation, the Red Group would most likely have gotten it correct. Yet in both their explanation and their answers to Sandra's questions, the children consistently resorted to following the rules they had learned without being able to explain why. The other two groups were able to relate multiplication to addition and to verify their answers that way. The Blue Group seemed to be farthest along in making sense out of the partial products. When urged to explain where the 380 came from, they wrote that it was the result of multiplying 19 × 20. The Purple Group, however, could justify the final algorithm as reasonable only because it worked to produce the correct answer. What do these children understand about multiplication?

In *School Science and Mathematics*, Thomas C. O'Brien and Shirley A. Casey (1983) reported the results of a study they conducted with fourth-, fifth-, and sixth-grade children. The children were asked to complete the following computations using paper and pencil:

$$\textit{1.6} \times \textit{3} = \underline{\hspace{1.5cm}}$$
$$\textit{16} \times \textit{3} = \underline{\hspace{1.5cm}}$$
$$\textit{60} \times \textit{1} = \underline{\hspace{1.5cm}}$$
$$\textit{13} \times \textit{16} = \underline{\hspace{1.5cm}}$$
$$\textit{3} \times \textit{60} = \underline{\hspace{1.5cm}}$$

Then the children were asked to write a story problem for 6 × 3.

The five computations yielded success rates of 82 percent in grade 4, 75 percent in grade 5, and 97 percent in grade 6. The story problems, however, yielded different results. Of the fourth graders, only 25 percent wrote a story problem that was multiplicative in context. For the fifth graders, the figure was 15 percent, and for the sixth graders, it was 69 percent. More than half of the nonmultiplicative responses involved stories that described $6 + 3$, not 6×3, even though many of these stories ended with the statement, $6 \times 3 = 18$. What did these children understand about multiplication?

A student who is able to perform paper-and-pencil computations for the operations shows procedural understanding, knowing what to do in a situation. This does not necessarily mean that the student understands the *why* of that procedure—why it works, why it makes sense, why it is useful to problem situations. Knowing *what to do and why* means understanding the arithmetic procedure in relation to its meaning and application.

The Red Group in Sandra's class demonstrated procedural understanding of the algorithm for multiplying 19×21. The students knew what to do to produce the correct algorithm and arrive at the correct answer. When asked to explain where the partial product of 380 came from, they resorted to the rule that dictates adding a zero on the second line in two-place multiplication: *two times 19 equals 38. (Remember, it's a rule to put a zero on the second line.)*

The Blue Group, however, was struggling to explain the meaning behind the same partial product, not just following a rule: *You multiply 19×20 to get 380. . . . The 20 is the 21 without the one because you times the one already.* Although these children's understanding was incomplete as shown in their written work, their reasoning indicated a *what to do and why* understanding beyond rules learned by rote.

Sandra tried a different experiment with her class the next year, again in December. This was a class of fifth graders. She gave them an individual assignment to complete: Work this problem, and when you think you have the correct answer, explain why you think your answer is reasonable.

Sandra had the children attempt this assignment before she did any formal instruction with them in multiplication. They had, however, been taught the multiplication algorithm the previous year. Nine of the students did the computation accurately, producing either of the two results shown below. Following are their actual explanations, with their misspellings, of why their answers were reasonable.

$$\begin{array}{r} 47 \\ \times 23 \\ \hline 141 \\ 940 \\ \hline 1{,}081 \end{array}$$

My answer was reasonable because I added 141 and 940.

I think my answer is reasonable because I worked it out carefully.

My answer is reasonable because it is right multiplying and adding.

$$\begin{array}{r} 47 \\ \times 23 \\ \hline 141 \\ 94 \\ \hline 1,081 \end{array}$$

My answer is reasonable because I checked it.
I think it's reasonable because I added the right numbers and timed the right numbers.
I think my answer is reasonable because I took my time and check it.
I think my answer is reasonable because if you estimated 47 it would become 50 and if you estimated 23 it would become 20. 20 × 50 = 1,000 and 1,000 is close to 1,081.
I think my answer is reasonable because twenty three is almost twenty, and forty seven is about fifty and fifty times twenty is 1,000. My answer is about 1,000.

The incorrect answers students gave varied, as did their explanations. For the following responses, see if you can identify the calculation errors that the students made.

$$\begin{array}{r} 47 \\ \times 23 \\ \hline 141 \\ 840 \\ \hline 981 \end{array}$$

My answer is reasonable because I know how to mutply this way.

$$\begin{array}{r} 47 \\ \times 23 \\ \hline 141 \\ 940 \\ \hline 1,161 \end{array}$$

My answer is reasonable because I know my times tabels and I was paying attention.

$$\begin{array}{r} 47 \\ \times 23 \\ \hline 141 \\ 94 \\ \hline 1,135 \end{array}$$

I think my answer is reasonable because I understud the problem.

$$\begin{array}{r} 47 \\ \times 23 \\ \hline 141 \\ 614 \\ \hline 755 \end{array}$$

My answer is OK because if you were to take the four and the two and times it you would get eight and the 755 and rounded it you would get 800.

$$\begin{array}{r} 47 \\ \times 23 \\ \hline 134 \\ 1480 \\ \hline 1,614 \end{array}$$

Its reasonbal because I did what Im saposto do.

$$\begin{array}{r} 47 \\ \times 23 \\ \hline 141 \\ 1210 \\ \hline 1,351 \end{array}$$

cause I worked it out four times

$$\begin{array}{r} 47 \\ \times 23 \\ \hline 141 \\ 8,140 \\ \hline 8,281 \end{array}$$

I think my answer is reasonable because I did the problem step by step and this is what I came out with 8,281.

$$\begin{array}{r} 47 \\ \times 23 \\ \hline 141 \\ \times 00 \\ \hline 1,083 \end{array}$$

My answer is reasonable because 141 × 23 is 1,083.

Most of the students, whether their answers were right or wrong, struggled with explanations in the context of the procedures, rather than in the meaning of the operation. Only three students tried to justify their answers by referring to the numerical quantities.

The Limits of Learning Rules

Learning rules and applying them are common to many children's experiences in mathematics. Children are taught to add the ones first and then the tens in two-place addition, to borrow in subtraction, to put a zero in the second line in multiplication, to start from the left when doing long division, to multiply across the numerators and denominators to find the product of two fractions, to divide the numerators and denominators of fractions by the same number to simplify them, to line up the decimal points before adding, to count up the decimal places to see where to place the decimal point in the answer to a decimal multiplication problem. A blatant example of teaching for *what to do* understanding is the two-line rhyme for division of fractions:

Yours is not to reason why;
just invert and multiply.

Sometimes the rules for algorithms do not even make sense to follow, yet children are asked not to veer from the prescribed procedure. For example, it is common for second graders to learn to add two-place numbers. This is usually first presented with no required regrouping and in vertical form:

$$\begin{array}{r} 34 \\ +21 \\ \hline \end{array}$$

The procedure taught is standard—first you add the ones and then you add the tens. When a teacher notices a child adding the numbers in the tens place first, the teacher will most likely redirect the child to add the ones first instead. Why? It certainly makes no difference which you add first to arrive at the correct sum.

The teaching rationale, however, is that if children learn correctly in this simpler example, they will more easily transfer their learning to the next, more complex, task of adding when regrouping is necessary. It seems as if the decision is made in the interest of supporting the children's learning. However, teaching what to do in this instance is mainly to make children's arithmetic pursuits easier a few pages farther on in the book.

What do children perceive from being taught this rule? Many merely learn to add the numbers on the right first, and then the numbers on the left, without thinking that first they are adding ones and then tens. To some children, a page of such problems looks much like a page of one-digit addition placed vertically, except that some of the numbers have been shoved together.

There is a danger in this instructional approach, even for those children who learn rules well. Such instruction teaches a child that it is OK for something not to make sense, that it is not necessary to understand the sense in what you are expected to do. This message is counterproductive to having children approach mathematics with the goal of understanding concepts and skills.

Other second graders, however, notice that they can do the exercises either way and get the same answer, but they know that they are supposed to add the right-hand column first. If they ask why, what might the teacher say? (What would you say?) The answer most likely will be a "This is the way we do it" answer or "This will make your life easier later" answer. There is no other reason.

Lacking in this instructional approach is support for the child who is trying to make sense out of the procedure. The most obvious message to children is that arithmetic requires that you follow rules. It would be a bleak and joyless arithmetic picture for second graders if they imagined all the rules they would have to face in the school years that stretched ahead! Fortunately for us, most children don't take this future view of life; hopefully, those that do will be forgiving.

Teaching what to do in mathematics is widespread practice. Check your students' mathematics textbooks for instances of teaching by procedural approaches. Recall your own elementary and high school mathematics learning. Can you remember being taught long division, or how to find the area of a circle, or how to multiply algebraic expressions such as $(x + 3)$ $(2x - 5)$ and not understanding why they worked? Think back on mathematics courses you have taken. Have you ever had the experience of passing a course, perhaps even with a good grade, yet feeling you did not really understand what you were taught?

There is nothing inherently or necessarily wrong in knowing rules and being able to apply them. It is important to realize, however, that teaching procedures and teaching procedures in relation to their meaning are two very different approaches to teaching arithmetic. When children do not have the broader understanding, they may lack the flexibility to deal with situations that differ even slightly from the particular situations learned.

The ideas in this book are firmly rooted in the belief that teaching for understanding is essential. Children must see their learning task as one of making sense of whatever they're studying. It is an irresponsible choice to teach children how to do a procedure without teaching them how to reason. Students should not be expected to do things by rote or be made to say things they do not honestly understand.

When children subtract in an example such as this:

$$\begin{array}{r} 3\,1 \\ -1\,6 \\ \hline \end{array}$$

it is not uncommon for them to arrive at the incorrect answer of twenty-five. They have "learned" to subtract, but when confronted with a problem that requires regrouping, children will frequently just take the smaller from the larger—a procedure they have been practicing in appropriate situations. They are following a rule they've learned but are applying it to the wrong situation.

Teaching What to Do versus Teaching What to Do and Why

Why is the practice of teaching the procedures of mathematics detached from meaning and applications of these procedures so pervasive in schools? There are a host of reasons that support the emphasis on teaching procedures. These reasons have to be understood before any widespread change in this practice will occur.

1. Learning what to do is usually easier than learning what to do and why.

Actually, learning what to do is sometimes much easier. Take the example of learning how to divide fractions. The standard algorithm is to turn the fraction on the right-hand side upside down and then multiply across the tops and bottoms. This rule is simpler to learn (and to teach) than the principle that division is the inverse of multiplication—or that dividing by a number is the same as multiplying by its multiplicative inverse, which in the case of dividing by a fraction means multiplying by its reciprocal. If the goal of the mathematics instruction is to prepare students to produce a page of correct answers, teaching the appropriate procedures will meet this goal more quickly and easily.

2. The textbooks emphasize the learning of procedures.

The basic goal of textbooks and workbooks is to teach students to write correct answers, rather than to think and understand. This may sound harsh. After all, no textbook publishers or authors say or even suggest that they do not care if students think as long as they get the answers on the pages correct. Teachers' guides urge instructors to teach for the underlying understanding and often provide additional suggestions for doing so. But the reality is there, implicitly or explicitly: Children will show their understanding by being able to complete the work on the pages. Writing correct answers is the primary goal of teaching what to do; thinking, understanding, and seeing relationships are the primary goals of teaching what to do and why.

3. The pressure of tests looms.

Standardized tests are another reality. Teachers are accountable for students' performance, and, in some communities, test scores are published in the local newspapers. For the most part, these tests evaluate students' proficiency with mathematical procedures. The procedures themselves are more quickly and efficiently learned by focusing specifically on how to do them. The fact that students continue to do poorly on test items that require more than rote learning does not seem to be a compelling enough reason to change the current emphasis on procedural mathematics.

4. It is difficult to assess if students understand the *why* of arithmetic.

It is not possible to tell what a student is thinking merely from the paper-and-pencil work she submits. Think back to the work of the Red Group in the fourth-grade class. Those students successfully performed the algorithm for multiplication but could explain what they had done only by resorting to rules they had learned. Judging their computational work alone would not have revealed this important information.

5. Some teachers do not understand the difference between teaching procedures and teaching reasoning in arithmetic.

Many teachers do not feel competent or comfortable with mathematics. Although proficient with the computational algorithms, they themselves were probably taught these algorithms without learning the underlying reasoning behind them. It has been shown that teachers generally teach as they were taught. Besides, teachers cannot teach what they do not truly understand. These circumstances seriously hinder the effort to offer children a thinking mathematics curriculum.

Other reasons could be cited as well. Parental pressure often affects what teachers teach. Changing a habit is in itself difficult, especially without consistent support. Also, students make demands. Many teachers have had the experience of explaining the meaning behind a procedure, only to have the students listen, wait patiently, and finally say, "If you'll just show me how to do it, I'll do it."

In contrast, what are the reasons for teaching arithmetic in the context of meaning and application, of teaching the *why* as well as the *what to do* in mathematics? These reasons, too, are important to consider.

1. When you understand why, your understanding and skills can be applied more easily to new tasks.

For example, teaching how to add, subtract, multiply, and divide decimals from the procedural approach focuses primarily on the various rules for what to do with the decimal points in each of the operations. When you add and subtract, you line up the decimal points; when you multiply, you count up the decimal places to figure where the decimal point goes in the answer; when you divide, you move decimal points when they appear in the divisor but not when they don't appear. Should you forget the rule for one particular operation, a rule from another has no bearing.

If, however, you learn why the rules for each of the operations make sense—if you learn to reason with decimals as well as to compute with them—then you will understand which answers are sensible in any situation. When learning procedurally, you have to memorize not only rules but also which problems the rules work for, and often you have to memorize different rules for each type of problem.

It's more important that children develop the kind of understanding that allows them to apply their learning to the new and different situations they will be sure to meet than that they develop the ability to follow rules. This requires they understand why as well as knowing how. It is not an either-or situation; both are necessary. Knowing only the rules for figuring percents is not sufficient for choosing the best savings or money market account, the type of mortgage that makes most sense, or the best way to finance a new car. These decisions require understanding and judgments that extend beyond algorithmic thinking.

2. Learning the meaning in arithmetic procedures makes them easier to remember.

When you understand the reasons behind rules, you are not keeping a large number of unrelated rules in your memory. A common error when adding fractions is for students to add the numerators and denominators; for example: $\frac{1}{2} + \frac{1}{3} = \frac{2}{5}$. Students who do this are merely following a rule, which unfortunately is totally inappropriate in this instance. Much of mathematics requires looking for the sense in the situation, not merely following a rule. It does not make sense to start with $\frac{1}{2}$, add to it, and wind up with an answer, $\frac{2}{5}$, that is less than the amount you started with. Yet many students do not notice this inconsistency or even think about looking for it.

Standards for arithmetic instruction are usually organized into bite-size pieces. This structure is often seen as making curriculum goals more manageable. However, it masks a pedagogical risk. Teaching children in bite-size pieces does not necessarily help them learn anything other than bite-size skills. Some children do make connections between the individual pieces. However, children who have difficulty usually have to repeat their experience with the pieces, as if a second go-around, or a third, will produce eventual success. Such instruction has never worked and never will work.

Breaking the learning of mathematics into tiny pieces is like giving children a heap of graham cracker crumbs and wondering why they have no concept of the whole graham cracker. It's an attempt to simplify learning that may seem to be in the interest of children. But it is, in fact, counterproductive and in conflict with what is known about how children do learn. It is wrong to think that children cannot deal with meaning and complexity.

3. Learning to reason is a goal effective in itself and leads to the continued support of learning.

All of us (hopefully) have experienced the joy of accomplishment that comes from figuring something out in order to produce a satisfying result. When children are taught to make sense out of mathematics, they receive support for seeing connections between ideas. Their connections can lead them to further learning in ways that do not occur when learning is approached as a series of unconnected events.

In his essay "Nature Closely Observed," David Hawkins (1983) describes the distinction ancient Greeks made in their language between what they called arithmetic and what they called logistic. He writes:

> Arithmetic was the investigation of the world of numbers; logistic was a set of rules, to be memorized, for doing rote sums, differences, products, quotients. Arithmetic was a kind of science, always fresh and open to endless investigation. Logistic was a dull art, needed for bookkeeping and other such practices, which you could learn by rote. If you understood something of arithmetic, you could easily master the rules of logistic; if you forgot those rules, you could reinvent them. What we mainly try to teach in all those early years of schooling is logistic, not arithmetic. We drag, not lead, and the efficiency of learning is scandalously low. (71)

The true measure of the failure of teaching only the *what to do* is the feeling of mathematical incompetence and negativity toward mathematics experienced by so many otherwise highly educated people. This rejection of mathematics, sadly so common, is a clear indication that something is very wrong. It is not possible to appreciate something you do not truly understand, and the charge to teachers is a crucial one—to teach mathematics so that children are encouraged to make sense out of all they learn to do.

Multiple Strategies for Computing

How can children be taught arithmetic so that they will learn both what to do and why? How can children learn procedures for solving arithmetic problems? What should be the role of algorithms?

First, a definition: Algorithms are systematic procedures that provide reliable and efficient ways to find accurate answers to computation problems and, therefore, simplify potentially difficult calculations. It's important for children to understand that algorithms are procedures that have been invented to carry out calculations that are done repeatedly. It's important for them to learn how algorithms are based in the structure and logic of our number system. But it's also important for children to understand that one particular algorithm may be no better or more efficient than another, and that many methods, including ones they invent themselves, are equally valid.

A major risk of instruction that emphasizes the teaching of algorithms is the risk of interfering with children's learning to make sense of numbers. When learning algorithms, children focus on learning sequences of steps to carry out procedures, rather than on thinking and reasoning to make sense of numerical situations. Teachers know that it's common for children, when using standard algorithms, to make calculation errors and not even notice when they reach absurd solutions. Also, children sometimes reach for paper and pencil to solve problems that they should be able to do easily in their heads.

Suzanne H. Chapin and Arthur Johnson address the role of algorithms in their book *Math Matters* (2006). They write: "In the best of circumstances, algorithms free up some of our mental capacity so that we can focus on interpreting and understanding a solution in the context of a problem. In the worst of circumstances, algorithms are used when a task could be done mentally or are applied by rote with little understanding for the bigger mathematical picture—why the calculation is important and how the answer will be used" (43).

Arithmetic instruction should focus students on multiple strategies for computing and help them explore the parallels and differences among them. Research suggests that students benefit from opportunities to invent their own strategies for calculating, with a focus on the meaning of the numbers involved and the goal of connecting to their own ways of thinking. Sense making is at the core. Teachers should not only give children the challenge of figuring out methods for calculating but also require them to explain the reasoning for their invented procedures. Teachers should provide time for students to present their methods to the class. Describing their methods helps students cement their thinking, while also giving students the opportunity to learn from one another.

Dee Uyeda's third graders in Mill Valley, California, learned about division through a problem-solving approach. Working in pairs and small groups, the children were asked to find solutions to division problems and to explain how they reasoned. They worked on problems with remainders along with problems without remainders.

For example, children were asked to figure out how to share seventeen cubes among four children, describe their method, and then use the cubes to test their solution. Several of the children added to get the answer. Verity, for example, wrote: *Each kid gets 4 cubes and 1 goes to the classroom. I figerd it out by 4 plus 4 is 8 and 8 plus 8 = 16.*

Joel used what he knew about multiplication. He wrote: *First I just gave one of the cubes to the good will. Then I devided 16 cubes. Because I know that 4 × 4 = 16 so 4 kids each get 4 cubes.*

Jenee drew seventeen cubes in a vertical line and then counted to divide them into four parts. She wrote: *They each get 4 cubes and there will be one left over.*

Rebecca wrote: *I'm going to draw pictures of 17 cubes and four baskets. I put one cube at a time in the basket. Each basket gets four cubes if you want it to be even. Since you have sixteen cubes in all the baskets, the extra cube can go to someone.*

Elliot wrote: *I'm going to do it in 2's. I will count 8 2's and have 1 left. Each child would get 4 cubes.*

Lisa decided to use a calculator. Her paper showed how she coped with her limited understanding of decimals. She wrote: *We each get 4. And put one in the box. How I did it: On the calculator, I pressed 17 ÷ 4 = that didn't work. Then I pressed 17 ÷ 2 = 8.5. .5 is a half. Two halfs is a whole. That is 8 + 9. Half of 8 is 4. And there is one left over.*

Some of the division problems Dee gave to the children involved money. Children were asked to share $5.00 among four children. All groups correctly solved this problem. Michelle, Michael, Timothy, and Alana's solution was typical. They wrote: *Each person gets $1.25. We think this because if each person got a dollar there would be one dollar left. And there are four quarters in a dollar. So everybody gets a $1.25.*

As groups finished their work, they were given the problem of sharing $0.50 among four children. Children found this problem more challenging. The numbers were more difficult for them and they had to decide what to do with the remainder. For their solution, the same group wrote: *We think each person gets 12¢ and there would be 2¢ left over that they could not split up, but they could buy bubble gum with the two cents and split the gum. We think this because we have to share the last two cents.*

Whenever possible, Dee used classroom situations to pose problems. For example, the children counted and found there were 163 pencils in the class supply. They were given the problem of figuring out how many pencils each child would receive if they were divided equally among them. Laura, Teddy, and Grace drew twenty-seven circles, one for each student, and used tally marks to distribute the 163 pencils. They wrote: *Everybody would get 6 and there would be 1 left over. We figured this out by drawing 27 circles. Grace put talley marks in them while Teddy and Laura counted. We proved it by adding 27 6 times and adding one.*

Kendra, Bryce, and Marina wrote: *We think that each child will get 6 pencils and there will be 1 left over. We think this because we made a circle for each kid and gave them each five pencils. We added it up. It came to 135 so we took 135 from 163 and there were 28 left. There are 27 kids in the class so each kid gets one more and there is one left.*

After children solved problems, they presented their results and methods to the class and discussed the different methods used. After discussing each problem, the teacher showed the children the standard notation for representing division: $17 \div 4$, $4\overline{)17}$, and $\frac{17}{4}$, for example. With more experience, the children began to use the standard symbols in their own writing.

When Cathy Humphreys taught percents to her seventh and eighth graders in San Jose, California, she did not teach them how to solve the three standard types of percent problems. As described in *A Collection of Math Lessons: From Grades 6 Through 8* (Burns and Humphreys 1990), Cathy organized the unit on percents around a series of problem-solving situations that called for applying percents. Students worked in small groups and presented their answers and methods to the class. For all problems, Cathy kept the emphasis on students' making sense of the situation and justifying the methods they used for their calculations. One such problem was the following:

A school has 500 students. If a school bus holds 75 students, is there enough room on one bus for all the school's left-handed students?

Cathy gave the class the information that from 12 percent to $12\frac{1}{2}$ percent of Americans are left-handed. After collecting information to compare their class data with the national statistic, students worked in pairs to solve the problem. They produced a variety of solutions.

Martin and Tony, for example, wrote: *There will be 60 left-handed students on the bus. Out of 100 12% would be 12 people. Since 500 is 5 × more than 100 you times 12 × 5 = 60.*

Marshal and Kiet wrote: *Yes, there are enough seats to hold all of the left-handed people because 10% of 500 is 50 people, 2% of 500 is 10 people, so 50 plus 10 is 60 people, and each bus holds 75 people.*

Liz and Audrey wrote: *To get the answer we multiplied 500 students by 12% and got 60 people and the bus can hold 75 people so there is enough room.*

Khalil and Gina took a completely different approach. They wrote: *We think you can because 75 is 15% of 500. We only have to put 12% on of the left handed people.*

Not all students' methods were appropriate. Jon and Phi, for example, divided five hundred by twelve and wrote: *After we did the problem we got 41.66 and it kept on going on so we rounded it off to 42 students. We then subtracted 75 into 42 and got 33. After we got 33 seats we knew all the left handed people could get on the bus.*

Raymond, Paula, and Stephanie also used division, but they divided twelve by five hundred. They wrote: *Yes, 12 ÷ 500 = 0.024 so out of 500 students 24 of them are left handed so the bus can hold all the left handed people.* Even though their reasoning was erroneous, the students who used division arrived at the correct conclusion. Correct answers can hide a lack of understanding— a reason for being sure to have students explain their thinking.

This lesson occurred near the beginning of the unit, and Cathy knew to expect this sort of confusion. As stated in the *Mathematics Model Curriculum Guide* (California State Department of Education 1987, 14): "We must recognize that partially grasped ideas and periods of confusion are a natural part of the process of developing understanding."

Cathy led a class discussion during which students presented their methods and the class discussed them. She kept the focus of the discussion on making sense of the procedures presented.

From many experiences during the unit with problems such as this one, students began to formulate their own understanding of how to work with percents. Teachers often fear that if they don't teach the standard procedures for percent problems, students won't learn to solve these types of problems. The reverse may be a greater worry, however. Teaching the standard procedures for percent problems can result in students being unprepared to reason with percents to solve problems.

Encouraging multiple strategies for computing requires a total commitment to making thinking and reasoning the cornerstone of mathematics instruction. It requires teachers to be curious about students' ideas, to take delight in their thinking, and to encourage them, at all times, to make sense of mathematics.

Questions from Teachers

Teachers working toward making such a change in their mathematics instruction have raised many questions. Following are the ones most often asked.

Should I ever teach the standard algorithms?

Just as students present their ideas for calculating, teachers can also present the standard algorithms, explain why they make sense, and offer them as another way to calculate. For older students, teachers may want to refer them to textbook presentations of algorithms and ask them to explain why the methods work.

It's important, however, that standard algorithms be presented with a light touch, not as better ways, or the real ways. The standard algorithms should not be mandatory procedures that students must use when calculating. The goal of instruction should be for students to find ways that are appropriate and make sense to them. In this way, arithmetic is taught through a problem-solving approach.

Also, know that your explanations of standard algorithms may not make sense to all students. Similarly, when students present their methods for calculating, it's unlikely that all the others in the class will understand them. It's difficult to follow others' reasoning. Encourage students to seek the meaning in others' ideas, continue to have students explain why their ideas make sense, and keep true to the principle that students are to do only what makes sense to them and to persist until it does.

What about learning the basic facts?

The instructional approach of having students invent their own algorithms does not eliminate the need for students to learn the basic facts. Being able to compute by any method, whether figuring an accurate answer, estimating, or justifying the reasonableness of a calculator answer, requires facility with addition and multiplication facts. Ideally, students would learn these facts from repeated use in problem-solving situations. However, additional practice is typically needed for students to commit basic facts to memory.

Several guidelines are important, however. It's not wise to focus on learning basic facts at the same time children are initially studying an operation. A premature focus gives weight to rote memorization, instead of keeping the emphasis on developing understanding of a new idea. The danger to avoid is having children believe that giving quick, right answers is really what is most important when learning arithmetic.

Also, when learning facts, children should build on what they already know and focus on strategies for computing. For example, the doubles in addition, such as $5 + 5$ and $8 + 8$, are easier for children to remember. It's helpful for children to see how other combinations, such as $5 + 6$ and $7 + 8$, relate to the doubles.

What about using timed tests to help children learn their basic facts?

Teachers who use timed tests believe that the tests help children learn basic facts. This makes no instructional sense. Children who perform well under time pressure display their skills. Children who have difficulty with skills, or who work more slowly, run the risk of reinforcing wrong learning under pressure. In addition, children can become fearful and negative toward their math learning.

Also, timed tests do not measure children's understanding. Teachers concerned with the results of timed tests necessarily maintain a vigorous and steady program of drill and practice. The danger in this pedagogical focus is that an instructional emphasis on memorizing does not guarantee the needed attention to understanding. It doesn't ensure that students will be able to use the facts in problem-solving situations. Furthermore, it conveys to children that memorizing is the way to mathematical power, rather than learning to think and reason to figure out answers.

Children's own numerical strategies are often cumbersome and inefficient. Doesn't it make more sense to help them learn the standard ways for computing?

The goal for arithmetic instruction must not be efficiency but the development of children's numerical capability and confidence. If efficiency were the goal of arithmetic instruction, then teaching any method other than using a calculator would be risky, less effective, and, therefore, foolish. Math instruction should seek to help children learn to think, reason, and make sense of numbers.

What kind of arithmetic drill and practice is appropriate?

Children benefit from many and varied opportunities to apply their computation and numerical reasoning skills. An instructional approach based on developing children's thinking and reasoning should address broader goals for arithmetic competency than mere computational facility. Children should be required to analyze problem situations, decide on the operations needed, choose appropriate numbers, perform needed calculations, and evaluate results. Arithmetic practice that focuses on isolated numerical exercises does not prepare students to apply their skills to unique and diverse problems.

One challenge of teaching mathematics is to emphasize in arithmetic instruction and practice the same approaches used in other areas of the mathematics curriculum so that children explore, justify, represent, solve, discuss, use, investigate, describe, develop, and predict. These actions are the heart of doing mathematics and should be incorporated into arithmetic drill and practice.

Relating Arithmetic to Real Life

Most daily math problems that adults face require reasoning that goes beyond mere computation. In real-life problems, all the needed information is rarely provided in one tidy package; often the data have to be collected, frequently from a variety of sources. There's rarely only one possible method or strategy for real-life problems; usually there are several viable ways to solve them. Often, there's no one solution that is the right or best one; life has no answer book.

One example of a real-life arithmetic problem arises annually at Thanksgiving time—the preparation of the traditional turkey. For the cook, the responsibility is a real and important one, calling for roasting a turkey that will be deliciously succulent, large enough to feed all the guests with enough leftovers for the following days, and ready to serve at the time planned for dinner.

One problem for the cook to solve is *What time should I get up in the morning to start the preparations so the turkey will be ready on time?* Although this may not seem to be an arithmetic problem, it is. Of course, other kinds of decisions need to be made in this endeavor, but the tasks also require the application of arithmetic skills.

First of all, what information do you have? You would like dinner to be served at 5 P.M.; the turkey you have purchased weighs 17 pounds, 8 ounces; according to the cookbook, it takes 15 to 18 minutes a pound for the turkey to roast (the longer time is for a turkey that has been stuffed). You know you plan to stuff the turkey. How much time do you estimate the turkey will need to be in the oven? How close do you need to be in this estimate?

Of course, you need to take the turkey out of the oven long enough before 5 P.M. to make the gravy and let the turkey cool before it is carved. And, of course, it will take time in the morning to make the stuffing and truss the bird, something that every cookbook cautions never to do the night before. Perhaps you have purchased packaged bread cubes for stuffing instead of planning to use leftover bread. This can save time but also may require another arithmetic decision. Each package provides enough to stuff a 12-pound bird. What do you do? Use one package and stretch it? Use two packages and cook the extra in a casserole? Use a package and a half and wrestle with some more arithmetic to adjust the recipe accordingly? How much time will all this take? And once you have made all your estimates, you then have to decide what time you really do need to get up in the morning to make it all happen on schedule.

When solving problems such as these in real life, you call on all the resources you have—knowledge, previous experience, intuition. You need to analyze, predict, make decisions, evaluate. And there are always factors of variability—how your oven behaves, how long this particular turkey will actually take to cook, how close your estimate is to the time it will take you to truss the bird.

Students would benefit from problems that reflect the spirit and intent of the Thanksgiving turkey problem. An example: *How much would it cost to raise a medium-size dog to the age of eleven?* The problem requires several phases to get to its solution:

1. *Decide what information is needed and where to collect it.* What are the costs that most likely will be encountered? What others are possible? How can you find out how much food, veterinarian care, licenses, and so on, will cost?
2. *Choose the numerical information to use.* Which of the amounts are reasonable to use? How can you predict possible changes in these costs over the eleven years? (Uncertainty and variability are always elements of problems in real life.)
3. *Do the necessary calculations.*
4. *Use judgment to interpret the results and make decisions about a possible solution.*

A problem of this sort is wonderfully suited for small groups of students. Working together gives children the opportunity to draw on the resources of other students, expand their individual views, and have the support needed for solving a complex problem. After completing the first phase, groups can compare decisions they made about what information is needed and decide if they have included all that is important. Similarly, they can later compare the information they collected and their final solutions.

There is no correct or absolutely verifiable answer to a problem such as this. However, a family trying to decide if they would like to add a dog to their household would benefit from having some sense of the potential cost. Exact accuracy is not possible, or necessary. Who can predict if your dog is going to gnaw on a leg of the dining room table or do some other damage for which repairs have to be made? How can you predict how often the family will take a vacation and will have to board the dog? What about unpredictable medical needs? There is value for students in tackling problems for which solutions will always be somewhat uncertain, and it will be important for them to defend the reasonableness of their solutions.

Other such problems may come directly from class or school situations. How much will it cost to have a class party? How many cars will be needed for a class field trip? What needs to be done to plan a school dance? What is a fair way to organize the scheduling of the computer room for the school? How can we divide our class into two fair teams for a track-and-field event?

Other examples of problems include How many Friday the 13ths can occur in one year? What is a fair allowance for a student in your grade level? How can we figure out how many buttons are on all our clothes or how many pockets we have altogether? How can we find out how many dogs live in our town? According to the newspaper shopping information, which is the most economical supermarket for buying groceries for a family of four?

In order to function in our complex and changing society, people need to be able to solve a wide variety of problems. Preparing children to become effective problem solvers requires broadening the typical classroom applications of arithmetic. The challenge is to provide motivating problems that spark children's natural curiosity and allow them to learn and use skills in situations that simulate the way arithmetic is really used in life.

How Can Arithmetic Understanding Be Developed?

Well-rounded instruction in arithmetic should be organized so that it

- introduces arithmetic concepts to students in real-world contexts;
- develops number sense and understanding of relationships among the operations;
- integrates arithmetic with the other strands of the mathematics curriculum;
- builds on children's own ways of thinking and language for describing their thinking;
- relies heavily on estimating and mental computation; and
- encourages children to use multiple strategies for arithmetic calculations.

The rest of Part 3 offers suggestions for teaching arithmetic organized into nine sections: "Beginning Number Concepts," "Place Value," "Addition and Subtraction," "Multiplication," "Division," "Extending Multiplication and Division," "Fractions," "Decimals," and "Percents." The teaching ideas in each section present whole-class lessons, independent activities, and ways to assess students' understanding. They are designed to serve as models for classroom instruction that builds children's understanding, confidence, and competence in arithmetic.

Beginning Number Concepts

Overview

Mathematics instruction in the early grades should make numbers an integral part of children's classroom experiences. Children need many opportunities to identify quantities, see relationships between numbers, and learn about the operations of addition and subtraction. When developing beginning concepts of number, children benefit from exploring concrete materials and relating numbers to problem situations. They also benefit from talking about their ideas and hearing how other children think. The learning activities should be varied in their contexts and involve the children directly in thinking, reasoning, and solving problems.

Whole-Class Lessons

Using Classroom Situations

Everyday classroom situations provide many opportunities for solving math problems. Relating math to classroom routines helps children apply mathematics in a real setting and helps them see the usefulness of mathematics.

For example, daily attendance taking can suggest a math problem. Once you ascertain how many children are absent, ask the children to figure how many are present.

When the children need partners for an activity or are lining up in pairs, have them figure out if everyone in the class will have a partner or if there will be an extra person. Also, ask them to figure how many pairs there will be.

If some children have returned their field trip permission slips, have the children figure out how many more slips need to be returned.

If children need recording booklets for a project, have them make them by folding 12-by-18-inch newsprint in half and making a cover from construction paper. Ask the children first to figure out how many sheets they will need so they'll have twelve pages to write on. (Decide first if children are to write on right-hand pages only or on both sides of the paper.)

Have the children figure out how many pairs of scissors are needed if each child shares a pair with a partner.

Show the children a can of juice, a box of crackers, a bag of apples, or some other item with which they are familiar. Ask them to guess how much it costs. After each guess, give a clue by telling the children whether the item costs more or less than the amount that was guessed.

If each pair of children needs one die for a math activity, have them figure out how many dice are needed in all.

In all situations, don't settle just for answers. Have children explain their reasoning.

Number Games

Games are fun and provide a relaxed setting in which children can think about number relationships. The following games give children experience with comparing, addition, and subtraction, and they also provide informal experience with ideas of statistics and probability.

How Many Reds?

This is a card game that provides valuable experience with representing ten as the sum of two addends. Introduce the game by having two children play while the rest of the class watches. Tell the children that they need twenty playing cards, ace through 10 of a red suit and a black suit. They also need a recording sheet. Show them how to fold a piece of newsprint or copy paper into ten areas, as shown:

Have two children model how to play. One child mixes the cards by placing them facedown and stirring them, then deals them out, ten to each person. They each count the number of reds they have, and one child records in one space on their paper. Take this opportunity to introduce or reinforce the standard way to record addition: 4 + 6, for example.

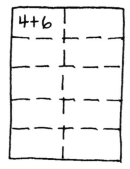

Now the other child mixes and deals the cards. Again, they count the number of red cards they have, and the other child records on their paper. When you feel comfortable that the class understands how to play, distribute cards and have all the children play in pairs.

Although it is obvious to adults that the total of red cards in both children's hands is always ten, this may not be obvious to the children. From playing this game, they have the chance to become familiar with the addends of ten in a game context.

For a statistical extension, make a class graph of the addends children recorded. By having the children speculate about why some pairs of addends come up more often than others, the activity incorporates thinking about probability as well.

Empty the Bowl

For this activity, you need twenty cubes or tiles in a small bowl and one die. Explain to the children that you are going to roll the die and that the number that comes up will tell how many cubes to remove from the bowl. Ask them how many rolls they think it will take to empty the bowl. Allow all children who have ideas to share them with the class.

Demonstrate the game. Choose a child to come to the board and record the numbers as they're rolled. Have different children take turns rolling the die and reporting the number of cubes you are to remove. (You don't have to go out exactly; that is, if there are two cubes left in the bowl, and a 3 is rolled, it's OK to remove the cubes so the bowl is empty.) Once the bowl is empty, you may want to ask the children to figure the sum of the rolls recorded on the board.

Leave the information about the rolls on the board, and play the game again several more times until you're sure the children understand the activity. Then ask the children some questions to probe their thinking about the game so far. Although all children won't be able to answer these questions, raising the issues sets the stage for the kind of thinking you would like them to do. Also, their responses give you information about what individual children understand.

> What do you think is the most number of rolls it could possibly take to empty the bowl?
> Why couldn't the bowl be emptied in just one roll?
> Why couldn't it be emptied in two rolls?
> What do you think is the fewest number of rolls you would need to empty the bowl?

On the board, list the numbers from *1* to *20*, and put tally marks to indicate how many rolls it took you to empty the bowl in each of the demonstration games. Tell the children that now they are to play five games in pairs and keep track of the numbers that come up each time, as you did on the board. After five games, they are to come up and tell you how many rolls it took for each game so you can mark the class graph. Recording on a class graph gives the children experience with collecting statistical data.

For children who finish their five games quickly, have them play some more and contribute additional information to the class graph. After all the children's data have been recorded, again discuss the questions you posed previously. Push the students to make a prediction about the fewest number of rolls they think generally would be needed to empty the bowl. Opinions may differ, and that's OK. Children can test their hypotheses on the *Empty the Bowl* menu task (see page 207).

Introducing Addition and Subtraction with Word Problems

When children are learning about the operations of addition and subtraction, it's helpful for them to see the connection between these processes and the world around them. Word problems accustom children to looking at groups of people or objects, help them see the actions of joining and separating, and give them experience figuring out sums and differences. Have children act out stories that involve addition and subtraction, either by pretending or using concrete materials to represent situations.

Acting Out Addition and Subtraction Stories

Tell stories in which the children pretend to be animals, people, or things. The following are examples:

_____, _____, _____, and _____ are clowns at the circus. _____, _____, and _____ are more clowns who also come to perform at the circus. How many clowns are in the circus?

_____, _____, and _____ are birds sitting in a tree. _____ and _____ flew away. How many birds are left in the tree?

_____ put four books on the reading table. _____ put two more books on the table. How many books are on the table altogether?

_____, _____, _____, and _____ are standing near the door. _____ and _____ are sitting at their desks. How many more children are standing than sitting?

Once the children are comfortable acting out stories, model how to record stories symbolically. Write the addition and subtraction equations so the children can see how symbols are used to represent the situations you present. When children understand how to connect stories and symbols, have them write equations to describe other stories.

Addition and Subtraction Stories with Cubes

Tell stories and have the children use interlocking cubes, such as Snap, Multilink, or Unifix cubes, to represent the people, objects, or animals in the stories. Have the children work on construction paper or tagboard or prepared counting boards on which you have drawn trees, oceans, corrals, and so on, to correspond to the stories you tell. The following are examples:

There were four ladybugs and three ants in the grass. How many were there altogether?

We gave our rat six kibbles. He ate four of them. How many kibbles were left?

There were eight horses in the pasture. Six were brown and the rest were white. How many white horses were there?

Seven cars were in the supermarket parking lot. Three more cars arrived. How many cars were in the parking lot altogether?

Beyond Word Problems

While routine word problems can serve to introduce children to the language and symbolization of addition and subtraction, nonroutine number problems require children to organize and stretch their thinking. Nonroutine problems contribute to building children's number sense and strengthening their ability to deal with new situations. The following suggests one problem-solving experience that supports children's learning about numbers.

The Necklace Lesson

This lesson involves the children with patterns, estimation, addition, graphing, and comparison of volume. To prepare for the lesson, mix red food coloring with rubbing alcohol, and dye enough macaroni to fill a pint jar. Fill another jar with macaroni that hasn't been dyed. Cut lengths of string long enough for necklaces, and dip one end of each in glue to make it easier for children to string the macaroni.

Model for the class how to make a necklace using the following pattern: one red, one white, two reds, one white, three reds, one white, and so on, ending with six red and one white. Explain the pattern as you make the necklace. Show how to tie the ends of the string.

Tell the children they each are to make a necklace following the same pattern. Before they get started, discuss the following questions:

Do you think I've brought enough macaroni?
Do you need more red or more white macaroni for your necklace?
 Why do you think that?
When you've all made your necklaces, will we have more red
 macaroni left over, more white, or about the same of each?
How would you describe the pattern you'll be using?

After the children have made their necklaces, ask the same questions again. Have the children compare the amounts of the remaining macaroni.

On another day, tell the children that they'll have the chance to make another necklace using the same macaroni pattern, but with a color other than red. Have them record on a class graph to indicate whether they would like to use yellow, blue, green, orange, or purple. The children can either sign their names or post colored squares on which they've written their names.

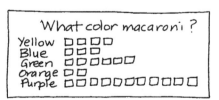

Process the graph, discussing which color was chosen most, which was chosen least, how many children chose each color, and so on. Then talk about how much of each color macaroni the class will need. Use the jar of red macaroni as a reference. The children's responses will reveal whether they can relate information from a graph to the practical problem of deciding on quantities of macaroni to dye.

Finally, dye the macaroni, using food coloring and alcohol, showing the children how to mix colors to get green, orange, and purple. Tell them they'll be able to make their necklaces the next day when the dyed macaroni has dried. Also tell them that in the meantime, they are to figure out how many white and how many colored macaroni they each need. You may want to prepare a sheet on which they can record their solutions and thinking. The next day, have children make their new necklaces.

Using Children's Books

Children's books can be valuable resources for math lessons. They capture children's imagination and interest and are effective vehicles for stimulating children's mathematical thinking and reasoning. The following suggestions model the kinds of activities that can be initiated from simple counting books. The five books mentioned in this section are only a few of the many children's books that help to develop young children's beginning number concepts. Four Math Solutions Publications books that present teaching lessons using children's literature are *Math and Literature, Grades K–1* and *Math and Literature, Grades 2–3* (Burns and Sheffield 2004a and 2004b); *Math and Literature, Grades 4–6, Second Edition* (Bresser 2004); and *Math and Literature, Grades 6–8* (Bay-Williams and Martinie 2004).

The Rooster's Journey

Rooster's Off to See the World, by Eric Carle (1991), tells the story of a rooster who decided one day that he wanted to travel. Strikingly illustrated with colorful collages, the book describes how the rooster was joined by two cats, three frogs, four turtles, and five fish. A problem arose, however, when night fell and the animals realized that no plans had been made for food or shelter. They all became hungry, cold, and afraid and decided to return home.

Read the book and then present the children with the problem of figuring out how many animals altogether set out to see the world. Tell the children they need to show how they figure out the answer and explain their reasoning. Children who have difficulty writing can dictate their explanations.

One Gorilla and More

One Gorilla, by Atsuko Morozumi (1996), received the New York Times Best Illustrated Children's Book Award. This counting book begins, "Here is a list of things I love." The list includes one gorilla, two butterflies, three budgerigars, four squirrels, and on up, to ten cats. The gorilla appears on each page, and children take delight in the illustrations.

This book suggests an extended version of the problem presented for *Rooster's Off to See the World*. Ask the children to figure out how many things the author loved, show their work, and explain their reasoning. For children who find the numbers too difficult, suggest the alternative problem of figuring out how many things he loved that could fly. This simplifies the problem to adding 2 + 3 + 9, the numbers of butterflies, budgerigars, and birds.

Many other children's books also suggest this same problem: *1 Hunter*, by Pat Hutchins (1982), and *The Midnight Farm*, by Reeve Lindbergh (1987), for example. Although the mathematical thinking required for all these books is similar, the change in context makes each a new problem for the children. Giving these problems to children over time gives you the opportunity to assess their progress.

Making Books with Dots

Donald Crews (1986) begins *Ten Black Dots* with a question: "What can you do with ten black dots?" He answers the question by incorporating black dots into colorful illustrations of everyday objects, beginning with one dot and continuing up to ten dots. Simple rhymes accompany the graphics. The book begins:

> One black dot can make a sun
> or a moon when day is done.
> Two dots can make the eyes of a fox
> or the eyes of keys that open locks.

After reading the book several times, ask the children what they might do with one, two, three, and so on, up to ten black dots. After all have had the opportunity to make their suggestions, have them begin making their own *Ten Black Dots* books. Plan for children to complete a page or two a day. Black adhesive dots, $\frac{3}{4}$ inch in diameter, are available at office supply stores and easy for children to use. Newsprint with an unlined top portion for illustrations and a lined bottom portion for their writing works well.

When children have completed and shared their books, have them figure out how many dots they each used. As for all problems, ask the children to show their work and explain their reasoning. To help them begin their explanations, write on the board: *We each needed _____ dots. I got my answer by _____.* More able children may be interested in figuring how many dots were used by the entire class.

Independent Activities (Menu)

Build a Stack

You need: interlocking cubes, about 12 per student

This activity is suitable for a small group of six to eight children. The children need interlocking cubes. Give a variety of directions that use more and less, and have the children build the stacks. For example:

"Build a stack that has one more than four."
"Build a stack that has two more than six."
"Build a stack that has one less than seven."

An easier version: "Build a stack of four. Now build a stack that has one more than four. How many did you use?"

More of a challenge: "What number do you think is one less than five? Let's build a stack and see."

Grow and Shrink

You need: cubes, 6 per student
cube numbered 1–6
Ten frame, 1 per student (see Blackline Masters)

The children take turns rolling a numbered cube. You and the children (who are able) call out the number rolled. Each child builds the number rolled on his or her ten frame.

Yarn Shapes

You need: yarn, enough for each student to cut a piece the same
length as his or her arm
tiles, about 100 per student

Each child cuts a piece of yarn as long as his or her arm and then uses the yarn to make a shape, covers the shape with tiles, and counts the tiles. Then he or she makes and covers other shapes. Ask the children to see what they can discover about shapes that hold more tiles and those that hold fewer tiles.

Spill and Compare

You need: two-color counters, 10 per child

Children take a given number of counters, spill them, and record which color comes up more or if there is an equal number of each. They keep track by making tallies on a chart as shown:

More red	Same	More yellow

Have children play the game first with six and then with different numbers of counters and notice which numbers never come up with both colors the same.

Trace and Compare

You need: tiles, about 50 per child

Have children trace around one of their shoes. Then have them predict which would take more tiles—to fill their foot shape or to place tiles on the outline like a fence. They then measure with the tiles to find out.

They repeat by tracing other shapes: a book, their hand, a chalkboard eraser, and so on.

Snap It

You need: interlocking cubes, 10 per child

Children each make a train of interlocking cubes using the same number. On the signal "Snap," they break their train into two parts and hold them behind their backs. They take turns showing the cubes in one hand and then in the other while the other children say the combination. (See also "Patterns and Addition," on page 368, for more on this activity.)

Extension

When students are able, each child shows the cubes in one hand and the others predict how many are in the other hand. The child then shows the other cubes for the children to check. Also, have children record addition sentences to describe how they broke apart their trains.

$$
\begin{array}{c}
1 \\
+5 \\
\hline
6
\end{array}
\qquad
\begin{array}{c}
3 \\
+3 \\
\hline
6
\end{array}
\qquad
\begin{array}{c}
2 \\
+4 \\
\hline
6
\end{array}
$$

Grab-Bag Subtraction

You need: a partner
                    cubes or tiles
                    paper bag

Children work in pairs. Select a number for the children to work with. One child fills the paper bag with the appropriate number of cubes or tiles (to be determined by the teacher). The other reaches in and takes out some, showing how many have been removed. Both predict how many they think are left. Then they check their predictions, and each records the equation.

Extension

Have the children use a 5–10 die or spinner to generate the number of cubes or tiles to put in the bag.

Assessing Understanding of Beginning Number Concepts

Observing Children

Observing children in class discussions and when they are working on independent activities provides information about their understanding of number concepts. Children's verbal responses to questions and reactions to others' ideas reveal their levels of interest and understanding. Also, children's written work can be an indication of their thinking, especially when they've explained their reasoning processes.

It's important to look not only at whether children's answers to problems are right or wrong but also at how they arrived at their solutions. Was the answer appropriate or reasonable? Did they have a strategy for finding a solution or were they guessing? What does their work reveal about their understanding of different-size numbers?

To continue to learn about children's thinking, continually probe by asking questions such as the following:

How did you figure that out?
Are you sure?
Can you explain why you're sure?
What made you think of that?
Can you think of another way to figure it out?

For example, seeing how children approach the problems in books such as *One Gorilla* (Morozumi 1996) tells you about their comfort with numbers and their ability to calculate. Looking at their solutions to the number of macaroni needed in *The Necklace Lesson* (page 200) can tell you about their ability and comfort with larger numbers. Observing their strategies as they play *Grow and Shrink* (page 204) can reveal their understanding about relationships between numbers.

Individual Assessments

This assessment gives a general idea about children's understanding of number relationships (Baratta-Lorton 1976). Also, children's responses indicate their confidence with number combinations.

TEACHER	CHILD	INTERPRETATION
"Count five blocks into my hand."	Child is able to do so.	Appropriate level. Shows ability to count with one-to-one correspondence.
	Child is unable to do so.	Inappropriate level. Try it with three blocks. If this is not possible, do not go on.
"How many blocks do I have in my hand?"	Child says "five" without counting.	Appropriate level. Child conserves for five. Ask next question.
	Child must recount.	Inappropriate level. Child doesn't conserve. Try with three blocks.
Hide some blocks in one hand and show the others. Ask: "How many am I hiding?"	Child answers instantly, correctly, and confidently.	Appropriate level. Check several other combinations, and then assess for six. As long as the level is appropriate, continue assessing up to ten.
	Child guesses wrong, or cannot guess, or does not know instantly with confidence.	Try several other combinations to make sure level is inappropriate. If so, try again with three blocks.

Place Value

Overview

Our place-value system, which allows us to represent any number with just ten digits, is complex for children to understand. Children need to learn to make groups of ten items and then count those groups as if they were single items. They must learn that digits have different values, depending on their position in numbers. The difference between 36 and 63, for example, though obvious to adults, is not always easy for young children to understand.

When learning about place value, children benefit from grouping concrete materials into tens and hundreds and linking their experience to standard numerical notation. Children also benefit from involvement with problem situations that call for estimating large numbers of things. This section suggests whole-class lessons and independent activities in which children estimate and count large quantities of objects, look for patterns in the numbers on 0–99 and 1–100 charts, learn several games, and explore geometric shapes. While the activities focus on the idea of place value, they also provide experience with probability, measurement, patterns, and logic.

Whole-Class Lessons

Counting Large Quantities

Engage the students in a variety of situations in which they estimate and count large numbers of objects. Plan lessons in which children figure out the following:

- how many buttons or pockets there are on all their clothing
- how many feet or thumbs or fingers there are in class altogether
- how many feet there would be if the adults living in all the children's houses came to the class at the same time
- how many cubes there would be altogether if each child put a handful in a box
- how many letters there are altogether in all the children's first or last names
- how many books are in the class library

Spacing such explorations throughout the year makes it possible to assess changes that occur over time in children's thinking about large numbers. It's important to remember that teaching children the usefulness and logic of grouping objects into tens to make sense of large quantities should not be a lesson objective. It's a long-range goal that must not be attached to one day's activity. Children need many experiences over time to learn to connect the idea of counting by tens (which many can do by rote) to our place-value system of representing quantities symbolically.

While children are learning, it's important they feel that their own methods for counting large numbers of objects are also valid. The pedagogical challenge is to make the connection between grouping by tens and our number system but to do so with a light touch. The goal is for children to have the chance to consider the connection, understand it, see its usefulness, and eventually use their experience to construct an understanding of our place-value system for themselves.

The following describes how two such explorations might be conducted in a classroom.

How Many Fingers?

Pose the problem of figuring out how many fingers there are on the children's hands altogether. Ask students for their ideas about ways to solve the problem. Also, ask children for estimates of what the answer might be.

Tell the class that when solving a problem, it sometimes helps to try a similar but smaller problem. Ask seven or eight children to come to the front of the room and hold up their hands. Ask the class for different ways to count their fingers. Typically, children will suggest counting by twos, fives, tens, and, perhaps, ones. As each way is suggested, have the class count aloud in unison.

Then ask how many children would be needed for there to be one hundred fingers altogether. For some children, this will be obvious; others may be uncertain or have no idea at all. If someone suggests ten children, have that many come to the front; otherwise use whatever number is offered. Go through the process of counting by twos, fives, and tens, and even ones, if the children want, to see how many fingers there are.

Ask: "Are there enough children in class to have two hundred fingers? More than two hundred fingers? More than three hundred?" Keep the discussion going, bringing up children to count and verify, as long as the class is interested. Record the final answer on the board. You may want to write this in several different ways; for example, *two hundred and seventy*, *27 tens*, *100 + 100 + 70*, and *270*.

How Many Pockets?

Ask the students how many pockets they think are on all the clothing they're wearing that day. Have them discuss this among themselves in pairs or small groups. Then have volunteers give estimates and have them explain why they think their estimates make sense.

Give the children interlocking cubes, such as Multilink, Snap, or Unifix cubes, and ask them to put one cube in each of their pockets. Collect the extra cubes, and then have the children remove the cubes from their pockets, snap them into trains, count how many they each have, and compare with the others in their group.

To figure out how many pockets there are in all, ask the pairs or groups to make trains of ten cubes and bring the trains to the front of the room. Have the class count aloud with you by tens. Then have children bring up their extra cubes and use them to make additional trains of ten. Again, have them count aloud by tens. Then have them count the extra cubes. Record the final answer on the board to connect their counting to the numerical representation; for example, *6 tens and 8 ones = 68.*

Tell the children they'll repeat the activity for the next few days to see if the number of pockets changes. Keep the activity going for as many days as the children are interested.

Note: Be aware that in a lesson such as this one, you are imposing on the children the structure of organizing by tens. It may seem that grouping by tens is the most efficient way to count the cubes, but left to their own choices, children may prefer to group objects in other ways, by twos or fives, for example. The method of grouping by tens is convenient because of its relation to our place-value system; however, do not expect this reason to be compelling or even make sense to all the students.

When doing other explorations, such as figuring the number of buttons or books, vary the materials. Use beans, for example, to represent buttons, and group them into tens in small cups. Use tally marks to record the number of feet in the room and, after counting by twos, draw circles to group them into tens.

Class discussions are useful for giving children opportunities to hear each other's ideas and also for helping you assess their understanding. Raise questions such as the following for children to discuss:

> If you group the cubes (or whatever) by twos or fives or tens, will you get the same number when you count how many there are altogether? Always? Explain your thinking.
> Some people say it's easy to count by tens. Why do you think they say that?
> Which takes fewer numbers—to count to one hundred by fives or by tens? Why? How else can you count to one hundred?

Using Money

Children's interest in money makes it a useful model for place value. The following game takes advantage of children's familiarity with money. Before introducing the game, however, review for the children the relationships of the denominations to each other.

Race for $1.00

For each group of four, prepare a zip-top bag with about sixty pennies, forty dimes, and four pretend dollar bills. Do not distribute them until you've explained the rules and played a game with one of the students.

To play, children take turns rolling two dice. They add the numbers that come up and take that many pennies. Then they pass the dice to the next person. If children have enough pennies to exchange for a dime, they may do so only when the dice are in their possession. The winner is the first person to get a dollar.

Play the game with a child to model the rules. Then provide the materials for each group and have them begin to play. Circulate to make sure they are playing correctly. Notice if children take shortcuts; that is, when they roll a sum larger than 10, such as 12, some may take one dime and two pennies rather than count twelve pennies. Others in the group may question this and ask if it's allowed. Respond that shortcuts are allowed only if everyone in the group understands what is being done and agrees. (See "Games with Money" on page 371 for another discussion of this game.)

A Logic Game

The game of *Digit Place* appears on page 142 in the "Logical Reasoning" section. The game focuses children on the importance of the digits' positions in numbers, while also challenging them to think logically. In the simpler version described below, the game is played with two digits instead of three.

Digit Place

To introduce the game, have the children gather near the board. Tell them that they'll learn a game in which they are to guess the two-digit number you are thinking about. Check to see if the children know what is meant by *two-digit number*. Ask for examples, and then ask if anyone can explain what *digit* means. Also, be sure to point out that although numbers such as fifty-five and ninety-nine are two-digit numbers, they aren't allowed in this game; the digits have to be different.

Play a practice game. Tell the class your number is seventeen. Show them how you would give clues for several pretend guesses. Tell them that each clue reveals how many of their digits are correct and how many of those are in the correct place. Then play a real game with the class, having children guess while you record the clues. Each time you give clues, ask the children what they know for sure. This encourages them to reflect on what the clues mean before they charge ahead with new guesses.

Guess	Digit	Place
74	1	0
16	1	1
84	0	0

Play a game or two each day for several days to help the children learn the rules.

Looking for Patterns

Writing numbers on a 10-by-10 grid arranges them in an orderly way, making it possible for children to see patterns and relationships in our counting system. This activity focuses children on patterns in the numbers from zero to ninety-nine and/or from one to one hundred.

Patterns on the 0–99 Chart

You need a 10-by-10 grid that is large enough for all the children to see. On the chart, write the numerals from *0* to *25*.

Then ask children questions such as the following:

What number would come next?
Where do you think forty will land? Fifty? Fifty-three? Sixty-three?
[*Point to a square.*] What number do you think belongs here?

Continue until you've filled in the chart completely.

Direct the children to study the chart quietly for a few moments and look for patterns. Then have them share what they noticed.

Typically, children will see patterns in the rows and columns. For example, the first column has all numbers that end in 0; all the numbers in the bottom row start with 9. Children don't often look for diagonal patterns. You can prompt this by saying: "I see a pattern in the numbers that have both digits the same."

Talk about other patterns, such as odd and even numbers, numbers with 6 in the ones place, and numbers for which the two digits add to ten. As you talk about these ideas, write them on the board.

odd numbers
even numbers
numbers with both digits the same
numbers with a 6 in them
numbers whose digits add to ten

Distribute recording sheets with a large 0–99 chart on them (see Blackline Masters). Have pairs choose one of the number descriptions you've recorded and color in the numbers. Together, they should write a description about the patterns of the numbers they've colored.

Note: If you prefer, do the same activity with the numbers from one to one hundred instead of zero to ninety-nine. This results in the last column having all the numbers that end in 0. (See also "0–99 Chart versus 1–100 Chart" on page 372.)

Independent Activities (Menu)

These activities use the idea of place value in a variety of situations that give children experience with several other topics in the math curriculum. Some of the activities require that children make an estimate. It's important to talk with the children about estimating to make sure they don't think estimates must be exact. Let the children know that the purpose of estimating is to give them the chance to think about numbers, better understand what they mean, and make guesses that they can then check.

Race for $1.00

You need: a partner
bag with 10 dimes, 20 pennies, and 1 pretend dollar
1–6 dice, 2

Players take turns rolling the dice and taking that many pennies. The game continues until one player collects ten dimes and exchanges them for one dollar. Record how much each player has at the end of the game.

Stars

You need: a partner
way to time 1 minute

Predict how many stars you think you can draw in 1 minute. Record your prediction.

    Make stars while your partner times 1 minute.
    Count. Record your answer. Describe how you counted.

Digit Place

You need: a partner

One player chooses a two-digit number. (The digits must be different.) The other player tries to guess the number. For each guess, the first player tells how many digits in the guess are correct and how many of the correct digits are in the correct place. (If only one digit is correct, do not tell which it is; just say that one is correct.)

A chart helps:

Guess	Digit	Place
27	0	0
13	1	1

Play again so that the other player can guess.

Fill the Cube (Version 1)

You need: Unifix cube
popcorn kernels, enough to fill the cube
lentils, enough to fill the cube

Predict how many kernels of popcorn you think will fill the cube. Record your prediction.

Fill the cube.

Count. Record your answer and describe how you counted.

Repeat with lentils. Use your popcorn count to make your estimate of lentils.

Five-Tower Game

You need: a partner
                 interlocking cubes, at least 120 per student
                 1–6 dice, 2

Roll the dice, add the numbers that come up, and take that many cubes. Snap them into a tower. Take turns doing this until you each have five towers.

Each of you now figures out how many cubes you have.

Compare your counts. See if one of you has more than the other or if you both have the same number of cubes. Report your findings.

Number Puzzle

You need: 10-by-10 square of half-inch grid paper (see Blackline
                 Masters)
                 envelope

Write the numbers from *0* to *99* on your grid.

Cutting only on the lines, cut the chart into seven interesting pieces. Write your name on the back of each piece.

Test your puzzle by fitting the pieces back together.

Put your puzzle pieces into an envelope. Write your name on the envelope, and place it in the puzzle box for others to try.

Choose someone else's puzzle to put together. When you solve it, sign your name on the back of the envelope. Return the puzzle to the puzzle box. **Note:** If you prefer, have students write the numbers from *1* to *100* instead of from *0* to *99*.

Pinch a 10

You need: small bag or bowl of kidney beans

Take a pinch of kidney beans and count. Did your pinch have fewer than ten, more than ten, or exactly ten? Make a chart as shown and record with a tally mark. Do this ten times.

(Tally like this: ⫶⫶⫶ ‖)

Fewer than 10	10	More than 10

Write a statement about your results.
Repeat and see if you get better at pinching tens. Or pinch popcorn.

Make a Shape

You need: a partner
crayon or marker
color tiles, 10 each of 4 colors

On a plain sheet of paper, draw a shape that both of you think can be covered with thirty-two tiles.

Test with color tiles. Use ten of one color, then use ten of another color, and so on, until your shape is covered.

Record the number of tiles you used.

Try this activity a second time, drawing a new shape that you think can also be covered with thirty-two tiles. Again, cover, count, and record.

Assessing Understanding of Place Value

Observing Children

When children are working on the independent tasks, circulate and observe them. Also, whole-class discussions can help reveal what children understand.

With *Race for $1.00*, notice how children organize their pennies and dimes. See if they exchange when possible and if they take shortcuts, such as taking one dime and two pennies when they roll a sum of 12. Interrupt them to ask who is winning and see how they compare their two quantities.

With *Stars, Fill the Cube (Version 1)*, and *Five-Tower Game*, see which children group the objects into tens and which group by twos and fives or persist in counting by ones. Ask children how many groups they would have if they grouped by tens. Don't insist that children group by tens; there's no point in children doing something mechanically without understanding. Encourage them, talk about grouping by tens, but respect their need to do what makes sense to them.

For *Fill the Cube*, ask children how they could use the information from their popcorn count to predict how many lentils the cube will hold.

When children count the beans in *Pinch a 10*, notice how they count—by ones, twos, or some other way.

Notice how children fit together the pieces from each other's puzzles from *Number Puzzle*. Ask questions such as the following: "What clues do you look for? How will you know when the puzzle is together correctly? What's easy and what's hard about the puzzle?"

Individual Assessments

Choose from the following suggestions to find out what children understand:

1. Give children twenty-four or so counters and ask them to put them into groups of ten. When they've done this, ask three questions:
   a. How many groups do you have?
   b. How many extras?
   c. How many counters are there altogether?
      Children who cannot tell without counting them one by one are not making use of grouping by tens and need more experience.
2. The following assessment appears in Part 1 of *Mathematics: Assessing Understanding*, a three-part videotape series (Burns 1993).
   a. Show the child sixteen counters and ask her to make a drawing of them.
   b. Then ask the child to write *16* with numbers on the same sheet of paper.
   c. Circle the 6 in 16 and ask the child to indicate in the drawing what six means. (Children usually correctly circle six counters.)
   d. Then ask what "this part" means, circling the 1 in 16. (Some children correctly circle ten counters; others erroneously circle one counter, indicating that they need more experience.)
   e. Then ask what "the whole thing" means, circling the 16. (Most children will circle all sixteen counters.)
   f. For children who circled only one counter in Part d, ask why "these" (the nine remaining counters) were not circled.

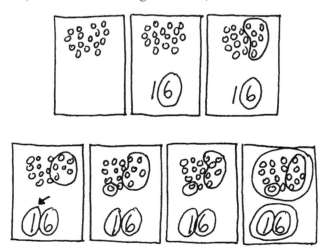

3. Check to see if children can count by tens to 100. If so, can they count to 150 or higher?
4. Give children two or three small cards with a different numeral on each. Ask them to arrange the numerals to make the largest number possible. Ask for the smallest.
5. Dictate several numbers for children to write.
6. Show children several numbers to read aloud.

Addition and Subtraction

Overview

This section focuses on having children use and compare two-digit numbers. The activities model ways to involve children with addition and subtraction of two-digit numbers in the context of problem-solving activities. The activities draw on ideas from various topics in the math curriculum: number and operations, probability and statistics, geometry, and measurement. In this way, while children are developing their understanding of number, they have opportunities to broaden their view of mathematics and see relationships among the different areas of the math curriculum.

In all activities, the emphasis is on having children use and explain their own strategies for adding and subtracting. As a regular part of their work, children are expected to justify their answers and explain why they make sense.

Whole-Class Lessons

A Statistical Investigation

Statistical investigations offer rich opportunities for children to develop their number sense. In this lesson, the lengths of the children's names are organized into two class graphs. The children interpret the data and compare the number of letters in their first and last names.

The Name Graphs

Ask each child to write his or her first name on a 3-by-3-inch sticky note. List the numerals from *1* to *10* on the board, and have the children, one at a time, come to the board and post their names next to the numeral that indicates the number of letters. In this way, the sticky notes are organized into a graph.

Discuss the graph with the children. This is a good opportunity to introduce the ideas of range and mode. On the graph shown, the range is five, the difference between the largest and smallest numbers of letters. The mode is also five because there are more names with five letters than with any other number of letters. You might want to talk about the idea of average by asking the children how long they think a "typical" name is.

Have the children estimate how many letters they think are in all their names together. Talk about how they might determine the total from the information on the graph. Have students work in groups to solve the problem and then share their answers and strategies.

To confirm the total concretely, and also give children experience with the idea of our place-value structure, have each child make a train using as many interlocking cubes as letters in his or her name. Ask groups to organize their cubes into trains of ten and bring the tens to the front of the room. Then call for the extra cubes, making additional trains of ten. Count the tens and extras to arrive at the total.

Then give each student another sticky note. Have them write their last names, and organize these into another graph. Ask the students to look at both graphs and describe how the shapes of the data compare. Ask if they can tell from looking at the graphs if there are more letters in their first or last names altogether. Have volunteers offer their opinions and explain their reasoning.

At a later time, as an independent task, have students use the information on the graphs to figure how many letters there are in their last names altogether and find the difference between the totals of letters in their first and last names.

Measurement Activities

In these activities, children's measurements provide both a purpose for adding and subtracting and the numerical data to use. Although children will be working with different numbers, and therefore arriving at different answers, they'll be thinking about the same problem situations.

How Much Ribbon?

This investigation involves students in figuring out how much ribbon or yarn they need to wrap a package. For this activity, you need a box for each pair or small group. Larger boxes, such as boxes for shoes, sweaters, blouses, kitchen mixing bowls, and large pitchers or vases, require children to combine larger numbers. Smaller boxes, such as those for candy, ties, and other smaller gifts, produce problems with smaller numbers.

You also need yarn or ribbon for this activity. Cut a length for each pair or group of children that measures about 1 yard. Also, have several rolls of yarn or ribbon available from which children can cut additional lengths as needed.

Begin by showing the children a box and asking them to estimate how much yarn or ribbon they think they need just for making a bow. Then give each pair or group a yard-long length and have them tie a bow around a pencil. Tell them that it's up to their group to decide on the size of the bow and the length of the ends. After they make a bow and trim its ends, they measure the length of the yarn they used. When all have completed this, have them show their bows and report their lengths. Record this information on the board.

Then give each pair or group a box. Tell them that their job is to figure out how many inches of ribbon or yarn they would need to wrap their box, including the bow. (They can use their own measurement for the bow or any other one that is reasonable according to the class list of bow measurements.) Write the following directions on the board:

1. *Talk about a plan to solve the problem.*
2. *Decide on the length of yarn you need.*
3. *Write about how you got your answer.*
4. *Measure and cut yarn to test.*

When all groups have completed the problem, have them present their results and procedures to the class. Presentations such as these help children learn about other ways to solve problems and work with numbers. After several presentations have been made, before subsequent groups present their findings, have the rest of the children look at their boxes and use the information they already have to predict a reasonable range for the solution.

How Big Is Your Hand?

This activity involves the children with measuring area. Have the children trace one of their hands, fingers together, on centimeter grid paper (see Blackline Masters) and figure its area. Talk with the children about the approximate nature of their answers and about dealing with the bits and pieces of squares. Have the children explain in writing how they did their calculations.

Typically, some children will avoid the incomplete squares. In cases such as these, have children pair up and share how they each solved the problem. Then give students a chance to revise or refine their work.

Also, talk with the children about how they think their measurements would compare if they traced their hands with their fingers apart. Have those who are interested try this experiment.

At a later time, as an independent task, have children figure the area of a kindergarten child's hand and an adult's hand and compare with their own measurements.

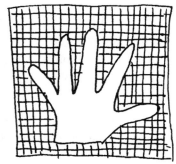

Probability Activities

Games of chance are always appealing to children. The two suggested here are sure favorites. Both are two-person games that involve children in mental addition and encourage them to think strategically. The first game gives practice with sums less than twenty; the second requires adding to one hundred. After the games are taught to the whole class, children can play them independently.

Roll 15

To play this game, each pair of children needs four cubes, two numbered 0–5 and two numbered 5–10. The object of the game is to get a score as close to 15 as possible.

Choose two students to demonstrate the game. The first player chooses any cube to roll, then rolls a second cube, and finds the sum of the two numbers rolled. (If the two numbers rolled are 3 and 4, the sum is 7 so far.) The player may now choose to stop or to roll a third cube. This third number is then added to the previous sum. (If the number rolled is a 9, the sum is now 16.) It's all right to go over 15. After the third roll, if the sum is still less than 15, the player may choose to roll the fourth cube. Then the second player rolls the cubes one at a time in the same way. Have the class decide which player's score is closer to 15.

Have the class play the game in pairs. Ask students to record each time they roll, keeping track of which cubes they roll, the numbers that come up, and the sums they have. Have them play five rounds.

Use the following questions for a class discussion: "How many times did you usually roll before stopping? Which cube did you use first? Second? How many times did you go over fifteen? What might you roll to produce a result of exactly fifteen?"

Have the children play five more rounds.

The Game of Pig

This game appears on page 99 in the "Probability and Statistics" section. Demonstrate the game by playing with a volunteer. Emphasize to the children that they are to keep the running totals mentally for each round, then record them, and add them to their previous totals. Also emphasize that children are to check each other's addition.

After a demonstration game, give each pair of children two dice and have them play the game. Give the children time over the next several days to play. Also, you might give them the homework assignment of teaching the game to someone at home.

When all the children are familiar with the game and have had the opportunity to play it several times, have a class discussion about their methods for adding mentally, their strategies for deciding when to roll and when to stop, and what they noticed about the sums that came up. Use the following questions: "How did you decide when to keep rolling and when to stop and keep your score? How often did a one come up? How often did doubles come up? Suppose you had a score of fifteen and rolled a sum of nine; What would your new total be? How did you figure that in your head? Suppose your score was nineteen and you rolled eleven; what would your score be now? [Give all children who have strategies the chance to share them.] What advice would you give to a new player?"

Independent Activities (Menu)

Children benefit from many opportunities to add and subtract numbers throughout the year. Three of the activities that follow are extensions of the whole-class lessons—*Last Names*, *Too Short*, and *Comparing Hands*. The others offer other problem situations that give children experience with adding and subtracting.

Last Names

You need: a partner
                the class graphs of first and last names

Figure out how many letters there are altogether in the last names in the class. Compare this with the total for the letters in the class's first names. Find the difference. Explain how you did this.

Too Short

You need: measuring stick, tape, or ruler
                gift boxes of varying sizes—for shoes, sweaters, ties,
                    and so on, 5
                3-yard roll of ribbon

Suppose you needed to wrap each of the five boxes and had only one 3-yard roll of ribbon. If you wanted to waste as little ribbon as possible, which would you choose to wrap with the ribbon you have? How much more ribbon would you need to buy?
    Explain your reasoning and defend your answer with numerical data.

Comparing Hands

You need: your hand traced on centimeter grid paper (see Blackline
                  Masters)
                the hand of a kindergarten student traced on centimeter
                grid paper

Find the area of the hand of a kindergarten child. Find the difference between the area of your hand and the area of the kindergarten child's hand. Explain how you figured this out.
    Record the difference on the class chart.
Homework: Trace one of your parent's hands on centimeter grid paper. Figure its area and compare that with yours. Is your hand half grown yet? Explain your reasoning.

How Old Is Ramona the Pest?

You need: a partner
              Ramona the Pest (Cleary 1968)

In the book *Ramona the Pest*, Ramona is in kindergarten, which makes her about five years old. According to the copyright date, the book was written in 1968. How old is Ramona now?

Estimate and Measure

You need: a partner
              interlocking cubes, about
                50 per student

Using cubes, measure the length of at least five different things. For each, do the following:

1. Make an estimate and record.
2. Measure.
3. Count and record.
4. Figure how far off your estimate was.

Record.

Estimate and Measure			
Object	Est.	Meas.	How far off?

In 1 Minute

You need: a partner
              way to time 1 minute

While your partner times 1 minute, write the letters of the alphabet. (If you get to Z before time is up, start over with A.)

Repeat, this time writing numerals, starting with 1 and continuing until time is called.

Switch so your partner writes letters and numerals while you keep time.

Each of you counts the number of letters and numerals you wrote. See if you wrote more letters or more numerals, and figure how many more. Record your results.

Compare your results with your partner's.

Extension

Predict how many letters and numerals you think you would write in half a minute. Time each other to test your estimates. Compare your results with your 1-minute data. Write about what you notice.

Billy Goes Shopping

You need: 9 dimes
               50 pennies

Billy wants to buy some new school supplies. He has nine dimes to spend. He needs to save 25¢ for the bus. Look at the price list and choose some things for Billy to buy. (He can buy different things or more than one of the same thing.)

List the items you chose, along with the cost of each. Find the total. Use the dimes and pennies to figure out the change.

Find at least three ways Billy can spend his money. Remember, he needs 25¢ for the bus.

Price List
Erasers 10¢
Rulers 29¢
Pencils 25¢
Pens 39¢
Book covers 20¢

Covering Covers

You need: color tiles, about 100
               books, 6

Choose two different books from the class or school library. Estimate which cover has the greater area. Measure each book cover with tiles and record. Figure out how many more tiles are needed for the larger cover and explain how you arrived at your answer.

Repeat for two other pairs of books.

Fill the Cube (Version 2)

(**Note:** This activity is similar to *Fill the Cube* on page 215 in the "Place Value" section. In this version, the children figure the difference between the two counts.)

You need: Unifix cube
                  popcorn kernels, enough to fill the cube
                  lentils, enough to fill the cube

Find out how many kernels of popcorn fill the cube. Record.

Predict how many lentils you think will fill the cube. Record your prediction and explain why you think it makes sense. Test your prediction.

Now figure out how many more lentils than popcorn kernels it took to fill the cube. Explain how you figured it out.

101 and Out

You need: a partner or small group
                  die or 0–9 spinner

This is a game for two or more players. Follow these rules:

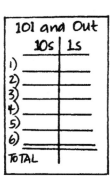

1. Each player makes a recording sheet as shown.
2. Take turns rolling the die or spinning the spinner to generate six numbers.
3. On each turn, all players write the number in either the tens column or ones column of their recording sheet. Once a number is recorded, it cannot be changed.
4. After six numbers, fill in any blank spaces in the ones column with 0s and add.
5. The player closest to 100 without going over wins.

Cross Out Singles

You need: a partner or small group
1–6 die or 0–9 spinner

This is a game for two or more players. Follow these rules:

1. Each player makes a recording sheet, as shown, for a game of three rounds.
2. To begin the game, one player rolls the die or spins the spinner.
3. All players write the number in a square on their first chart. Once a number is recorded, it cannot be changed.
4. Another player now rolls or spins to generate a number for everyone to record in another square. Take turns rolling or spinning until players have filled all nine squares on their charts.
5. Players then find the sums of the rows, columns, and diagonal, and record them in the respective circles.
6. Players examine their sums. Any sum that appears in only one circle must be crossed out.
7. The total of the sums that are *not* crossed out is the player's score for that round. For example:

SCORE: 51

8. Play two more rounds. Then compare totals.

Extensions

1. Find ways that produce a 0 score.
2. Using the numbers 1 to 9 once each, what is the highest score you can get?
3. Discuss strategies for how to place numbers.

Assessing Understanding of Addition and Subtraction

Observing Children

Class discussions can reveal how students think. For example, students' strategies for adding in the game of *Pig* reveal information about their number sense and ability to add mentally. How they deal with the incomplete squares when figuring the area of their hands gives information about their understanding of fractional parts. How they decide whether there were more letters in their first or last names provides information about their number sense and ability to interpret statistical data. Although some of this information may not relate specifically to comparing quantities or the processes of addition and subtraction, it contributes to your understanding of each child's mathematical thinking.

When children are working on the independent tasks, circulate, observe, and, at times, question children about their thinking and reasoning. The following are suggestions for your observations: What methods do children use for the calculations in the various tasks? Are the methods children use for one task similar to their methods in other tasks? Are there children who deal effectively with small numbers but are lost with large numbers? Which children rely on their mental calculations and which use other methods? How do the children use calculators?

Individual Assessments

To find out about children's understanding of addition and subtraction and their abilities to compute, give them problems to solve similar to those they have been working on in class. Be sure to ask children to describe their thinking processes and explain why their answers make sense.

Such assessments are the same as learning tasks. However, looking at a class set of such papers gives you information about the abilities of the class in general and the progress of specific students. The following are some suggestions:

1. Give children problems to solve that use information from two or three of their results from *Estimate and Measure*. For example: *Lindsay and Laura measured Lindsay. Their estimate was 86. Their measurement was 69. How far off was their measurement?*
2. Give them the copyright date on one of their library books. Ask them to figure out how long ago the book was written.
3. Ask them to write a paper titled "What Is Addition?" or "What Is Subtraction?"

4. Ask that they write an addition (or subtraction) word problem that follows two rules:
   a. It must end in a question.
   b. The question must be one that's possible to answer by adding (or subtracting).
   Have them solve their word problem in as many ways as they can.

Multiplication

Overview

Traditionally, instruction in multiplication has focused on two objectives: learning the multiplication facts and developing computational facility. After memorizing the times tables, children learn to multiply with paper and pencil, first practicing with one-digit multipliers and then progressing to two-digit and three-digit multipliers. Word problems are usually the vehicle for giving students practice with applying multiplication in problem situations.

The ideas in this section provide a shift toward a broader view of multiplication and a more active approach to learning. The activities introduce multiplication from several perspectives: geometric, numerical, and through real-world contexts. To integrate multiplication with the rest of mathematics, the activities include ideas from the topics of number and operations, geometry, statistics, and patterns and functions.

The standard mathematical representation for multiplication is introduced in the context of the activities, helping children connect the abstract representations to their own experiences. Also, rather than teaching the standard computational algorithm for multiplying, the activities give students the challenge of creating their own procedures for computing.

Whole-Class Lessons

Multiplication in Real-World Contexts

Having children investigate groups of objects in a real-world context helps them link the idea of multiplication to the world around them. It also helps them avoid the pitfall of seeing mathematics as totally abstract and unrelated to their lives. Too often, math exists for children only on the pages of textbooks and worksheets. They need opportunities to see mathematics as integral to their daily experiences.

The Chopstick Problem

Use this problem to initiate the exploration of multiplication in a context. First, make sure children know that when people use chopsticks to eat, two are required. Then pose a problem for class discussion: *How many chopsticks are needed for four people?* Hear from all children who want to respond, asking them to explain how they arrived at their answers.

Then pose another problem: *How many chopsticks are needed for everyone in the class?* Ask the children to discuss and solve this problem in small groups. Then have individuals report their answers, again asking them to explain their reasoning. Record on the board the methods they report, modeling for the children how to use mathematical notation to represent their ideas. Keep the emphasis on children's different approaches for solving the problem.

Things That Come in Groups

Collect the materials needed for this activity: a 12-by-18-inch sheet of newsprint for each small group of children and eleven sheets of 9-by-12-inch drawing paper. Post one 9-by-12-inch sheet of paper and title it *Things That Come in 2s.*

Have the class brainstorm things other than chopsticks that come in twos. List their suggestions. It's common for children to think of examples from their bodies—eyes, ears, hands, feet, thumbs, and so on. If they are limited by a particular category, such as their bodies, offer a few suggestions to broaden their thinking—wheels on a bicycle, wings on a bird, slices of bread in a sandwich.

Give the class the problem of making lists for other numbers. Have the children work in small groups and think of objects that come in threes, fours, fives, and so on, up to twelves. Give each group a sheet of 12-by-18-inch newsprint on which to organize its list.

Post the additional sheets of 9-by-12-inch paper and label them for the numbers from three to twelve. Have groups take turns reading items from their charts. After a group reads an item, the others guess the list on which it belongs. Should uncertainty or a dispute arise about items, such as sides on a stop sign or wings on a butterfly, start a separate "research" list and resolve the questions at a later time. Continue having groups report until all their findings have been offered. Keep the lists posted for the remainder of the unit to provide a resource of subjects for problem solving.

Also, encourage the children to continue thinking about other items to add to the lists. You may choose to give children the homework assignment of asking their parents to help think of additional items.

Multiplication as Combining Equal Groups

Because children learn in different ways, it's helpful to include a diversity of approaches in lessons. The following game suggests a way to introduce children to multiplication as combining equal groups, often referred to as repeated addition, with the additional benefit of providing a visual representation of multiplication. In this game, the children interact with the idea of multiplication pictorially (by drawing circles and stars), symbolically (by writing the multiplication equations), and verbally (by reading the equations).

Circles and Stars

Collect the materials you need for the game: one die for each pair of children, a sheet of unlined paper (such as copier paper) for each child, a pair of scissors for each child or pair of children, and two or three staplers.

Tell the children that you're going to teach them how to play a game called *Circles and Stars* that they will then play in pairs. To model how to play, invite a child to be your partner and join you at the board.

Begin by rolling a die and reporting to the class the number that comes up. Draw that many circles on the board, pointing out to the class that you're drawing the circles large enough to be able to draw stars inside. Then have the child who is your partner roll the die and draw the appropriate number of circles. Roll the die again, report the number to the class, and draw that many stars in each of your circles. Have your partner roll the die and draw the correct number of stars. Ask the class to figure out how many stars each of you drew. Write the correct number of stars underneath each drawing. Play another round to be sure the children understand, and then ask the volunteer to be seated.

Tell the class that a complete game takes seven rounds. Demonstrate how to fold a piece of paper into fourths, cut it apart, and staple it into a booklet. Write *Circles and Stars* and your name on the front. Have the children count as you show that seven pages remain for playing. Tell the children that although they can see who wins each round by comparing how many stars each player drew, the winner of the game is the person who has more stars altogether in the booklet. After seven rounds, children are to figure out the total and record it on the cover.

Have the children make their booklets and play the game. Those who finish more quickly can make a second booklet and play again.

When all the children have played at least one complete game, show them how to record a multiplication equation on each page. First draw on the board a sample page of three circles with two stars in each and underneath write: *3 × 2*. Explain to the children that this is a way to write three sets of two or three groups of two with math symbols. Tell them that you can also read it as "three times two," and it means the same thing. Show

how adding = 6 tells how many stars there are in all. Write on the board the three ways to read 3 × 2 = 6:

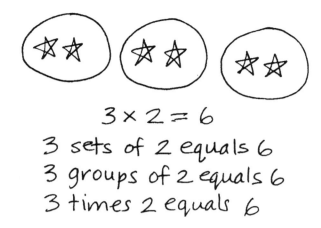

3 × 2 = 6
3 sets of 2 equals 6
3 groups of 2 equals 6
3 times 2 equals 6

Then ask the children to work with their partners and agree on the math equation to write on each page of their booklets. Tell them that as they write the math equations, they should read them aloud to each other in two different ways. Also tell them that when they complete recording in a booklet, they should save it for later analysis and data collection.

After all the children have played at least one game, have them work in small groups and compare the number of stars on each page of their booklets. Ask them to look for the different numbers of stars that came up, which numbers of stars on a page came up frequently, and the different ways they got them. Have children present their findings in a class discussion. On a later independent task, they will more formally analyze the possible numbers and ways to get them.

For homework, have children teach someone at home how to play *Circles and Stars*.

A Geometric Model for Multiplication

Investigating rectangular arrays introduces children to a geometric model for multiplication. The students investigate rectangular arrays as they research how to package candy. The "candies" are 1-inch square tiles that are packed one layer deep in rectangular boxes. Children use the tiles to identify various dimensions of boxes for different numbers of candies.

Candy Boxes

Collect the materials you need for this activity: color tiles (at least twelve per child), half-inch grid paper (see Blackline Masters), scissors, and tape or glue.

Distribute tiles so that each pair of children has twenty-four. Explain that the tiles are pretend candies that come in rectangular or square boxes and are always packed in just one layer. Tell the children that a sampler box has four candies in it. Ask each child to take four tiles and see how the candies might be arranged to fit into a box.

Typically in a class, students produce the two possible options. Draw them on the board. If only one is found, however, show the other and have the children build it with the tiles. If children suggest an L-shaped arrangement, remind them that the boxes must be rectangular or square. This is a good opportunity to point out that squares are really special rectangles because each of their sides is the same length.

Write the dimensions *2 × 2* and *1 × 4* inside each rectangle you drew.

Read them aloud as "two rows of two" and "two by two" and "one row of four" and "one by four" and explain to the children that the numbers tell how many tiles there are on adjoining sides. Then, using half-inch grid paper, cut out the two different arrays and record the dimensions on each.

Next, pose the research problem: Each pair of students is the design research team of the candy company. The president of the company has asked for a report about the different boxes possible for six, twelve, and twenty-four candies. Give the children three directions.

1. For each number, use the tiles to find all possible rectangles.
2. Cut out each rectangular shape as you find it, using half-inch grid paper.
3. Write a memo to the president explaining what you've learned about boxes for each quantity and what shape box you recommend. Include your cutout boxes with your memo.

Have children report their findings and recommendations in a class discussion.

Independent Activities (Menu)

The independent activities provide children with a variety of experiences with multiplication. Three of the activities—*Patterns in Multiples, More Circles and Stars*, and *Candy Box Research*—extend the whole-class lessons. Two versions of *Candy Box Research* are included; the first version is simpler for children to do.

The other activities—*Billy Wins a Shopping Spree*, *Calculator Patterns*, *Multiplication Stories*, *Times Tables Plaids*, *How Long? How Many?*, *How Many Were Eaten?* and *The Factor Game*—provide additional ways for children to learn about multiplication.

Patterns in Multiples

You need: "Things That Come in Groups" charts (see page 234)
large 0–99 charts, 2 (see Blackline Masters)

Choose an item from one of the "Things That Come in Groups" charts. List at least twelve multiples and write multiplication sentences.

Color in the multiples on a 0–99 chart. Then continue the pattern to the end of the chart.

Write about the patterns you see in the numbers on your list and on the 0–99 chart.

Repeat for an item from a different list.

Candy Box Research (Version 1)

You need: a partner
color tiles, 36
half-inch grid paper, several sheets (see Blackline Masters)
bag with numbers

Pick a number from the bag.

Using color tiles, build all the rectangular boxes possible for that number of candies. Cut out each from the grid paper and label its dimensions. Tape on the class chart. Repeat for another number from the bag.

Note: The bag has slips of paper numbered from 1 to 36, excluding 4, 6, 12, and 24. The class chart is a large horizontal chart with spaces marked for the numbers from 1 to 36. The students already investigated rectangular arrays for the numbers four, six, twelve, and twenty-four; post the rectangles for each of these numbers.

Candy Box Research (Version 2)

You need: a partner or small group
                color tiles, 36
                half-inch grid paper, several sheets (see Blackline
                   Masters)
                large newsprint, several sheets

Use color tiles to build the rectangular boxes possible for all the numbers from one to thirty-six. Cut out each from the grid paper and label its dimensions. Tape the rectangles on newsprint ruled into sections for each number.

When you've completed your chart, write answers to the following questions:

1. For which numbers are there rectangles that have sides with two squares on them? Write the numbers from smallest to largest.
2. For which numbers are there rectangles that have sides with three squares on them? Write the numbers from smallest to largest.
3. Do the same for numbers with rectangles that have four squares on a side.
4. Do the same for numbers with rectangles that have five squares on a side.
5. Which numbers have rectangles that are squares?
6. How many squares are in the next larger square you can make?
7. What is the smallest number with exactly two different rectangles? Three different rectangles? Four?
8. Which numbers have only one rectangle? List them from smallest to largest.

More Circles and Stars

You need: a partner
                1–6 die

Make a booklet and play *Circles and Stars* as you did before.

After you play, make tally marks on the class chart to show the number of stars you drew on each round.

Note: The class chart should list the numbers from 1 to 36.

Billy Wins a Shopping Spree

You need: a partner

Billy won a $25.00 shopping spree at the Science Museum Store. He could choose items from the price list shown. Decide what Billy could buy. Record your choices.

PRICE LIST

$3.00	$4.00	$5.00
1. Origami paper	1. Kaleidoscope	1. ball
2. Crystal and gem magnets	2. Large magnifying bug box	2. Glow-in-the-dark solar system stickers
3. Furry stuffed seal pups	3. Sunprint kit	3. Inflatable world globe
4. Prism	4. Inflatable shark	4. Wooden dinosaur model kit

Make a receipt that shows how many items of each price Billy bought. Show the total he spent and the credit he has left, if any.

Extension
Find the combinations of differently priced objects that Billy could buy and spend $25.00 exactly. Note that buying five balls is the same price combination as buying three balls and two dinosaur model kits because in each case, Billy is buying five items at $5.00 each.

Calculator Patterns

You need: calculator

Enter a number from 2 to 12. Press the + key. Press the = key. (You should see the same number you first entered.) Keep pressing the = key. Each time you press it, list the number displayed. Continue until there are at least twelve numbers on your list. Write about the patterns you notice.

Multiplication Stories

Write a multiplication story that follows two rules:

1. It must end in a question.
2. The question must be one that's possible to answer by multiplying.

Solve your story problem in as many ways as you can.
Exchange papers and solve each other's problems.

Times Table Plaids

You need: multiplication table (see Blackline Masters)

Choose a number from 2 to 12. List the multiples of the number up to 144. (You may use a calculator and the method described in *Calculator Patterns* on page 240.)

On a multiplication chart, color all the multiples on your list. Check with other students to compare your pattern with patterns generated from the multiples of other numbers. Write about the similarities and differences among the patterns.

How Many Were Eaten?

You need: candy box with 7 cubes inside

There are seven candies left in the box. Figure out how many were eaten. Show your work and explain your reasoning.

Note: Have several different-size candy boxes, each with seven cubes inside, from which students can choose. Some may be interested in solving the problem for more than one candy box.

How Long? How Many?

You need: a partner
                    Cuisenaire rods, 1 set
                    1–6 die
                    centimeter grid paper, 1 sheet (see Blackline Masters)

Two versions of the game are described below. Try both versions.

Version 1

Each player uses a different 10-by-10 square of centimeter grid paper. Take turns. On your turn, roll the die twice. The first roll tells *how long* a rod to use. The second roll tells *how many* rods to take.

Arrange the rods into a rectangle. Trace it on your grid and write the appropriate multiplication sentence inside.

The game is over when one of you can't place your rectangle because there's no room on the grid. Then figure out how many of your squares are covered and how many are uncovered. Check each other's answers.

Covered —
Uncovered —

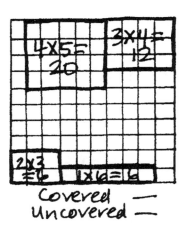

Covered —
Uncovered —

Version 2

Both of you use one notebook-size piece of centimeter grid paper. The goal is to cover as much of the paper as possible. As in the first version, take turns rolling the die and taking the appropriate rods. Together, decide how to form them into a rectangle and where to trace it on the paper. Continue until you can't place the rectangle for the numbers you rolled. Figure out how many of your squares are covered and how many are uncovered.

The Factor Game

You need: a partner
markers, 1 each of two different colors
sheet of paper with the numbers 1 to 30

```
The Factor Game
 1  2  3  4  5
 6  7  8  9  10
11 12 13 14 15
16 17 18 19 20
21 22 23 24 25
26 27 28 29 30
```

Each player uses a different-colored marker. One player selects a number and circles it with his or her marker. The other player finds all the proper factors of the number, circling each with his or her marker. The process alternates between the two players until there are no factors left for the remaining numbers. Players add the numbers they circled. The winner is the player with the larger score.

Caution: Selecting a number with no factors left is an illegal move. If you make an illegal move, you get to add the number to your score . . . but you lose your next turn to select a number.

Assessing Understanding of Multiplication

Observing Children

When children are working on the independent tasks, circulate, observe, and, at times, question them about their thinking and reasoning. When children play *Circles and Stars*, for example, some figure out how many stars there are on a page by counting each star. Others count by twos, or add, or know the multiplication fact. Asking children to explain how they figured the number of stars on one or more pages can give insights into their thinking. For *Candy Box Research*, ask children how they know when they've found all the possible rectangles for a particular number. For *Billy Wins a Shopping Spree*, notice how children do the calculations when they decide what Billy can buy or how much he spent.

The children's stories for *Multiplication Stories* reveal whether children can relate contextual situations to the idea of multiplication. Their solutions from *How Many Were Eaten?* help you see if they can interpret multiplication geometrically.

Talk with children about the patterns they are noticing in *Candy Box Research*, *Patterns in Multiples*, *Calculator Patterns*, and *Times Table Plaids*. After they have the opportunity to play *How Long? How Many?* have children explain their strategies for filling as much as possible of the centimeter grid paper.

Individual Assessments

Rather than testing the children on the times tables or having them do arithmetic calculations, give assessments that help reveal their thinking. The following are several suggestions.

1. Before beginning instruction, ask students to write what they know about multiplication. Have them do this again at the end of the instructional unit. Return both papers to the students and ask them to reflect on their learning.
2. Give the children a multiplication fact—6 × 5 or 7 × 6, for example. Ask them to explain how to figure out the answer. If students say they already know the answer, ask how they would tell a younger child how to figure it out.
3. Give children a word problem to solve and ask them to find the answer in as many ways as possible and explain why their solutions make sense.

Overview

There are two different types of division. One is sharing or partitioning, which involves dividing a collection of objects into a given number of equal parts. Sharing twelve candies among three friends is a division situation of this type. The second type is grouping, dividing a collection of objects into groups of a known size. Figuring how many $0.15 pencils can be purchased with $1.00 is an example of division by grouping.

Children should become familiar with both types of division. Their formal instruction with division should begin with problem situations for them to solve. The situations can then be related to the standard symbolic representations. Also, children's understanding of division becomes more powerful when they begin to see the connection between sharing and grouping and between division and the other operations.

Whole-Class Lessons

Introducing Division Through Problem Situations

Presenting children with problem situations helps develop their familiarity with the language and process of division. Be sure to present problems for each type of division. Have children work with partners or in small groups so that they have opportunities to talk about their thinking. For all problems, when children present answers, have them explain their reasoning orally and in writing. Link the situations and solutions to mathematical symbols so that children learn the standard notation. The following are samples of problems to present to students throughout the year.

Division Sharing Problems

Tell the children the following story:

> *While walking to school one day, four children found a $5.00 bill. When they arrived at school, they told their teacher, and she asked them to tell the principal. The principal thanked the children and told them she would try to find out who lost the money. A week later, the principal called the children back to her office, and told them no one had claimed the money and that it was theirs to keep. However, they first had to figure how to share it equally among the four of them.*

Have the children work together to solve the problem. Ask them to record their solution and explain their reasoning. It may help to write the following prompt on the board for the children to follow:

Each person gets _____. We think this because _____.

For groups who finish first, ask them to solve a similar problem. Choose one with a remainder. For example: *If four children found 50¢ on the way to school, how much would each get if they had to share it equally?*

Have children share their solutions. Show them how to record the stories and solutions mathematically:

$$50¢ \div 4 = 12¢ \ R \ 2¢$$

$$4 \overline{)50¢} \ \overset{12¢ \ R \ 2¢}{}$$

On other days, continue with stories about the four children who find things on the way to school. They can find a bag of marbles with fifty-four marbles, a train of seventeen interlocking cubes, a bag with twenty-two apples, and so on.

Also, give problems with other divisors. For example:

Suppose someone gives the class a gift of 100 pencils. If they are divided among all the students, how many pencils will each student get?

If eight children were at a birthday party, and there were a box of cookies with three packets of ten cookies each, how many cookies could each child get?

The Doorbell Rang

The Doorbell Rang (Hutchins 1986) provides children the opportunity to think about several division problems. The book begins with two children who are about to have a snack. There is a plate of a dozen cookies. Have the class figure how many cookies each child could eat.

Just as the children are about to divide the cookies between them, however, the doorbell rings. Two more children enter. Have the class figure how many cookies they each could then have.

Then, just before the four children begin to eat their cookies, the doorbell rings again, and two more children enter. Have the class figure how many cookies each child could then have.

The six children are about to eat their cookies. But the doorbell rings once more. This time, six more children arrive. There are now twelve children and twelve cookies.

The doorbell rings again and the children sit frozen. When the door opens, it is Grandma with a plate of freshly baked cookies!

Read the story a second time, this time recording on the board the mathematical sentences for each problem.

$$12 \div 2 = 6$$
$$12 \div 4 = 3$$
$$12 \div 6 = 2$$
$$12 \div 12 = 1$$

$$2\overline{)12}^{6} \qquad 4\overline{)12}^{3}$$
$$6\overline{)12}^{2} \qquad 12\overline{)12}^{1}$$

Have children practice retelling the story, referring to the mathematical sentences for cues. In this way, they see mathematical symbols related to the action of a story.

Division Grouping Problems

Tell the children the following story:

> *There were two cartons in the refrigerator with a dozen eggs in each, plus three extra eggs in the holders in the refrigerator door. Mom liked to eat an omelette each day and used two eggs in each omelette. How many days could she make omelettes before she had to buy more eggs?*

As with the other problems, have the children work in pairs or small groups, figure the answer, and explain their reasoning. Represent the story and solution with the correct mathematical symbols:

$$27 \div 2 = 13\ R\ 1$$
$$2\overline{)27}^{13\ R\ 1}$$

Present other grouping division problems. Keep the emphasis on the children's thinking. Have them share their reasoning processes and explain why their methods and answers make sense. As children present their solutions, represent the problems and their solutions mathematically on the board so that children see the mathematical symbols related to a variety of problem situations. The following are examples:

- Bring a loaf of sliced bread to class. Choose a loaf that is packaged in a clear wrap so children can count the slices. Ask them to figure how many sandwiches can be made from the loaf.

- Tell the class that for a math activity, each student needs eight tiles. A box has two hundred tiles. Have them figure out if everyone in the class can participate in the activity at one time.
- Talk with the children about the way paper is packaged. Tell them that a ream contains five hundred sheets. Present this problem: *If each student needs 20 sheets of paper to make a recording book, how many books can be made from a ream of paper?*
- Tell the children about a person with an apple tree who had a giveaway celebration to get rid of fifty extra apples. She offered three apples to each person who asked. How many people could get free apples?

When solving problems, children often use a combination of operations. For example, consider the following problem:

A woman decided to knit socks for holiday presents for her family. She was able to knit one sock a week. One year, she began knitting on January 1, and knit steadily until December 15. She then stopped to wrap each pair of socks. How many presents did she wrap?

Some children will solve the problem by counting to fifty by twos and keep track of how many twos they count. Record this on the board by writing 2, 4, 6, 8, . . . , 50, and also by recording the multiplication and division notations that relate:

$$25 \times 2 = 50$$
$$50 \div 2 = 25 \qquad 2\overline{)50}\,^{25}$$

Other children solve the problem by a combination of multiplying, adding, and subtracting: For 10 people, she would use 20 socks. For 10 more, another 20. That's 40 socks altogether. So she has 10 socks left. That's enough for 5 more people. So add 10 + 10 + 5, and she has socks for 25 people. Record these ideas with several mathematical sentences:

$$10 \times 2 = 20$$
$$20 + 20 = 40$$
$$50 - 40 = 10$$
$$10 \div 2 = 5$$
$$10 + 10 + 5 = 25$$

Some children approach the problem differently: Each person needs two socks, and half of fifty is twenty-five. That means twenty-five people get presents. Record this as follows:

$$\frac{1}{2} \text{ of } 50 = 25$$

It's important that children understand that a situation such as this one presents a division problem. However, it's also valuable for students to know that there are a variety of ways to find the answer. Although children may use different operations when calculating, they are finding the answer to a division problem in a legitimate way.

Don't shy away from problems with large numbers or with remainders. The wider the variety of problems, the more support children have for developing number sense and the more mathematically flexible they will become.

A note about calculators: Calculators should be readily available to children. Even if children use a calculator to find or verify an answer, have them explain why the answer makes sense. In problems with remainders, calculators are valuable for introducing children to decimals. Using a calculator to solve the problem of sharing 17 cubes among four children, for example, gives the answer of 4.25. This may be the first introduction to decimals for some children. Talk about 4.25 being a number that is greater than 4 but less than 5.

Investigations with Raisins

Read about this investigation on page 161 in the "Number and Operations" section. The lesson involves the children with estimating, statistical reasoning, and whole number operations, and presents the sharing problem of dividing raisins equally.

Relating Division to Multiplication

Seeing the relationship between division and multiplication helps deepen children's understanding. In the section on multiplication, several activities were suggested in which students learned about multiplication through exploring "candy boxes" that were rectangular arrays. If students engaged in those activities, the following extension can relate their experience to division.

Candy Box Sales Guides

Present the following problem:

> *Customers reported to the candy company that they sometimes had problems sharing the candy at home. The candies don't split into pieces. So when a family with five people buys a box with six candies, there is one extra candy. This sometimes causes squabbles. Not only is it a family problem, but it is a company problem, because the people might not want to buy the candy anymore.*

The problem for the students to solve is to prepare a guide for salespeople in the candy stores. When customers want to buy candy, the salesperson first asks how many people are in their family. Then he checks in the guide for suggestions about an appropriate quantity of candies to buy. In this way, he provides advice for a squabble-free purchase.

Have children design such a guide. Since it's unreasonable to provide suggestions for every possible family size, have the class graph how many people live in the students' houses. Use that information to decide which size families are most typical.

As an extension, have children find which size box is a good recommendation that would work for most families—for families of two, three, four, five, and six, for example.

A Division Game

The following game of chance gives children experience with sharing quantities into equal groups and relating the action to the appropriate mathematical representation.

Leftovers

Children play in pairs. Each pair needs one die, one piece of paper for recording, six 3-by-3-inch squares of construction paper, and fifteen color tiles or other counters.

The first player rolls the die, puts out that number of 3-by-3-inch paper squares, divides the fifteen tiles equally on the squares, and keeps any tiles that remain. The second player records a mathematical sentence to describe what occurred, as shown on the next page.

The children then change roles. The second player removes the tiles from the squares (there may be fewer than fifteen if the first player had a remainder and therefore kept the extra tiles), rolls the die, puts out the correct number of 3-by-3-inch squares, and divides the tiles among them. The first player records.

The game continues until no tiles are left to divide. The players count the tiles they each have. On a class chart, they record their sentences with remainders of zero. (Ask children to record only those sentences that haven't already been recorded on the chart.)

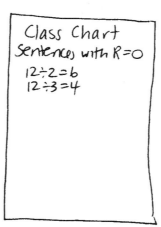

Independent Activities (Menu)

The independent activities give children additional experiences with division. Three of the activities—*Leftovers with 20, More Candy Box Research*, and *The Doorbell Rings Again*—extend whole-class lessons. The other activities—*Division Stories, Chocolate Bars*, and *The Kings-and-Elephants Problem*—give children further opportunities to learn about division.

Leftovers with 20

You need: a partner
die
color tiles, 20
3-by-3-inch squares of construction paper, 6

Play the game as before, following these rules:

1. The first player rolls the die, takes that number of 3-by-3-inch squares, and divides the tiles among them. If there are leftover tiles, the first player keeps them.
2. The second player writes the math sentence.
3. Switch roles. Continue until there aren't any tiles left.

   When you're finished: On the class chart, record all sentences with R≠0. (Only record sentences that haven't already been recorded.)

More Candy Box Research

You need: candy box sales guides

List the numbers of candies that can be shared equally among two, three, four, five, and six people. Examine these lists and see what patterns you notice and which numbers appear on more than one list.

Suppose there were a box with one hundred candies. On which lists would it fit? What about a box of fifty candies? Forty-eight? Do the same exploration for other numbers.

Division Stories

Write a division story that follows two rules:

1. It must end in a question.
2. The question must be one that's possible to answer by dividing.

Solve your story problem in as many ways as you can.
Exchange papers and solve each other's problems.

The Kings-and-Elephants Problem

You need: *17 Kings and 42 Elephants*, by Margaret Mahy (1987)

This book tells the story of seventeen kings and forty-two elephants going on a journey through a jungle. Figure out how seventeen kings could divide up the work of taking care of forty-two elephants. Explain your reasoning.

Write other math problems that use the information in the story. For example: How many elephant feet were there altogether?

The Doorbell Rings Again

You need: *The Doorbell Rang*, by Pat Hutchins (1986)

Write another version of this story. You may change the number of cookies on the plate and also the number of children who arrive each time. Illustrate your story. Then read it to someone else.

Assessing Understanding of Division

Observing Children

When children are working on the independent tasks, circulate, observe, and, at times, question them about their thinking and reasoning. When they are playing *Leftovers*, for example, ask children if they can predict whether there will be a remainder before they divide the tiles. The game gives children concrete experience with division problems that have a quotient of zero; make sure children understand when zero is an appropriate answer.

    The children's stories for *Division Stories* reveal whether they can relate contextual situations to the idea of division. *More Candy Box Research* gives you information about children's comfort with numbers. If children are interested and able, discuss rules for divisibility with them.

Individual Assessments

The following written assignments offer ways to find out about children's understanding of division.

1. Before beginning instruction, ask students to write what they know about division. Have them do this again at the end of the instructional unit. Return both papers to the students and ask them to reflect on their learning.

2. Give the children a division problem—24 ÷ 3 or 65 ÷ 5, for example. Ask them to explain how to figure out the answer. If students say they already know the answer, ask how they would tell a younger child how to find out.

3. Ask the children to solve 21 ÷ 4 in four different situations. For each, they are to report an answer, show how they arrived at it, and explain why the answer makes sense.

   a. *Share 21 cookies among 4 children.*

   b. *Share 21 balloons among 4 children.*

   c. *Share $21.00 among 4 children.*

   d. *Do 21 ÷ 4 on a calculator.*

4. Assign a problem, such as one of those suggested for whole-class lessons. Ask children to present a solution in writing and explain their reasoning.

Extending Multiplication and Division

Overview

In the upper-elementary grades, students develop skills with which to estimate and calculate accurately when multiplying and dividing with large numbers. Students should be able to compute mentally as well as with paper and pencil and make estimates that allow them to judge the reasonableness of answers. When confronted with problem situations, they should know when it's necessary to be accurate and when an estimate will suffice.

Traditionally, instruction related to multiplying and dividing large numbers has focused primarily on computing accurate answers proficiently using paper-and-pencil algorithms. Unfortunately, the result of this focus has been that many students learn the algorithms for multiplication and long division without understanding why these algorithms make sense. Also, little emphasis has been given to calculating mentally.

In contrast, instruction should help students develop a repertoire of strategies for multiplying and dividing with large numbers both by figuring mentally and using paper and pencil. Learning different strategies requires that students understand several important ideas—how to multiply and divide by ten, powers of ten, and multiples of powers of ten; how to apply the distributive property to multiplication and division problems; and how multiplication and division relate to each other. When emphasis is placed on understanding and using these ideas, the role of paper and pencil expands beyond performing standard algorithms to using paper and pencil as tools for keeping track of numerical reasoning and calculating in ways that relate to the specific numbers at hand. Standard algorithms may be part of instruction, but they should be presented as one way to perform computations, not as the only or best way. Too often, for example, when faced with calculations like 463×100 and $360 \div 20$, students will reach for pencil and paper to apply the algorithm they learned rather than reason that for these problems, figuring mentally is more useful, appropriate, and efficient. Proficiency with multiplication and division should not be judged by students' ability to perform one particular algorithm but by their ability to calculate answers to multiplication and division calculations accurately and efficiently using approaches that are appropriate to specific problems.

Whole-Class Lessons

Multiplying by Ten and Powers of Ten

Because of the structure of our base ten number system, multiplying by 10 is made simple, calling merely for adding a zero. Six times 10, for example, is 60; 13 times 10 is 130; 247 times 10 is 2,470; and so on. Learning this pattern allows students to multiply by 10 in their heads easily. It's important, however, that even when students know the pattern of adding a zero they can also verify answers in other ways. For example, they might reason that 13 times 10 is 130 because 10 10s are 100, 3 more 10s is 30 more, and 100 plus 30 is 130. Or they can verify that 25 times 10 is 250 by thinking that 25 times 2 is 50, doubling that for 25 times 4 gives 100, doubling again for 25 times 8 gives 200, and adding two more 25s makes 250 altogether. Using these and other strategies not only helps students develop computational flexibility but also helps them verify that applying the shortcut makes sense.

The pattern of multiplying by 10 extends to larger powers of 10. Multiplying by 100, for example, results in adding two zeros, so that 12×100 is 1,200. (In this and similar problems, it seems to help students make sense of them if they read 1,200 as "twelve hundred" rather than as "one thousand two hundred" or think of 3,700 as thirty-seven hundred rather than three thousand seven hundred.) Again, although students know the pattern of adding two zeros, they should be expected to verify answers using other reasoning; for example, 4×100 is the same as 4 groups of 100—$100 + 100 + 100 + 100$.

It's a good idea to devote whole-class discussions to solving just a few multiplication and division problems with ten and powers of ten. Encourage students to think of multiple approaches and record their ideas on the board as they present them. Recording their reasoning models for students how to represent their thinking symbolically.

$25 \times 2 = 50$
$50 + 50 = 100 \quad (25 \times 4)$
$100 + 100 = 200 \quad (25 \times 8)$
$200 + 50 = 250 \quad (25 \times 10)$

$10 \times 10 = 100$
$10 \times 10 = 100$
$5 \times 10 = 50$
$100 + 100 + 50 = 250$

5 tens $= 50$
Count by 50 five times
50, 100, 150, 200, 250

Keep the emphasis of discussions on how students reason as well as on verifying correct answers. Start a class list of strategies. Talking about which strategies are better suited for specific problems is a way to have students think about the efficiency of certain methods. Keep in mind that the goal of this instruction is to develop students' ability to reason mentally both accurately and efficiently. Follow your class discussions with small-group work and individual assignments, asking students to solve a few problems in several different ways. Use the work students do in completing assignments as the basis for subsequent class discussions in which they tell how they used paper and pencil to keep track of and explain their numerical reasoning, making a bridge between reasoning mentally and using paper and pencil.

Using the Distributive Property

It's helpful to have frequent whole-class discussions about strategies for mentally multiplying and dividing specific problems, presenting problems that traditionally have been relegated to paper-and-pencil solutions. Present the class with a problem, give students the chance to think individually for a bit, have them share their ideas with a partner or in a small group, and then ask volunteers to report their ideas.

When asked to calculate mentally the answer to 13×5, for example, one student may report that 10 times 5 is 50, 3 more 5s is 15, and 50 plus 15 is 65. Another student may reason that 6 times 5 is 30 and another 6 times 5 makes 60 altogether; this takes care of 12 5s, and 1 more 5 makes 65. Or a student may think that 13 times 2 is 26, so 13 times 4 is twice that, or 52, and 1 more 13 makes 65. As described in the previous section about multiplying by 10 and powers of 10, record on the board as each student reports.

$$13 \times 5$$

$10 \times 5 = 50$	$6 \times 5 = 30$	$13 \times 2 = 26$
$3 \times 5 = 15$	$6 \times 5 = 30$	$13 \times 4 = 52$
$50 + 15 = 65$	$30 + 30 = 60$	$52 + 13 = 65$
	$60 + 5 = 65$	

Be sure to talk with the class about how recording is a useful tool for keeping track of and describing how you reason, not only for following a formerly learned procedure. In each of the previous strategies, students do simpler multiplications, getting partial products, and then combine the results for a final answer. This is similar to what students will do when multiplying by ten and powers of ten, but other numbers provide new challenges. At first, if students do not offer strategies like these, jump-start their thinking by encouraging students to begin with what they know. Or give them a suggestion about a place to start, such as multiplying ten times five, and have them talk in partners or small groups about how that might help. Or model one way as an example and then ask students to think of other approaches. Thinking about multiplying or dividing in this way is new for some students, and they need time to expand their computational repertoire to include ways other than using the procedures they may have learned and practiced.

Also, relating multiplication to rectangular arrays (see page 236) is a way to show why a particular way to reason numerically makes sense and offers a geometric interpretation of multiplication that can help students see how the areas of number and geometry can relate to each other. For example, a 5-by-13 array can be split into a 5-by-10 array and a 5-by-3 array, as shown below:

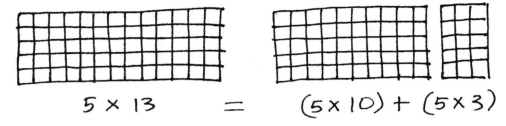

$$5 \times 13 \quad = \quad (5 \times 10) + (5 \times 3)$$

All of the strategies described for multiplying 13×5 make use of the distributive property of multiplication over addition. This means that instead of thinking of 13×5 as one multiplication, we split the problem into two or more problems. For example, by thinking of 13 as $10 + 3$, we can distribute multiplying by 5 over the two addends by doing 10×5 and 3×5.

Similarly, for division, students can figure the answer to $150 \div 6$ by using the distributive property, this time distributing the division over addition. One way to do this is to think about 150 as $60 + 60 + 30$. Divide 60 by 6 to get 10 and then divide 60 by 6 for 10 more. This accounts for 120 of the 150, leaving $30 \div 6$ for 5 more. Adding 2 10s and 5 gives 25, the answer to $150 \div 6$.

Making use of the distributive property helps students develop strategies for computing and, because applying the distributive property depends on the specific numbers involved, develops students' number sense as well. For example, when thinking about dividing 150 by 6, as explained above, choosing to think of 150 as $60 + 60 + 30$ helps make the problem more manageable. If the problem called for dividing 150 by 7, however, it might make more sense to think of 150 as $70 + 70 + 10$ or $140 + 10$. Making decisions like these focuses students on the particular characteristics of numbers and helps refine their number sense.

The distributive property is also the basis of why standard algorithms work, producing partial products for multiplication and the individual digits in quotients of long-division problems. However, the focus of lessons should be on finding ways to make complicated computations simpler and more manageable, not on learning what the distributive property is. (I remember learning about the distributive property by being shown that $a(b + c) = ab + ac$, but never understanding why it was important or how it might be useful.) Keep the emphasis on the specifics of numerical calculations. It's fine to identify that what your students are doing is applying the distributive property, but don't make the distributive property the goal of instruction.

Relating Multiplication and Division

Jars, scoops, and various sizes of dry beans are easily accessible materials that are effective for engaging students with multiplication, division, and the relationship between them. The emphasis of lessons using these materials should be on having students solve problems for which they can use multiplication and explain how they reasoned. Lessons like these can be done from time to time during the year, varying the problems as well as the sizes of the jars, scoops, and beans. Following are several examples.

A Long-Division Activity

As described in *50 Problem-Solving Lessons* (Burns 1996), this lesson gives fourth and fifth graders the opportunity to invent their own ways to divide, thus creating procedures that make sense to them. To prepare for the lesson, fill a jar with coffee scoops of beans, and count the number of scoops. Show the class the coffee scoop and the jar filled with beans, and ask the students to estimate the number of scoops they think it took to fill the jar. After revealing the number of scoops the jar holds, tell the class how many beans are in the jar and ask them to figure out how many beans will fill the scoop. Let the students solve the problem and have them describe their methods in writing. Then lead a class discussion about the different procedures they used. Finally, give groups of students a scoop of beans with which to verify their answers. Of course, the number of beans in different scoops will vary, giving the students the chance to talk about the problem as one for which an accurate answer doesn't make the most sense but for which an estimate will suffice or be even more appropriate.

To vary Bonnie's lesson, rather than asking the students to figure the number of beans that will fill a scoop, give each pair or group one scoopful of beans and have them use the information to figure out the number of scoops they think are in the jar. Because students' scoops will vary slightly, they may arrive at different answers. After discussing their solutions and methods, empty the jar and then refill it with scoops as the students count.

How Many Beans?

Show the class an empty jar, a scoop, and a bag of beans. Ask the students to estimate about how many beans they think the jar will hold. After listening to their estimates, fill the scoop and pour the beans on one student's desk so she or he can count them. Talk with the class about how to use the number of beans in one scoop to figure out the total number of beans in the jar. After the students determine that multiplying the number of beans in one scoop by the number of scoops in the jar will produce a reasonable estimate, fill the jar with scoops of beans, stopping after several scoops to ask the students to calculate mentally the number of beans in the jar so far and discuss their methods. Continue adding scoops and having students calculate the number of beans until the jar is full. Repeat the activity with different-size beans and jars, sometimes giving the students writing assignments to explain how they figured.

A variation of this lesson is to give each pair or group of students a scoop of beans to count rather than having a student count just one scoop. The counts will vary, but they will all be close. Record the counts on the board and discuss with the class how to determine which number is the best estimate to use for how many beans a scoop holds. Doing this incorporates instruction about averaging into the lesson and can engage the students in using division to figure the mean.

Multiplication and Division Through Real-World Problems

Using situations that call for multiplying and dividing with large numbers as the basis for whole-class discussions provides opportunities for students to explain their strategies and listen to strategies other students have used. As much as possible, choose contexts that relate to students' lives or are familiar to them. Also, ask students to make up their own multiplication and division problems to solve.

As described in *50 Problem-Solving Lessons* (Burns 1996), David Ott created problems for his sixth graders to solve that involved data collection and measurement as well as multiplication and division. Here are three of them:

> *Replacing Floor Tiles.* Figure out the number of floor tiles needed
>   to tile the floor of our classroom. Then calculate the number of floor
>   tiles needed for our wing and for all the classrooms in the school.
> *Stacking Chairs.* If we stacked all of our chairs on top of one another,
>   how high would the stack reach?
> *Head to Heels.* Figure out the length of your group if all of you were
>   to lie head to heel. Then use that information to approximate the
>   length of all the students in our class lying head to heel.

Here are some other examples of real-world problems:

> *School Days.* About how many days are students expected to come
>   to school each month? How many school days are there each year?
> *What's in a Name?* What is the average length of the first names
>   of students in our school? What is the average length of last names?
> *Milk Money.* How much do students in our class spend to buy milk
>   for lunch weekly? In the entire school year? How much do all students
>   in school spend on milk weekly? In the entire school year?
> *Soccer Statistics.* If our town has eight teams in the soccer league, how
>   many players are needed altogether?

Using Games

Games are useful for instruction because they motivate students, offer a change of pace, and stimulate both thinking and practice. The following games provide students practice with multiplying and dividing. Students can play them either by figuring mentally or with paper and pencil. The purpose of using these and other games should be to help students learn about new strategies for computing and to refine and reinforce the strategies they already know.

Hit the Target (Version 1)

In *Developing Number Sense, Grades 3–6* (Bresser and Holtzman 1999), the authors present a full classroom vignette of this game, along with samples of student work and extensions.

Students play this game in pairs. The goal of the game is to hit a target range in as few tries as possible. To start, the first player picks a number between one and one hundred. The second player then chooses a number to multiply this initial number by, with the goal of reaching the target range. Player 2 does the multiplication mentally and then Player 1 checks and records it. If the product isn't in the target range, Player 2 chooses another number to multiply the original number by. Play continues until the product hits the target. Players repeat the game, alternating roles.

To introduce the game to the class, write on the board *Target Range: 800–850* and choose a student to play with you. Post the rules for the game and follow them. Let the student be the first player. When it's your turn, ask for suggestions from the rest of the class about what you might do. For example, if the student chooses 12 as the initial number, ask the class to suggest a number you can multiply by 12 to get a product between 800 and 850. Asking students to explain how they would do the multiplication keeps the emphasis of the game on strategies for mental multiplication.

Then have students play the game in pairs. You can also play the game again with the class from time to time, changing the target range and/or the possible range for the initial number. After students have had experience playing the game, lead a class discussion about which initial numbers were easy and which were difficult and why. Also ask students to describe the strategies they used for calculating mentally.

Leftovers from 100

Leftovers from 100 is a version of the division game *Leftovers* (see page 250) that uses larger numbers. Students play in pairs and keep one recording sheet for the team. The starting number for the game is one hundred, and the goal of the game is to get the highest score possible. The numbers one through twenty are available for divisors; each number may be used only once in a game. Players should write the numbers from *1* through *20* at the top of their recording sheet and cross out numbers as they use them.

The first player chooses one of the numbers from one through twenty, divides one hundred by that number, and keeps the remainder as his or her score. The second player records the division sentence and marks the sentence with the first player's initial (see the illustration below). Both players then subtract the remainder from one hundred to determine the next starting number. (Having both players do this is a way to check the subtraction.) Students then change roles. The second player chooses a number from one through twenty (as long as it isn't the number already used), divides the new starting number by it, and keeps the remainder as his or her score. The first player records the division sentence. Again, both players subtract the remainder to get the new starting number. Play continues with the players alternating roles until the starting number becomes zero or it's no longer possible for either player to score. Players then total the remainders they scored.

Leftovers from 100

1 2 3 4 5 6 7 8 9 10
11 12 13 14 15 16 17 18 19 20

Starting Numbers		
100	100 ÷ 17 = 5 R 15	S
85	85 ÷ 18 = 4 R 13	B
72	72 ÷ 20 = 3 R 12	S
60	60 ÷ 16 = 3 R 12	B
48	48 ÷ 19 = 2 R 10	S
38	38 ÷ 13 = 2 R 12	B
26	26 ÷ 14 = 1 R 12	S
14	14 ÷ 8 = 1 R 6	B
8	8 ÷ 5 = 1 R 3	S
5	5 ÷ 3 = 1 R 2	B
3	3 ÷ 2 = 1 R 1	S
2	2 ÷ 1 = 2 R 0	B

S — 53 points   B — 45 points

Use the following questions for a class discussion after students have played the game enough times to feel comfortable with the rules and the kinds of numerical reasoning expected:

1. What is the best number to use for a first move? Why?
2. What strategies did you use to decide which number was the best to use?
3. When a game is finished, the total of both players' scores, plus the last starting number that remains, if it's more than zero, should add up to the original starting number of one hundred. Why is this so?

4. How would your strategies change if the starting number was ninety-nine?
5. How do you think the game would change if the divisors were limited to one through fifteen or included one through twenty-five? Try these versions to see which would be the best game.

As an extension, have students try the game with a different original number or by changing the possible divisors. Also, suggest that students use calculators to see whether this makes the game easier to play and, if so, how. Having students use calculators to play the game gives them the chance to think about the relationship between the whole number remainders used in this game and decimal remainders represented on calculators. For example, dividing 100 by 8, 12, and 16 all produce a whole number remainder of 4; on a calculator, however, $100 \div 8 = 12.5$, $100 \div 12 = 8.333[...]$, and $100 \div 16 = 6.25$.

Independent Activities (Menu)

Independent activities give students additional experience with multiplication and division of large numbers. After students have had experience with the independent activities, lead whole-class discussions to have them present what they learned. *Hit the Target* and *Larger Leftovers* extend whole-class lessons.

The Largest Product

You need: 1–6 die

Roll the die four times, recording the number that comes up each time. Use the four numbers to make a multiplication problem that produces the largest possible product. For example, if you roll 2, 5, 6, and 1, some problems you could make are 52 × 61, 51 × 62, and 612 × 5. Which has the largest product?
   Repeat for at least five sets of numbers. Then investigate the following:

1. If you rolled the same number four times, for example four 2s, your choices are 22 × 22 or 222 × 2. Which gives the larger product? Does the same configuration of any number rolled four times give the larger product?
2. Repeat the activity, trying to make the smallest product each time.
3. Repeat the activity rolling five times.
4. Do the activity with a 0–9 die or spinner so that you have more numbers to use.

Larger Leftovers

You need: a partner
             1–6 dice, 2

This game is an adaptation of *Leftovers from 100* (see page 261). As with the previous game, the goal is to get the highest score possible. Play the game using the following rules:

1. Agree on a starting number between two hundred and five hundred.
2. The first player rolls the two dice and uses the numbers to make a two-digit divisor. For example, if the player rolls a 3 and a 5, the player can use thirty-five or fifty-three as the divisor. The player divides the starting number by the divisor and keeps the remainder as his or her score. The second player records the division sentence, marking the sentence with the first player's initial.
3. Both players subtract the remainder from the starting number to determine the next starting number.
4. Switch roles. The second player rolls the dice, forms a number, divides the new starting number by it, and keeps the remainder as his or her score. The first player records the division sentence. Both players then subtract the remainder to get the new starting number.
5. Continue switching roles and playing until either the starting number becomes zero or it's no longer possible for either player to score.
6. Total your remainders.

Remainders of Zero

You need: 1–6 die

Roll the die four times, recording the number that comes up each time. Use the four numbers to make division problems that have a remainder of zero. For example, if you roll 2, 5, 6, and 1, one problem that you could make is 156 ÷ 2. See how many different problems you can find for the four numbers. If you are convinced that it isn't possible to make any problem with a remainder of zero, explain why you think this is so. Then do the following investigations:

1. Repeat the activity, trying to make problems with the largest remainder possible.
2. Repeat the activity, rolling five times.
3. Do the activity with a 0–9 die or spinner so that you have more numbers to use.

Hit the Target (Version 2)

You need: a partner
1–6 die

The goal of the game is to hit the target range in as few steps as possible. Play the game as on page 261, except use a die to determine the target range, as explained in Step 1:

1. To choose a target range, roll the die three times (or four times to use larger numbers). Arrange the three or four numbers into the largest possible number; this is the lower end of your target range. (For example, if you roll 2, 6, and 3, then the number you make is 632.) Add fifty to your original number to determine the upper end of your range. (In the case of the example, the target range is 632–682.)
2. Player 1 chooses a number between one and one hundred (fourteen, for example).
3. Player 2 chooses another number to multiply the first number by, and Player 1 verifies and records the result (14×50, for example).
4. If the product doesn't hit the target range, Player 2 goes back to the original number and multiplies it by any another number. Player 1 verifies and records the result.
5. Players repeat Step 4 until the product falls within the target range.
6. Players repeat the game, this time alternating roles.

Sample Game Scenario

Target Range: 632–682

Starting Number: 14

$14 \times 50 = 700$	The number is too high.
$14 \times 40 = 560$	The number is too low.
$14 \times 45 = 630$	The number is closer but still too low.
$14 \times 46 = 644$	The number is within the target range.

Assessing Understanding of Multiplication and Division with Large Numbers

Observing Children

During class discussions and when students are involved with independent activities, circulate among them, observe what they are doing, and talk with them about their numerical reasoning. When students are engaged in small-group or individual written assignments, ask them to explain what they have written.

Individual Assessments

1. Assign a multiplication or division problem and ask students to show at least three different ways to figure the answer and explain their reasoning.
2. Give students real-world problems along the lines of the examples suggested for whole-class lessons. Ask students to present their solutions in writing and to explain their reasoning.

Fractions

Overview

Children's introduction to fractions initially occurs outside of school. They hear adults use fractions in a variety of circumstances:

- I'll be back in three-quarters of an hour.
- I need two sheets of quarter-inch plywood.
- The recipe says to add two-thirds of a cup of water.
- The trim calls for two and a half yards of ribbon.
- There's a quarter moon tonight.
- The dishwasher is less than half full.

Also, children have learned to use the language of fractions to describe events in their own lives:

- You can have half of my cookie.
- Here, use half of my blocks.
- It's a quarter past one.
- I need half a dollar.

From their experiences, a number of ideas about fractions take shape informally in children's minds. However, children's understanding of fractions typically is incomplete and confused. For example, they often think of half as any part of a whole, rather than one of two equal parts, and they often refer to one half as being larger than another. (It's common to hear children say: "My half is bigger than yours.") They may be familiar with $\frac{1}{2}$, $\frac{1}{3}$, and $\frac{1}{4}$ of a unit, but not with $\frac{2}{3}$ or $\frac{3}{4}$. They may not have noticed relationships between fractions, that $\frac{2}{4}$ of an hour is the same as $\frac{1}{2}$ of an hour, for example, or that $\frac{3}{4}$ of an inch is $\frac{1}{4}$ less than 1 inch. Also, children's informal learning has most likely not been connected to the standard symbols of fractional notation.

Classroom instruction should build on children's previous experiences and help children clarify the ideas they've encountered. It should provide many opportunities throughout the year for children to make sense of fractions, use fractional language, and learn to represent fractions with the standard symbols. Children should deal with fractions concretely and in the context of real life before they focus on symbolic representations.

Some of the activities suggested in this section present fractions as parts of a whole, while others present fractions as parts of sets of objects. Various concrete materials are used so that the children do not link the concepts to the attributes of any particular material. (It may seem ludicrous to think children might generalize that fractions are round, but if their experiences with fractions deal only with fraction "pies," that misconception is not so improbable.)

The essential topics for instruction in fractions include naming fractions, comparing fractions, studying equivalence of fractions, and performing operations with fractions. It seems that fractions with a numerator of 1 do not pose much of a problem for students. Yet when fractions such as $\frac{2}{5}$ and $\frac{3}{4}$ enter the picture, so does confusion. Also, children have difficulty deciding which of two fractions, $\frac{2}{3}$ and $\frac{4}{5}$, for example, or even $\frac{1}{8}$ and $\frac{1}{16}$, represents more, and why fractions such as $\frac{3}{6}$ and $\frac{4}{8}$ describe the same part of a unit. These types of difficulties indicate the need for further concept development with concrete materials and real-life situations.

When they teach older students who lack basic understanding of fractions, it's not uncommon for teachers to feel the pressures of time and the demands of the curriculum. In that situation, it's often a temptation to speed up instruction and to teach the rules for operating with fractions. Some teachers resort to telling students, for example, that multiplying the numerator and denominator by the same number gives an equivalent fraction, or that in order to divide you invert the fraction on the right and multiply across the tops and across the bottoms.

Giving students rules to help them develop facility with fractions will not help them understand the concepts. The risk is that when students forget a rule, they'll have no way to reason through a process. Try this test with your students: Give students a fraction problem they're "supposed" to understand, $\frac{1}{2} + \frac{1}{3}$, for example. Ask them to show you what the problem means with any concrete material, or a drawing, or by relating it to some real-life situation. Watch the students' responses, and let their responses guide you when making instructional choices.

One last note: It's important to provide a variety of ways students can learn about fractions—with concrete materials, from a geometric perspective, with a numerical focus, and related to real-life situations. Let the students know that different people learn in different ways, and that they should pay attention to the kinds of activities that help them develop understanding. Encourage them to try activities with which they are less comfortable. Do not expect immediate results from any one activity. Students need time to absorb new ideas and integrate them with the understanding they already have.

Whole-Class Lessons

Introductory Lessons

Children need many opportunities to talk about fractional parts, see examples, work with concrete materials, and relate their experiences to the standard mathematical notation. Such experiences are best done over time, so that children can develop familiarity and understanding.

Introducing Fractions as Parts of Sets

The following are suggestions for introducing fractions and their symbols. These lessons can help children understand the structure of fractional notation.

Bring a six-pack of soft drinks to class. Remove one can from the pack and tell the children: "If I drink this soft drink, I can write a fraction that shows what part of the six-pack I drank." On the board, write $\frac{1}{6}$. Tell the children that this is read as "one-sixth" and means one of six parts. Then pose the following questions:

What do you think the six refers to?

What do you think the one stands for?

Why does this mathematical notation make sense?

What could I write to show the fractional part of the rest of the six-pack, the part I didn't drink?

Have students explain their thinking. Correct any erroneous notions. If this is the first time students have been introduced to this notation, remember they'll need time to understand and become comfortable with it.

Remove another can and ask the same sorts of questions. Continue, introducing three-sixths, four-sixths, five-sixths, and six-sixths. Be sure to point out that six-sixths equals one whole six-pack. Follow the same procedure for other sets of objects: a pack of five sticks of gum, a bunch of seven bananas, a box of crackers with three separately wrapped packages.

Also, have similar discussions about sets that contain different things. The following are examples:

- Ask a group of eight students to come to the front of the room. Ask: "What fraction of the group are boys? Girls? Are wearing blue? Are wearing long sleeves?"
- Show a box of colored birthday candles. Ask: "What fraction of the candles in the box are pink? Blue? Green?"
- Show a set of pencils, some sharpened and some unsharpened. Ask: "What fraction of the set are sharpened? Unsharpened? Have good points? Have erasers?"
- Stack about a dozen textbooks on a table. Ask: "What fraction of the set are math books? Science books? Social studies books?"
- Have nine students each take off one shoe. Set them on a table at the front of the room, or have students gather so all can see them. Ask: "What fraction of the set are tennis shoes? Have laces? Don't have laces? Have bumpy soles?"

- Bring to class a bag of apples, some red and some green. Ask: "What fraction of the set are red? Green?"
- Take a handful of color tiles, with some each of red, yellow, blue, and green. Ask: "What fraction of the set are red? Yellow? Blue? Green?"

Fractions with Two-Color Counters

Distribute twelve two-color counters to each student. (Two-color counters are plastic disks that are red on one side and yellow on the other. Coins would also work or any counters with sides of two different colors.) Give students the directions and questions that follow. Have them discuss the questions in small groups and then present their answers to the entire class, explaining their reasoning for each.

1. Divide the 12 counters into 3 equal groups with all yellow sides showing. What fractional part of the whole set is represented by each group? How many counters are in $\frac{1}{3}$?

2. Flip the counters in one group. What fractional part of the whole set is red? Yellow? How many are in $\frac{1}{3}$? In $\frac{2}{3}$?

3. Rearrange the counters into six equal groups with all yellow sides up. Flip the counters in one group. What fractional part of the whole set is red? Yellow? Flip another group. What fractional part of the whole set is red? Yellow? Flip another group. What fractional part of the whole set is red? Yellow? Continue until all groups have been flipped.
4. Arrange the counters so $\frac{1}{4}$ of them have red sides showing. What fractional part of the whole set is yellow? Show another set with fewer than 12 counters that also has $\frac{1}{4}$ of the set with red sides showing. See how many different solutions you can find.
5. Show a set of counters that has $\frac{2}{6}$ of them with their yellow sides showing. Find as many different solutions as you can that use 12 or fewer counters. (Continue for other fractions: $\frac{2}{8}$, $\frac{5}{6}$, $\frac{3}{5}$, and so on.)

The Fraction Kit

This activity introduces students to fractions as parts of a whole. Organize students into pairs or small groups. Each student needs five 3-by-18-inch strips of construction paper in five different colors, a pair of scissors, and a number 10 envelope. (Four strips can be cut from a 12-by-18-inch sheet of construction paper.) Also, prepare fraction dice—cubes with the six faces labeled as follows: $\frac{1}{2}, \frac{1}{4}, \frac{1}{8}, \frac{1}{8}, \frac{1}{16}, \frac{1}{16}$; each pair or group needs one.

Give students directions to cut and label the strips. Ask students to take a strip of a particular color, fold it in half, and cut it into two pieces. Have them label each piece $\frac{1}{2}$. (Review the rationale for the notation by explaining that the whole has been divided into two pieces of the same size, that each piece is one of the two pieces, and that the $\frac{1}{2}$ notation means one of two equal pieces.)

Then choose a color for the second strip and have the students fold and cut it into four equal pieces. Talk about each piece being one of four, or one-fourth, and ask students to label each piece $\frac{1}{4}$. Then have them fold, cut, and label a third strip into eighths and a fourth strip into sixteenths. Students leave the fifth strip whole, and label it *1* or $\frac{1}{1}$.

Each student now has a fraction kit to use. Having students cut and label the pieces helps them relate the fractional notation to the concrete pieces and compare the sizes of fractional parts. They can see that one-fourth, for example, is larger than one-sixteenth, and they can measure to prove that two of the one-eighth pieces are equivalent to one-fourth. Finally, have students label the backs of their pieces with their initials. Give them envelopes in which to keep their kits.

Following are activities for children to do in pairs or small groups.

Cover Up. This is a game for two or more players. Each player starts with a whole strip. The goal is to be the first to cover the whole strip completely with other pieces of the fraction kit. No overlapping pieces are allowed. Following are the rules for play.

1. Children take turns rolling the cube labeled with fractions.
2. The fraction faceup on the cube tells what size piece to place on the whole strip.

3. When the game nears the end and a student needs only a small piece, such as $\frac{1}{8}$ or $\frac{1}{16}$, rolling $\frac{1}{2}$ or $\frac{1}{4}$ won't do. The student must roll exactly what is needed.

Uncover. This game gives children experience with equivalent fractions. Each student starts with the whole strip covered with the two $\frac{1}{2}$ pieces. The goal is to be the first to uncover the strip completely. Following are the rules for play.

1. Children take turns rolling the cube.
2. A child has three options on each turn: to remove a piece (only if he or she has a piece the size indicated by the fraction faceup on the cube), to exchange any of the pieces left for equivalent pieces, or to do nothing and to pass the cube to the next player. (A player may not remove a piece and trade on the same turn, but can do only one or the other.) It's important for children to check that each other trades correctly.

At this time, the only fractional symbols the fraction kit activities have used are $\frac{1}{2}$, $\frac{1}{4}$, $\frac{1}{8}$, and $\frac{1}{16}$. After students are familiar with both games, they can be introduced to fractions with numerators other than 1. They have probably already used the language of those fractions in their games: "I've got just three more sixteenths to take off," or "I can exchange this one-half piece for two fourths." The symbolism for these fractions needs to be connected to students' concrete experiences.

Recording Cover-Ups. Ask the students to cover their whole pieces with whatever smaller pieces they choose. Record several of their examples on the board. For example, if a child used three $\frac{1}{4}$ pieces and two $\frac{1}{8}$ pieces, record: $\frac{1}{4} + \frac{1}{4} + \frac{1}{4} + \frac{1}{8} + \frac{1}{8} = 1$. Then explain how to shorten the equation by counting the fourths and writing $\frac{3}{4}$, and counting the eighths and writing $\frac{2}{8}$: $\frac{3}{4} + \frac{2}{8} = 1$. Have children help you shorten several other of the recordings on the board. Then have them each cover their whole strip with at least five different combinations of pieces and record on a worksheet, with and without shortening their lists. Have students exchange and check each other's papers.

Fraction Sentences. Give the students incomplete fraction sentences and have them use their fraction kits to decide how to complete them. This is fairly standard fraction practice, but in this case it is related to the students' concrete experience with the fraction kits. In all cases, have students explain, orally and in writing, why their answers make sense.

Such exercises can have several forms:

- Give pairs of fractions and have students write >, <, or = to make a true sentence.
- Ask students to supply the missing number to make the fractions equivalent.
- Have students write other fractions that are equivalent to the one you give.
- Have students find a way to write one fraction to complete a sentence. They can use their fraction kits for this by covering the pieces with all pieces of the same size so the length can be represented with one fraction.

$$\frac{1}{2} + \frac{1}{4} + \frac{1}{8} = \frac{7}{8}$$

Using Graphs to Build Understanding of Fractions

Use data from class graphs for class discussions about fractions. Over time, such discussions help students develop and secure their understanding of fractional concepts. The graphing ideas that follow present variations on graphs about names. Check the list of graphs on pages 105–106 in the "Probability and Statistics" section for other graphing ideas that you may find useful.

Is your last name longer, shorter, or the same length as your first name?
(Ask: "What fraction of the class has last names that are longer?
Shorter? The same length?")

First and Last Names
Make a tally. (卌 ‖)

My last name is longer.	My names are the same.	My last name is shorter.

How many letters in your last name? (Ask: "What fraction of the class
has last names with more than five letters? More than seven? Fewer than
six?")

Letters in Last Names
Color in a square.

2										
3										
4										
5										

How many syllables in your first name? (Ask: "What fraction of the class
has one syllable in their first names? Two? Three? More? What fraction of
the class has fewer than three syllables in their first names?")

Syllables
How many syllables are in
your first name? Write your
name in the correct column.

1	2	3	4

Do you have a middle name? (Ask: "What fraction of the class has a
middle name? What fraction does not?")

Middle Names
Do you have a middle name?
Make a tally. (卌 ‖)

Yes	‖
No	‖

Were you named after someone special? (Ask: "What fraction of the class was named after someone special? What fraction was not?")

Exploring Fractions Through Sharing Problems

Students benefit from a variety of sharing problems that call for fractional solutions. They can use circles to share cookies, squares to share brownies, and rectangles to share apple crisp bars. Although the problems presented for each of the shapes can be the same, for some students, changing the shapes seems to change the problem and to present a new challenge. The following are models of sharing problems.

Sharing Cookies

In this investigation, children share different numbers of "cookies" among members of a group. It's important they know that each person should get the same amount. For younger children, you might introduce this task by presenting the following problem: *If I gave each group of four children four cookies to share, how much would each person get?* This will most likely be obvious to them, but it will give you the chance to discuss what is meant by "sharing equally." Then have children solve the problems of sharing one, two, three, five, and six cookies among four people.

Provide the children with paper circles to represent cookies (see Blackline Masters). Ask that they cut the circles, paste each person's share on a sheet of paper, and record how much each person got. Have groups present and explain their solutions.

Extend the investigation by changing the number of cookies they are sharing, by changing the size of the group to six or eight people, or by substituting rectangular "bars" (see Blackline Masters) for the round cookies.

Sharing Brownies

This activity uses grids made of 4-by-4 squares (see Blackline Masters). Using the context of brownies, students figure out different ways to divide the grids into halves, fourths, and eighths. Although these are the same fractional parts the students investigated when they constructed fraction kits, using grids gives them another way to build their understanding.

Begin with halves. On the board or a projected overhead transparency, draw several 4-by-4 grids. Ask students how to divide the grids in half so that two people would each get the same amount of brownie to eat. Students typically suggest the following three ways.

If students don't offer other ways, suggest that they think of ways that don't use one straight cut but that still produce two pieces the same size. Show an example.

Then have students work in pairs or small groups to find as many other ways as they can to divide the brownies into halves. Distribute worksheets of 4-by-4 grids on which they can record their work. In a class discussion, ask students to show their favorite solutions and explain how they know the two parts really are halves.

Repeat for fourths and again for eighths.

To extend the activity, use 6-by-4 grids (see Blackline Masters) and ask students to share these rectangular brownies among 2, 3, 4, 6, and 8 people. This provides experience with halves, thirds, fourths, sixths, and eighths.

Comparing and Ordering Fractions

Learning to compare and order fractions is an important aspect of developing an understanding of fractions. Students must recognize that the size of the denominator affects the size of fractional parts of the same whole—the larger the denominator, the smaller the pieces. Students must also be able to determine when fractions are equivalent—that two-fourth, for example, represents the same part of a whole as does three-sixth, four-eighth, and so on.

Put in Order

Write twelve fractions (see below) on 4-by-6-inch index cards, one per card, large enough for everyone to see. Prop one card on the chalkboard tray. Tell the students that their task is to place the rest of the fractions in order from smallest to largest. Then show the cards one at a time, each time asking a student to place it. Students should also explain their reasoning.

Put in Order is an appropriate follow-up to the fraction kit activities after students have made kits and have played *Cover Up* (page 271) and *Uncover* (page 272). It's helpful for students to use their fraction kits when first encountering *Put in Order* to help them reason. The following set of fractions works well for a first lesson with this activity. Begin by propping on the chalkboard tray the card with $\frac{1}{2}$ on it, giving students a familiar landmark fraction to use.

$$\frac{1}{16}, \frac{1}{8}, \frac{3}{16}, \frac{1}{4}, \frac{3}{8}, \frac{1}{2}, \frac{5}{8}, \frac{3}{4}, \frac{15}{16}, \frac{1}{1}, \frac{9}{8}, \frac{3}{2}$$

Repeat the activity with different sets of fractions or using previous sets but presenting the fractions in a different order. When making sets of cards, avoid including equivalent fractions so students don't try to order two fractions that have the same value.

$$\frac{1}{8}, \frac{1}{6}, \frac{1}{4}, \frac{1}{3}, \frac{1}{2}, \frac{2}{3}, \frac{3}{4}, \frac{15}{16}, \frac{8}{8}, \frac{17}{16}, \frac{7}{6}, \frac{4}{3}$$
$$\frac{1}{16}, \frac{1}{12}, \frac{2}{8}, \frac{3}{8}, \frac{3}{6}, \frac{3}{4}, \frac{7}{8}, \frac{11}{12}, \frac{3}{3}, \frac{17}{16}, \frac{9}{8}, \frac{5}{4}$$

After the class is familiar with the activity, have students work in pairs or small groups to create sets of fractions to present to the class. Have them first justify in writing the order of their fractions; after you check their reasoning, have them lead the activity for the rest of the class.

Who Ate More?

Build on the experience children have gained through thinking about fractional parts of circles in *Sharing Cookies* (page 275) by having them compare shares of pizza. Vary the problems by changing the number of pieces cut and eaten. Either present the problems to the whole class, or first ask pairs or small groups to consider them before leading a class discussion.

Joey and Roberta each had individual pizzas that were the same size. Joey cut his into four pieces and ate three of them. Roberta cut hers into six pieces and ate four of them. Who ate more pizza?

Mario cut his pizza into eight pieces and ate two of them. Kim cut hers into four pieces and ate one of them. Who ate more pizza?

William cut his pizza into eight pieces and ate five of them. Elissa cut hers into six pieces and ate four of them. Who ate more pizza?

Sara cut her pizza into three pieces and ate one of them. Tomas cut his into eight pieces and ate two of them. Who ate more pizza?

Mental Calculation with Fractions

A great deal of emphasis traditionally has been put on paper-and-pencil algorithms for addition, subtraction, multiplication, and division of fractions. Too much focus is often put on how to do the problem rather than on what makes sense. The following suggestions offer ways to have students calculate mentally with fractions. The emphasis shifts from paper-and-pencil computation with the goal of arriving at exact answers to mental calculation with the goal of arriving at estimates and being able to explain why they're reasonable.

Closest to 0, $\frac{1}{2}$, or 1?

Give students fractions that are less than 1—$\frac{3}{8}$, $\frac{1}{6}$, or $\frac{5}{7}$, for example—and have them decide if the fraction is closest to 0, $\frac{1}{2}$, or 1. Have students discuss in groups and then report back to the class, explaining their reasoning. You may want to give groups a collection of a dozen or so fractions to sort into three groups: closest to 0, closest to $\frac{1}{2}$, and closest to 1. They should record their answers and write about the methods they used to sort their fractions.

Fractions in Contexts

Give students problems for which they are to find estimates mentally. Have students work in groups so they can talk about their ideas. As with all activities, have students defend their answers by explaining their methods.

Finding Fractional Parts. In order to do these problems, students should be able to figure mentally such fractional parts as $\frac{1}{3}$ of 30, $\frac{1}{2}$ of 24, and $\frac{1}{4}$ of 32.

A full tank of gas holds 14 gallons. The fuel gauge reads $\frac{1}{4}$ full. About how many gallons are left? (If you get 20 miles per gallon, how much farther can you drive?)

Jill's mother and aunt together have agreed to split equally $\frac{1}{2}$ of the cost of a baseball glove with Jill. The glove costs $25.99. About how much does Jill need to contribute?

A $7.98 shirt is on sale at $\frac{1}{3}$ off. About how much will Tony save if he buys it?

Have students make up situations such as these for their classmates to solve.

Fraction Word Problems. Have students try the following problems. Be sure to keep the emphasis on reasonable answers and on the different methods they used.

A bookshelf measures $2\frac{1}{2}$ feet. How many could you fit against a wall that measures $14\frac{1}{2}$ feet?

If it takes $1\frac{1}{4}$ yards of fabric to make a cape and each of the six people on the cheering squad needs a cape, how much fabric should you buy?

Then have them try some of their textbook word problems, not to calculate exact answers, but to arrive at acceptable estimates and to be able to explain their reasoning.

Strategies for Operations

Encourage students to invent their own strategies for mentally estimating sums and differences. You may want to present a sample strategy to the class. For example, estimating whether fractions are close to 0, $\frac{1}{2}$, or 1 can help in estimating sums. To estimate $\frac{12}{13} + \frac{4}{9}$, you could think $\frac{12}{13}$ is close to 1 and $\frac{4}{9}$ is close to $\frac{1}{2}$, so the sum is about $1\frac{1}{2}$. But it's a little less, since the actual numbers were less than 1 and $\frac{1}{2}$. Try some exercises with the whole class and then give small groups problems to discuss and estimate together.

In the same way, model techniques for estimating products and quotients. For example, to estimate the answer to $2\frac{7}{8} \times 15\frac{3}{4}$, you can say that $2\frac{7}{8}$ is close to 3 and $15\frac{3}{4}$ is close to 16, and 3×16 is 48. So you know the answer is close to but less than 48.

Independent Activities (Menu)

Following are activities that engage students with fractions. Several activities suggest ways to use manipulative materials for investigating fractions. Have students work on the activities in pairs or small groups. Then have whole-class discussions in which students present their findings, the different methods they used, and difficulties they encountered.

Fractions Close to $\frac{1}{2}$

For each situation, decide whether the best estimate is more or less than one-half. Record your conclusions and reasoning.

1. When pitching, Joe struck out 7 of 17 batters.
2. Sally made 8 baskets out of 11 free throws.
3. Bill made 5 field goals out of 9 attempts.
4. Maria couldn't collect at 4 of the 35 homes on her paper route.
5. Diane made 8 hits in 15 times at bat.

Make up three situations and exchange papers with a classmate.

Building Rectangles

You need: color tiles, about 10 of each color
half-inch grid paper, several sheets (see Blackline Masters)
markers or crayons, 1 each of red, yellow, green, and blue

Use tiles to build a rectangle that is $\frac{1}{2}$ red, $\frac{1}{4}$ yellow, and $\frac{1}{4}$ green. Record and label it on grid paper. Find at least one other rectangle that also works. Build and record.

Now use the tiles to build each of the rectangles below. Build and record each in at least two ways.

$\frac{1}{3}$ green, $\frac{2}{3}$ blue
$\frac{1}{6}$ red, $\frac{1}{6}$ green, $\frac{1}{3}$ blue, $\frac{1}{3}$ yellow
$\frac{1}{2}$ red, $\frac{1}{4}$ green, $\frac{1}{8}$ yellow, $\frac{1}{8}$ blue
$\frac{1}{5}$ red, $\frac{4}{5}$ yellow
$\frac{1}{8}$ red, $\frac{3}{8}$ yellow, $\frac{1}{2}$ blue

These rectangles show two solutions for $\frac{3}{4}$ red, $\frac{1}{4}$ yellow.

Fraction Riddles

You need: color tiles, about 10 of each color
half-inch grid paper, several sheets (see Blackline Masters)
markers or crayons, 1 each of red, green, blue, and yellow

(A suggestion: First try the activity *Building Rectangles* on page 280)

Riddle 1: A rectangle is $\frac{1}{2}$ red, $\frac{1}{5}$ green, $\frac{1}{10}$ blue, and the rest yellow. How much of the rectangle is yellow? Draw the rectangle on grid paper and record the fraction that tells which part is yellow.

Riddle 2: A rectangle is $\frac{3}{5}$ red. The rest is blue and yellow but not in equal amounts. What could the rectangle look like? Record.

Riddle 3: A rectangle is $\frac{1}{2}$ red and $\frac{1}{3}$ blue. Also, it has one green tile and one yellow tile. What could the rectangle look like? What fractional part is green? Yellow? Record.

Make up three riddles like these for others to solve.

Rod Relationships

You need: Cuisenaire rods, 1 set

The yellow rod is half as long as the orange rod. (Prove this to yourself with the rods.) This relationship can be written:

$$\tfrac{1}{2}\,o = y$$

Find all the other pairs of halves you can with the rods and build them. Record each.

Then do the same with thirds. For example, it takes three light green rods to make a train as long as the blue rod, so light green is one-third of blue. (Prove it with the rods.) Record like this:

$$\tfrac{1}{3}\,e = g$$

Find all the fractional relationships you can for halves, thirds, fourths, fifths, and so on, up to tenths. Explain why you think you've found them all.

Build the Yellow Hexagon

You need: pattern blocks, 1 set

Find all the different ways you can build the yellow hexagon from different assortments of blocks. Count only different combinations of blocks. For example, if you use two blues and two greens, that combination counts as only one way even if the arrangements look different.

These count as one way.

Use fractions to record the different ways you found. For example, the green triangle is $\frac{1}{6}$ of the hexagon and the red trapezoid is $\frac{1}{2}$ of the hexagon. Therefore, if you build the hexagon using one red and three greens, you can record as follows: $\frac{1}{2} + \frac{1}{6} + \frac{1}{6} + \frac{1}{6} = 1$. Also, you can shorten that by combining the three greens into one fraction: $\frac{1}{2} + \frac{3}{6} = 1$. Record each of the ways you built the yellow hexagon, recording each in different ways.

Wipeout

You need: a partner
                pattern blocks, 1 set
                cube with faces marked $\frac{1}{2}, \frac{1}{3}, \frac{1}{3}, \frac{1}{6}, \frac{1}{6}, \frac{1}{6}$

This is a two-person game. The goal is to be the first to discard your blocks. You each should start with the same number of hexagons, either one, two, or three. Follow these rules:

1. Take turns rolling the cube.
2. You have three options on each turn: to remove a block (only if it's the fractional part of the hexagon indicated by the fraction faceup on the cube), to exchange any of your remaining blocks for equivalent blocks, or to do nothing and pass the cube to your partner. You may not remove a block and trade on the same turn; you can do only one or the other.

Be sure to pay attention to each other's trades to make sure they are done correctly.

Assessing Understanding of Fractions

Observing Students

During class discussions and when students are working on the independent tasks, circulate, observe, and question them about their thinking and reasoning.

Individual Assessments

The following written assignments offer ways to find out about children's understanding of fractions.

1. Before beginning instruction, ask students to write what they know about fractions. Have them do this again at the end of the instructional unit or even midway through. Return papers to the students and ask them to reflect on their learning.
2. Assign problems such as those suggested for whole-class lessons. Ask students to present solutions in writing and explain their reasoning.
3. Ask the students to draw pictures to show the following fractional parts:

   a. $\frac{2}{5}$ of a set of circles are shaded

   b. $\frac{4}{5}$ of the squares are red

   c. $\frac{3}{4}$ of the triangles are blue

   d. $\frac{1}{3}$ of the balls are footballs

   e. $\frac{4}{9}$ of the fruit are apples

4. Show students a pattern block design made with three green triangles, six blue parallelograms, three red trapezoids, and one yellow hexagon (see right).

   Ask students to respond in writing to the problem: *What fraction of the design is blue?* (Caldwell 1995).
5. On the 1982 National Assessment of Educational Progress (NAEP), thirteen-year-olds were given the following item: *Estimate the answer to $\frac{12}{13} + \frac{7}{8}$.*

   a. *1*

   b. *2*

   c. *19*

   d. *21*

Only 24 percent of the students answered correctly, with approximately equal numbers of students choosing each of the wrong answers. (Can you explain to yourself what the thinking was behind each of the erroneous choices?) See how your students respond to this question.

Decimals

Overview

Decimals make it possible to use our place-value system of notation to write fractions, as long as they are expressed as tenths of a unit, hundredths, thousandths, and so on. The activities in this section assume that children have learned about fractions and have a base of understanding that can be expanded to incorporate the symbolism of decimals. They suggest ways to connect students' former experiences to the new notation.

When students are learning about decimals, it's helpful to distinguish between the way decimals are commonly read and what they mean. It's natural to read decimals such as 2.7 and 0.34, for example, as "two point seven" and "point thirty-four." However, students should know that these decimals can also be read as "two and seven-tenths" and "thirty-four-hundredths," and they should be able to relate decimal fractions to common fractions. Paying attention to this difference reinforces the fact that decimals are fractions written in different symbolic notation.

The lessons in this section suggest several ways to introduce students to decimal numerals and to help them discover how decimals relate to our number system. The emphasis is on helping students make sense of decimals in several different ways and building a foundation of understanding from which students later can learn about repeating decimals, scientific notation, and other related topics.

Whole-Class Lessons

Investigations with Calculators

The calculator is a useful tool for helping students learn about decimals. Following are several suggestions for using calculators to introduce decimals. Encourage students to make discoveries and to draw conclusions from their investigations.

Using Division Problems to Introduce Decimals

Give students a division problem such as the following: *The library had extra copies of 50 books. The librarian decided to divide the books equally among the 12 classrooms in the school. How many books would each class get?* Have students talk about this in small groups and then present their solutions to the class.

Then ask what answer they think they'd get if they did this problem on a calculator. Have them try it. They'll probably get an answer such as 4.1666666 or 4.1666667, depending on the particular calculator they use. Tell them that this number is called a decimal numeral and is the calculator's way to represent a number that is greater than 4 but less than 5. Have the students try other divisions and compare the answers they figure themselves with the answers they get when they use a calculator. Have them report what they discover about decimal numerals.

Relating Fractional Remainders as Decimals

For another experience with division, give the children problems for which they can use fractions to express the remainders. For example, when sharing 7 cookies between two children, there is one extra cookie. Most children solve the problem by suggesting that each child get an additional half, giving them each $3\frac{1}{2}$ cookies. Give the students other such sharing problems that have remainders and ask them to represent the remainders as fractions. The following are examples.

> *Share seven cookies among three children. How much does each child get?*
> *Divide nine apples between two people. How much does each person get?*
> *Share five brownies among four children. How much does each child get?*
> *Share seven brownies among four children. How much does each child get?*
> *Divide a whole pie among ten people. How much does each person get?*

After you've discussed the answers to these problems with the children, return to the first problem of sharing seven cookies between two children. Ask the students what answer they think they would get if they did this problem on a calculator. Then have them do it. As in the previous activity, tell them that 3.5 is how the calculator represents a number that is greater than 3 but less than 4, that it means the same as $3\frac{1}{2}$, and that it's called a decimal numeral. Have the students use calculators to solve the other problems. Then ask them to make up additional problems to solve mentally, finding fractional remainders, and then solving with a calculator. Have them record discoveries they make about decimals.

A Geometric Perspective on Decimals

Some students benefit from being able to visualize decimals. A 10-by-10 grid is useful for helping students see the relationship between decimals and common fractions and make sense out of operating with decimals. For these activities, students need 10-by-10 grids (see Blackline Masters) and markers or crayons.

Decimals on Grids

Introduce decimal notation by beginning with tenths. On the board or overhead, draw several 10-by-10 grids. Talk with the students about the grids—the number of rows, columns, and small squares. Although it may seem obvious to you that there are ten rows, ten columns, and one hundred small squares, this may not be obvious to the students.

On one grid, shade three columns of squares. Ask: "What fractional part of the grid have I shaded?" Students may respond with three-tenths or thirty-hundredths. Record the fractions and have the students explain why those fractions make sense. If they suggest only one possibility, then record the other and have them discuss why this also makes sense. Then show the class how to record these fractions as decimals: 0.3 and 0.30. Talk about the differences between these two numerals.

Now do another example. Shade just three small squares and again ask: "What fractional part of the grid have I shaded?" As before, record the common fraction, $\frac{3}{100}$, and the decimal fraction, *0.03*. Choosing this example gives you the opportunity to discuss the importance of the placement of the digits.

Continue by shading other amounts. For example, shade two columns of ten squares and seven additional squares on the next column. Have students explain why $\frac{27}{100}$ makes sense and show them how to write it as a decimal. Also point out that this could be written as $\frac{2}{10} + \frac{7}{100}$. Ask students to discuss why this makes sense. Write both representations as decimals: *0.27* and *0.2 + 0.07*.

When you feel they are ready, give students blank 10-by-10 grids and have them make up their own problems. They should shade any amount they like and record. In these investigations, encourage students to be flexible and to look for all the different ways to record symbolically the portion of the grid they shade.

It's useful to relate the decimal notation you've presented to our system for recording money. Ask them to think of the 10-by-10 grid as $1.00; relate pennies to hundredths and dimes to tenths. Compare notations to see how they are alike and different. For example, on a grid, 0.14 can be described as one column and four extra squares or as fourteen squares; similarly with money, $0.14 can be one dime and four pennies or fourteen pennies. However, while three columns on a grid can be represented as 0.3, three dimes isn't written as $0.3, but as $0.30. These are social conventions that students must learn.

The following are suggestions for extensions.

- Introduce how to write mixed numerals in the same way. For example, use three grids to show $2\frac{3}{10}$, or 2.3.

- Have students use the grids to compare decimal numerals. When they focus on the visual representations of decimals, they are less apt to mistakenly interpret that 0.52, for example, is more than 0.6. Also, coloring on grids helps reinforce that decimals such as 0.4 and 0.40 are equivalent.

    Give students pairs of decimal numerals to compare, or several to put in order, such as 0.15, 0.2, 0.46, and 0.3.
- Talk with students about how to use decimal numerals to represent common fractions that are not expressed as tenths or hundredths. Because of students' familiarity with money, begin with one-fourth, one-half, and three-fourth.
- Introduce students to using rectangular arrays to multiply tenths by tenths. It may be necessary to review how arrays model multiplication of whole numbers.

$$3 \times 4 = 12$$

Below are two examples of using grids to multiply decimals. Examples such as these may help students see why multiplying tenths by tenths produces hundredths.

$$.5 \times .7 = .35 \qquad 1.3 \times .5 = .65$$

Mental Calculation with Decimals

A great deal of emphasis traditionally has been put on paper-and-pencil algorithms for addition, subtraction, multiplication, and division of decimals. The focus is often put on how to do the problem rather than on what makes sense. The following suggestions offer ways to have students calculate mentally with decimals. The emphasis shifts from paper-and-pencil computation with the goal of exact answers to mental calculation with the goal of arriving at estimates and being able to explain why they're reasonable.

Closest to 0, 0.5, or 1?

Give students decimal numerals that are less than 1—0.4, 0.15, or 0.7, for example—and have them decide if they are closest to 0, 0.5, or 1. Have students discuss these in groups and then report back to the class, explaining their reasoning. Include decimals with tenths, hundredths, and, if the students are able, thousandths.

Decimals in Contexts

Give students problems for which they are to find estimates mentally. Have students work in groups so they can talk about their ideas. As in all activities, have students defend their answers by explaining their methods.

Jenny started jogging. Her dad clocked her distances by car. On Monday, she ran 1.5 miles; on Tuesday, she ran 2.1 miles. How many miles did she run in the two days?

Raul bought three small bags of potato chips that cost $0.69 each. How much did they cost altogether?

Maria had $4.65 in nickels. How many nickels did she have?

Then have students try some of their textbook word problems, not to calculate exact answers, but to arrive at acceptable estimates and be able to explain their reasoning. Have them check their estimates with calculators.

Strategies for Operations

Encourage students to invent their own strategies for mentally calculating. You may want to present a sample strategy to the class for estimating products and quotients. For example, to estimate the answer to 3.24×4.9, you can say that 3.24 is close to 3 and 4.9 is close to 5, and 3×5 is 15. Then you can decide if the answer will be greater than or less than 15. Try some exercises with the whole class and then give small groups some problems to discuss and estimate together. After students make estimates, they can check with a calculator to see how close they were.

Independent Activities (Menu)

Following are activities in which students use decimals. They suggest additional ways for students to continue exploring decimal numerals.

Decimals in the Newspaper

You need: newspaper

Look for articles in which decimals are used. Choose one to present to the class. In your presentation, explain the meaning of the decimals.

Multiplication Puzzlers

You need: calculator

For each problem shown on the right, find the missing number by using your calculator and the problem-solving strategy of guessing and checking. Don't solve the problems by dividing, but instead see how many guesses each takes you. Record all of your guesses as shown.

    For example, to solve 4 × _____ = 87, you might start with 23 and then adjust. Below is a possible solution that shows how you are to record.

    Try the following:

    5 × _____ = 96
    6 × _____ = 106
    4 × _____ = 63
    8 × _____ = 98

$4 \times \underline{} = 87$

$4 \times 23 = 92$
$4 \times 22 = 88$
$4 \times 21 = 84$
$4 \times 21.5 = 86$
$4 \times 21.6 = 86.4$
$4 \times 21.7 = 86.8$
$4 \times 21.8 = 87.2$
$4 \times 21.74 = 86.96$
$4 \times 21.75 = 87$ ★
It took 9 guesses

Adding to 1

You need: calculator

Enter a number. Press the + key and then press the = key. (You should see the same number you entered.) However, if you continue to press the = key, each time the calculator will add the same number you entered over and over.

Your task is to find numbers to enter so that by following this procedure of pressing the + key and then pressing the = key over and over, the display will eventually show a total of 1. For example, enter .5 and then press the + key, followed by pressing the = key twice. The total is 1. You can record this: *.5 + .5 = 1.*

Find as many different ways as you can to repeat the same addends and get a total of 1. Record each.

The Place-Value Game

You need: a partner or small group
1–6 die or 0–9 spinner

The goal of this game is to make the largest number possible. Each player should draw a game board as shown:

— — — . — —

Players take turns rolling the die or spinning the spinner. Each time a number comes up, every player writes it in one space on his or her game board. Once written, the number cannot be moved. Whoever has the largest number and is able to read it is the winner.

Assessing Understanding of Decimals

Observing Students

During class discussions and when students are working on the independent tasks, circulate, observe, and, at times, question them about their thinking and reasoning. Look and listen for evidence of students' understanding of decimals and their relation to fractions.

Individual Assessments

The following written assignments suggest ways to find out about students' understanding of decimals.

1. Before beginning instruction, ask students to write what they know about decimals. Have them do this again at the end of the instructional unit or even midway through. Return papers to the students and ask them to reflect on their learning.
2. Ask students to write about the ways our systems for decimals and money are alike and different. Ask them to include examples.
3. Assign problems such as those suggested for whole-class lessons. Ask students to present solutions in writing and to explain their reasoning.

Percents

Overview

Students have many experiences with percents before they study them formally in school. They know that a 50 percent sale means that prices are cut in half and that a 10 percent sale doesn't give as much savings. They understand what it means to earn a 90 percent grade on a test. They hear on TV that some tires get 40 percent more wear, that a tennis player gets 64 percent of her first serves in, that there is a 70 percent chance of rain tomorrow. Common to these sorts of experiences is that percents are presented in the context of situations that occur in students' daily lives.

The goal for instruction in percents should be to help students learn to use percents appropriately and effectively in problem situations. This means that, when given a situation that involves percents, students should be able to reason mathematically to arrive at an answer, to explain why that answer is reasonable, and to make a decision about the situation based on the answer.

The activities presented in this section are designed to build on what students already know and to help them extend their understanding of how to reason with percents. The ideas do not provide a comprehensive guide for teaching percents. Rather, they offer models of ways to introduce ideas about percents, suggest problem situations that engage students, and give alternative methods for assessing what students understand.

Whole-Class Lessons

Introducing Percents in Contexts

It makes sense for formal lessons on percents to build on what students already know. Instructional activities should expand students' knowledge from their daily life experiences into more general understanding.

Sense or Nonsense?

Students are to decide whether the statements are reasonable and why. You can discuss each of the statements in a whole-class discussion or have small groups of students discuss and write about them and then present their explanations to the class. For another class activity or for homework, have students write additional statements like these and use them for further class discussions.

1. Mr. Bragg says he is right 100% of the time. Do you think Mr. Bragg is bragging? Why?
2. The Todd family ate out last Saturday. The bill was $36.00. Would a 50% tip be too much to leave? Why?
3. Joe loaned Jeff a dollar. He said the interest would be 75% a day. Is this a pretty good deal for Joe? Why?
4. Cindy spends 100% of her allowance on candy. Do you think this is sensible? Why?
5. The Never Miss basketball team members made 10% of the baskets they tried. Do you think they should change their name? Why?
6. Sarah missed 10 problems on the science test. Do you think her percent is high enough for her to earn an A? Why?
7. Rosa has a paper route. She gets to keep 25% of whatever she collects. Do you think this is a good deal? Why?
8. The weather reporter said, "There's a one hundred percent chance of rain for tomorrow." Is this a reasonable prediction for this month? Why?
9. Ms. Green was complaining, "Prices have gone up at least two hundred percent this past year." Do you think she is exaggerating? Why?
10. A store advertised, "Best sale ever, 10% discount on all items." Is this a good sale? Why?

The Harper's Index Problem

As a regular feature, *Harper's Magazine* includes Harper's Index, a listing of statistical information about a variety of world issues (see *www.harpers.org/ HarpersIndex.html*). An item in the October 1989 magazine read: "Percentage of supermarket prices that end in the digit 9 or 5: 80%."

Use this statement for a class investigation in which students collect and analyze data in order to test its validity. Ask students to bring supermarket receipts to class. In small groups, have students examine their receipts to see whether they support the statement. Ask groups to write a report about their investigation that includes the following:

data (shown in a neat and organized manner)
calculations (with an explanation about why the procedures they used make sense)
conclusion (explained clearly and concisely)

Have groups present their findings. **Note:** Students in one class raised the issue that while fruit, vegetables, and meat might have prices per pound that end in nine or five, the cost on the receipt won't necessarily reflect this for different amounts purchased. Therefore, they did a second study of their data in which they eliminated items in this category. The discussion about this gave the students experience with the kinds of difficulties that arise in real-life statistical investigations.

A Geometric Perspective on Percents

This activity presents students with a spatial model for thinking about percents. It introduces students to the idea that percents are parts of one hundred and gives them the opportunity to estimate areas and to express their estimates in terms of percents.

What Percent Is Shaded?

Make transparencies of the sheet of 10-by-10 grids (see Blackline Masters) and cut them apart so each student has one grid. Also, prepare a sheet of shapes such as the ones shown below.

Before distributing any of the materials, do several sample problems with the class. Draw a square on the board and shade part of it. Ask the students to estimate the percent of the square that is shaded. Have them

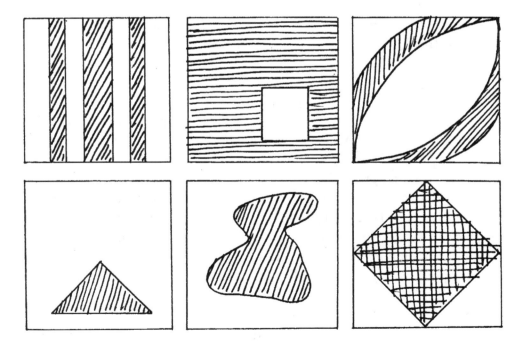

discuss this in small groups and then report their estimates and explain their reasoning. Do this for several shapes. Shade regions for which a range of responses is reasonable so that the emphasis is on students' reasoning, not on finding an exact answer that can be proved right or wrong.

Show students one of the transparent 10-by-10 grids. Ask them to discuss among themselves how to use the grid to estimate what percent of a square is shaded. It's important to introduce students to the idea that percent means "part of one hundred." Since there are one hundred small squares on the grid, the number of small squares that are shaded tells what percent of the grid has been shaded.

When you feel that students understand the task, distribute a worksheet of shapes and the transparent grids. Ask them to estimate the percent of each square that is shaded and use their transparent grids to check their estimates. Have students do this individually and then compare their answers in small groups. Have a class discussion about any they couldn't resolve.

Have students make up shapes for others to try. Having them put their shapes on index cards is an easy way to create a class set of problems.

Using Graphs to Build Understanding of Percents

The questions that follow are ideas to be used for class graphs. The graphs suggested have been chosen so that students can compare the statistical result of their class samples with the percentages reported for the population at large. Use the graphs to initiate discussions about percents. For each, ask the following types of questions:

How many students indicated _____?
Is this more or less than fifty percent?
About what percent of our class reported _____?
How did you figure that percent?
The national statistic is _____. How does our class sample compare with this national statistic?

The following statistics are from *American Averages*, by Mike Feinsilber and William B. Mead (1980).

1. Do you bite your fingernails? (Between 25 percent and 36 percent of college students do.)
2. How many hours a day do you sleep? (Sixty-three percent of adults sleep between seven and eight hours a day.)
3. Do you get a regular allowance? (Fifty percent of twelve- to seventeen-year-olds do.)

4. Do you view smoking as a sign of weakness? (Seventy-five percent of Americans do.)

5. Are you wearing athletic shoes or sneakers? (Twenty-five percent of shoes worn by Americans are athletic shoes or sneakers.)

6. Which do you generally take, a shower or a bath? (Fifty-nine percent of teenage girls and seventy-eight percent of teenage boys take showers rather than baths.)

7. What is your favorite animal? (Nine percent of children report that the horse is their favorite animal.)

8. What animals live in your home? (Thirty-three percent of U.S. households have a dog; 12.5 percent have a cat; 10 percent have both.)

9. Do fish live in your household? (Just 6.2 percent of households have fish.)

10. Have you ever taken piano lessons? (Forty percent of American children take piano lessons at some time or another.)

11. How many TVs are there in your home? (Fifty percent of households have two or more TVs.)

12. Which soft drink would you order: Coke, Pepsi, Dr. Pepper, 7-Up, other? (Twenty-six percent of Americans order Coke; 17 percent order Pepsi; the rest order something else when ordering a soft drink.)

13. Is there a child in your family under the age of six? (Twenty-five percent of American families have at least one child under the age of six.)

14. Is there a dishwasher in your home? (There are dishwashers in 40.9 percent of homes.)

15. How are the dishes done in your home most often: by hand or by a dishwasher? (In 58 percent of American homes, dishes are done by hand.)

16. Are you right- or left-handed? (Twelve percent of Americans are left-handed.)

Mental Calculation with Percents

It's useful for students to learn to calculate mentally with percents and to find strategies for doing so that make sense to them. Initiate a discussion about this by asking the students: "What is fifty percent of one hundred dollars?" Have volunteers respond, and ask each to explain how he or she knows that $50 is the correct answer. It's important for students to know that you value their thinking, not just their right answers. Don't stop after just one student's explanation, but have others also explain their reasoning.

Then ask: "What is twenty-five percent of one hundred dollars?" Again, have students give answers and explain their reasoning. Typically, fewer students are sure about this problem. If no one can explain, offer several ways for them to think about it: that 25 percent is half of 50 percent, so the answer is half of $50.00, that there are four $0.25 in $1.00 and similarly there are four $25.00 in $100.00, that 25 percent is one-fourth of 100 percent and one-fourth of $100.00 is $25.00.

Continue the same sort of discussion for 10 percent, 5 percent, and 1 percent. Then write the following on the board:

100% of $200 is _____.   *10% of $200 is* _____.
50% of $200 is _____.   *5% of $200 is* _____.
25% of $200 is _____.   *1% of $200 is* _____.

Have students work in small groups to find the answers. Then have a class discussion in which they present their answers and reasoning.

Give the students other problems to solve by changing the $200 to another number: $500, $300, or $75, for example. Also, give the students problems such as the following:

Financing a loan costs approximately 11% a year. About what is the interest charge for a $400 loan?

A poll reported that 97.6% of a town's voters support the mayor. The voter population of the town is 12,500. About how many voters support the mayor?

If dinner in a restaurant costs $37.90, how much is a 15% tip?

Independent Activities (Menu)

Have students work on independent activities in pairs or small groups. Then have whole-class discussions in which students present their findings, the different methods they used, and the difficulties they encountered.

Percents in the Newspaper

You need: newspaper

Look for articles (not advertisements) in which percents are used. Choose one to present to the class. In your presentation, explain the meaning of the percents.

Figuring Tips in Restaurants

Read the following story.

Four people went to a restaurant for pizza. They ordered two medium pizzas: one pepperoni and one plain. They each ordered a soft drink. The waitress brought their drinks right away, which was good since they were all thirsty. The pizzas were ready soon afterward, and she brought them right over, with a stack of extra napkins for them to use. The bill was $18.90 without tax.

Answer two questions:

1. What percent tip would you give?
2. How much money would you leave?

Explain your reasoning for each.

Write a restaurant story for others to solve.

Comparing Advertisements

You need: assortment of magazines or newspaper supplements that contain advertisements

Clip four advertisements that offer discounts for items and paste them on a sheet of paper. Include one that indicates the percent the customer will save, one that gives the sale price, and two of your choice. Decide which of the advertisements gives the customer the best deal. Record your decision on the back, including an explanation of your reasoning.

Trade with other groups and decide on the best deal for the advertisements they clipped. Compare your decisions.

The Photocopy Problem

You need: copies of a cartoon or drawing, including 1 full-size copy, 3 reductions, and 2 enlargements

Figure what percent was used for each reduction and enlargement. Record your solutions and explain the procedures you used.

The Discount Coupon

You need: discount hamburger coupon

About what percent discount do you get with this coupon? Show your work and explain why your method and answer make sense.

Find one or two other coupons or advertisements that could be used for the same sort of investigation. Figure the percent discount for each of them.

Try the investigation for coupons other students have found.

Block Letters

You need: 10-by-10 grids, 1 sheet (see Blackline Masters)

Make block letters on 10-by-10 grids, trying to make each one so it covers as close to 50 percent of the grid as possible.

The Warehouse Problem

For the following problem, explain your thinking and show all the work that helps make your explanation clear.

A warehouse gives a 20% discount on all items, but you also must pay 6% in sales tax. Which would you prefer to have calculated first—the discount or the tax? Does it matter?

Percent Stories

Write a percent story problem that follows two rules:

1. It must end in a question.
2. The question must require that percents be used to answer it.

On a separate paper, solve your problem. Show your work and include an explanation of why your method makes sense.
Exchange papers and solve each other's problems.

Assessing Understanding of Percents

Observing Students

During class discussions and when students are working on the independent tasks, circulate, observe, and, at times, question them about their thinking and reasoning. Look and listen for evidence of students' ability to calculate with percents and relate percents to contextual situations.

Individual Assessments

The following written assignments offer ways to find out about students' understanding of percents.

1. Before beginning instruction, ask students to write what they know about percents. Have them do this again at the end of the instructional unit or even midway through. Return papers to the students and ask them to reflect on their learning.
2. Assign problems such as those suggested for whole-class lessons. Ask students to present solutions in writing and to explain their reasoning.

Mathematical Discussions

Introduction

This section addresses the mathematics underlying some of the problems presented in this book. The problems included here were chosen for a variety of reasons—the topics involved, the problem-solving approaches used, the skills required, the connections offered to other ideas and activities, or the amount of mail we've received from teachers asking for help with them. Whatever the reason, all the problems selected are vehicles for delving more deeply into ideas that are important to K–8 mathematics.

Since you can't teach what you don't understand, this section offers those of you who have limited mathematics backgrounds a chance to learn more about some specific areas of mathematics and, in general, about thinking mathematically. And those of you with more mathematical experience will find either that the explanations confirm your own way of thinking or offer other approaches to solving some of the problems.

There are dangers in offering answers and explanations: answers often put an end to thinking, and other people's explanations can be hard to follow. However, there is even more danger in not understanding, especially as we work to help children become mathematically proficient. The purpose of these explanations is to model one way to think about the mathematics in the problems and, by so doing, make the mathematics more accessible. In the spirit that answers without understanding do not serve learning, the answers included are offered as checkpoints for your own learning.

To benefit from these explanations, merely reading them isn't enough. You have to think about the ideas and make sense of them for yourself. It may help to write or make sketches as you read to keep track of your reasoning or explore a new idea. You might read a paragraph or two and then go back and try to solve the problem on your own. Or you might work with a friend or small group on a particular challenge.

It's important to remember that we all learn in individual ways and on our own timetable. All of us have math problems we haven't yet solved and ideas we haven't yet learned. The goal is to stay involved as learners of mathematics. Doing so will make us all better mathematics teachers.

Measurement Problems

Squaring Up [page 79]

I was mathematically flabbergasted the first time I encountered this problem. Following the directions of the *Foot Area and Perimeter* activity (see page 78), I traced my foot and figured its area by counting the whole centimeter squares and approximating areas of the partial squares. I also carefully cut a piece of string equal in length to the perimeter.

When I formed the perimeter string into a square, I thought, This a much more efficient way to figure the area of my foot than dealing with all those bits and pieces of centimeter squares. But I was shocked when I found that the area of the square was so far off from the area I'd calculated earlier. Whoa, I thought, what did I do wrong? Why is the area of the square so much more than the area of my foot? I recalculated the areas of my foot outline and of the square. The difference was still substantial.

The best way to describe myself at this time is that I was experiencing *disequilibrium*. (Read pages 27–32 to learn about disequilibrium.) I was confused because I believed that two shapes with the same-length perimeter should have the same area, but my measurements contradicted this belief.

It turned out that my belief was wrong. I learned this from immersing myself in other investigations. I did *The Perimeter Stays the Same*, on page 80. I experimented with my perimeter string, first shaping it into a pencil-shaped rectangle, long and skinny. It had hardly any space inside at all, so its area was much less than the area of the square and of my foot. But when I shaped the string into a rectangle with more footlike dimensions, the area was closer to the area of my foot. My understanding shifted. I no longer erroneously believed that shapes with the same-length perimeter had to have the same area. But don't just take my word for it. There's no substitute for firsthand experience, so try some investigations for yourself.

About the *Giant Foot* extension: The problem doesn't specify whether the giant foot should be twice the area of yours or a foot that's twice as long and twice as wide as yours. The wording is intentionally vague, providing another opportunity to think about area and perimeter in relationship to each other. Enlarging a foot so that it's twice as long and twice as wide as yours gives it an area that's much more than twice as large! Making it just twice as long doubles the area, but makes for a very long, thin foot. The challenge is to make a foot that is the correct shape with an area twice as large.

It's a bit tricky. It may help to try to draw a square with twice the area of another and see how the lengths of the sides compare.

Box Measuring [page 81]

To solve this problem, I began by cutting 20-by-20-centimeter squares from centimeter grid paper, cutting squares from the corners, and then folding so that the cornerless squares formed boxes. If you haven't done this, I recommend doing so before reading further. I think it will help make my explanation clearer.

By following the directions and cutting the same-size square from each corner, cutting only on the lines so that the squares you're removing measure a whole number of centimeters on a side, you can make nine different-size boxes. Cutting a 1-by-1-centimeter square from each corner and folding what remains results in a very flat box that measures 18 centimeters by 18 centimeters by 1 centimeter. As pictured on page 81, cutting a 2-by-2-centimeter square from each corner results in a box not quite as flat. The larger the square you cut from each corner, the taller the resulting box.

You can cut squares from each corner up to 9 by 9 centimeters. (If you try cutting 10-by-10-centimeter squares, you wind up with four separate pieces and no box at all!) The nine boxes nest nicely, but merely looking at them isn't sufficient for comparing their volumes. (Students generally figure out from this activity that multiplying the three dimensions of a box gives its volume.)

The following table, which compares the volume of each box with the dimension of the square cut from each corner, shows that cutting a 3-by-3 square from each corner results in the box with the largest volume.

Side of corner square (cm)	Dimensions of box (l × w × h)	Volume of box (cm³)
1	18 × 18 × 1	324
2	16 × 16 × 2	512
3	14 × 14 × 3	588
4	12 × 12 × 4	576
5	10 × 10 × 5	500
6	8 × 8 × 6	384
7	6 × 6 × 7	252
8	4 × 4 × 8	128
9	2 × 2 × 9	36

Suppose, however, that you weren't restricted to cutting squares that measured a whole number of centimeters on a side. (You didn't think this was the end of the problem, did you?) If you cut a 3.5-by-3.5-centimeter square from each corner, for example, the resulting box would be 3.5 centimeters tall and have a 13-by-13-centimeter base. Its volume would be 591.5 cubic centimeters ($13 \times 13 \times 3.5 = 591.5$). This is larger than any of the boxes already cut. You might want to investigate what size square to cut from each corner to get the box of maximum volume.

You might also compare the surface areas of the boxes. Removing squares from each corner reduces the surface area left to form a box, but a box with less surface area can have a greater volume!

Round Things [page 81]

I wish I had been introduced to this activity when I studied circles in elementary school. I remember learning that pi was about 3.14, or $3\frac{1}{7}$. But I don't remember learning that it described a relationship that exists in all circles. If you divide the circumference of any circle by its diameter, the result is pi, or about 3.14, or $3\frac{1}{7}$. Another way to say this is that pi is the ratio of the circumference to the diameter of a circle. Any circle.

Because measurement is never exact, dividing the circumference by the diameter of the circular objects you chose to measure didn't produce identical results, but they should all have been close to one another and to 3.14. If you got an answer that was way off, check your measurements.

Wraparound [page 81]

If you're stumped about how to proceed with this problem of making a measuring tape that when wrapped around a tree or pole or other circular object tells you the diameter of that object, it might help if you first do the *Round Things* activity, on page 81.

Here's an approach that makes sense to me. First, I made a table similar to the one suggested for *Round Things*, with data organized as shown below:

Diameter	Circumference
1	3.14
2	6.28
3	9.42
⋮	⋮

I then marked a tape in intervals of 3.14 inches, but labeled them to match the related diameters; that is, I labeled the 3.14-inch mark *1*, the 6.28-inch mark *2*, and so on. (I could have made it a metric measure by marking off intervals of 3.14 cm each.) Of course, since measurements are never exact, my tape produced only approximations, but they were close approximations.

Double the Circumference [page 83]

If this problem had been called *Double the Perimeter* and asked you to investigate a square instead of a circle, it would have been easier to solve. You wouldn't need to find a square object to trace, but could draw any size square. To make the investigation easy, you could decide that the area of the square you'd draw would be 1 square unit. Then you wouldn't need string to measure its perimeter—its perimeter would be 4 units, 1 unit per side. Doubling the perimeter would be 8 units, and a square with a perimeter of 8 units would have 2 units per side. The area of the larger square would be four times that of the smaller. Halving the original perimeter to 2 units would produce a square that measured $\frac{1}{2}$ unit on a side with an area of $\frac{1}{4}$ square unit.

Trying this for other size squares would show that doubling the perimeter consistently produces a square with an area that is four times as large and halving the perimeter consistently produces a square with an area that is one-fourth as large.

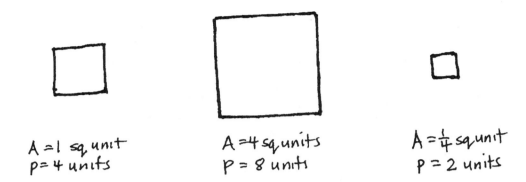

A = 1 sq. unit
p = 4 units

A = 4 sq. units
p = 8 units

A = ¼ sq. unit
p = 2 units

The examples you try may be convincing to you, but they're not enough for an acceptable proof. You also need a convincing argument. Algebra is a useful tool for proving that doubling the perimeter of a square always results in a square with an area that is four times as large. Suppose we call the side of the first square s. Its perimeter is $s + s + s + s$, or $4s$; its area is $s \times s$ or s^2. Doubling the perimeter to $8s$ results in a square with each of its four sides measuring $2s$. The area of this new square is $2s \times 2s$, or $4s^2$. And $4s^2$ is four times greater than s^2, no matter what s measures.

Try using algebra to prove that halving the perimeter produces a square with an area that is one-fourth as large.

What about circles? If you double the circumference of a circle, will the area of the new circle be four times as large? And if you halve it, will the area be one-fourth as large? Yes. As the activity suggests, you can experiment to see that this seems to be so. And you may notice as you investigate that doubling the circumference of a circle doubles its radius. The area of a circle with a radius r is $\pi \times r^2$, or πr^2. For a radius of 3 inches, the area is $\pi \times 3^2$, or $\pi \times 9$, which is about 28.26 square inches. Double the radius to 6 inches and the area is $\pi \times 6^2$, or $\pi \times 36$, which is about 113.04 square inches. And 113.04 is four times as large as 28.26.

The area of a circle with a doubled radius of $2r$ is $\pi \times (2r)^2$, which is $\pi \times (2r \times 2r)$, which is $\pi \times 4r^2$, or $4\pi r^2$. And $4\pi r^2$ is four times as large as πr^2. It's possible to use the same logic to verify that halving a circumference results in a circle with an area one-fourth as large.

A sticky part of this reasoning is to be convinced that doubling the circumference of a circle really does double its radius. The circumference of a circle is equal to π times the diameter. Since the diameter is the radius doubled, the circumference can be thought of as $2\pi r$. Doubling this circumference makes it $4\pi r$. This means that, for the larger circle, $4r$ is its diameter, so the radius is $2r$, which is twice the original radius of r.

If you find this explanation confusing, let this be a reminder about how difficult it can be to follow someone else's reasoning. You have to turn ideas around in your head to make sense of them in your own way. This reasoning works for me, and I've gotten clearer about it as I've worked to get it down in writing. It may help you to talk with a colleague about my thinking or to try writing down your own explanation.

The Area Stays the Same [page 84]

This activity is one of my favorites for several reasons. It's extremely versatile. I've had success with it in third through eighth grades. I like the fact that children create for themselves different-shape figures that all have the same area. I like using the shapes they make to introduce the terminology for polygons—*triangle*, *quadrilateral*, *pentagon*, *hexagon*, and so on. And comparing the perimeters of the figures they make themselves seems to offer convincing evidence to students that shapes with the same area can have different perimeters. *The Perimeter Stays the Same* (page 80) is a wonderful companion activity. (The Math By All Means unit *Area and Perimeter* [Rectanus 1997] uses these and other activities to help students learn about these ideas.)

Probability and Statistics Problems

Shake and Spill [page 101]

In this problem, you investigate what to expect when you shake and spill six two-color counters. Shaking and spilling six counters can result in seven outcomes:

six yellow	⦾ ⦾ ⦾ ⦾ ⦾ ⦾
five yellow, one red	⦾ ⦾ ⦾ ⦾ ⦾ ●
four yellow, two red	⦾ ⦾ ⦾ ⦾ ● ●
three yellow, three red	⦾ ⦾ ⦾ ● ● ●
two yellow, four red	⦾ ⦾ ● ● ● ●
one yellow, five red	⦾ ● ● ● ● ●
six red	● ● ● ● ● ●

Shaking and spilling the six counters twenty-five times typically produces the evidence that these outcomes are not equally likely. Six yellow or six red come up much less frequently than do three yellow and three red, or four of one color and two of the other.

To understand why this is so, it may help to think about what happens when you shake and spill just one counter. For each counter there are two possibilities—red or yellow—and a fifty-fifty chance for either to come up. The two possibilities are equally likely. With six counters, however, and an equal chance for each counter to come up yellow or red, it's rare for all six to come up the same color on the same spill. It's more likely that some of the six counters will come up yellow and some will come up red.

Does this mean that there's a fifty-fifty chance that you'll get three yellow and three red when you shake and spill six counters? No, it's not that simple. If you're interested in learning about figuring the probabilities of three yellow and three red, all red, four yellow and two red, or any of the other possibilities, the discussion under "Shake and Spill Revisited" (page 312) offers an explanation. But first read the following explanation for *Two-Coin Toss*. It will help set the stage for your thinking.

Two-Coin Toss [page 97]

Two-Coin Toss is similar to doing *Shake and Spill* with only two counters. That's because coins and two-color counters both have two equally likely possibilities—heads and tails, or red and yellow. You can say that there's a fifty-fifty chance a coin will come up heads, or that the probability of a coin coming up heads is $\frac{1}{2}$. The same is true for tails.

When tossing two coins, or two two-color counters, there are three possibilities:

two heads	two yellow
one head, one tail	one yellow, one red
two tails	two red

It may seem that each of these possibilities is equally likely, so that there's a $\frac{1}{3}$ chance of getting two of the same or one of each. But that's not so, because there are two different ways that one head and one tail, or one yellow and one red, can come up. To understand this, think about tossing two different coins, a penny and a nickel, for example. For one head and one tail to come up, it either can be heads on the penny and tails on the nickel or vice versa. If you were tossing two pennies, unless they had different dates and you noted them, it wouldn't be obvious that there are two ways for one head and one tail to come up.

So there are *four* equally likely outcomes when tossing two coins:

two heads
heads on Coin 1, tails on Coin 2
tails on Coin 1, heads on Coin 2
two tails

This means that there is a $\frac{1}{4}$ chance that both coins will come up heads, a $\frac{1}{4}$ chance that both will come up tails, and a $\frac{1}{2}$ chance that one will come up heads and the other tails. (Note that the sum of the probabilities of all the equally likely possibilities for tossing two coins—$\frac{1}{4} + \frac{1}{4} + \frac{1}{2}$—adds to 1. The same holds true for tossing only one coin—$\frac{1}{2} + \frac{1}{2}$ adds to 1. The sum of the probabilities of all the equally likely possibilities always adds to 1.)

These probabilities don't imply that if you toss two coins four times, then both heads are sure to come up once, both tails once, and one of each twice. The probabilities are theoretical. They imply, but do not guarantee, that if you toss two coins many times, you can expect them to land with one head and one tail showing about twice as often as landing with two heads showing or two tails showing, and that two heads or two tails should come up about the same number of times.

Shake and Spill [page 101] Revisited

Let's go back to thinking about two-color counters. Shaking and spilling two counters is mathematically the same as tossing two coins—there are four equally likely outcomes. In order for this to make sense, it may help if you thought about labeling the two counters so you could tell one from the other, perhaps by writing a small *1* on both sides of one of them and a small *2* on both sides of the other. The four equally likely outcomes and the probability of each are:

two yellow ($\frac{1}{4}$)
yellow on Counter 1, red on Counter 2 ($\frac{1}{4}$)
red on Counter 1, yellow on Counter 2 ($\frac{1}{4}$)
two red ($\frac{1}{4}$)

Labeling helps you make an accurate count of what really is possible. Without labeling the counters 1 and 2, the two different ways that one of each color would come up would be indistinguishable, but it would still be a more likely possibility:

two yellow ($\frac{1}{4}$)
one yellow, one red ($\frac{2}{4}$, or $\frac{1}{2}$)
two red ($\frac{1}{4}$)

Now let's think about shaking and spilling three counters. Labeling them *1*, *2*, and *3* helps you list all of the equally likely possibilities:

three yellow
yellow on Counters 1 and 2, red on Counter 3
yellow on Counters 1 and 3, red on Counter 2
yellow on Counters 2 and 3, red on Counter 1
yellow on Counter 1, red on Counters 2 and 3
yellow on Counter 2, red on Counters 1 and 3
yellow on Counter 3, red on Counters 1 and 2
three red

There are eight equally likely possibilities, so each has a probability of $\frac{1}{8}$. Ignoring the labels, I could combine the possibilities into four categories, and combine the probabilities:

three yellow ($\frac{1}{8}$)
two yellow, one red ($\frac{3}{8}$)
one yellow, two red ($\frac{3}{8}$)
three red ($\frac{1}{8}$)

Adding the probabilities—$\frac{1}{8} + \frac{3}{8} + \frac{3}{8} + \frac{1}{8}$—produces 1, ensuring that I've taken into account all the possible outcomes.

You can continue in this way to analyze what happens when shaking and spilling four two-color counters, then five, and finally six. Here's how I analyzed the situation for six two-color counters:

six yellow ($\frac{1}{64}$)

five yellow, one red ($\frac{6}{64}$)

four yellow, two red ($\frac{15}{64}$)

three yellow, three red ($\frac{20}{64}$)

two yellow, four red ($\frac{15}{64}$)

one yellow, five red ($\frac{6}{64}$)

six red ($\frac{1}{64}$)

While it's more likely for three of each color to come up than any other possibility, the probability of getting three yellow and three red is $\frac{20}{64}$, which is closer to a probability of $\frac{1}{3}$ than it is to $\frac{1}{2}$.

If you follow my reasoning, congratulations (to both of us)! If not, then you may need more time, more experience, the help of a friend, or another way to look at the situation. We all learn in our own ways and on our own timetables.

One more mathematical connection that may help: Instead of writing lists of the possibilities for shaking and spilling different numbers of counters, I could arrange the possibilities in a way that produces interesting patterns. For two counters, for example, I would arrange the possibilities like this:

YY YR RR
    RY

For three counters, I put those with two yellows and one red in one column, and those with two reds and one yellow in another:

YYY YYR YRR RRR
     YRY RYR
     RYY RRY

For four counters, I would arrange the possibilities like this:

YYYY   YYYR   YYRR   YRRR   RRRR
        YYRY   YRYR   RYRR
        YRYY   YRRY   RRYR
        RYYY   RYRY   RRRY
                RYYR
                RRYY

Now examine the number of entries in each column in relation to the probabilities for the possibilities. For two counters, the probabilities for each of the three columns are $\frac{1}{4}$, $\frac{2}{4}$, and $\frac{1}{4}$. For three counters, the probabilities for the columns are $\frac{1}{8}$, $\frac{3}{8}$, $\frac{3}{8}$, and $\frac{1}{8}$. For four counters, since there are sixteen possibilities altogether, the probabilities for the columns are $\frac{1}{16}$, $\frac{4}{16}$, $\frac{6}{16}$, $\frac{4}{16}$, and $\frac{1}{16}$. (Try it for five counters and see how the pattern extends.)

Now look at Pascal's triangle as shown on page 163:

$$
\begin{array}{ccccccccccc}
 & & & & & 1 & & & & & \\
 & & & & 1 & & 1 & & & & \\
 & & & 1 & & 2 & & 1 & & & \\
 & & 1 & & 3 & & 3 & & 1 & & \\
 & 1 & & 4 & & 6 & & 4 & & 1 & \\
1 & & 5 & & 10 & & 10 & & 5 & & 1
\end{array}
$$

The numbers in this pattern relate to the way I arranged the possibilities above and the numerators of their probabilities! For example, the numbers in the fourth row of Pascal's triangle are the numerators of the combined probabilities for shaking and spilling three counters—$\frac{1}{8}$, $\frac{3}{8}$, $\frac{3}{8}$, $\frac{1}{8}$. For five counters, the numbers are 1, 5, 10, 10, 5, and 1. And if you extend Pascal's triangle, the next row has the numbers 1, 6, 15, 20, 15, 6, and 1—the numerators of the probabilities for shaking and spilling six counters listed earlier. Connections like these help us see how mathematical ideas relate to one another. And while figuring the probabilities generates the numbers in Pascal's triangle, you can also continue the pattern of numbers by adding any two adjacent numbers to get the number underneath. Try to figure out how extending Pascal's triangle can help you think about what happens when you shake and spill more than six counters.

Got a Match? [page 97]

This problem invites you and a partner to spin two identical spinners, predict how often your results will match, and then test your prediction by spinning and recording the matches that come up in twenty-four spins. No specific spinner is suggested, but let's consider the problem with the 1-2-3 spinner shown on page 88. My method for thinking about this spinner can be applied to any other spinner.

One complication with using the 1-2-3 spinner is that it's twice as likely that 3 will come up than either 1 or 2. In order to think about this problem, I need to figure out a way to compare equally likely outcomes. I can do this with the 1-2-3 spinner by imagining that it's divided into four quarters, with the number 3 in two of the quarters. To be clear, I'll label them *3a* and *3b*. This gives four equally likely outcomes from spinning—1, 2, 3, and 3— and is the same as having three outcomes with the 3 twice as likely.

When I spin two spinners, I can get either a match or a nonmatch, and I need to investigate how often each of these options occurs. To do so, I'll make a list of all the possibilities. Here's how I reason.

If a 1 comes up on the first spinner, there are four equally likely possibilities for what will come up on the second spinner—1, 2, 3a, or 3b. This means that a 1 on the first spinner produces either 1-1, 1-2, 1-3a, or 1-3b. This isn't so good for a match—only one out of four possibilities. The same holds true if a 2 comes up on the first spinner—2-1, 2-2, 2-3a, or 2-3b—only one more possible match. This is not looking good for matches. Maybe the 3s will help.

If I spin 3a on the first spinner, then the four possibilities after spinning the second spinner are 3a-1, 3a-2, 3a-3a, 3a-3b. Ah, things are looking up. Since 3a and 3b are the same number, this produces two matches. And the same is true if I spin 3b on the first spinner. There are two matches in the four possibilities—3b-1, 3b-2, 3b-3a, 3b-3b.

I count up the total number of ways the two spinners could match (1-1, 2-2, 3a-3a, 3a-3b, 3b-3a, 3b-3b)—there are six. Then I count up the total ways that the two spinners wouldn't match (1-2, 1-3a, 1-3b, 2-1, 2-3a, 2-3b, 3a-1, 3a-2, 3b-1, 3b-2)—there are ten. Of the sixteen possible ways, there is a $\frac{6}{16}$ chance of getting a match and a $\frac{10}{16}$ chance of not getting a match.

The X-O Problem [page 99]

I found choosing a strategy for this problem perplexing. I first thought about the problem in a certain way, then decided I was wrong, and finally I decided on the strategy that would be most effective. I offer my experience to reinforce the concept that erroneous ideas are often opportunities that lead us to correct thinking.

My first idea was this: There are three cards—one with an X on both sides, one with an O on both sides, and one with an X on one side and an O on the other. OK, that means there are three Xs and three Os altogether. If I draw one card at random and look at what's marked on just one side, I "use up" one of the marks. So if I see an X, what's left are two Xs and three Os. And since there are more Os left, I'll predict that the other side of my card will be an O. I tested my strategy by playing thirty times, as directed in the activity, each time predicting the opposite of the mark that was showing. My prediction was correct less than half of the time. I played another thirty times; the results were about the same. I wasn't satisfied.

I mulled over the situation. I talked with friends. I mulled some more. I was stuck, frustrated, and took a break from thinking about the problem. When I came back to it, I decided to try a different approach, one that had been suggested by several other people. Instead of focusing on the numbers of Xs and Os, one friend suggested, consider that two of the cards have the same mark on both sides—both X or both O—and only one card has a different mark on each side. When you draw one of the cards at random, she told me, there's a $\frac{1}{3}$ chance that you'll draw the card with an X on one side and an O on the other and a $\frac{2}{3}$ chance that you'll draw a card with the same mark on both sides. A probability of $\frac{2}{3}$ is twice as likely as a probability of $\frac{1}{3}$, so predict the mark you see.

I was skeptical, although I could see the logic of her approach. I just couldn't see why it was better than my initial idea. But I decided to try it by predicting, each time I drew, that the same mark I saw would be on the other side, assuming that two-thirds of the time I would draw a card with either X on both sides or O on both sides.

Again, I played thirty times, as directed in the activity, each time predicting the same mark as the one showing. My prediction was correct twenty-three times, more than two-thirds of the draws. I played another thirty times; my prediction was correct eighteen times, less than two-thirds but more than half. Now I was satisfied that if I predicted what I saw I'd do better in the long run. When I compiled my data with the data others collected in their trials, I was even more convinced. Not only did I have a theoretical prediction that made sense, but the prediction was consistently supported by actual data. Case closed.

Some final notes. I thought more about why my initial idea was wrong. I decided that thinking about the Xs and Os as separate entities didn't make sense since they weren't independent of the cards on which they were drawn. My idea would make sense if there were six cards, three marked X and three marked O, but my idea didn't relate to the game in this problem.

Also, I've observed participants in classes choosing strategies different from either of the two I tried. Some have decided to alternate predictions between X and O, not paying attention to what came up first, but sticking to an X, O, X, O pattern. I saw one person toss a coin each time, predicting

X on heads and O on tails. I've observed people predicting randomly, depending on a whim for each draw, feeling that it wouldn't make any difference because it was a game of chance. In these cases, while there were occasional short runs of success, overall results were dismal. Remember, the larger the sample, the more reliable the data to substantiate a prediction or theory.

How Many Throws? and How Many Ways?
(pages 100 and 101)

These two activities offer several ways to think about the probabilities that result from throwing two dice. From experiences they've had playing games with dice, many people learn that when throwing two dice, it's harder to get sums of 12 or 2 than sums of 6, 7, or 8. Also, some learn that in general it's harder to get a sum by rolling a double; for example, it's less likely to get a sum of 8 from throwing two 4s than it is from throwing 5 and 3 or 6 and 2. Experience is an excellent teacher for building our intuition about probabilities. Collecting and analyzing data about throwing two dice as suggested in these activities helped me fully understand the probability involved.

In *How Many Throws?* one of the charts presented is an addition table for adding the numbers one through six to get thirty-six sums. The activity directs you to complete the chart by entering each sum as it comes up from throwing two dice and also to keep track of the number of throws it took to complete the entire chart. An important part of completing the chart is to use dice of different colors (red and white are suggested in the activity) or different sizes so that you can easily distinguish the dice and record sums correctly.

RED

	1	2	3	4	5	6
1	2	3	4	5	6	7
2	3	4	5	6	7	8
3	4	5	6	7	8	9
4	5	6	7	8	9	10
5	6	7	8	9	10	11
6	7	8	9	10	11	12

(WHITE, vertical label on left side)

Take the sum of 4, for example. You can get a sum of 4 by throwing 3 and 1 in two different ways—3 on the first die and 1 on the second die, or 1 on the first die and 3 on the second die. Each of these possibilities is represented by a different location on the addition table. Also, you can get a sum of 4 by rolling 2 on both dice. There's only one way for this to happen—2 on the first die and 2 on the second die—and therefore there's only one place on the chart to enter this sum. For the sum of 4, there are a total of three possible ways, with double

2s being half as likely as getting 3 and 1. Understanding this is the key to understanding the probabilities when throwing two dice.

When you complete the addition table, you've recorded all of the thirty-six equally likely outcomes possible when throwing two dice. Of these sums, you can count and see that the sum of 7 can be made in six different ways—more ways than any other sum, but not much more. The sums of 6 and 8 each come up in five different ways. The sums of 2 and 12 can each come up only one way—either double 1s or double 6s. This is why it's more likely to roll sums of 6, 7, or 8 than 2 or 12. Of course, when throwing dice to complete the chart, you may roll sums of 2 or 12 several times each, but according to probability theory, in a large sample of throws, 2 and 12 will each come up only about one–thirty-sixth of the time, while the sum of 7 will come up six–thirty-sixths of the time.

The probabilities of the sums are

$$P(2) = \frac{1}{36}$$
$$P(3) = \frac{2}{36}$$
$$P(4) = \frac{3}{36}$$
$$P(5) = \frac{4}{36}$$
$$P(6) = \frac{5}{36}$$
$$P(7) = \frac{6}{36}$$
$$P(8) = \frac{5}{36}$$
$$P(9) = \frac{4}{36}$$
$$P(10) = \frac{3}{36}$$
$$P(11) = \frac{2}{36}$$
$$P(12) = \frac{1}{36}$$

While 7 is your best bet when throwing two dice, a probability of $\frac{6}{36}$ means that you have only a $\frac{1}{6}$ chance of throwing a sum of 7. These aren't very good odds, so take care when applying this knowledge.

The chart suggested for *How Many Ways?* is a different way of organizing the same information that appears on the addition table. Some people find it a clearer way to display what happens; others prefer the first way. One of the goals when studying mathematics is to learn to think flexibly, so it's a good exercise to try to make sense of both charts.

Possible Totals	2	3	4	5	6	7	8	9	10	11	12
	1,1	1,2 2,1	1,3 2,2 3,1	1,4 2,3 3,2 4,1	1,5 2,4 3,3 4,2 5,1	1,6 2,5 3,4 4,3 5,2 6,1	2,6 3,5 4,4 5,3 6,2	3,6 4,5 5,4 6,3	4,6 5,5 6,4	5,6 6,5	6,6
Total Ways	1	2	3	4	5	6	5	4	3	2	1

There are other ways of making sense and displaying the information about what happens when you throw two dice. For example, some people reason as follows: Suppose a 1 comes up on the first die. Then there are six possibilities for the second die—1, 2, 3, 4, 5, and 6. This accounts for six possible sums when a 1 comes up on the first die—2, 3, 4, 5, 6, and 7. If 2 comes up on the first die, again there are the same six possibilities for the second die—1, 2, 3, 4, 5, and 6. The possible sums with 2 on the first die are 3, 4, 5, 6, 7, and 8. Continuing in this way will identify the thirty-six possible sums. Below is a way to diagram this way of thinking, often called a *tree diagram*.

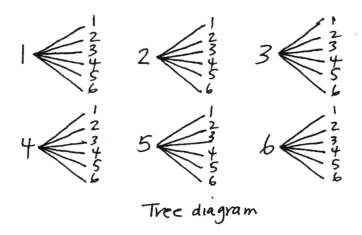

Tree diagram

Fair Game 1 [page 102]

This game of paper, scissors, rock as described is not fair! One way to analyze why is first to account for all of the equally likely possibilities and then see which player has an advantage.

There are three possibilities for what each person shows on a turn—paper, scissors, or rock. A player could show the same sign over and over again, but to analyze the game, you need to think of them as three equally likely random choices.

To analyze the possibilities, I made a list using *p*, *s*, and *r* to stand for paper, scissors, and rock. I also labeled three columns *A*, *B*, and *C* to represent the three players. I listed the following twenty-seven equally likely possibilities (see page 320).

<u>A B C</u>

```
p  p  p  *
p  p  r
p  p  s
p  r  p
p  r  r
p  r  s  !
p  s  p
p  s  r  !
p  s  s
r  p  p
r  p  r
r  p  s  !
r  r  p
r  r  r  *
r  r  s
r  s  p  !
r  s  r
r  s  s
s  p  p
s  p  r  !
s  p  s
s  r  p  !
s  r  r
s  r  s
s  s  p
s  s  r
s  s  s  *
```

In these twenty-seven possibilities, the same sign comes up only three times, a probability of $\frac{3}{27}$. (I marked these with an asterisk.) Two players showing the same sign comes up eighteen times, a probability of $\frac{18}{27}$. All players showing different signs comes up six times, a probability of $\frac{6}{27}$. (I marked these with an exclamation point.) To be sure that I counted correctly, I added the three probabilities—$\frac{3}{27} + \frac{18}{27} + \frac{6}{27}$. The sum is 1, which indicates that I've accounted for all of the possibilities. To make the game fair, you either need to decide on new rules that give each person the same chance of winning or keep the rules as they are and change the number of points each person gets when his option comes up.

Fair Game 2 [page 102]

Two versions of this dice game are suggested. In the first, Player A scores a point if the sum is even and Player B scores a point if the sum is odd. There are eleven possible sums when rolling two dice—2, 3, 4, 5, 6, 7, 8, 9, 10, 11, and 12. Six of these sums are even; five are odd. But that's not enough information for deciding who has the advantage, because the sums aren't equally likely. You need to compare the combined probabilities for the even sums with the combined probabilities for the odd sums. For example, there is a $\frac{1}{36}$ chance of rolling a 2, a $\frac{3}{36}$ chance of rolling a 4, $\frac{5}{36}$ for 6, $\frac{5}{36}$ for 8, $\frac{3}{36}$ for 10, and $\frac{1}{36}$ for 12. Adding these results in a probability of $\frac{18}{36}$ for rolling an even sum. That's the same as $\frac{1}{2}$, leaving $\frac{1}{2}$ for rolling an odd sum. (You can check by adding the probabilities for the odd sums.) So this is a fair game.

Thinking about the products requires collecting new information about dice. I did this by creating a multiplication table instead of the addition table suggested in *How Many Throws?* (page 100). The multiplication table not only reveals the possible products—1, 2, 3, 4, 5, 6, 8, 9, 10, 12, 15, 16, 18, 20, 24, 25, 30, and 36—but lets you count how often each occurs. (Remember, you have to account for all thirty-six possible ways the dice can come up.)

	1	2	3	4	5	6
1	1	2	3	4	5	6
2	2	4	6	8	10	12
3	3	6	9	12	15	18
4	4	8	12	16	20	24
5	5	10	15	20	25	30
6	6	12	18	24	30	36

But before listing and counting all the ways, I began to wonder if there was an easier way to think about the problem. (Mathematicians often—and gladly—spend more time seeking an "easier" way to solve a problem than it would take to do what's obvious but laborious.) I thought about what happens when you multiply even and odd numbers. If you multiply any number by an even number, the product will be even. That means that you get an even product from even × even, even × odd, and odd × even. The only time you get an odd product is when you multiply two odd numbers. So, hey, I'd rather have the even products. Forget the listing and counting of the thirty-six possibilities; I'm satisfied. Are you?

Geometry and Spatial Sense Problems

The Tangram Puzzle [page 111]

Extension 1: Area and Perimeter

This activity offers another way to look at the mathematical ideas in *Squaring Up* (page 79), *Double the Circumference* (page 83), and *The Area Stays the Same* (page 84) from the "Measurement" section. The tangram pieces allow you to think about how area and perimeter relate by comparing shapes instead of resorting to standard units of measurement.

To compare the areas of the square, parallelogram, and middle-size triangle, rearrange the two small triangles to make each of the shapes. The areas of these three shapes are the same. Then match their edges to compare their perimeters. The parallelogram and middle-size triangle have the same-length perimeters, but the perimeter of the square is shorter. This is because the same amount of area is squashed together more compactly in a square, requiring less perimeter. If you rearranged the same area into a long, skinny rectangle, you'd need a longer "fence" to surround it and the perimeter would therefore be longer. If you made a circle of the same area, however, the circle's circumference would be shorter than even the square's perimeter; the circle is the most economical shape for minimizing the distance around.

Extension 3: Using All Seven

This activity asks you to use all seven pieces of the tangram to make different convex shapes. A convex shape is one with all of its interior angles measuring less than 180 degrees. Shapes with at least one interior angle greater than 180 degrees are called concave.

It's easy to spot them—children have told me, "They go in and out," or "They have dents."

The shapes you build with the tangram pieces are all polygons. A polygon is a closed shape (which means it encloses an interior region the way a fence encloses a yard) made of connecting straight line segments. Sometimes a polygon is defined as a "simple closed curve." This seems contradictory, since the sides

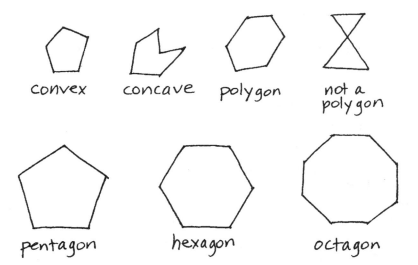

convex   concave   polygon   not a polygon

pentagon   hexagon   octagon

of a polygon are all straight line segments, but the definition has been in common use for quite some time. The "simple" part of the definition is important. It means that the line segments enclose one contiguous interior region; the inside of a polygon can't be divided into smaller regions. One way to think about this is to think of the corners where line segments meet—the vertices—as fenceposts. Only two segments of the fence can touch each fencepost.

The directions for this extension could have asked you to use the seven tangram pieces to investigate convex polygons, instead of convex shapes. It's hard to decide when to use standard mathematical terminology or more common language. A good pedagogical approach is to use both—common language to provide access to an idea and correct terminology to help learners extend their mathematical vocabulary.

One more comment about the convex polygons you search for in this activity. Polygons are categorized by the number of sides they have—triangle, quadrilateral, pentagon, hexagon, heptagon, octagon, and so on. Any shape with four sides—a square, a parallelogram, a rectangle, and so on—is a quadrilateral. When a polygon has all identical sides and angles, it's called a regular polygon. A square is a regular polygon; so is an equilateral triangle. When we see pictures of pentagons, hexagons, and octagons, we typically see pictures of them as regular polygons.

The convex shapes you make in this activity, except for the square, are not regular. The rectangle shown below, for example, was made from the seven tangram pieces, but it isn't a regular quadrilateral because its sides aren't all the same length:

When doing this activity, be sure to name the different polygons you make.

Extension 4: Making Squares

I know it isn't possible to form a square from six tangram pieces. I can't remember where I heard this, but my own experience experimenting with the tangram pieces led me to believe that it is true. However, for a long time I wasn't able to explain why. (It's not enough to assert that I tried really hard to make a square from six pieces and couldn't—a proof calls for a convincing argument.) I was stymied. I don't mean to imply that I spent a lot of waking hours thinking about why I couldn't arrange six tangram pieces into a square. But I remained intrigued by this fact and wondered about it whenever I taught a lesson using the tangram puzzle.

In 1990, I raised this question at the annual retreat I hold with Math Solutions instructors. I formed a panel of four people who had a good deal of mathematical expertise, experience, and confidence but who hadn't yet thought about this particular problem and asked them to think about it together, out loud, while the rest of us observed. My idea was that it would be interesting not only to learn about why a square can't be formed from six tangram pieces but also to have the chance to see mathematical thinkers in action.

So we observed four people rummage for ways to approach the problem. They cut tangram pieces; they moved pieces about; they exchanged ideas; at times, one person would retreat into private thoughts and then reemerge to share discoveries; others would build on these ideas, as interested in how the others thought as they were in their own ideas. The group functioned in the way I want groups of students in the classroom to function.

Because of this experience I finally learned why making a six-piece square isn't possible. I offer my understanding knowing that it's hard to follow someone else's reasoning but hoping that my explanation will be useful to you and, perhaps, get you interested in this problem if you haven't been up to now.

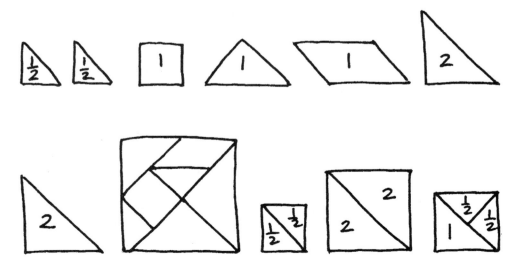

Think about the small square tangram piece as having an area of 1 square unit. As you may have learned from the first extension activity, the parallelogram and middle-size triangle have the same area—also 1 square unit. The two small triangles that together form the square, parallelogram, and middle-size triangle each have an area of $\frac{1}{2}$ square unit. Since the large triangles can be made from a square and two small triangles, they each have an area of 2 square units. Using these values, the square formed by all seven tangram pieces has an area of 8 square units. (Check to make sure you are with me this far; this information will be important a bit later.)

Now think about making a square with 2, 3, 4, 5, 6, and 7 tangram pieces. First, you can make a square with 2 pieces by using the 2 small triangles. This square is the same size as the small square tangram piece and therefore has an area of 1 square unit. And because you can find the area of a square by multiplying the length of a side by itself, it measures 1 unit on a side. If you use the 2 large triangles to make a square, however, each side measures 2 units (it's equal in length to two sides of a square), and its area is 4 square units. (Use your tangram pieces to check that this is so.) This also makes sense because $2 \times 2 = 4$.

What about using three pieces to make a square? The chart on page 111 shows how to use two small triangles and the middle-size triangle to make a square. Its area is 2 square units. Each of its sides is equal in length to the long side of the small triangle—its hypotenuse. This is more than 1 unit but less than 2 units. How much is that, exactly? Although 2 is a small number that's generally easy for computations, in this situation it's easier to figure the length of a side for squares with larger but more cooperative areas. For a square with an area of 49 square units, for example, the sides are 7 units (since $7 \times 7 = 49$). For a square with an area of 64 square units, the sides are 8 units. In these examples, 49 and 64 are square numbers. (Take forty-nine or sixty-four pennies and you could arrange either number into a square array.) And 7 and 8 are the square roots of 49 and 64. We could say that the sides of those two squares are, respectively, $\sqrt{49}$ and the $\sqrt{64}$. Finding the square root of 2 isn't so friendly, so we could use a calculator, pressing 2 and then the square root key (my calculator displays 1.4142135, which makes sense because it's in between 1 and 2). Or we could just say that the side is $\sqrt{2}$ long.

Another way to figure the length of this side is to recall the Pythagorean theorem, which states that for a right triangle (and all of the tangram triangles are right triangles because they all have a right angle), the hypotenuse (the long side) is equal to the square root of the sum of the squares of the other two sides. The theorem is often written as $a^2 + b^2 = c^2$. The illustration of a right triangle with sides that measure 3 and 4 and a hypotenuse that measures 5, and showing the sides squared, may help you see how the Pythagorean theorem makes sense. And the theorem can be a helpful clue for understanding this problem. To use the Pythagorean theorem to figure the length of the hypotenuse of the small tangram triangle, I use the information that the shorter sides are each 1 unit, the same as the length of the side of the small square. The hypotenuse is the square root of $1^2 + 1^2$, which is $\sqrt{2}$. Then I use my calculator as I did earlier to get that messy number of 1.4142135.

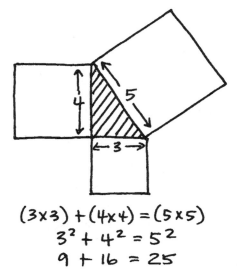

$$(3 \times 3) + (4 \times 4) = (5 \times 5)$$
$$3^2 + 4^2 = 5^2$$
$$9 + 16 = 25$$

Another clue is that if you examine the sides of all the tangram pieces, they either are 1 unit, twice that (2 units), $\sqrt{2}$ units, or twice that ($2\sqrt{2}$ units). (Again, use your tangram pieces to make sense of this information.)

On to making a square with four pieces. Ah, that's possible. First I make a two-piece square using the two large triangles and then I replace one of the triangles with three pieces—the two small triangles and the square. The resulting four-piece square still has an area of 4 square units and measures 2 units on a side.

four pieces

A five-piece square can be made from the five small pieces. It's the same size as the four-piece square—4 square units—and its sides measure 2 units.

I already know about the seven-piece square. That's the square made from all seven tangram pieces. Its area is 8 square units and each of its sides is the length of the long side (the hypotenuse) of the large tangram triangle piece. This is the same as twice the hypotenuse of the small triangle, which measures $\sqrt{2}$. So each side of the seven-piece square measures $\sqrt{2} + \sqrt{2}$, which can also be written as $2\sqrt{2}$.

five pieces

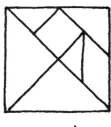

seven pieces

For a square to be formed from six pieces, one piece of the tangram puzzle has to be eliminated. The choices are to eliminate either one of the small triangles, $\frac{1}{2}$ square unit; the square, parallelogram, or middle-size triangle, 1 square unit; or a large triangle, 2 square units. So the area of a six-piece square would measure either $7\frac{1}{2}$ square units, 7 square units, or 6 square units. The side of a six-piece square, therefore, would have to measure either $\sqrt{7\frac{1}{2}}$, $\sqrt{7}$, or $\sqrt{6}$. But there aren't any tangram pieces with sides any of those lengths or combinations of those lengths. All we have are sides of lengths 1, 2, $\sqrt{2}$, and $2\sqrt{2}$, so it isn't possible to form a square with six tangram pieces.

Convinced? If not, give it time. Remember that I thought about this problem for a long time—years—before finally making sense of it for myself. Try again when you're interested and rested. And don't forget the tangram pieces; they contain many of the clues to thinking about this problem.

That's Just Half the Story [page 112]

This is the first of several activities that use the uppercase alphabet letters for geometric explorations. *That's Just Half the Story* investigates which of the letters have mirror symmetry, also called line symmetry. Some teachers make cutout block letters available, and children fold them to test for symmetry instead of using mirrors. This works well.

The letters that work only one way have exactly one line of symmetry— A, B, C, D, E, K, M, T, U, V, W, and Y.

Some letters have more than one line of symmetry—H, I, O, and X.

And some letters have zero lines of symmetry—F, G, J, L, N, P, Q, R, S, Z.

It's also possible for a shape to have an infinite number of lines of symmetry. If the O is formed as a perfect circle, for example, as long as a fold goes through the center of the circle, the two halves will match. Any line that goes through the center of a circle is a line of symmetry.

When children do this activity, they're often surprised and unsettled to find that N, S, and Z do not have lines of symmetry. I think this is because the letters appear to have a kind of balance that letters like F and G, for example, don't have. While N, S, and Z don't have mirror symmetry, they have rotational symmetry. This means that if you imagine each as a cutout letter attached to a surface with a pin through its center, you can rotate the letter 180 degrees so that it's upside down and it will look the same. Notice that the letters that have more than one line of symmetry also have rotational symmetry.

A note about rotational symmetry: Shapes can have rotational symmetry at other than 180 degrees. A square, for example, has rotational symmetry at 90 degrees, and an equilateral triangle has rotational symmetry at 120 degrees.

Interior Regions [page 112]

It's generally easy for children to sort the letters into those that do and don't have interior regions, so there's not much to discuss about this activity. But in the spirit of looking for connections among activities, I revisited this activity after writing the discussion for Extension 3, *Using All Seven*, from *The Tangram Puzzle*, which had made me wonder whether any uppercase letters were polygons. (If you aren't sure what a polygon is, read the explanation for *Using All Seven* on page 111.) The only letter formed only by straight line segments that enclose an interior region is A, but it has extra "tails," a feature that eliminates it from the polygon classification. Some of the letters that don't have interior regions would be polygons if their two dangling line segments were joined. For example, L and V would become triangles; M and W would become pentagons, actually concave pentagons. (Again, read the *Using All Seven* explanation if you're not sure what makes a shape concave.)

Straight or Curved? [page 112]

Deciding which of the uppercase letters have only straight line segments, curves, or both is another easy sorting activity. Converting the chart to a Venn diagram, however, may be something new. A Venn diagram is a clever way to display sets of information when there is information that belongs in more than one set. (Venn diagrams are named for John Venn, a British mathematician [1834–1923], who worked in statistics, probability, and logic.)

If this activity is your class's first experience with a Venn diagram, it may help to use cutout letters and two circles of different-colored yarn. First form the two circles so that they don't overlap, then designate one for letters with straight line segments and one for letters with curves. The problem of where to put letters that have both straight line segments and curves comes up fairly quickly. Ask the children for suggestions. Some may suggest a third yarn enclosure, but that doesn't solve the problem of a letter such as B belonging in all three sets. Some students may suggest making three Bs; you can counter that you have only one of each letter and push them to think of an easier way than cutting out more.

If no one suggests overlapping the circles, then tell them about Venn's idea. Put the B in the intersection and have them verify that it's in both the yarn circle for letters with straight line segments and the yarn circle for letters with curves. While ideas like making three Bs might work, Venn diagrams have become accepted convention for displaying information like this, so children should become familiar with how they work.

No-Lift Letters and More No-Lift Letters [page 113]

The house shape shown in *No-Lift Letters* is one that fascinated me as a young child. Once I realized that I could draw the house without lifting my pencil or retracing a line if I drew it in a certain way, I practiced and practiced until I could do it correctly every time. Then I experimented with other shapes.

Much later, from doing an activity like *More No-Lift Letters*, experimenting convinced me that the only shapes that could be drawn this way were those with zero or two odd vertices. Now I had a way to predict before I tried whether it was possible to draw a shape without lifting the pencil or retracing any line.

It was even later that I began to understand why it was possible to draw shapes with zero or two odd vertices without lifting the pencil or retracing any line. It seemed so strange that this was a rule that worked. Then I engaged in a different kind of experimenting, trying to understand why shapes with one, three, or more odd vertices didn't work. I came to see that an odd vertex was a dead end to be avoided, so zero odd vertices was best. Two odd vertices are OK because they provide places to begin and end. More than two odd vertices are trouble. And I haven't yet figured out how to draw a shape with just one odd vertex; maybe it's not possible.

My personal passage through this investigation shows how the same mathematical experiences can be appreciated in different ways at different ages. I returned to this problem over and over again for years. The discovery about odd and even vertices wouldn't have interested me as a young child trying to master how to draw a shape without lifting my pencil or retracing any line. Later, however, learning the rule was exciting to me, like uncovering a secret. But it wasn't until even later that I became interested in why the rule made sense. And perhaps there's still more to think about with this investigation—it wouldn't surprise me.

I sometimes hear teachers worry that students have done an activity in a previous year and therefore will no longer be interested. That hasn't been the case for me. I've found that children often enjoy returning to things they've previously learned. I've also found that revisits offer children the opportunity to see a situation in new ways and to bring to it their new maturity, experience, and learning.

Square Partitioning [page 117]

This activity demonstrates how rummaging around and getting immersed in a problem can reveal useful patterns that aren't obvious at first. At least that's what happened to me. For example, from fiddling with this activity, I discovered a tried-and-true system for partitioning squares into any number of smaller squares in this sequence—4, 7, 10, 13, 16, 19, and so on—with the numbers continuing to increase by three. When you divide a square into four equal-size squares, the change from one square to four squares represents an increase of three squares, so the system is to divide any existing square into four equal-size squares. All of the numbers in the sequence are one more than a multiple of three.

The next one that seemed easy to do was to partition a square into nine smaller squares, making a 3-by-3 array. Once I had nine squares, I could divide any square using the system I had discovered before and get three more squares. So this took care of 9, 12, 15, 18, 21, and so on. Or I could divide any of the nine squares into nine more squares, which added eight more squares, to solve the problem for 17, 25, 33, 41, 49, and so on.

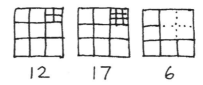

But I was getting ahead of the problem with these large number solutions. What about partitioning a square into six, eight, or eleven squares? I stumbled into six from erasing some lines from the nine-square. And I found eight and eleven from dividing a square into a 5-by-5 array and then erasing some interior lines.

But enough. The fun in a problem like this is the discovering—if you like that sort of thing. I do. Once I have systems, I'm no longer interested, although at times I become delighted all over again when someone gives me a completely new way to look at a problem I thought I completely understood. The lesson is—be mathematically curious. It's a key to becoming mathematically competent.

So what's the story with five? It's not possible to partition a square into five smaller squares, a reminder that not every mathematical problem has a solution.

The Banquet Table Problem [page 117]

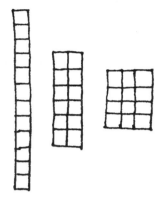

This problem uses the context of arranging tables for a banquet to explore the ideas of area and perimeter. Different arrangements of twelve square tables all have the same area but have different perimeters and, therefore, can seat different numbers of people. For example, putting all twelve tables in one row to make a long, thin table seats the most people—twelve on each side and one at each end for a total of twenty-six. Arranging the tables into a 6-by-2 rectangle results in seating for sixteen people—six on each side and two at each end. A 4-by-3 arrangement seats fourteen people—four on each side and three on each end. These are the only rectangular arrangements that I had in mind when I wrote the problem. However, students have found ways to arrange the tables in other ways, leaving holes in the center.

From time to time, students interpret a problem in a different way from the one intended. It's difficult to give precise directions all the time. My first impulse when a student built a table with a "hole" was to clarify that this wasn't what I meant, that I had meant only "filled-in" rectangles. I was locked into the goal I had for the lesson, for students to see the relationship between the number of small tables and the pairs of factors of that number. (For 12, the pairs of factors are 1×12, 2×6, and 3×4.) I wanted them to see that long, thin tables had longer perimeters than did more squarelike tables. When a student suggested a banquet table with a hole, and then others argued about whether or not people could sit inside the hole, I felt that I was losing mathematical control over the lesson.

I relaxed, however, and decided to see the diversion not as a potential disaster but as a way for students to follow their curiosity. The students continued to search for all possible tables and record their findings. Later, in a class discussion about the banquet tables made from twelve, twenty-four, and one hundred small tables, I asked them to consider just those tables that were filled-in rectangles. This focused us on looking at the mathematics I felt was important.

For additional activities that also address area, perimeter, and relationships between them, see *Squaring Up*, on page 79, and *The Area Stays the Same*, on page 84. Also, *Spaghetti and Meatballs for All!* (1997), a children's book I wrote, uses the context of a family reunion to show how rearranging tables can affect seating.

The Four-Triangle Problem [page 122]

This problem is an extremely versatile investigation that is valuable for and accessible to children at all grade levels. It helps students explore geometric concepts, learn geometric vocabulary in context, and develop spatial reasoning skills.

The triangles used for the investigation are right triangles; they all have one square corner. This is because the triangles come from cutting squares on the diagonal, leaving one of the square's right angles intact in each triangle. Also, all of the triangles are the same size, making them congruent right triangles. It's possible to arrange four congruent right triangles into a larger triangle and also into five different quadrilaterals, two different pentagons, and six different hexagons.

If you're interested in reading more about how to use this activity in the classroom, see Chapter 9 (pages 99–106) in *A Collection of Math Lessons: From Grades 1 Through 3* (Burns and Tank 1988) for a description of the lesson in a first-grade class. And the Math By All Means unit *Geometry, Grades 3–4* (Rectanus 1994, 16–25 and 77–82) offers a detailed explanation of the activity with older children.

Geoboard Line Segments [page 127]

There are fourteen different-length line segments you can make on the geoboard by stretching rubber bands so that pegs of the geoboard are the end points of the segments. Four of them are parallel to the sides of the geoboard, measuring 1, 2, 3, and 4 units. Then there are four that are on the diagonal from one side or corner to the opposite side or corner. Children often think that the diagonal line segments are also 1, 2, 3, and 4 units, but that's not right. The line segment from a peg to the next diagonal peg is longer than the line segment from a peg to the peg directly above or below it. You can use a ruler or string to test that this is so. Or you can think about the Pythagorean theorem, since the diagonal is the hypotenuse of the right triangle. (You can read about the Pythagorean theorem in the explanation about Extension 4 of *The Tangram Puzzle, Making Squares*, on page 111.)

In addition to these eight line segments, there are six more, not parallel to any of the eight I described so far. The line segment that goes from one of the bottom corner pegs to the opposite top corner peg is the longest on the geoboard. The next-to-the-longest line segment goes from one bottom corner peg to the peg just under the opposite top corner peg. I think this is correct because the diagonal line segments are all hypotenuses of right triangles, and this particular one is the hypotenuse of a right triangle whose sides measure 4 units and 3 units. Use the Pythagorean theorem to calculate that this hypotenuse is 5 units, longer than the longest segment that is parallel to the sides of the geoboard. No other right triangle, except for one with both sides 4 units, has sides this large.

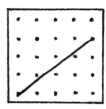

Area on the Geoboard [page 127]

If you can figure the area of the twenty-six shapes on page 127, you can probably figure the area of any shape on a geoboard. To do so, there are a few techniques that are useful.

One is to get good at spotting halves of squares. In Shape A, for instance, there are two whole squares and half of another; its area is $2\frac{1}{2}$ square units. In Shape B, there is one square intact topped by a parallelogram that is formed from two half-squares. Keep an eye out for those halves and you'll do fine with Shapes A through E. You can also confirm these areas by using small paper squares the size of square units, cutting them in half, and fitting them together to make all of the shapes from A to E.

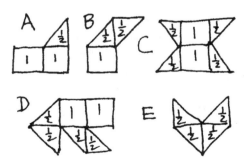

The next shapes get tricky. You can continue to use small paper squares, cutting them to fit the odd-looking shapes and adding up the bits and pieces. One problem with this approach is that measurement is never exact, and the lack of precision will be frustrating. Trust me, it's better to use your head than paper and scissors, at least for these problems.

Here's my advice. Think about rectangles. They're the easiest to figure because you have to count only whole squares. Look at Shape F. It's not a rectangle, I realize, so I make it into one. The rectangle I draw has 2 square units; F is half of it; therefore, F is worth 1 square unit. (OK, if you'd like, verify this by the paper-and-scissors method.)

Look at L. If I "rectangulate" it, the rectangle will have an area of 4 square units, so the area of L is 2 square units.

Nice work, you say, but you took the easy ones. What about M? Or N? Or O or P?

My advice is this: Relax and rectangulate. My additional advice is that it's always easier to figure out what's outside the shape but inside your rectangle. Look at what happens when I draw a rectangle to enclose M. Its area is 8 square units. The triangle on the right side is the same as L and, therefore, has an area of 2 square units. The triangle on the left is half of the rectangle, so its area is 4 square units. Subtract these two areas from the whole rectangle, and you're left with 2 square units for M.

If you do N, O, and P the same way, you'll find that they each have an area of 2 square units. Does it seem peculiar that L, M, N, O, and P all have the same area? It made sense to me once I noticed that they all have the same length base and the same height (which is the perpendicular distance from the base to the opposite vertex). Also, I know that you can figure the area of a triangle by multiplying the base times the height and dividing by two ($A = \frac{bh}{2}$). Looking at the illustration of rectangulating L helps show this; the area of the rectangle can be found by multiplying its base times its height ($A = bh$), and the triangle is half as big. Because L, M, N, O, and P all have the same base and height, their areas are also all the same.

With these techniques—rectangulate, figure out what's outside the shape but inside the rectangle, then subtract—I can figure the area of all the shapes on the page. Following are the answers (all in square units) so that you can check the answers you get.

A = $2\frac{1}{2}$	L, M, N, O, P = 2
B = 2	Q = $3\frac{1}{2}$
C = 4	R = 3
D = 4	S = $2\frac{1}{2}$
E = 2	T = 6
F = 1	U = $6\frac{1}{2}$
G = 2	V = $4\frac{1}{2}$
H = 1	W = 8
I = $3\frac{1}{2}$	X = 4
J = $3\frac{1}{2}$	Y = 9
K = $5\frac{1}{2}$	Z = $8\frac{1}{2}$

King Arthur's Problem [page 132]

The way I made sense of this problem was to investigate where the safe seat would be if there were only two knights, then three, then four, then five, and so on. For example, for five knights, here's what I did:

> I wrote the numerals *1* through *5* in a circle.
> I put my pencil on the 1 and said, "You live."
> I then moved my pencil to the 2, said, "You die," and crossed it out.
> I moved to the 3 and said, "You live."
> I then moved my pencil to the 4, said, "You die," and crossed it out.
> I next moved my pencil to the 5 and said, "You live."
> I then moved to the 1, said, "You die," and crossed it out. Only the 3 and 5 were left.
> I moved to the 3 and said, "You live."
> I moved to the 5, said, "You die," and crossed it out.
> The 3 was left, so it was the safe seat with five knights.

I recorded my findings on a table, hoping to find a pattern that would allow me to stop figuring and, instead, have a way to predict where the safe seat would be for any number of knights. On the following page is the table up through twenty knights.

Number of knights	Safe Seat
1	1
2	1
3	3
4	1
5	3
6	5
7	7
8	1
9	3
10	5
11	7
12	9
13	11
14	13
15	15
16	1
17	3
18	5
19	7
20	9

A confession here: I didn't actually apply the method I described above to all twenty numbers. I started looking for patterns after ten knights. I noticed that Seat 1 was the safe seat when there were one, two, four, and eight knights. I recognized the pattern of these numbers, that each was the double of the previous one. (These numbers are the powers of two.) That discovery led me to predict that with sixteen knights, Seat 1 would again be the safe one. I tried sixteen and found that I was correct.

I also noticed that even-numbered seats were never safe. This makes sense because the live-die pattern alternates the same way even and odd numbers do. Knights in the even-numbered seats get killed in the first pass around the circle.

And I noticed that the odd-numbered safe seats followed a predictable pattern—1, 3, 5, 7, and so on—until the next power of two. After sixteen knights, Seat 1 would again be safe when there were thirty-two knights, and the safe seat numbers after sixteen knights would go 3, 5, 7, 9, and so on up to when there are thirty-one knights. At that point, right before Seat 1 again became the safe seat, Seat 31 would be the safe seat.

OK, this is all interesting, but the power of patterns is that they allow you to predict beyond the information you currently have. What if there were 50 knights at the table? How would I figure out the safe seat without writing the numerals in a circle and applying my crossing-out method? Here's how I thought about this. I know that Seat 1 is safe for 32 knights, and the next time that Seat 1 will be safe is for 64 knights. The safe seats for 33 to 63 knights will be consecutive odd numbers—3, 5, 7, 9, . . . , 63. So, where will 50 hit? If you start with 32 (when the safe seat is 1) and count to 50, you count 19 numbers. (Check this out for yourself. I know that the difference between 32 and 50 is only 18, but I have to count both 32 and 50.) So the safe seat for 50 knights is the nineteenth consecutive odd number. The tenth consecutive odd number is 19, the twentieth consecutive odd number is 39 (see a pattern?), so the nineteenth consecutive odd number is 37. It's my bet that 37 is the safe seat for 50 knights. I checked my prediction by making a partial table, from 50 up to 64, where I knew 1 would be the safe seat again. If Seat 63 was safe for 63 knights, I'd be satisfied.

Number of Knights	Safe Seat
50	37
51	39
52	41
53	43
54	45
55	47
56	49
57	51
58	53
59	55
60	57
61	59
62	61
63	63
64	1

Hurray!

OK, now what if there are 100 knights at the table? Again, I start with what I know, that after 64 knights, the next time that Seat 1 is safe is for 128 knights. I also know that from 64 through 127 knights, the safe seat numbers will go in consecutive odd numbers—3, 5, 7, 9, . . . , 127. All I need to figure out is how many consecutive odd numbers there will be to get from 64 to 100. The difference between 64 and 100 is 36, but I have to count both 64 and 100, so I need to find the 37th consecutive odd number. I remember that the 10th odd number is 19 (1 less than twice 10) and the 20th odd number is 39 (1 less than twice 20). I try a few smaller examples to check this pattern. The 3rd odd number, 5, is 1 less than twice 3; the 4th odd number, 7, is 1 less than twice 4. So I'm comfortable figuring that the 37th odd number is 1 less than twice 37, or 73. So Seat 73 is the safe seat for 100 knights.

More people have written to me about *King Arthur's Problem* than any other problem in *About Teaching Mathematics*. Some write short desperate pleas for help. Others write longer letters, often explaining in their own words what I have just offered. Both the long-letter writers and the short-letter writers make the same request—*What's the formula?*

Sorry, but it isn't possible to reduce every math problem to a formula that you can use to get the answer you want. Well, I could concoct a formula for King Arthur. Let me see. Let n represent the number of knights. Let s be the safe seat. Let p be the power of two that is closest to but less than n. Then, the number of consecutive odd numbers to count would be $n - p + 1$, and to figure out what the safe seat number is would be $2(n - p + 1) - 1$. Mush the variables and you get $s = 2n - 2p + 2 - 1$, or $s = 2n - 2p + 1$. So, if you like formulas, there you go.

But here's what I know. I may not—and probably won't—remember that formula, but I know that I'll always be able to figure out how to solve the problem. And that's what counts in mathematical thinking.

The Prison Problem [page 135]

This problem has generated almost as much mail as *King Arthur's Problem*. When I first encountered it, I decided to solve a related but smaller problem. This technique often helps with math problems. Instead of thinking about a jail with one hundred cells, suppose the jail had only ten cells. What could I learn?

I wrote the numbers from *1* to *10* in a row to represent the cells. I followed the warden's first order, unlocked them all, and wrote U (for unlocked) under each number.

I then followed the warden's second order, left the first cell unlocked, locked the second, left the third unlocked, and so on. I wrote Us and Ls to indicate what I had done.

1	2	3	4	5	6	7	8	9	10
U	U	U	U	U	U	U	U	U	U
U	L	U	L	U	L	U	L	U	L

I continued following the warden's orders until I had to turn the key just in the tenth cell, keeping track as I went.

	1	2	3	4	5	6	7	8	9	10
Unlock	U	U	U	U	U	U	U	U	U	U
Leave 1	U	L	U	L	U	L	U	L	U	L
Leave 2	U	L	L	L	U	U	U	L	L	L
Leave 3	U	L	L	U	U	U	U	U	L	L
Leave 4	U	L	L	U	L	U	U	U	L	U
Leave 5	U	L	L	U	L	L	U	U	L	U
Leave 6	U	L	L	U	L	L	L	U	L	U
Leave 7	U	L	L	U	L	L	L	L	L	U
Leave 8	U	L	L	U	L	L	L	L	U	U
Leave 9	U	L	L	U	L	L	L	L	U	L

Boy, this was tedious. Clearly I had to do some fast thinking. I certainly didn't want to do this for one hundred cells. What could I learn from what I had done so far?

For ten cells, the ones that remained unlocked after all I did were Cells 1, 4, and 9. But would they stay unlocked for the rest of the time if we did this for one hundred cells? Well, I knew that Cell 1 would for sure. It was unlocked the first time around, was skipped ever since, and would continue to be skipped no matter how many cells there were. And since I was now up to skipping the first ten cells before turning the lock in any of them, all of the cells from 1 through 9 would now remain untouched.

Now I began to rummage in my mind. One clue: What I was doing by following the warden's orders was a kind of jailhouse version of skip-counting. Skip-counting is related to multiplication. The answer must have something to do with multiplication. Another clue: The numbers of the unlocked cells—1, 4, and 9—are square numbers. What do I know about square numbers and multiplication?

OK, 1, 4, and 9 are square numbers because $1 = 1 \times 1$, $4 = 2 \times 2$, and $9 = 3 \times 3$. There's a tie to multiplication. I also know that square numbers are the only numbers that have an odd number of factors. All other numbers have pairs of factors. Think about 12, for example. Its factor pairs are 1×12, 2×6, and 3×4; 12 has six factors—1, 2, 3, 4, 6, and 12. Each factor is paired with a different number to make 12. But with square numbers, you can multiply a number by itself, so one of its factors has itself as a partner, resulting in an odd number of factors. Think about 16, for example. Its factor pairs are 1×16, 2×8, and 4×4; 16 (a square number) has five factors—1, 2, 4, 8, and 16.

So, what does this have to do with the locking-unlocking pattern? With the skip-counting method, each cell will have its lock turned once for each of its factors as it comes up in the warden's screwy system. For numbers that are not square, which all have an even number of factors, the lock will be turned an even number of times. It started locked, and after an even number of turns, it will again be locked. The only way it could be left unlocked would be if the lock were turned an odd number of times, which can happen for only the square numbers. For me, the problem was resolved.

The Three-Sacks Problem [page 136]

When I start a problem like this, I first try to establish what I know for sure. In this situation, because each sack is mislabeled, I know the following:

- The sack labeled All Red has either only blue cubes or a mixture of red and blue cubes.
- The sack labeled All Blue has either only red cubes or a mixture of red and blue cubes.
- The sack labeled Red and Blue has only one color of cubes in it.
- I have to determine what really is in each sack by reaching into just one sack, removing one cube, and using only that information.

That's all I know.

To get started, I think about what might happen if I reach into the sack labeled All Red and pull out a red cube. I'd then know that the sack must have both red and blue cubes in it, or else it wouldn't be mislabeled. This would solve the problem! The sack labeled All Blue would then be the one with only red cubes, leaving the Red and Blue sack the one with only blue cubes. But . . . what if I reached into the sack labeled All Red and pulled out a blue cube? I wouldn't be sure if the sack had all blue cubes or a mixture. I'd be stuck.

I'd be in the same situation if I decided to pull a cube out of the sack labeled All Blue. If the cube I pulled was red, I wouldn't know if all of the cubes in the sack were red or if there were some blue in the sack as well. Again, I'd be stuck.

I guess I have to pull a cube from the sack labeled Red and Blue. But what would this tell? Since this sack is mislabeled, I know it has only one color in it—either only red or only blue cubes. Suppose the cube I pulled was red. Then the sack labeled Red and Blue should really be labeled All Red. Of the two sacks left, one must have all blue cubes and one a mixture. The sack mislabeled All Blue can't have all blue cubes, or else it wouldn't be mislabeled. So it must have a mixture and, therefore, should be labeled Red and Blue. And the sack mislabeled All Red must have all blue cubes. And if I pulled a blue cube from the sack labeled Red and Blue, I could still identify what the other two contain following this same logic.

The best way to test my logic is to set up the three sacks, label them incorrectly, and try it.

The Orange Juice—and-Water Problem and the Two-Color Problem [page 139]

The problem about orange juice and water causes fiercely passionate discussion in classes, with staunch believers on three sides—some convinced that there's more orange juice in the water glass than water in the orange juice glass, some believing the reverse, and some sure that there's the same amount of each in each. My position is that after taking spoonfuls back and forth three times—or any number of times—there will always be the same amount of orange juice in the water glass as there is water in the orange juice glass.

The way I reason is that after moving spoonfuls, there's still the same amount of liquid in each glass, allowing some small difference for imprecise measuring technique. We started with the same amount of orange juice as water, but just mixed the two. Now, the quantity of water in the orange juice glass has replaced the same amount of orange juice, which is now in the water glass.

It may help, if my reasoning doesn't hold water (oops, sorry), to think about the next problem in the book, *The Two-Color Problem.* In this situation, you have two sacks, one with ten objects of one color and one with ten objects of another color. You move the same number of objects back and forth, mixing the sacks each time. When you're done, you still have ten objects in each sack, most likely a mixture of colors. If there are now three blues in the red sack (or whatever colors you used), for example, there have to be three red objects replacing those blues in the blue sack. As long as you wind up with the same number of total objects in each sack, the number of red in the blue sack and vice versa will be the same. I'm thoroughly convinced that this is the same as the orange juice–and-water situation.

Riddles with Color Tiles [page 141]

I've done this activity successfully with students as young as second graders as well as with middle school classes, adjusting the number and the complexity of clues to fit the situation. (If you're interested, vignettes of this lesson appear in two Math Solutions Publications books in the Collection of Math Lessons series. See Chapter 3 in the book for grades 1–3 [Burns and Tank 1988] and Chapter 1 in the book for grades 6–8 [Burns and Humphreys 1990].)

Aside from the logical reasoning skills that these riddles promote, they also help develop or reinforce vocabulary—*more than*, *fewer than*, *half of*, and so on. With second graders, a clue such as "I have twice as many blue tiles as yellow tiles" often reveals that you need to teach children what *twice* means.

For the riddles on page 141, the color tiles in Riddle 1 included four tiles of each color; for Riddle 2 there are two yellow tiles and four blue tiles.

Patterns, Functions, and Algebra Problems

The Handshake Problem [page 156]

This is another problem that generates a fair amount of mail from readers. I include this long-winded explanation as an example of how to approach, in general, the problems in the "Patterns, Functions, and Algebra" section.

Typically, letters about *The Handshake Problem* don't request help with figuring out the number of handshakes for successive numbers of people; that seems to be something that readers are able to do from acting it out, making a drawing, or using some other strategy. Here's the table completed for up to ten people:

PEOPLE	HAND-SHAKES
1	0
2	1
3	3
4	6
5	10
6	15
7	21
8	28
9	36
10	45

People usually include in their letter their discoveries about how to continue the table by following the pattern in the Handshakes column. The number of handshakes increases each time by one more than the previous increase—from 0 to 1 is 1 more, from 1 to 3 is 2 more, from 3 to 6 is 3 more, from 6 to 10 is 4 more, and so on. Continuing the pattern, there are 9 more handshakes for 10 people than there were for 9 people (45 − 36 = 9), so the number of handshakes for 11 people would be 10 more than for 10 people. Since 45 + 10 = 55, if 11 people were each to shake hands with everyone else, there would be 55 handshakes in all.

Three questions are asked most frequently in the letters I receive: (1) Why do handshakes generate this pattern? (2) How can you figure out how many handshakes there will be for a large number of people, say one hundred or more, without making a long table? and (3) What's the formula for this pattern?

In a way, all three questions are the same. The answer to Question 1 is the rationale for the pattern of handshakes. This rationale can be applied to any number of people to answer Question 2. And a rationale can often be expressed as an algebraic formula, which would answer Question 3.

A rationale first. Suppose you are one of the people in the room. With how many other people will you shake hands? This depends, of course, on the number of people in the room and therefore changes for different numbers of people. What stays the same, however, is that you'll shake hands with everyone in the room except yourself. That means that the number of handshakes for you will be one less than the number of people in the room. The same is true for everyone else in the room: each person in the room shakes hands with one less than the total number of people.

If there were five people in the room, for example, each of the five people will do four handshakes. You can try this by drawing five people in a circle and drawing hands connecting each person to every other person.

Every person shakes hands with four others. And if five people each do four handshakes, I reasoned, that makes twenty handshakes altogether. Right?

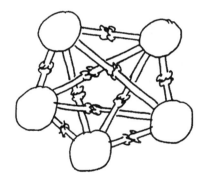

Wrong! Look at the table on the previous page. According to the table, for five people, there are ten handshakes, not twenty.

When I first encountered this problem, it took me a while to figure out where the glitch was in my thinking. Then I had a lucky realization—a mathematical "Aha!" Counting all twenty handshakes was twice as many as there should be because I was counting each handshake twice. For example, if you were in the room, then I counted shaking hands with you as one handshake. But I also counted your shaking hands with me as one handshake. This is double trouble.

So I refined my rationale. First I reasoned that each person shakes hands with one less than the total number of people. Then I figured out how many handshakes that makes altogether (by multiplying the number of handshakes each person makes by the number of people). Finally, I cut the number in half.

I tried my refined rationale for another number. For six people, for example, each person shakes hands with five others. That makes thirty handshakes, which is twice as many as there really are, since each handshake has been counted twice. Half of thirty is fifteen. Check the chart! Also, try my rationale for other numbers to be sure it holds true.

Now I can answer Question 2. Suppose there are one hundred people in the room. Each person shakes hands with ninety-nine others. If one hundred people do this, it seems that there would be 9,900 handshakes, but that's double the correct answer of 4,950 handshakes.

To answer Question 3, I need to translate my rationale to an algebraic equation. The number of people varies from room to room, and therefore we need to use a variable to represent it. Also, the number of handshakes depends on the number of people, so we need to use a variable to represent it as well. How about p for people and h for handshakes? Each person in the room shakes hands with one less than the total number of people, so each person makes $p - 1$ handshakes. With p people altogether, that makes p times $p - 1$ handshakes, which we can write in algebraic shorthand as $p(p - 1)$. But that's twice as many handshakes as we need, so I have take half of $p(p - 1)$, or divide $p(p - 1)$ by 2 to get the number of handshakes. Here are two ways to write a formula that works:

$$h = \tfrac{1}{2} p(p-1)$$
$$h = \frac{p(p-1)}{2}$$

If you followed this, great. If you didn't, maybe you'd like another way to think about the problem. Here's another rationale. (Remember, there's usually more than one way to think about any math problem.) Well, it's not a totally different rationale. Go back to the way I began thinking about the problem, supposing that you're one of the people in the room, and figuring out that you'll shake hands with one less than the number of people in the room. So you do $p - 1$ handshakes.

Now suppose that I'm also in the room and I have to shake hands with everyone else. But I already shook hands with you. To avoid that double trouble later, I won't shake hands with you again and will, instead, shake hands with everyone else *except* you. This means I do $p - 2$ handshakes.

Now the third person shakes with everyone else except for you and me— $p - 3$ handshakes.

Continue thinking in this way and then add up the handshakes. For five people in a room, for example, you shake hands with the four others. Then

I go around the room, skipping you and shaking hands with the three others. Then the third person skips both you and me and shakes hands with the two others. The fourth skips you, me, and the third person and shakes hands with the only other person in the room—the fifth person. The fifth person then doesn't have to do any more handshaking since he (or she) already shook hands with you, me, and the other two people. Total the handshakes—four for you, three for me, two for the third person, and one for the fourth person—$4 + 3 + 2 + 1 = 10$. Yup, it works.

Try it for six people. The 1st does 5 handshakes; the 2nd does 4; the 3rd, 3 handshakes; the 4th, 2 handshakes; the 5th, 1 handshake; the 6th is finished. Add $5 + 4 + 3 + 2 + 1$ and you get 15.

This method will also work for 100 people—$99 + 98 + 97 + 96 + 95 + 94 + 93 + \cdots + 1$. Bleh. If I had to do this much adding, I might as well just finish the table and have the answers for all of the numbers up to 100.

A friend told me another way to think about the problem, however, that also led to a viable formula. Suppose everyone shook hands with everyone else, including shaking hands with themselves. For five people, that would be five handshakes per person, which is five times five, or twenty-five handshakes. For six people, this reasoning means six handshakes per person, which is six times six, or thirty-six handshakes. For any number of people (p), it's p times p or p^2 handshakes.

Ridiculous, I protested. That's way too many handshakes, and people don't shake hands with themselves.

OK, my friend said, let's subtract the extras. Take out one handshake per person to eliminate the self-handshakes. For five people, that means subtracting five handshakes; for six people, that means subtracting six handshakes; for p people, that means subtracting p handshakes. So now we're down to $p^2 - p$.

No way, I protested again. For 5 people, that's $25 - 5$, or 20 handshakes; for 6 people, it's $36 - 6$, or 30 handshakes. These numbers are twice as big as they should be.

Ah, my friend said, I counted each handshake twice, as you did before. So I'll just take half of $p^2 - p$ and I'll have the right answer. I used this logic to write two versions of the formula:

$$h = \tfrac{1}{2}(p^2 - p)$$
$$h = \frac{p^2 - p}{2}$$

I tried the formulas for several other numbers. Bingo!

Now I had four options for formulas:

$$h = \tfrac{1}{2} p(p-1)$$

$$h = \frac{p(p-1)}{2}$$

$$h = \tfrac{1}{2}(p^2 - p)$$

$$h = \frac{p^2 - p}{2}$$

If you recall how to work with algebraic expressions, you can verify that these four options are really all the same.

Two last thoughts. The first one is a mathematical connection: *Dot Connecting* (page 149) is mathematically identical to *The Handshake Problem*. Take a look. The sketches I made for *Dot Connecting* are just like the sketches I made for figuring out handshakes of people in a room, except they have just lines, not little hands. Ten lines connect five dots on a circle, for example, just as there are ten handshakes for five people in the room.

My last suggestion is to use the pairs of numbers on the table—(1, 0), (2, 1), (3, 3), (4, 6), and so on—to mark points on a coordinate graph. Look at the example about tricycles and wheels on page 147 if you need a reminder about how to do this. The points on page 147 go in a straight line, but the points for *The Handshake Problem* go in a curve. When you have $p \times p$, or p^2, in a formula, it's called a quadratic equation and makes a curve that's called a *parabola*. If this is a new idea for you, remember that learning something invariably leads to learning something new. Keep your mind open to learning about parabolas and other curves that come from graphing formulas. It may open a whole new aspect of math for you.

Number and Operations Problems

Number Sums [page 158]

This problem asks primary-age children to find all the possible ways to represent small numbers as the sum of addends. When I listed on page 158 the seven ways to write four as the sum of addends, I used an orderly approach to be sure to account for all the possible ways. I started by using all ones as addends, then I listed the different combinations with twos, and then I used threes. My system isn't the only useful approach, but it works for me. I used the same system to find the fifteen possible combinations for the number five:

$$1 + 1 + 1 + 1$$
$$1 + 1 + 1 + 2$$
$$1 + 1 + 2 + 1$$
$$1 + 2 + 1 + 1$$
$$2 + 1 + 1 + 1$$
$$1 + 2 + 2$$
$$2 + 1 + 2$$
$$2 + 2 + 1$$
$$1 + 1 + 3$$
$$1 + 3 + 1$$
$$3 + 1 + 1$$
$$1 + 4$$
$$4 + 1$$
$$2 + 3$$
$$3 + 2$$

When I do this problem with young children, however, I typically find that the children don't use a logical approach but merely rummage to find different combinations. I sometimes show a class how I think about making a list to account for all the possibilities, but I do so with a light touch and don't push them to solve the problem my way. I've learned that as children get older, they're more inclined to think in a logical fashion. Besides, children's rummaging is valuable. It engages them in thinking about combinations of different numbers, which is useful addition practice. The activity also gives children informal experience thinking about commutativity and associativity.

While the addition is simple enough for older children, the problem can still be interesting for them, especially if the focus is on predicting how many ways there are to write sums for larger numbers. The summarizing section of the problem asks for predictions about the number of ways to write sums for 6, 7, and 8. The information in the table on page 159 helps in making these predictions. The numbers of ways to write sums for 3, 4, and 5 are 3, 7, and 15. The numbers of ways are odd. They're also each 1 less than a power of 2. (The powers of 2 are 1, 2, 4, 8, 16, and so on, the numbers that are so useful for *King Arthur's Problem*, on page 132.) Using this information, my prediction is that for the number 6 there are 31 possible sums (because 31 is 1 less than 32, the power of 2 that follows 16); for the number 7 there are 63 possible sums; for 8 there are 127.

My predictions also make sense if I evaluate the existing data another way. Look at the differences between 3, 7, and 15, the numbers of sums for 3, 4, and 5. The difference between 3 and 7 is 4; the difference between 7 and 15 is 8. These differences—4 and 8—are powers of 2. In a logical progression, the difference between 15 and the next number should be 16, the next power of 2. That would make the number 31, which is consistent with the prediction I made. The difference between 31 and 63 is 32, the next power of 2; and the difference between 127 and 63 is 64.

I didn't include in the problem thinking of all the ways to write sums for the number two. Maybe I should have, but it didn't seem interesting, since there's only one way to write two as a sum—1 + 1. But if I add that information to the table, I can see that it preserves the patterns I used for predicting, since one is one less than a power of two.

Number	How Many Sums?
2	1
3	3
4	7
5	15
6	31
7	63
8	127
⋮	⋮

A teacher suggested to me that an easier problem for children would be to consider the different combinations of addends for each number without worrying about the reversals, so that 2 + 1 and 1 + 2 would be considered the same since they use the same addends. For the number three, then, there would be only two possibilities:

$$1 + 1 + 1$$
$$1 + 2$$

In this version of the problem, the number four has four possibilities:

$$1+1+1+1$$
$$1+1+2$$
$$1+3$$
$$2+2$$

The number five has six possibilities:

$$1+1+1+1+1$$
$$1+1+1+2$$
$$1+2+2$$
$$1+1+3$$
$$1+4$$
$$2+3$$

Make a table of this information and predict the number of sums for six, seven, and eight.

Either version of the problem is fine, and you may think of another. What's important is that the problem engages children in practicing addition and also looking for patterns.

Making Change [page 162]

Using the context of money, this problem calls for making a list of all possible ways and, in that way, it's similar to *Number Sums*, on page 158. The problems are also similar in that both involve thinking about different addition combinations. I approached solving the problem the same way I did for *Number Sums*, making a list in an orderly fashion that would exhaust all the possibilities for making change for $0.25, $0.50, and $1.00.

Instead of making a list, actually, I made a chart, writing the coins at the top and using each line for a different combination, indicating how many of each coin I would use. For $0.25, for example, I made the following chart, which produced twelve ways to make change:

10¢	5¢	1¢
2	1	0
2	0	5
1	3	0
1	2	5
1	1	10
1	0	15
0	5	0
0	4	5
0	3	10
0	2	15
0	1	20
0	0	25

I've learned to watch for patterns when I tackle a problem. In examining the chart above, I noticed a 2-4-6 pattern in the dimes column. There are two ways to use a dime twice, four ways to use a dime once, and six ways not to use a dime at all. This isn't a great discovery, but one that gave me some comfort that there was some order to what I was doing.

For $0.50, here is part of the chart I made (this chart has an additional column to account for quarters as well as dimes, nickels, and pennies):

25¢	10¢	5¢	1¢
2	0	0	0
1	2	1	0
1	2	0	5
1	1	3	0
1	1	2	5
1	1	1	10
1	1	0	15
1	0	5	0
1	0	4	5
1	0	3	10
⋮	⋮	⋮	⋮

I found forty-nine ways to make change for $0.50. The 2-4-6 pattern emerged again in the dimes column when one quarter was used, and also a 1-3-5-7-9-11 pattern in the dimes column when no quarters were used. Hmmm.

On to making change for $1.00. I knew that there would be many more ways to make change for $1.00, and I wondered if there was a way to find them other than starting another chart. Making such an elaborate list was going to be pretty exhausting.

I decided to use what I knew about making change for $0.50. I added a first column to the chart for using a 50¢ coin, using a different-colored pen to keep my previous work intact. Then I thought: If I added a 50¢ coin to each of the forty-nine ways for $0.50, each would then be worth $1.00, and that makes forty-nine ways. Also, I could make $1.00 using only two 50¢ coins, so now I have fifty ways and, I think, have taken care of all possibilities using one or two 50¢ coins. Now I had to figure out the ways to make change for $1.00 without using any 50¢ coins.

I thought that if I used the chart I'd made for making change for $0.50 and doubled the quantities for each coin, the amount on each line would double from $0.50 to $1.00. That would give another forty-nine ways, bringing my total up to ninety-nine ways. I wondered if doubling would take care of every other possibility, however. I realized that the ways I had considered so far used four quarters once and two quarters twenty-four times, but I hadn't considered any possibilities using one or three quarters. Oops. I went back to construct those.

It wasn't hard to figure that there were twelve ways with three quarters: I reasoned that because three quarters makes 75¢, I need 25¢ more, and I learned earlier that there are 12 ways to make change for 25¢. So if I added three quarters to each of those 12 ways, I'd have 12 new ways to make change for $1.00. That changed my total from 99 to 111 ways.

Now I thought that all I had to do was figure the ways using one quarter. With one quarter, I need 75¢ more. Maybe I can use the chart for $0.25 again, this time tripling the quantities for each coin so that the amount on each line would triple from $0.25 to $0.75. That would produce 12 more ways to make change for $1.00 using one quarter, bringing the total to 123.

Was this saving time? Should I just have made the list to begin with? How did I know whether I had accounted for all the possible ways? I didn't feel right about this number 123. I don't know why, but I felt there were other possibilities. I took a break. I fixed a cup of tea and a snack. I phoned a friend (about something completely unrelated). I went to the store to do an errand.

Then it came to me. I was thinking that there were only 12 ways to make change for $1.00 using one quarter, but that couldn't be right. That would be the same as saying that there were twelve ways to make change for $0.75 if I used only dimes, nickels, and pennies. But there were twelve ways to make change for $0.25 with dimes, nickels, and pennies, so there should be lots more ways to make change for $0.75 with these same coins. I went back to work, this time making a chart for the ways to make change for $0.75 with dimes, nickels, and pennies. I found seventy-two ways! (And 72 is the sum of $2 + 4 + 6 + 8 + 10 + 12 + 14 + 16$, an extension of the 2-4-6 pattern I had noticed earlier.)

My chart included those 12 ways from tripling the quantities in my old chart for $0.25, so I eliminated that step, went back to the previous total of 111 and added on the new 72 ways, to get a total of 183.

At this point I was sorry that I had ever put this problem in *About Teaching Mathematics* and even sorrier that I had committed to offering solutions. Now I had heaps of paper on my desk and an answer of 183, in which I had little confidence. I decided that I needed to give the problem a fresh look, but this was not the time. I took another break and didn't return to the problem for several days.

When I returned to the problem, rested, I took a new approach. To make change for $1.00, I thought, I could use two 50¢ coins; that was one way. Or if I used one 50¢ coin, then my former logic made sense that there were 49 ways to make $0.50 with quarters, dimes, nickels, and pennies; adding the 50¢ coin to the ways I already had would bring each total to $1.00. So now I had fifty ways so far, as I had before. So far, so good.

OK, I eliminated the 50¢ coins and thought about what happened with quarters. I could make $1.00 with four quarters, three quarters, two quarters, one quarter, or no quarters.

Four quarters is easy; there's only one way.

For three quarters you need $0.25 more to make $1.00, and there are twelve ways to make that.

For two quarters, you need $0.50 more, and there are forty-nine ways to make that. But I couldn't count the ways on my list of forty-nine that already used one or two quarters, because those ways used three and four quarters total, which I had already counted earlier. This eliminated thirteen possibilities and left me with thirty-six more ways.

For one quarter, I needed $0.75 more. Let's see, the answer to that was somewhere in my heap of papers. (I hadn't thrown out anything.) There it was—using only dimes, nickels, and pennies, there were seventy-two ways to make $0.75.

There was only zero quarters left. How many ways could I make change for $1.00 with only dimes, nickels, and pennies? I started a chart. A 1-3-5-7 . . . pattern emerged for using ten dimes, then nine dimes, then eight, and so on. I didn't write all of the possibilities; I merely added the odd numbers from 1 through 21 and got 121. Boy, I love patterns. So I went with 121 ways to make $1.00 using only dimes, nickels, and pennies.

What was my total this time? I had to add 50, 1, 12, 36, 72, and 121, which gave a total of 292. I hope this is right. But please write if you have a quarrel with my answer or my reasoning. I'd like to hear from you. Really. (I'll save my papers.)

How Many Sums? [page 163]

Egads, I thought, another problem of finding all the different possible sums. But this time there are only five possible addends, so it should be easier.

I began by making a list of the possible combinations using two addends. I found ten:

$$19 + 21$$
$$19 + 15$$
$$19 + 17$$
$$19 + 13$$
$$21 + 15$$
$$21 + 17$$
$$21 + 13$$
$$15 + 17$$
$$15 + 13$$
$$17 + 13$$

I knew that I didn't need to reverse these combinations, because I was interested in different sums, and reversals would produce the same set of sums. Hey, I then thought, this is like *The Handshake Problem*, on page 156—if five people shake hands with each other, there will be ten handshakes altogether. It's also like *Dot Connecting*, on page 149—with five dots, I can draw ten lines connecting each one to every other one. (Keep an eye out for connections like these. They help build your mathematical intuition.)

I was feeling pleased with myself, but only for a moment. What if I was allowed to use the numbers more than once? Then I'd have to include 19 + 19, for example, and the other sums with both addends the same. But what did the problem call for?

I read it again. It wasn't clear. I could go either way. Well, it's my book, I thought. Which way was I thinking? I couldn't remember. (After all, I wrote the first edition of this book quite a while ago.) But I could remember why I included the problem. It gave practice with addition in a way that also called for logical reasoning. Either version does that. So there really are two problems here, one in which you use each number only once and one in which you can use each number as many times as you'd like.

I opted to continue the way I started and went on to make a list of the possible combinations of three addends, using each number only once in each combination. Again, I found ten.

$$19 + 21 + 15$$
$$19 + 21 + 17$$
$$19 + 21 + 13$$
$$19 + 15 + 17$$
$$19 + 15 + 13$$
$$19 + 17 + 13$$
$$21 + 15 + 17$$
$$21 + 15 + 13$$
$$21 + 17 + 13$$
$$15 + 17 + 13$$

For possible combinations of four addends, I found five ways.

$$19 + 21 + 15 + 17$$
$$19 + 21 + 15 + 13$$
$$19 + 21 + 17 + 13$$
$$19 + 15 + 17 + 13$$
$$21 + 15 + 17 + 13$$

For five addends, there's just one way:

$$19 + 21 + 5 + 17 + 13$$

All in all, there were twenty-six combinations of addends. But I wasn't done, because the problem asked for different possible sums, not different possible combinations of addends.

I returned to the ten combinations with two addends and figured the sums:

$$19 + 21 = 40$$
$$19 + 15 = 34$$
$$19 + 17 = 36$$
$$19 + 13 = 32$$
$$21 + 15 = 36$$
$$21 + 17 = 38$$
$$21 + 13 = 34$$
$$15 + 17 = 32$$
$$15 + 13 = 28$$
$$17 + 13 = 30$$

The sums were all even, which makes sense, because whenever you add two odd numbers, the sum is even. And there were duplicate sums. I looked again at the numbers and realized that they were consecutive odd numbers—13, 15, 17, 19, and 21. If I added the first and the last, the sum would have to be the same as if I added the second and the fourth because I would be increasing one addend by two and decreasing the other addend by two. So there's more to discuss with students than merely calculating sums; there's also seeing relationships among pairs of addends. For two addends, there were ten possible combinations, but only seven different sums. That's because 19 + 13 = 15 + 17; 19 + 15 = 21 + 13; and 19 + 17 = 21 + 15.

To think about the sums with three addends, I tried using this information to see which would be eliminated. First of all, I knew that all the sums would be odd, since adding three odd numbers always produces an odd number. That guaranteed that there wouldn't be any matches with the first set of sums, which were all even. But again there were duplicates in this set, which left me with seven different sums, making fourteen altogether so far.

The combinations with four and five addends produced unique sums, which added five more. The grand total: twenty possible sums.

I'm done—unless I want to do the other version of the problem and use the numbers more than once. Well, not right now. Maybe later.

Change from a $10.00 Bill [page 163]

I found eleven solutions for the amount I could spend: $0.95, $1.85, $2.75, $3.65, $4.55, $5.00, $5.45, $6.35, $7.25, $8.15, and $9.05. The first one in the list has given people trouble because of the 0 in the dollar place.

Multiplication Possibilities [page 164]

I used to view this as a ho-hum problem, just a twist on providing students with multiplication practice. Using trial and error to test different numbers certainly does support practice, but this problem can also help develop students' number sense and logical reasoning skills.

The first thing I wondered about was how to get a 6 in the ones place of the answer. In order for that to happen, the product of the one-digit multiplier and the ones digit in the three-digit top number had to end in a 6. I wondered about which pairs of numbers made this possible. I started a list with 1 × 6. Then I thought about 2 as a factor, and came up with 2 × 3. For 3,

3×2 was obvious. For 4, I came up with 4×4, which made me realize that I was being fairly narrow with 1, 2, and 3, thinking only about how to get to a product of 6. I had skipped over 2×8. And if 6 and 16 are possible products that end in 6, so are 26, 36, 46, 56, 66, 76, 86, and 96. Now I began to think of ways to reach those products with two single-digit factors. My list evolved:

$$1 \times 6$$
$$2 \times 3$$
$$2 \times 8$$
$$3 \times 2$$
$$4 \times 4$$
$$4 \times 9$$

I skipped over 5. I knew that 5 times any number ends in either 5 or 0, so it wouldn't be a possibility. I continued.

$$6 \times 1$$
$$6 \times 6$$
$$7 \times 8$$
$$8 \times 2$$
$$8 \times 7$$
$$9 \times 4$$

I couldn't think of any others, but a dozen was a good start. OK, I thought, now what do I do?

I'm a just-get-started kind of problem solver, happy to try something and think about it afterward. I put a 1 in the box to use as the multiplier. Aha, that works if I use 966 as the top number. I put a check next to 1×6 on my list.

I then tried 2 as the multiplier. Ah, I thought, this works if I use half of 966 as the top number. (Do you see why that makes sense?) Since 966 is even, that's possible. Now I had two possibilities. I put a check next to 2×3.

Next on the list was 2×8. Well, if I used 2 as the one-digit multiplier, I already knew the answer—483—so 2×8 wouldn't work. I crossed it off my list. But what if I used 8 for the one-digit multiplier and the 2 in the ones place on top? What times 8 equals 966? Here's where knowing how multiplication and division relates helps. Dividing 966 by 8 gives 120.75, and that won't fit in the three boxes for the top number, so 8 can't possibly be a multiplier. I crossed off 8 × 2 and 8 × 7. My list now looked like this:

Now I started to wise up. I knew that 1 and 2 were possible single-digit multipliers; I knew that 8 was impossible; the only other numbers I needed to test were 3, 4, 5, 6, 7, and 9. I didn't really have to make that list after all. I could have merely tried those numbers, using what I know about the relationship between multiplication and division.

Also, I could use what I knew about divisibility. A number is divisible by 3 if its digits add to a multiple of 3. I added 9 + 6 + 6 and got 21; since 21 is a multiple of 3, I knew that 3 would work. And I knew that 6 would also work, because even numbers that are divisible by 3 are also divisible by 6.

I did the divisions and found what I think are the only possibilities—966 × 1, 483 × 2, 322 × 3, 161 × 6, 138 × 7. (Where's the answer book to check my work?)

I began to wonder what other problems like this one would be good for students to try. That got me thinking more about the 966 problem. Judging by all the thinking it sparked for me, it seems that 966 was a good choice of number. What other factors would produce a product of 966? How could I think about that? I identified the prime factors of 966—2, 3, 7, and 23.

Then I rearranged and combined the factors in different ways, applying the commutative and associative properties. I came up with other problems—(2 × 3 × 7) × 23, or 42 × 23; (2 × 7) × (3 × 23), which is the same as 14 × 69; and 21 × 46. None fit the three-digit times one-digit format, but all produced the answer of 966. Who ever thought that I'd get so involved with 966?

So, what other numbers would be good to use in a problem like this to replace 966 and spark thinking? Here are three I tried that you might be interested in tinkering with. Or you can make up some of your own.

$$\begin{array}{r} \square\ \square\ \square \\ \times\ \square \\ \hline 5\ 1\ 0 \end{array} \qquad \begin{array}{r} \square\ \square\ \square \\ \times\ \square \\ \hline 8\ 7\ 0 \end{array} \qquad \begin{array}{r} \square\ \square\ \square \\ \times\ \square \\ \hline 5\ 9\ 4 \end{array}$$

The Postage Stamp Problem [page 167]

The arithmetic calculations required in this problem aren't particularly challenging, which makes it accessible to some primary students as well as to upper-elementary students. And the patterns that emerge are interesting to students of all ages. I offer here how I thought about the problem of the possible postage to make with 3¢ and 5¢ stamps, and then with 5¢ and 8¢ stamps. I leave it to you to think about what happens with stamps of other denominations.

If I use only 3¢ stamps on an envelope, then the possible postage amounts are multiples of 3—3¢, 6¢, 9¢, 12¢, 15¢, and so on. Using only 5¢ stamps produces postage amounts that are multiples of 5—5¢, 10¢, 15¢, 20¢, 25¢, and so on. Combining both denominations produces other possible amounts. For example, one 3¢ stamp and one 5¢ stamp makes 8¢; two 3¢ stamps and one 5¢ stamp makes 11¢; three 3¢ stamps and one 5¢ stamp makes 14¢. These begin a pattern that increases by 3¢ each time and results in all new totals—8¢, 11¢, 14¢, 17¢, 20¢. Oops, there's a repeat, caused because it uses five 3¢ stamps, which is the same as three 5¢ stamps. So there will be some new amounts and some repeats from using one 5¢ stamp with different numbers of 3¢ stamps.

It seems way too complicated to figure out all of the possible amounts. Maybe it would be easier to think about the amounts that aren't possible. Maybe there's a pattern there that would give a tidy solution.

OK, I know from a bit of testing that it's not possible to use the stamps to make the amounts of 1¢, 2¢, 4¢, or 7¢. What is the next impossible number?

I listed the amounts from 1¢ to 25¢ and decided to try which I could make. After 7¢, all the amounts were possible, so I concluded that 1¢, 2¢, 4¢, and 7¢ were the only impossible amounts. The way I did my figuring was first to use trial and error to find solutions for all of the sums from 8¢ to 17¢. The next number, 18¢, was 10¢ more than 8¢, an amount I had already solved, which meant I could do 18¢ with two more 5¢ stamps. And 19¢ was 10¢ more than 9¢, another amount for which I had solution. Every subsequent number would be 10¢ more than something I had already done, which meant adding on two more 5¢ stamps to a previous solution. Actually, I could have done even less arithmetic and stopped once I found three consecutive numbers in a row with solutions—8¢, 9¢, and 10¢. Then all I had to do was add a 3¢ stamp on to 8¢ to make 11¢, then 3¢ to 9¢, and so on, to make every subsequent amount. But adding 10 seems so friendly.

There are four impossible amounts using 3¢ and 5¢ stamps, and the largest is 7¢. Done.

Well, not really done. Next the problem asks me to use only 5¢ and 8¢ stamps. Hoo-hah, this was harder. I was looking for a consecutive string of five numbers with solutions so I could apply the same logic, this time adding a 5¢ stamp to make all subsequent amounts. I finally found a string—28¢, 29¢, 30¢, 31¢, and 32¢. There were fourteen impossible amounts, all smaller— 1¢, 2¢, 3¢, 4¢, 6¢, 7¢, 9¢, 11¢, 12¢, 14¢, 17¢, 19¢, 22¢, and 27¢, with 27¢ being the largest impossible amount.

The problem suggests also investigating what happens with other combinations of stamps. I fiddled with some and was intrigued by the differences when both stamps were even or odd, or when there was one of each. The problem can get complex. But the beauty of it is that the only skill you need to get started is addition, and adding gets you pretty far. In a classroom, some students won't progress beyond adding to find solutions while others will search for patterns to reveal what's happening. There's something here for everyone.

	3¢	5¢
1	—	—
2	—	
3	1	o
4	—	—
5	o	1
6	2	o
7	—	
8	1	1
9	3	o
10	o	2
11	2	1
12	4	o
13	1	2
14	3	1
15	)8̅	3̅
16	2	2
17	4	1
18	1	3
19	3	2
20	o	4
21	2	3
22	4	2
23	1	4
24	3	5
25	)8̅	5̅

Arrow Arithmetic [page 167]

In this activity, each arrow tells you to move one square on a 0–99 chart in the direction that the arrow is pointing. I like this activity and have had success with it in primary classes as well as in middle school classes; students generally delight in figuring out what the arrows mean. Doing this activity with students has taught me not to take for granted that the patterns that seem so obvious to me on the 0–99 chart are also obvious to students. Some students, even older ones, need to refer to the chart to check predictions, if not actually to arrive at answers. But I've found that when they are given time to explore the activity, students make numerical discoveries that serve them beyond the arrow problems.

Young students typically continue to use the 0–99 chart as a reference for finding answers. Older students, however, either visualize the chart or translate the arrows to arithmetic calculations—an arrow pointing right results in adding one to the starting number; an arrow pointing down results in adding ten; an arrow pointing diagonally down to the right results in adding eleven; and so on. Thinking arithmetically helps students develop strategies for adding and subtracting eleven and nine, which is good practice for developing their mental arithmetic ability.

Teachers sometimes ask me why I use the 0–99 chart instead of the 1–100 chart. The activity works equally well with either version, but on the 0–99 chart all of the numbers in the same decade, the twenties or thirties, for example, are on the same line. But this is a small preference, not a biggie. Take your pick of charts. (For more in this topic, see "0–99 Chart versus 1–100 Chart" on page 372.)

We're used to having one right answer to most math problems, and the extension problems offer the refreshing possibility for different interpretations. For 9→, for example, I've heard of three different answers from students, all of which made sense according to how they reasoned.

1. The answer is 10, because → means *add 1*, and 9 + 1 = 10.
2. The answer is 0, because I think how the chart would look pasted on a cylinder, like a can of vegetables or soup. If you go one space to the right, you'll be back at the beginning of the same row.
3. There is no answer. Not all math problems can be solved, and this is an example of one of them.

All of these answers show reasonable mathematical thinking. The system of arrows suggested in this problem isn't one that has been established as a conventional part of mathematics. Different answers to potentially ambiguous situations can exist as long as they are justified.

Questions Teachers Ask

Introduction

Over the years, I've responded to many questions sent to me by teachers and parents (my responses have become more manageable because of the ease of email). We've posted some of these questions and my responses on our website and I've used others to inform articles that I've written. For this section, I rummaged through my file (now quite large), picked out those questions that I thought had the most general appeal, and included them here along with my responses.

Different from the mathematical questions I received that led to Part 4, the questions in this section are pedagogical queries that address classroom management and instructional issues. But as in Part 4, I tried to keep my responses here conversational, offering help more in a sharing tone than a definitive one. Also similar to Part 4 is that my answers are meant to offer just one way to think about the question at hand—a way to spark ideas for teachers so they can use my responses in their own ways with the special needs of their own students at the forefront.

I organized the questions according to the grade levels of the teachers writing to me. However, because most questions can apply to other grade levels as well, I suggest that you scan the title I provided for each to hint at its content. Also, I've included one question I received from a parent for two reasons. One is because the issue—memorizing multiplication and division facts—is one that teachers have raised as well. The other reason is because it models a way to communicate with parents about an issue that often concerns them.

I've enjoyed responding to teachers' queries. Writing answers sometimes gives me the opportunity to share my experiences, and at other times it helps me clarify my thinking, expand on my ideas, or reflect on new issues. Also, teachers' questions have helped me stay in touch with what is on the minds of teachers trying to make changes in their classroom mathematics instruction.

Using Fingers for Computing

Q I teach first grade and I encourage children to use their fingers when adding or subtracting. My daughter's teacher has a "strict rule" against using fingers when adding. Can you clear this up for me? —Grade 1

A I think that we need to consider counting on fingers in the context of our larger goals for children's arithmetic competence. Our goals for children include that they learn to add, subtract, multiply, and divide accurately and efficiently and also learn to reason flexibly and confidently with numbers. Skills for computing are best built on a solid base of understanding and rely on repeated experiences over time.

That said, I do not think it's harmful for children to use their fingers when first learning to compute. Their fingers are their way of making numbers concrete and being sure of their answers. As their confidence develops, children's reliance on their fingers diminishes and, finally, ends completely. Rather than ban the use of fingers, I prefer to find ways to develop children's understanding, confidence, and skill with computing. For example, it's important for first graders to develop strategies for adding. Counting on is a beginning strategy that a child might use; for example, a student might find the answer to a problem like 9 + 3 by saying, "Nine, . . . ten, eleven, twelve," thus counting on three more from the nine. Making a ten is another strategy; for 9 + 3, a child may think, "Nine and one more from the three makes ten, and then I have to add two more to get twelve." Children often learn the doubles first, such as 3 + 3 and 4 + 4. While using doubles isn't particularly useful for 9 + 3, it helps with a problem like 6 + 7, when a child might think, "Six and six is twelve and one more is thirteen." Emphasizing strategies like these helps build children's understanding, number sense, and confidence.

From my forty years of teaching experience, I've learned that children learn at different rates and on their own time schedules. The support we offer children should always aim at building their understanding and nurturing their interest in learning. I worry that banning fingers is asking your child to give up what makes sense to her at this time. I don't see any problem with letting children use their fingers in first grade.

Math Centers

Q I am a first-grade teacher with twenty very lively students in my classroom. How can I incorporate math center activities into my daily schedule? —Grade 1

A Spend the time it takes to establish routines so that children know how to operate during math time. One way to begin is to introduce just one math center activity. For example, a center might involve the children in measuring several objects with interlocking cubes and counting to see how many cubes they used. Place the materials the children need—cubes, objects to measure (lengths of different-colored yarn, books, a paintbrush, and so on), and a supply of recording sheets—in a box or container. Gather the children and demonstrate what they are to do. Show them where the materials will be placed and tell them how many children may be at the center at one time. Talk about how to put the materials back when they are done and what to do with their paper. Then, ask for volunteers to try the activity while you work with the rest of the class. Have them do so for ten or fifteen minutes. Then gather the class again and have the children who worked at the center report on their experiences. Allow time for others to ask questions. Over the next several days, give all of the children a chance to go to the center.

Next introduce two other activities to the whole class. Again, demonstrate and set the parameters—how many children can work at one time, where they are to work, how they are to record, and so on. This time, have two groups try the centers while you work with the rest of the class.

If you work in this way, you'll soon be able to have enough math center activities set up so that all of the children can work at a center at the same time.

Patterns

Q I've always given my students experiences with snapping cubes together and describing the repeating patterns in the colors they use. I'm wondering about the purpose of doing the sort of repeating patterns I've been doing. And is it OK to stop there or should I also give them experiences with growing patterns? —Grade 1

A Involving children in making and describing patterns provides them with important and valuable mathematical experiences, and both repeating patterns and growth patterns have their place. One important similarity between patterns that repeat and patterns that grow is that both kinds of patterns provide the wherewithal to generalize and make predictions beyond the information currently available. For example, if you have a repeating red-blue-red-blue-red-blue cube pattern (*ababab* . . .), or a pattern that goes yellow-yellow-green-yellow-yellow-green (*aabaabaab* . . .), you can use the repeating aspect of the pattern to predict the color of cubes that are farther along in the train. For example, young children can extend the patterns to figure out the color of the tenth cube, while older students can think about what color the hundredth cube will be. In the same way, if you have a pattern that grows, such as the number of wheels on any number of tricycles, once you see the pattern of the number of wheels for one tricycle, two tricycles, three tricycles, and so on (3, 6, 9, 12, 15, . . .), you can predict the number of wheels you need for ten or one hundred tricycles. Young children may have to draw the tricycles and count the wheels; older children can think about multiplying by three.

Actually, both kinds of patterns deal with repeating, though in different ways. For the cube patterns, it's the color of the cubes that repeats in an orderly way. For the tricycles, the pattern that repeats in an orderly way is the relationship between the number of wheels and the number of tricycles—there are three wheels for every tricycle.

Is it enough to give first graders experiences only with repeating patterns? I don't think so. I think that one aspect of the mathematical experiences that we provide children should be to help them develop flexibility in their thinking. I wouldn't want children to encounter only repeating patterns and think, therefore, that these constitute the full world of what patterns offer. A second reason for incorporating growth patterns is because they involve children with problem-solving experiences that help the development of their numerical reasoning. In this way, work with growth patterns supports children's work with numbers. And along with developing flexibility and supporting numerical reasoning, thinking about growth patterns is important for building a foundation for the development of children's algebraic thinking.

For more about patterns, see the section "Patterns, Functions, and Algebra" on page 144.

Patterns and Addition

Q I tried a variation on *Snap It*, an activity in the "Beginning Number Concepts" section of *About Teaching Mathematics* (see page 206). I gave my students two colors of cubes and asked them to build different trains all with six cubes. I was hoping they would see the pattern of 0 + 5, 1 + 4, 2 + 3, and so on. They didn't! But they liked building the trains. Any ideas about what I might do differently to help them see this pattern? —Grades 1–2

A I had a similar experience when I asked second graders to build different two-color trains with seven cubes each. (I asked them to build trains, not towers, and place them flat on their desks. I've found that this avoids the toppling that typically happens with towers.) My goal was the same as yours except for the number seven—I wanted to focus students on the different pairs of addends for the number seven and see the pattern of addends that you described for the number six. And my experience was also the same as yours—the students didn't discover the pattern.

Also, many of the students enjoyed building trains with alternating colors (for example, *RBRBRBR* or *RRBBRRB*) rather than keep the red and blue portions of their trains together, as I had envisioned. And no one built a train that was all red or all blue; not only were they following my direction to build two-color trains, but I don't think they found a one-color train particularly interesting.

Here's what I did to reveal the pattern after they had built their trains. I called on a student to hold up one train and describe it, and I modeled how to describe the train another way, with an addition equation. I continued with other students doing the same, creating a list of equations:

$$1 + 5 + 1 = 7$$
$$3 + 4 = 7$$
$$6 + 1 = 7$$
$$5 + 2 = 7$$
$$1 + 1 + 1 + 1 + 1 + 1 + 1 = 7$$

And so on.

Then we played a game I called *What's a Matching Train?* I pointed to an equation on the list and the students would see if they had a matching train. If they did, they would hold it up for everyone to see (and check). This activity reinforced for children how the trains they had physically constructed with the cubes could be mathematically represented with equations. When I pointed to $3 + 4 = 7$, some students held up a train with three red and four blue cubes and others held up a train with four red and three blue cubes. We talked about how both of these possibilities were OK.

Then, to reveal the pattern that you mentioned, I did a follow-up activity, *What's a Matching Equation?* I explained, "This time I'm going to walk around the room and pick up trains that fit a pattern I'm thinking about. For each train, you'll tell me the matching equation and I'll write it on the board. As we continue, see if you can figure out my pattern. One thing you need to know is that for this pattern, the first number in the equation should always match the red cubes in the train I pick."

I walked around the room, chose a train that had six red cubes and one blue cube, held it up, and had the students talk with their partners about what a matching equation might be. I called on a student to report and wrote on the board $6 + 1 = 7$. I repeated this, next choosing a train that had five red cubes and two blue cubes, and writing $5 + 2 = 7$. I continued until I had recorded equations for six trains.

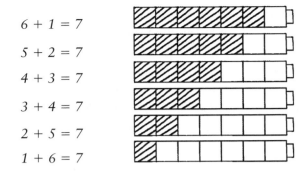

$$6 + 1 = 7$$
$$5 + 2 = 7$$
$$4 + 3 = 7$$
$$3 + 4 = 7$$
$$2 + 5 = 7$$
$$1 + 6 = 7$$

I asked the students what patterns they noticed, both in the list of equations and in the trains, and I gave all who wanted to a chance to report. They noticed that in the equations, the first numbers went down, the second numbers went up, and every equation ended with a seven. They commented that the trains had a zigzag pattern and looked like a staircase.

I asked them what equation I might write next if I wanted to follow the pattern. After they talked in pairs, I called on a student to report, and I added $0 + 7 = 7$ to the list. We talked about the matching train having seven blue cubes. Then we added an equation to the top of the list—$7 + 0 = 7$.

Money

Q Many of my students are confused about the value of coins and the counting of money. Do you have any activity ideas to help? —Grade 1

A Instruction about money not only helps children learn about our monetary system but also can promote and develop children's number sense. It's a win-win effort. I think that beginning instruction about money should focus children's learning in three areas—the names of coins, the values of coins, and how to represent amounts of money symbolically.

For a whole-class activity, I like to give children each a penny, a nickel, and a dime. I ask them to examine each coin to see what's the same and different about them. (If you have magnifying lenses, this is a good time to have the children use them.) We discuss our discoveries and then I pose coin riddles:

Which coins have a building on the back?

There's a picture of a U.S. president on the front of each coin.
On which two coins do the presidents face the same way?

Which coin says ONE CENT on the back? [I write ONE CENT on the board.]

Which coin says FIVE CENTS on the back? [I write *FIVE CENTS* on the board.]

Which coin is a penny? A nickel? A dime?

Games with Money

I find games to be useful for teaching money concepts. For one two-person game, each pair needs a small paper bag with nine coins in it—three pennies, three nickels, and three dimes. One child names a coin—penny, nickel, or dime. The other reaches into the bag and, without peeking, tries to remove the specified coin. They take turns.

For a harder version of the game that also focuses on the values of coins, I prepare a set of cards for various money values that can be made from three of the coins in their bag—1¢, 5¢, 10¢, 3¢, 6¢, 12¢, 21¢, 25¢, and so on. I choose amounts that I think are appropriate for them and sometimes vary the way I write the amounts, including some written as $0.01, $0.05, $0.10, and so on. One child chooses a card, the other reaches into the bag to remove the coins without peeking, and together they count up how much money they have to see if they match. If this game is too hard, I have the children put the coins in a container, choose a card, and work together to pick out the coins. For either game, they can record their answers by writing the values, using money stamps, or drawing coins to represent the coins they chose.

When they are ready, I like to teach children to play *Race for $1.00*, a two-person game that helps them learn about place value as well as money (see page 212). Children need two dice and a zip-top bag with thirty pennies, twenty dimes, and two play dollars. They follow these rules:

1. On your turn, roll the dice, add the numbers, and take that number of pennies. If you have enough pennies, exchange ten pennies for a dime.
2. Give the dice to your partner.
3. Play until one player can exchange ten dimes for a dollar.

I model the game for the class by playing with a child, being especially careful to emphasize that they are to watch each other's moves and to exchange only when they have the dice.

To involve parents in supporting children's learning about money, it's useful to send home a note asking parents to empty the change from their pockets or purse each night and, with their children, count the coins.

Experiences with money should be ongoing during the year. I think that it's ideal for children to use actual coins for activities and worth the time to help children develop the responsibility necessary for dealing with money in the classroom. For the activity with magnifying lenses, real coins are essential, but play money will work for the other activities.

0–99 Chart versus 1–100 Chart

Q I notice that sometimes you use a 0–99 chart for an activity, sometimes you use a 1–100 chart, and sometimes you suggest that either will do. How do you decide? —Grade 2

A For many years, I used only the 0–99 chart and had several reasons for doing so. I wanted to be sure that children learned that zero is a number, not merely a placeholder, and also that it is an even number. Having zero on the chart helps to give it status as a number that, as other numbers, tells how many. (Zero is the answer to the question How many elephants are in the room? I like to ask this question and then ask children to think of other questions for which the answer is zero.) And including zero presents the opportunity, when talking about whether numbers are even or odd, to establish zero correctly as an even number by helping children see that it fits the same pattern as all of the other even numbers on the chart.

Also, I'm always fascinated to hear second graders' responses when I ask, "How many numbers are on the zero to ninety-nine chart?" Some insist that there are ninety-nine "because the last number is ninety-nine." Others reason that it's one hundred, most often "because there are ninety-nine but you have to count the zero, too," and sometimes "because you can count by tens since there are ten numbers in each row." A wonderful discussion typically results.

However, more recently I've thought about several features that I especially like about the 1–100 chart, which I typically refer to as "the hundreds chart," and I've shifted to using it, too. The 1–100 chart begins with the first counting number. (Zero isn't considered a counting number.) Also, it includes the number one hundred, which is an important landmark number; continues the counting pattern into the first three-digit number; and allows for a natural extension to a two hundred chart, a three hundred chart, and so on.

So I now use the two different charts interchangeably and have even posted one of each and asked students to talk about the similarities and differences between them. For activities that use these charts, see *The 0–99 Chart* (page 163) and *Arrow Arithmetic* (page 167) as well as "Looking for Patterns" on page 213.

The Language of Math

Q Do you have any ideas for reinforcing the "language" of math for students? —Grade 2

A This question is appropriate for all grade levels. Acquiring new language in any subject, not just in mathematics, calls for hearing words and phrases used in contexts that help bring meaning to them. I remember when a friend came to visit with her young daughter, Maria. As we settled in to chat, my friend said to Maria, "Please sit on the sofa." Maria looked around, not yet familiar with the word *sofa*, and noticed several things to sit on. Not sure what to do, she perched on an ottoman. "No, honey," Maria's mother said, "you can sit over there, on the sofa." She pointed to the sofa. This one experience with the word *sofa* wasn't enough. Maria would need to hear the word *sofa* more times before she would be comfortable knowing what it meant, and even more times before she would be comfortable using it herself.

It's no different with mathematical language. It's important, as often as possible, for teachers to use the standard terminology of mathematics and to encourage children to do so as well. When children are introduced to pattern blocks, for example, they often describe the blue block as a diamond. I point out to them that this blue block has other names, too; I introduce the terminology of *parallelogram* and *rhombus* and encourage children to use these labels.

In a geometry lesson with fourth graders, Todd asserted that he thought that all squares were the same but that rectangles could be different. I wrote his idea on the board so that everyone could think about it: *All squares are the same, but rectangles can be different.* Then I pressed Todd to explain his idea further. He said, "All squares look the same, but rectangles can be fat or skinny."

Ella said that she disagreed with part of what Todd said. "Some squares are bigger than others, so they're not really the same."

Alma, however, defended Todd's idea. "But you can still tell that they're squares because their sides are the same."

The discussion continued with others weighing in with their ideas. Finally we agreed that while all squares have the same shape, no matter if they are large or small, all rectangles don't have the same shape. In the context of this discussion, I introduced the mathematical terminology of *similar*. "When shapes look the same, even if they are different sizes, they're called *similar*," I explained. I wrote *similar* on our "Math Words" chart and drew two squares of different sizes next to the word as a reminder. I asked the students to say the word aloud. I asked them to think of other shapes that would be mathematically similar. They thought of circles, some triangles, regular hexagons, and others.

One of the challenges of mathematical vocabulary is that often the words have other meanings in common usage, as does *similar* and words such as *even*, *odd*, *multiply*, *factor*, *prime*, and *power*. It's important to talk about the difference in meanings when common words have special mathematical meanings.

Also, after introducing new vocabulary, it's important to use the words often and in the context of experiences. I had the students explore similarity further. (Pattern blocks are good for this since the students can build larger and mathematically similar versions of all of the blocks with the exception of the yellow hexagon.) Sometimes I ask students to write the definition of a math term in their own words, but I do so only after they've had many experiences with the terminology.

Finally, keep in mind that language acquisition takes time and occurs from connecting words to experiences. (For more on this subject, see the section "Teaching Math Vocabulary" on page 42.)

Addition

Q **I teach second grade and am looking for a way to teach addition that helps children really understand why they are regrouping. —Grade 2**

A Building children's number sense is the key. Make sure to give your students ample experience taking numbers apart in various ways. For example, they should know that 10 can be broken into 6 + 4 or 9 + 1 and that it's also possible to break 10 into more than two parts, such 2 + 3 + 5. It's important that children are comfortable doing this for all numbers up to 10, and especially important for the number 10 as preparation for regrouping for larger numbers.

It's also important that children can easily find the answers to problems like 10 + 7 and 10 + 3, where they are adding a number onto 10. The pattern seems obvious to us as adults, but it often takes time for children to see and trust it. Try working with a 1–100 chart so children can see that going down to a number underneath is the same as adding 10.

As children begin to think about larger numbers, they need to see how tens fit into larger numbers. They should see that 15, for example, is 10 + 5 and that 26 is 20 + 6.

Finally, children should be asked to figure out their own ways to add larger numbers. In my experience, most begin by adding the tens first. For example, to add 15 to 26, they typically add the tens to get 30, then add the ones to get 11, and finally combine 30 and 11 to get 41. While this isn't the standard procedure that we teach, it is efficient and shows good number sense.

Give children a good deal of practice adding problems in their own ways and sharing their methods. Introducing the standard procedure before they have a base of understanding runs the risk of having them think about *what to do* instead of *how to make sense.*

Subtraction

Q **My second graders have difficulty counting up to subtract. They seem to equate counting up with addition. How can I help students so they don't have to count backward? —Grade 2**

A In general, subtraction is hard for students. I think this is because there are several different meanings of subtraction, each of which relates to a different situation but all of which can be represented the same way arithmetically. One is the traditional take-away meaning, which has a built-in action: *You have seven pencils and give away four of them. How many do you have left?* Another is a how-many-more interpretation, which has no action but calls for comparing part of a set to the entire set: *I have three pencils but I need six pencils. How many more do I need?* And a third is a comparing meaning, which also has no action but calls for finding the difference between two sets: *You have seven pencils and I have five. How many more pencils do you have than I do?* Also confusing is that two of the meanings use the language of "how many more," one involving finding the difference between two sets and the other involving increasing one set to get to another number.

I agree that counting backward isn't a useful strategy for children to use for any of the subtraction situations. For many years, I assumed that because children could count forward, they could automatically count backward. But it doesn't seem to be so. (This makes sense when I realize that although I know the alphabet really well, I can't easily say the letters backward from Z to A!)

It's useful for children to be introduced to examples of each of the different situations, and it's helpful for them not only to figure out answers but also to explain how they reason. Typically, they will draw on different strategies for different situations. Also, working with situations helps them develop mental models that they can later apply to abstract problems.

Another important goal is for children to see how addition and subtraction are related, that the how-many-more and comparing situations, for example, can be represented both as subtraction ($6 - 3 = ?$) or as addition ($3 + ? = 6$). In this way, counting up or counting backward both work, and children should be encouraged to choose a method that fits the situation, that is easy to use, and that makes sense.

Decimals

Q My third graders have trouble understanding the concept of decimals. They do not understand tenths, hundredths, and numbers smaller than one. They also have trouble transferring this knowledge to money; they'll write *$3.5* for three dollars and five cents. —Grade 3

A Over the years, I've learned that the most effective way to introduce math concepts or skills that are new for students is a two-pronged approach: build on their prior knowledge and give them concrete experiences with the new ideas. Once students have a base of understanding, I help make the connections to the mathematical symbolism and vocabulary.

In order to introduce decimals, for example, I find it useful to rely on children's prior knowledge about money—specifically pennies, dimes, and dollars—and also to provide them the concrete tools of pennies and dimes (real or play) and replicas of $1 bills. First I check to be sure that the children understand the relationships between pennies, dimes, and dollars—for example, 10 pennies are equivalent to 1 dime, and 100 pennies are equivalent to 1 dollar, and 10 dimes are also equivalent to 1 dollar. I also check that students can represent these amounts symbolically. I typically find that while students use the dollar sign to show 1 dollar ($1), they rely on the cents sign to show amounts less than 1 dollar (e.g., 10¢, 23¢).

Then I teach a game using the money that builds their number sense and lays the foundation for introducing decimal notation. *Close to $1.00* works well. Students play in pairs. Each pair needs a 1–6 number cube, a supply of about twenty dimes and twenty pennies, and two play dollar bills. Also, each player makes a recording sheet (see below, left).

They take turns rolling. When players roll the cube, they take either that many pennies or that many dimes and write their choice on their recording sheet. After six rolls, they each figure out how much money they have and record their total. They check each other's figuring and see who got closer to $1. (It's OK to go over $1.) For an extra bit of mathematical oomph, they also record how far each total is from $1.

When first teaching the game, don't focus the students on the notation, but rather have them learn the rules and become comfortable with the game. Then use their familiarity with the game to introduce the decimal notation for money. Here's where you establish that the number of each of the coins has its own place in the number. Have them practice reading different amounts—$0.35, $0.71, $0.05, and so on. Have them write amounts that you give them. Then have them play again, this time using a recording sheet that has them record with the notation (see below, right).

Close to $1.00

	Dimes	Pennies
Roll 1		
Roll 2		
Roll 3		
Roll 4		
Roll 5		
Roll 6		
Total:		

Close to $1.00

Roll 1 $0._____

Roll 2 $0._____

Roll 3 $0._____

Roll 4 $0._____

Roll 5 $0._____

Roll 6 $0._____

_____

Total: $__._____

To change the game, have them play *Close to $2.00*. The rules stay exactly the same but the new goal of $2 requires them to change their numerical strategy.

As the children become more comfortable, you can add in information about the values of the places and the relationship of these decimal numbers to the whole numbers they're already familiar with. All of their learning is based on place value, one of the most important big ideas of children's mathematics learning and an idea with which third graders need many experiences to help them cement and extend their understanding. We've traditionally asked students to demonstrate their place-value knowledge by identifying the place a digit in a particular number holds. For example, we might ask students, *How many hundreds are there in 3,412?* or *What place does the 4 hold in 3,412?* A correct response to either of these types of questions would indicate that the student knows where the hundreds place is. But a correct response does not necessarily mean that the student understands the meaning of the 4, that it represents four groups of one hundred. This sort of understanding develops from children exploring how to group different numbers of objects, seeing that when they have 132 objects, they can make one group of 100, three groups of 10, and have 2 extras.

Money can also be helpful for giving third graders experience with adding and subtracting decimals. For example, present a problem: *If you want to buy an apple for $0.39 and raisins for $0.25, how much money do you need?* First ask the students to estimate if they need more or less than $1.00. (Playing the games should have helped them think about making an estimate.) Then have them figure, using the coins if needed. Finally, connect their reasoning to the correct terminology and record both horizontally and vertically:

$$\$0.39 + \$0.25 = \$0.64 \qquad \begin{array}{r} \$0.39 \\ + 0.25 \\ \hline \$0.64 \end{array}$$

Interpreting Multiplication

Q While I was at a math conference, the speaker of a session I attended emphasized that in "real" life, 12 × 2 is not the same as 2 × 12. He used the example of sending a kid to the store for twelve packages of two eggs or two packages of twelve eggs. I know this is getting picky, but in order for students to do well in upper grades, I believe the foundation has to be solid in every way. Should I address this with my students? —Grade 3

A I agree with the speaker, that in real-world situations, 12 × 2 is not the same as 2 × 12, and I don't think this is a picky distinction. I think it's important. One way to interpret 12 × 2 is as twelve groups of two or twelve twos; another way to interpret it is as twelve two times. Using addition, the first interpretation can be represented as $2 + 2 + 2 + 2 + 2 + 2 + 2 + 2 + 2 + 2 + 2 + 2$ and the second as $12 + 12$. Since both interpretations produce the same correct answer, and multiplication is commutative, it's just an issue of mathematical semantics. When you think about 12×2 abstractly, out of any context, the interpretation is arbitrary.

Most elementary instructional programs use the first interpretation, referring to the times sign ($\times$) as "groups of." If I were asking children to think about the number of eggs in two dozen, I would use 2×12 to represent the total number of twenty-four eggs—two groups of twelve or two twelves. When students think about multiplication in a context, it's important for them to be able to explain how the symbolism relates to the situation.

Patterns in Multiples

Q **Year after year, as part of my multiplication instruction, I teach my students to find the patterns in the multiples of sixes, eights, and so on. Why do we teach children to do this? —Grade 3**

A I think there are several reasons for asking students to find patterns in the multiples of sixes, eights, and so on. One is that the exploration reinforces for students that mathematics is, in large part, based on patterns, and the search for patterns in all areas helps us better understand mathematical ideas. A more specific benefit is that when looking for patterns in multiples, students are getting experience with those particular multiples, thus helping build their mathematical intuition as well as helping them become more familiar with these basic facts.

Multiplication and Division Word Problems

Q **Do you have a strategy for multiplication and division word problems? Code words can be fickle. Any help would be greatly appreciated. —Grades 3–4**

A I agree that relying on code words isn't a wise pedagogical strategy. Instead of focusing on particular words, our teaching challenge is to help children make sense of a situation and then connect it to the appropriate operation or operations. Addition situations generally relate to putting groups together. Subtraction situations can be taking groups apart, taking away, comparing two groups, or thinking about how many more are needed.

For multiplication and division, the key is dealing with equal-size groups. While addition problems can involve combining quantities of different sizes, multiplication calls for combining several groups of the same size. Division calls for either figuring out how many groups there are (with each group being the same size) or how many there are in each equal-size group.

Some problems can be interpreted by more than one operation. For example: *Mary, Luis, and Rory each decorated four eggs. How many eggs did they decorate altogether?* A child can represent this situation mathematically as 4 + 4 + 4 = ? or as 3 × 4 = ?. I want students to be able to do both and also to know when multiplication wouldn't be appropriate; for example: *Mary decorated three eggs, Luis decorated five, and Rory decorated two. How many eggs did they decorate altogether?* Multiplication doesn't work here; there aren't equal-size groups to combine.

Some addition and subtraction situations can also be interpreted and represented in more than one way. For example: *Sally has six birthday candles, but she needs ten. How many more does she need?* Children may represent this situation as addition (6 + ? = 10) or with subtraction (10 − 6 = ?).

Representing situations with appropriate operations is only one aspect of solving word problems. The other is performing the calculation to get the correct answer. A child may write *10 − 6* and then add or count on to arrive at a solution. Or a child who writes *3 × 4* may think, "Two fours are eight and four more make twelve." Computation strategies differ, especially when children are encouraged to figure mentally, which I think is a valuable skill for them to develop.

Multidigit Multiplication

Q **What do students need to understand to be successful with multidigit multiplication? How can I help my students? —Grade 4**

There are three instructional ideas of fundamental importance that I introduce to students to build a foundation of understanding for multidigit multiplication. I introduce these ideas by having students practice figuring out the answers to carefully chosen multidigit multiplication problems. I have them figure mentally, rely on their number sense, and use paper-and-pencil recording to keep a record of their reasoning. I keep their focus on making sense of the computations.

Idea 1: Multiplying any number by ten results in adding a zero.

To teach this pattern, I assign each pair of students a "times ten" multiplication problem to solve. I don't tell them the pattern—merely memorizing the trick isn't sufficient. Rather, I have them figure out the answer by counting by tens or in some other way that makes sense to them. As each pair reports the answer and explains how they figured, I record a multiplication equation:

$$6 \times 10 = 60$$
$$2 \times 10 = 20$$
$$13 \times 10 = 130$$

And so on.

Then we talk about the pattern being a useful shortcut to figuring. It's also important for students to extend this pattern to multiplying numbers by one hundred, one thousand, or any power of ten. I repeat this process for "times one hundred" multiplication problems—$6 \times 100 = 600$, $13 \times 100 = 1,300$, and so on. And then I repeat it once again for "times one thousand" multiplication problems.

Idea 2: When multiplying, a useful strategy is to split numbers into smaller parts, multiply each part, and then combine the partial products.

Solving a problem such as 14×6, for example, is possible to do mentally if you think of 14 as $10 + 4$, multiply each part by 6 to get $60 + 24$, and then add the partial products to get 84:

$$10 \times 6 = 60$$
$$4 \times 6 = 24$$
$$60 + 24 = 84$$

Or you could solve 14×6 by splitting 14 into $7 + 7$, then multiplying 7×6 twice, and adding $42 + 42$, which also results in 84:

$$7 \times 6 = 42$$
$$7 \times 6 = 42$$
$$42 + 42 = 84$$

I give students practice with this strategy, first recording their thinking with equations as shown and then having them record. I emphasize that I use paper and pencil to keep track of how I (or they) reason. I've found that splitting numbers and distributing the multiplication over smaller numbers is accessible to students, and I choose the problems carefully to give them access to this strategy. Good beginning problems involve multiplying a number in the teens (12, 13, 14, or 15) by a single-digit number (3, 4, 5). Then I increase the size of the factors. When students use this strategy, they are applying the distributive property, distributing the multiplication over addends that are friendlier numbers. However, I don't focus at this time on formalizing the name and generalization of the distributive property; rather, I focus on their experience with using the idea of splitting.

Idea 3: Students should learn to multiply mentally by multiples of ten—twenty, thirty, forty, and so on.

For 7×50, for example, students may think of 50 as 5×10, then multiply 7×5 to get 35, and then multiply 35×10 for the answer of 350. When they do this, students are actually changing the problem from 7×50 to $7 \times (5 \times 10)$ and then applying the associative property to solve the problem by thinking of it as $(7 \times 5) \times 10$. As with the other ideas, I give students enough experiences for them to see the patterns and become skilled at using them.

Rounding

Q Rounding is very confusing for my students. Is there anything that I can do to help them? —Grade 4

A Rounding is a skill we rely on often. We round when we decide how much tip to leave for a meal in a restaurant, budget money for a trip, and figure out how many rolls of wallpaper we need or how much fertilizer to mix for the garden. On our government tax forms, we round amounts to dollars and eliminate the cents.

In a fundamental way, rounding relates to estimating. In our daily lives, we always understand the purpose of rounding, and we rely on interpreting situations to figure out what makes sense. While children's daily needs aren't the same as ours, the instruction they receive in school about rounding should engage them in the same ways—interpreting situations and figuring out answers when being exact isn't essential.

Rules by themselves won't lead to understanding or develop adequate skills. It's important first for children to have many and varied experiences estimating and rounding. Here are some ideas that have worked for me.

Friendly Numbers

I talk with students about "friendly" numbers. "They're numbers that are easy to think about," I tell them. Then I ask a variety of questions.

What are some examples of numbers that you think are friendly?

Typically students choose 1, 5, 10, and 100; older students include 25 and 1,000. I ask them to explain the reasons for their choices. I point out that

1, 10, 100, and 1,000 are landmark numbers for our number system, and we discuss why.

Which do you think is friendlier, seventy-three or seventy?

Typically students agree that seventy is friendlier. "You get to seventy by counting by tens," Alan told me, "but you can't get to seventy-three that way." We count by tens—ten, twenty, thirty, forty, and so on—and I identify these friendly numbers as multiples of ten.

What's a friendly number that's close to fifty-seven?
One hundred thirteen? Four hundred eighty-seven?

Multiple answers are possible for questions like these, so I'm sure to have students explain their reasoning. For example, Robert thought that 113 was close to 100, but Lindsay argued that it was closer to 110, which was also a friendly number. I pointed out that if you were thinking about the hundreds part of the number, then 113 was closer to 100 than 200, but if you were thinking about the tens part, then 113 was closer to 110 than 120.

Then, for individual assignments, I give students "closer to" problems, choosing numbers that are appropriate for the students. Then I talk more with the class about rounding numbers to the closest ten or the closest hundred. Following are examples:

> *Is 163 closer to 160 or 165?*
> *Is 163 closer to 160 or 170?*
> *Is 163 closer to 100 or 200?*
> *Is 163 closer to 150 or 200?*

Mental Math Problems

I use regular classroom routines to present problems to the class that encourage them to round numbers and make estimates. We talk both about their solutions and how they reasoned. I phrase some questions so that they have one right answer. For example:

> *Eighteen children bought milk for lunch. Did we collect more or less than $10?*

> *If everyone in the class took out four books from the library, would we take out more or less than one hundred books altogether?*

I phrase other questions so more than one right answer are possible. For example:

> *I measured the hallway and it is 94 feet plus some more inches. About how long is it?*

Some children think that 94 feet is a good estimate, some say 95 feet, and others vote for 100 feet.

Some questions suggest longer investigations. For example:

About how much do you think our class spends for milk in a week?

About how much does our year's supply of pencils cost?

About how many buttons do we have altogether?

About how many letters are there altogether in our first names? Our last names? Our first and last names together?

Connecting to the Language of Rounding

Once students are comfortable answering questions like the ones in the previous section, I address rounding directly. One way I've done this is to write on the board a number in the hundreds; for example, 138. Then I ask two questions:

What friendly number that ends in zero is closest to 138?

What friendly number that ends in two zeros is closest to 138?

I repeat this with other numbers between 100 and 900.

Then I introduce the typical language of rounding. I tell them that "rounding a number" means "finding a friendly number that is close to your original number." I explain how "ends in a zero" relates to tens while "ends in two zeros" relates to hundreds. To give them practice, I ask the same kinds of questions I did before, this time rephrasing to use the standard language of rounding.

Assessment in the Classroom

Q Other than the district tests we have to give, how do you recommend that I assess my students? —Grade 4

A Assessing what students are learning is essential for knowing whether the instruction we're providing is accessible and effective for all students. Different from once-a-year district-level tests, the assessments I'm referring to are ongoing, are an integral part of instruction, and inform me about what and how students are learning from the instruction I'm providing.

I assess students in various ways—by listening to them during whole-class discussions, observing and listening to them as they work in pairs or small groups, and reviewing assignments that students complete individually. And while all of these are useful, I find that individual assignments are essential for providing me with specific evidence about students' learning. Over the years I've been teaching, I've learned more about the sorts of assignments that are effective for giving me insights into what students understand, what they don't yet know, and how they are thinking.

These individual assignments are vastly different from the kinds of quizzes I gave when I first taught, where I mostly asked students to figure answers. Now I ask students to write, explain, include diagrams or sketches when appropriate, communicate about their confusion as well as their knowledge, and provide as much information as possible so that I have a view into their thinking.

I pore over papers to understand students' thinking, revisit papers from time to time, draw from them when planning follow-up instruction, use them for parent conferences, and keep them as a way to track each student's year-long progress. I'm lost without student work. Not only does students' work serve to help me assess individual students' progress, but it also helps me assess my own instruction in ways that I never was able to do in my earlier years. (For more on assessment, see "Linking Assessment and Instruction" on page 47.)

Learning Multiplication and Division Facts

Q My fourth-grade daughter is struggling to learn her multiplication and division tables. She takes timed tests at school and doesn't do very well. How can I help her? —Grade 4

A Your daughter's problem isn't uncommon, and I've found that getting assistance at home is a wonderful way to help children shift from being discouraged to developing confidence and experiencing success. Following are some ideas I hope will be useful.

First, it's important your daughter sees the usefulness of memorizing the multiplication and division tables. Without having these committed to memory, all calculations, whether done mentally or with paper and pencil, will be difficult and laborious. If you think that your daughter would benefit from some encouragement to think about reasons for learning the tables, you might check in the library for a book titled *Amanda Bean's Amazing Dream*, by Cindy Neuschwander (1998). The book was written by a third-grade teacher who wanted to motivate her students to think about multiplication. At the end of the book are activities I wrote for parents to do with their children. While the book and activities focus on multiplication, they also provide a good foundation for thinking about division.

Two other books that also would be helpful are *One Hundred Hungry Ants* (1999) and *A Remainder of One* (1995), both by Elinor J. Pinczes. These don't provide specific activities for you to do with your daughter, but they can spark discussion about both multiplication and division.

I like using children's books to support children's math learning. They help make abstract math ideas real and help stimulate children's imaginations. I know that they won't in themselves solve your daughter's problem, but they're a good starting place.

When helping your daughter, it's important to keep in mind that not only should students understand why memorizing basics is important but a focus on memorization should follow understanding the concepts of multiplication and division. Children should first learn how multiplication relates to repeated addition, how to interpret division, and how multiplication and division relate to each other. When I work with students, I check first that a child can figure out the answers to single-digit problems, such as 7×8 or $24 \div 3$, before they focus on memorizing answers. I want to be sure that a child knows that 7×8 can be interpreted as seven eights, or $8 + 8 + 8 + 8 + 8 + 8 + 8$, and that thinking about the problem as adding eight sevens, or $7 + 7 + 7 + 7 + 7 + 7 + 7 + 7$ will produce the same answer. For division problems like $24 \div 3$, a child should understand that the answer can be found by putting twenty-four into groups of three, by sharing twenty-four into three groups, or by relating the problem to multiplication and thinking, "Three times what number gives twenty-four?" The goal for your daughter is clear—quick and effortless recall of products and quotients with factors from one to twelve. But the memorization should follow learning the concepts.

After checking that your daughter has developed understanding of the concepts, you might look together at the multiplication table (see Blackline Masters). Look for patterns in the rows and columns of numbers. Notice which products appear only once, exactly twice, or more than twice. Find the product that appears most often and talk about why this is so. Think about numbers that aren't products—like seventeen and thirty-one, for example—and talk about why these don't appear. Find out if there are more even or odd products and, again, discuss why.

Use a calculator to help familiarize your child with multiples. Most calculators have the capability to do repeated additions. Try it with a calculator you have at home. Press 8, then +, then =, and the display should show 8. Press the = key again, and you should see 16 on the display. Keep pressing the = key and the display will continue to show multiples of 8—24, 32, 40, 48, and so on. Have your daughter predict what number will show next before she presses the = key each time. Doing this will familiarize your daughter with the multiples of 8. Start with other numbers to practice other multiples.

Brainstorm with your daughter all of the possible ways she might memorize the table. Have her choose one way to try with just one set of numbers, say the eights. When she's ready, quiz her. Together decide if the method she used to study helped or if she'd like to switch to a different method for another number.

Good luck—to you *and* your daughter!

Math Portfolios

Q I'd love advice on how to set up well-rounded math portfolios. How can I start this process at the beginning of the year so that I can have a good picture of a child's abilities for assessment and conferences? —Grade 4

A I've tried many different systems over the years for saving and organizing students' math work. I always look for a system that gives me access to a chronological view of each student's progress through the year and provides a sampling of student work that's useful for parent conferences. Also, because I believe that it's appropriate and beneficial for students in the intermediate grades to reflect on their own learning, I want a system that allows students to review their own progress from time to time. Finally, I know that a system must be easy to manage in order for it to have staying power in the classroom.

One system that I've found to work well is to set up a file box with a folder for each student. The logistics first: To make managing the folders really easy, arrange them in alphabetical order according to the students' first names, and then number them. As a regular routine for headings on papers, ask students to write their number after their name. This makes for easy filing later and for easy locating of their folders. Keeping the box on a counter makes the folders easily accessible both to you and to the students.

Next explain to the students how you plan to use these folders. I tell students, "It's important that I know as much as possible about what you are learning during the year, so I'm going to ask you to put into this math folder some of the math assignments you do. You won't file all of the work you do, but I'll pick assignments that are especially useful for showing what you are thinking, how you are reasoning, what you're learning, and what additional help I might give."

I also tell students, "Later in the year, we'll have a chance to look over your work and talk about your progress. Also, we'll be able to share your work with your parents so they also can see how you're doing in math."

There are times when students work in pairs on an assignment that I'd like them to include in their folders. Sometimes I'd like students also to take their papers home to share with their families. And sometimes students would like to take a particular paper home to share. In these instances, I make copies of the papers so that they can serve each of these purposes.

To get the folders started, try a beginning assignment that gives you information about how the students feel about math and their own math learning. You might ask them to write a math autobiography about their math experiences in school so far. Or you might ask them to record something they especially like about math or think is easy and something they don't like about math or think is hard. Or begin by assigning a problem that's useful for assessing students' mathematics understanding and also how they can organize themselves on paper. For example, asking them how they might make change for one dollar using quarters, dimes, and nickels will inform you about their understanding of money and their number sense. (Ask older students to find all the possible ways, but don't expect third graders to do so.) For an assignment that focuses on place value, ask the students to write down as many numbers as they can think of between five hundred and eight hundred that have one zero in them. (Again, ask older students to find all the possible numbers, but not third graders.) To focus on addition and learn about students' numerical comfort, ask them to find five numbers that add up to an odd number. (Also ask older students what they know about the five numbers and see if any come to the conclusion that one, three, or all five of the numbers have to be odd.)

Typically, I review a class set of papers in order to decide whether or not to file them. When I find a set that is useful for revealing students' strengths and weaknesses, I bring them back to class and ask a student to file them. Doing this over the year provides a chronological record of each student's math progress for each reporting period and for the entire year. Different from using a portfolio as a sampling of best work, this is a system that can show progress over time. Also, looking at the portfolios together gives me a sense of different students' experiences with the instruction I offered. I don't have a rule about how many papers to keep, but I think that about one a week is a general average so I have about thirty-five or so per student by the end of the year.

If you're not sure about what sort of work to save, you might start by saving all of the students' papers for several weeks. Then, after a month or so, look through the files and see which papers give you insights into how students reason, what their strengths are, and where they are having difficulty. Save these and use them as a guide for selecting future assignments that are useful for assessing your students' progress.

Also, be sure that the students know that work they do that you don't ask them to file is also important. Explain that all that they do has value, but you're looking particularly for work that shows you how they are thinking. Also, if a student has a piece of work that he or she wants to file, that's fine. The more involvement students have with collecting samples of their work, the more attention they give to their own learning.

Meeting the Needs of All Students

Q How can I challenge my students who are above grade level, but still teach to the whole class? —Grade 5

A We all have students who learn quickly and can handle additional challenges, while others require more time to learn and often need additional attention on the basics. Here are three ideas for dealing with this in the classroom.

1. Make math choices available.

Provide options that can keep students mathematically engaged in ways that support your learning focus. Post a large sheet of drawing or chart paper, title it *Math Choices*, and explain to the students that you'll list activities that are available to them when they finish assignments and have extra time. That way, you'll have time to work with students who need additional help. To begin, list just one or two activities, and change the list to keep up students' interest. Also, avoid one-shot activities and instead include activities that students can do multiple times. For example, to help build second graders' familiarity with the number ten and also think about combining three addends, introduce the whole class to *All About 10*. Give each child ten interlocking cubes or other counters and have students organize them into three groups. Ask a child to report, and record his arrangement as an addition equation, for example,

$$10 = 3 + 3 + 4$$

Repeat for several other children's arrangements. Then have children work on their own to record as many different equations as they can. Once the children are familiar with the activity, list variations as math choices—*All About 12* and/or *All About 20*—choosing numbers that are appropriate for your students. Also, as an extension, have them write equations with four or more addends.

I'm careful, however, that math choices aren't available only to the more capable students; I want all students to have opportunities to make choices. To accomplish this, I sometimes give choice time to the entire class. Not only is it useful for me to observe which activities students choose, but it also gives me the chance to observe how students work independently and give help as needed.

2. Teach games.

Games are also useful, especially when they offer variations that provide for additional options. For practice with multiplication facts combined with the chance to spark thinking about probability, teach your students how to play *Multiplication Bingo*. Give each student a blank 5-by-5 grid with the center marked FREE, as in regular bingo, and tell children that they are to fill in their own numbers on the other twenty-four squares. Explain the rules: Once they have their cards filled in, you'll roll two dice and they will multiply the numbers that come up. If the product is on their grid, then they cross it out. The winner is the first to get a bingo, as in the regular game. (Keep track of the numbers rolled so you can check the products the students crossed out.) While all children can easily play the game and get practice with basic multiplication facts, some students will be challenged to figure out the best numbers to write on their cards.

To vary the game, instead of using standard 1–6 dice, use 1–10 dice, or one 1–6 die and one 5–10 die. Also to vary it, have students play *Baby Bingo Blackout* using 3-by-3 grids with no free space. Again, they first fill in their own grids. For this game, the winner is the first player to cross out all nine numbers.

After introducing the games to the whole class, you can add them to the list of math choices for students to play independently in pairs or small groups.

3. Give assignments that allow students to set the parameters.

It's helpful if assignments are appropriate for different students' levels of proficiency and also provide information about their mathematical skill and comfort. For example, for an assignment for fifth graders on comparing fractions, I listed on the board six pairs of fractions:

$\frac{1}{2}$ *and* $\frac{1}{3}$ $\qquad$ $\frac{2}{3}$ *and* $\frac{3}{4}$ $\qquad$ $\frac{3}{8}$ *and* $\frac{1}{4}$

$\frac{3}{8}$ *and* $\frac{1}{3}$ $\qquad$ $\frac{5}{6}$ *and* $\frac{7}{8}$ $\qquad$ $\frac{6}{8}$ *and* $\frac{4}{5}$

I explained the directions: "Choose one pair of fractions to compare, copy it on your paper, circle the fraction that's larger, and explain how you know in two ways using numbers, pictures, and/or words." This kind of assignment works for any set of problems with varying difficulty. As a variation, ask students to choose any two or three of the problems to solve instead of just one.

For another example, to provide practice for third graders learning about multiplication, write on the board:

Which Has More Wheels?

7 bicycles
5 tricycles

Ask students to figure in their heads which has more wheels and check their answer with a partner. (For older students, use larger numbers—seventeen bicycles and twelve tricycles, or forty bicycles and twenty-five tricycles.) Have a student explain his or her reasoning. Then have students make up three more *Which Has More Wheels?* problems, choosing their own numbers and solving them. Having students exchange papers to check one another's work provides additional practice.

Long Division

Q Is there a way to teach long division so that students understand what is happening? My students have difficulty understanding the steps involved. —Grade 5

A Long division is hard. First of all, after students go through many years of learning to compute by starting at the right, with the numbers in the ones place, the standard long-division procedure asks them to start at the left. Also, even though the procedure is for division, students learn that, after they divide, they have to multiply, then subtract, and finally bring down a number to start the process all over again. Children wonder why division also involves multiplying and subtracting, and what "bringing down" really means. It's no wonder that few people can explain why the long-division method works, even when they can do it correctly.

Key to all of children's mathematical learning is that they do what makes sense to them, look for the sense in all situations, and persist in their thinking until something does make sense. And this is also true for long division. Let's try it. Think about this problem:

$$6\overline{)875}$$

The standard long-division algorithm calls for beginning by asking: How many 6s are there in 8? Asking this question calls for looking just at one digit in 875 and doesn't focus on the meaning of 875. Another way to think about this problem is to begin by asking: About how many 6s can fit into 875? The word *about* is important here. We're looking for an estimate that's a number that's friendly and easy to think about. Then we can refine. I know, for example, that there are more than 100 6s in 875 because 100 6s is only 600, and that's less than 875. But it's a place to start, so I write *100* to keep track of part of the answer. Now I've "used up" 600, with 275 still left. (That's where the subtraction comes in, to find out how much is still left to deal with.) Next I think, About how many 6s are in 275? I know that there are at least 10, so I write *10* as another part of the answer. That takes care of 60, which leaves 215 more. Ten more 6s work, so I write another

10 and subtract 60 to find out that now 155 is left. Now I can take out 120, which is 20 6s, so I write *20*. Now with only 35 left, I can figure that there are 5 more 6s, or 30, so I write *5* in the answer. There's less than 6 left, so there's a remainder of 5. What's the answer? Add up all the parts—100 + 10 + 10 + 20 + 5. The answer is 145 R5. Here are two ways to record:

$$
\begin{array}{r}
\left.\begin{array}{r} 5 \\ 20 \\ 10 \\ 10 \\ 100 \end{array}\right] 145\ R5 \\
6\overline{)875} \\
-600 \\ \hline
275 \\
-60 \\ \hline
215 \\
-60 \\ \hline
155 \\
-120 \\ \hline
35 \\
-30 \\ \hline
5
\end{array}
\qquad
\begin{array}{r}
145\ R5 \\
6\overline{)875} \\
-600 \;\; |100 \\ \hline
275 \\
-60 \;\; |10 \\ \hline
215 \\
-60 \;\; |10 \\ \hline
155 \\
-120 \;\; |20 \\ \hline
35 \\
-30 \;\; |5 \\ \hline
5
\end{array}
$$

Will this be easy for students to learn? Not for all students—the reality is that math is hard and that some students learn more easily than others. But at least this method is one that I can make sense of for myself and, therefore, help students understand, something that I've found difficult to do with the divide-multiply-subtract-bring-down procedure for long division. If you're interested in trying it, you will find instructional strategies in *Teaching Arithmetic: Lessons for Extending Division, Grades 4–5*, a book I wrote with Maryann Wickett (2003).

Test Prep

Q **Do you believe in test prep? If so, what do you do? —Grade 5**

A All students benefit from being prepared to take high-stakes tests. What's important to me is that I relate any test prep to students' math learning. I've had success using a type of activity I call hands-on-the-table math. Here's how I did this a few years ago when I was teaching fifth graders on a part-time basis, using the practice test booklet we were given. Here is one of the examples from the booklet:

Amy is paid $4 per hour for her first 10 hours of work one week. She earned $8 per hour for an additional 6 hours of overtime work. Which number sentence would you use to determine how much money Amy earned for the week?

> A. $(16 + 12) = x$
> B. $[(4 \times 10) + (8 \times 6)] = x$
> C. $(10 + 6)(4 + 8) = x$
> D. $[(4 \times 10) + (8 + 6)] = x$

I copied on the board just the first sentence from this test question:

Amy is paid $4 per hour for her first 10 hours of work one week.

(**Note:** Sometimes I used an overhead projector and ahead of time wrote the entire problem on a transparency. Then I'd merely show this sentence, covering up the rest.)

Then I asked, "What do you know so far?" I gave everyone who wanted to respond the chance to do so. Then I wrote the next sentence underneath:

She earned $8 per hour for an additional 6 hours of overtime work.

I asked, "What do you know now?" Again, I let all who were interested respond.

Then I asked, "What do you think the question is?"

For this problem, the general consensus was How much money did Amy earn? I gave the students time to figure out the answer, allowing them to talk with a partner, but doing it as hands-on-the-table math. That is, they had to figure mentally, without paper and pencil. I had several students explain how they figured out that Amy earned $88.

Then I wrote on the board the actual question from the text sample:

Which number sentence would you use to determine how much money Amy earned for the week?

The students were surprised by the question. I asked them to talk with their partners about what might be a number sentence for figuring out how much money Amy earned (still without paper and pencil). After a few moments, I interrupted them and asked to hear their ideas. As students reported, I recorded their suggestions on the board.

I then wrote on the board the choices from the test sample:

A. $(16 + 12) = x$
B. $[(4 \times 10) + (8 \times 6)] = x$
C. $(10 + 6) (4 + 8) = x$
D. $[(4 \times 10) + (8 + 6)] = x$

I said, "Talk with your partner about which you think is the correct answer." The students identified B.

Then we discussed why the others didn't work. They pointed out that in D, there was a plus sign where there should have been a times sign. For C, some of the students weren't familiar with the convention for multiplication shown by the expressions in the two parentheses without a times sign, and this gave me the chance to talk about it with them. And for A, they giggled when a student pointed out that sixteen was the sum of the hours Amy worked, and twelve was the sum of four dollars and eight dollars.

After a discussion like this one, I talk with the students about how this experience differs from what they'll face when they take the standardized test. I tell them that on the test, the good news is that they'll have paper and pencil to do their figuring. I also tell them that the not so good news is that they won't have the chance to talk about their ideas with a partner or discuss them with the class.

I repeated this same experience for one or two problems a day for several weeks. This helped prepare students for the format of the test items, and it also focused them on paying attention to the information given and the questions asked.

Connecting Fractions and Decimals

Q I know that fractions and decimals connect and I'm struggling for ways to help my students see the connection. Any suggestions? —Grade 6

A Helping students make connections among all of the mathematical ideas they are learning is important, and the best way to learn something new is to connect it to something you already know. In this light, what students already know about common fractions is a useful springboard for introducing decimals. Like fractions, decimals represent numbers less than one or numbers that are in between two whole numbers. Students' initial learning about decimals can build on what they already know about fractions and introduce them to another convention for representing these numbers.

Here's something I've done with students. I draw a pizza on the board, "cut" it into four equal-size pieces, and write $\frac{1}{4}$ in one of the pieces. Then I ask students to think about why mathematicians decided to use this symbolism to represent each part of the cut-up pizza—what the 4 means and what the 1 means. We discuss their ideas and I reinforce what the two numbers represent. Then I draw another pizza, divide it into just two equal-size wedges, and ask the students how to label one piece. I repeat for a pizza cut into ten pieces.

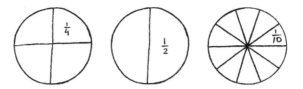

Now to make the connection to decimals: I focus the students on the pizza divided into ten slices and introduce the students to the decimal representation for $\frac{1}{10}$. I write on the board *0.1* and explain that this is another way to write the fraction $\frac{1}{10}$. When I introduce this notation, I am consistent in reading both $\frac{1}{10}$ and 0.1 as "one-tenth." (Later I'll introduce "point one" as another way to *say* 0.1, but I always emphasize that it *means* one-tenth.) We talk about how $\frac{2}{10}$ can be written as 0.2, $\frac{3}{10}$ can be written as 0.3, and so on. I list on the board:

$$\frac{1}{10} = 0.1$$
$$\frac{2}{10} = 0.2$$
$$\frac{3}{10} = 0.3$$
$$\frac{4}{10} = 0.4$$
$$\frac{5}{10} = 0.5$$
$$\frac{6}{10} = 0.6$$
$$\frac{7}{10} = 0.7$$
$$\frac{8}{10} = 0.8$$
$$\frac{9}{10} = 0.9$$
$$\frac{10}{10} = 1.0 = 1$$

I explain that the decimal point is a mathematical convention that indicates an important shift in a number. With money, it separates the dollars from the cents. With measurements, it separates whole units from the parts of units. With numbers, it allows us to describe numerical quantities that are less than one or that are in between whole numbers.

Then I return to the pizza on the board that is divided into two pieces. We talk about $\frac{1}{2}$ being equivalent to $\frac{5}{10}$, so another way to write $\frac{1}{2}$ is 0.5.

Depending on the class, I may continue on to hundredths and then talk about how to represent $\frac{1}{4}$ as a decimal, or I may wait to do that another day. Relating to money is a good way to talk about why 0.25 makes sense.

While the decimal point is mathematical convention, it also has a logical underpinning that's important for students to understand. For example, the meanings of the 0 and the 4 in 3.04 are based on the logical structure of our place-value system, extending the pattern that each place is a successive power of ten. Decimals may be difficult to grasp for students who do not yet fully understand the structure of our place-value system with respect to whole numbers but have only learned the pattern of writing numbers.

Changing Instruction

Q **I am trying to implement changes into my math teaching so that I do less telling my students what needs to be done and more fostering their thinking. But I worry that they won't learn all that they need. I would appreciate any ideas that would bring my math class alive. —Grade 6**

A I remember clearly how hard it was for me to shift away from teaching by telling. We tend to teach the way we were taught, and I was certainly schooled under a teaching-by-telling regime. And I also know how hard it is to change well-entrenched habits. (Why do people have to start diets or give up smoking over and over again?)

That said, I'd like to offer some general thoughts about making changes.

1. It's hard to make changes by yourself.

It's very, very difficult to make changes in the classroom when you're working by yourself. It's hard enough to take the plunge and risk trying something new, and it's especially hard to do so alone. Most of my own thinking about what makes sense in the classroom has developed from collaborating with others and getting support from colleagues. I urge you to find another teacher with whom you can talk about planning lessons, analyze about how they went, look at student work, discuss management issues, or talk about whatever else you'd like to examine.

2. Focus on one teaching change at a time.

As a beginning middle school teacher (actually, it was junior high school then), I taught five classes each day and spent a good deal of time preparing and honing my lessons. At the time, my goal was getting better at explaining what it was that students needed to learn. Then I shifted my goal to seeing the benefit of not doing all of the explaining myself, but asking questions and eliciting responses from students. My classes came alive in a new way.

After making this one change, I learned at a workshop about *wait time* and decided that I wasn't allowing students enough time to think after I asked a question. I was so eager to hear a response and move on to the next question I had ready that I tended to call on the same few students who raised their hands quickly and waved them enthusiastically. So I decided to try what I had learned at the workshop. After I'd ask a question, I'd say to the class, "Raise your hand when you're ready to answer." Then I'd stand silently and slowly count to ten as I looked around the room. Sometimes I'd wait longer before calling on anyone, until at least more than half of the students had a hand raised. The change was amazing. Students realized that I was expecting them all to think, that they couldn't rely on those few who were always eager to reply. It took time and discipline for me to change my former habit, but I did it.

Sometime in the next few years, I put students into groups of four for the first time to facilitate even more of them contributing in class. (This was an idea I learned in another workshop.) When the students were in groups, not only did more students have a chance to talk, but I was able to hear more of their thinking as I circulated in the room. It was hard at first to enforce the procedure of not responding to a student until everyone in the group had the same question, but with practice that, too, became a regular part of my teaching. Later I moved to having students work in pairs, and I found that easy to manage and in some cases more productive for the students.

I became a better teacher for these changes, but it took a year or so to make each of them staples in my instructional repertoire. Since then, each year I've found at least one way to improve my classroom teaching.

3. Look at the questions you ask.

Once I incorporated questioning, wait time, and small-group work into my instructional practice, I began what I think was the most significant shift in my classroom teaching—I broadened my attention from what I was teaching to figuring out what the students were really learning. I began this shift by rethinking the questions I posed to students. I did this in stages. First I made a concerted effort to avoid asking questions students could answer merely with *yes* or *no* and, instead, began formulating questions that required students to explain their thinking. (And when I reverted to a yes-or-no question, I followed it with "Can you explain why you think that?") Then I moved to questions that didn't have a right answer but aimed to find out how a student was thinking. Finally, in my most profound change, I began to focus more intently on what students were saying, shifting my emphasis from listening for what I hoped to hear to listening to how the students were thinking and what they were understanding. It took several years of work to get my teaching skills in this area to where they are now.

I applaud your determination for changing your teaching. Keep in mind that making substantive changes typically takes time. Good luck.

Order of Operations

Q Our grade-level objectives include teaching the order of operations. I've been using the sentence "Please excuse my dear aunt Sally" to teach this. Is there another way that will help my students understand as well as remember the right order to use? —Grade 6

A Ah, the order of operations. The sentence you mention may be as good as anything for helping students remember. But that said, along with remembering, students should at least realize why such a convention is needed to avoid confusion. Point out that the value of an expression like $3 + 4 \times 5$ can be either 35 or 23, depending on whether you do $(3 + 4) \times 5$ or $3 + (4 \times 5)$. The order of operations defines what to do if there isn't any punctuation and avoids the problem of having two possible answers.

After receiving your question, I checked with several colleagues and then tried a lesson with fifth graders, called *Four Strikes and You're Out*. I didn't tell the students that the idea came from a book written for a lower grade level (Tank and Zolli 2001) but instead just told them the name. Trent protested, "But you're only supposed to have three strikes."

I responded, "Let's play the game once with four strikes and then see if a three-strike version would be better." I introduced the activity as suggested in the book, by writing on the board:

$$\underline{}\ \underline{}\ +\ \underline{}\ \underline{}\ =\ \underline{}\ \underline{}$$
0 1 2 3 4 5 6 7 8 9

I explained the rules: "You choose a digit from zero to nine and I'll cross it off the list. Then I'll write the digit in the problem wherever it appears. If the digit isn't in my problem, you get a strike. See if you can figure out my problem before you get four strikes." I had written the problem—$24 + 48 = 72$—on a piece of paper that only I could see. "There are many possible problems," I added, "but you have to guess the one that I've selected." The students were successful. The best part was when they had partially solved the problem—$24 + 4\_ = \_2$—and reasoned to figure out the remaining digits.

Now that they understood how to play, I chose an example that led us to talk about the order of operations. I wrote on the board:

$$\underline{\hspace{1cm}} + \underline{\hspace{1cm}} \times \underline{\hspace{1cm}} = \underline{\hspace{1cm}} \ \underline{\hspace{1cm}}$$
0 1 2 3 4 5 6 7 8 9

On my paper, I had written $1 + 5 \times 7 = 36$. I purposely left out parentheses, which certainly would have clarified the problem, so that I could talk about the order of operations. There was a protest when the problem came to this: $1 + 5 \times \underline{\hspace{0.5cm}} = \underline{\hspace{0.5cm}}6$. "You have to write the six on the left side, too," Andy said. "It *has* to be thirty-six." He was thinking that $1 + 5$ was 6, and that 6×6 was 36.

"No, what I've written matches the equation on my paper," I responded. After some more guesses, the students finally got the equation. Then there was some outrage, which gave me the opportunity to talk about the order of operations and the use of parentheses. We then played several more rounds of the game that gave them practice with applying the rules.

The students decided that they needed all four strikes, so I didn't change that rule of the game.

Homework

Q **I am a middle school math teacher. I grade nearly every homework assignment that I assign. I know math teachers who have their students grade work in class prior to collecting it. I have done this in the past but felt that students were not accurate in their grading or, at times, were even dishonest. I feel that by grading most assignments, I have a strong feel for where each and every student is comprehension-wise. But I also feel that my job is taking over my life. I would like some insights into the best ideas to approaching homework assessment/assigning a homework grade. —Middle School**

A My suggestions for dealing with homework come from my experience in working with middle school students. (I taught eighth-grade math for six years.) Although these suggestions don't deal extensively with the grading issue, they do deal with how to process homework more efficiently and in ways that will both inform you and provide opportunities for students to learn from each other. I hope you find something to try that is consistent with your interest in supporting student learning *and* making your life a bit easier.

Get students involved in talking about their homework. Here are some of the ways we processed homework:

- In pairs and sometimes groups of four, students talked about their homework problems and worked on coming to consensus on their answers or solutions. I walked around, listening to conversations and, at that time, noting who had not done the homework assignment. This process allowed students access to other students' ideas and a chance to correct their own mistakes. Also, those who didn't do the assignment had the opportunity to learn.

- Often I had the pairs or groups record problems they were uncertain about on the board so that we could talk about them as part of a class discussion. We could skip or deal quickly with those that didn't appear on the list, giving us time to dig into those that were difficult for students.
- Sometimes I had students come to consensus on their homework papers and I took one paper from the group to represent the thinking of the group.

One final thought: I gave only a few problems for homework so that there would be time to process them in some way the next day and then get on to that day's lesson.

Math Homework That Counts, Grades 4–6, written by Annette Raphel (2000), is a book that has been helpful to me in thinking about homework. It asks and explores such questions as "What constitutes good and meaningful math homework?" "What are the purposes of math homework?" "What makes a 'good' worksheet?" and "What does research say about homework?" Although the examples given are for grades 4–6, you, too, might find the resource thought provoking.

Supporting Small-Group Work

Q How can I get my students to participate in and enjoy group work?
—Middle School

A I began teaching as a middle school math teacher and taught eighth graders for six years. For the first few years, my classroom lessons followed a standard format: I'd go over the homework from the night before, teach a new lesson, give some class work to check that students understood, and finally assign homework for them to do that night. Within this format, I used the inquiry or discovery approach that I had learned in my teacher preparation, posing questions during lessons to lead students to new understandings and skills. Students sat at individual desks, and during the whole-group part of the lessons, only I or just one of the students was talking. When I assigned class work, students worked by themselves and I circulated, giving help to individuals as needed. Sometimes, this part of the lesson was particularly hectic if many students needed help.

My teaching life began to change after I attended a workshop at a math conference where a teacher presented how she organized her students into groups of four and allowed them to work together. I was intrigued and tried it during the part of my lessons when students were doing class work. What a difference! Now, because students were working together on assignments instead of individually, the lesson wasn't as hectic because students were able to help one another. The room was noisier, for sure, but the noise was mostly productive noise. Of course, from time to time, I had to interrupt the students and ask that they all lower their voices, but this problem was overshadowed by the involvement I observed.

After that, group work became a staple of my classroom instruction. I began having students sit in groups all of the time and using small-group work during my whole-class instruction. Previously in my lessons, I'd pose a question to the class and allow wait time to give students a chance to think and raise their hands; then I'd call on a student to respond. Now, after posing a question and allowing time for students to think about it on their own, before I'd call on someone to respond, I'd ask them to "turn and talk" in their groups. The room would burst with conversation as students shared their thinking with one another. Then, after a few moments, I'd interrupt them and ask for someone to report to the entire class. Discussions became much more lively, and more students were engaged.

Some days, after going over the homework but before teaching a whole-class lesson, I'd assign a problem for students to work on first in groups. In this way, students had the chance to interact with the ideas I was planning to teach, which better prepared them for the lesson. At times, I'd ask them to work individually on the problem but to feel free to ask others in their group for help. Other times, I'd give them a problem to solve jointly, expecting each to contribute as much as possible.

Then I began using groups even for going over their homework assignments from the night before, beginning class by asking students in groups to compare their work and talk about any disagreements. Then we'd discuss differences they couldn't resolve. As the groups talked, I circulated and checked off who had and hadn't completed the assignments. A particular benefit was that students who hadn't completed assignments were still involved because they were able to participate in the small-group discussion.

Over the years, I've found small-group work to be invaluable for supporting student learning, maximizing student involvement, reducing isolation among individual students, and establishing a classroom environment that values student thinking, reasoning, and participation. I communicate these ideas to the students so that they understand why I'm expecting them to be productive group members. Also, over the years, I've honed my skills at successfully managing small-group work so that my math instruction goes as smoothly as possible. Following are some tips.

Make the rules clear.

Present the rules, explain them, post them, and review them often, especially just before students' beginning experiences with working in groups. I've changed the rules from time to time, but here is a good starting set:

1. You are responsible for your own work and behavior.
2. You must be willing to help any group member who asks.
3. You may ask the teacher for help only when everyone in your group has the same question.

The first rule isn't new, but I think it's useful to discuss it in the context of group work. Students now have a new option when doing their work; that is, to ask a group member for help. I clarify the second rule by pointing out the benefit that they all have willing helpers available at all times, without having to wait for help from me. Rule 3 is an incredible boon for helping with procedural as well as learning questions. Typically when I gave an assignment for students to do individually, I'd have to dash about and review or clarify what students were to do. Now students had to rely on their group first before receiving help from me. At the beginning, staying true to the third rule was the most difficult for me in that I worried about not being responsive to my students' needs. However, following this rule and being disciplined about not giving group help until all hands were raised resulted in students become more independent as they learned to rely on one another.

Identify a procedure for establishing and changing groups.

Teachers have reported different ways to put students into groups. Some do it randomly, such as identifying groups with playing cards—ace, 2, 3, and so on for as many groups as needed. Select the corresponding cards, distribute the cards, and have the students reorganize. Some teachers make the assignments themselves, setting up groups that they think will work well together. Other teachers, at times, let students select whom they would like to work with. Whatever system you use, be sure it's clear to the students. Also, it's helpful to let students know when you'll change groups—weekly, monthly, at report periods, when you start a new unit, or for some other reason.

Start with partner work.

It's easier for some students to stay on task when they are working with just one other classmate. Then, after they have some experience working in pairs, you can give them the opportunity to work in larger groups. To make the transition from partner to group work, choose a problem for which they clearly see the benefit of having more people available to contribute. For example, collecting data for a probability investigation is easier when more students are cooperating. Or read the following sections to learn about *The Consecutive Sums Problem*. Also, there have been classes for which I've stuck just with partner work because I found that this was more effective and supportive for the particular students involved.

Choose first experiences carefully.

For their first experience, give students a problem to work on that will be accessible to all of them and will also engage their interest. I have several favorites for students' initial experiences with group work. One is *The Consecutive Sums Problem*, a problem for them to work on jointly. To introduce the problem, first establish that consecutive numbers are numbers that go in order—for example, 1, 2, 3, 4 or 11, 12, 13. Then ask: "How can we write nine as the sum of consecutive numbers?" The typical response is $5 + 4$ (or $4 + 5$, which you should consider to be the same). Record this, and then underneath write another solution:

$$9 = 5 + 4$$
$$9 = 2 + 3 + 4$$

Then ask the students, in their groups, to find all the ways to write each number from 1 to 25 as the sum of consecutive numbers. Tell them that some numbers are impossible, but don't reveal which; rather, challenge them to find the pattern of those numbers. (They are the powers of 2—2, 4, 8, 16, and so on.) Give them large sheets of newsprint for recording. Ask them to look for patterns about which numbers can be written in only one way (such as 5), in two ways (such as 9), or in more ways. (For more on this problem, see page 57.)

Have an extension ready for groups that finish quickly.

Groups will finish at different times, so it's good to have a challenge planned for those that work more quickly. For *The Consecutive Sums Problem*, if a group finishes work to your satisfaction, ask it to predict how many ways thirty-six can be written as the sum of consecutive numbers. As a further extension, ask the group to predict for any number.

Lead whole-class discussions.

After groups have had a chance to complete an assignment you've given, be sure to have them present their ideas in a whole-class discussion. Use their work to teach ideas that are important to the curriculum. For example, *The Consecutive Sums Problem* gives you a way to discuss the powers of two—the numbers that are not possible to represent as the sums of consecutive numbers—and to use exponents to represent these numbers: $2^1, 2^2, 2^3, 2^4$, and so on.

Blackline Masters

- **Centimeter Grid Paper**
- **Area and Perimeter Shapes**
- **Half-Inch Grid Paper**
- **Hexagon Fill-in Puzzle**
- **Pattern Block Triangle Paper**
- **Toothpick Dot Paper**
- **Isometric Dot Paper**
- **Large Geoboard Dot Paper**
- **Medium Geoboard Dot Paper**
- **Small Geoboard Dot Paper**
- **Area on the Geoboard**
- **Inch Grid Paper**
- **Large 0–99 Chart**
- **Palindrome Recording Sheet**
- **Small 0–99 Charts**
- **Addition Chart**
- **Ten-Frames Recording Sheet**
- **Large 1–100 Chart**
- **Small 1–100 Charts**
- **Multiplication Table**
- **Fractions with Cookies**
- **Fractions with Bars**
- **Fractions on Grids (4-by-4 Squares)**
- **Fractions on Grids (6-by-4 Rectangles)**
- **10-by-10 Grids**
- **Shake and Spill**
- **2-Centimeter Grid Paper**

Centimeter Grid Paper

Area and Perimeter Shapes

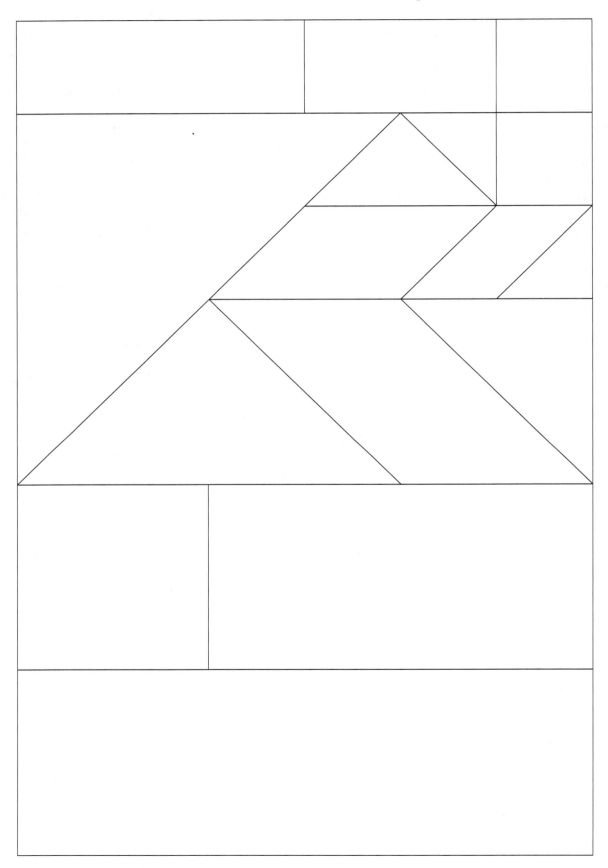

Half-Inch Grid Paper

Hexagon Fill-in Puzzle

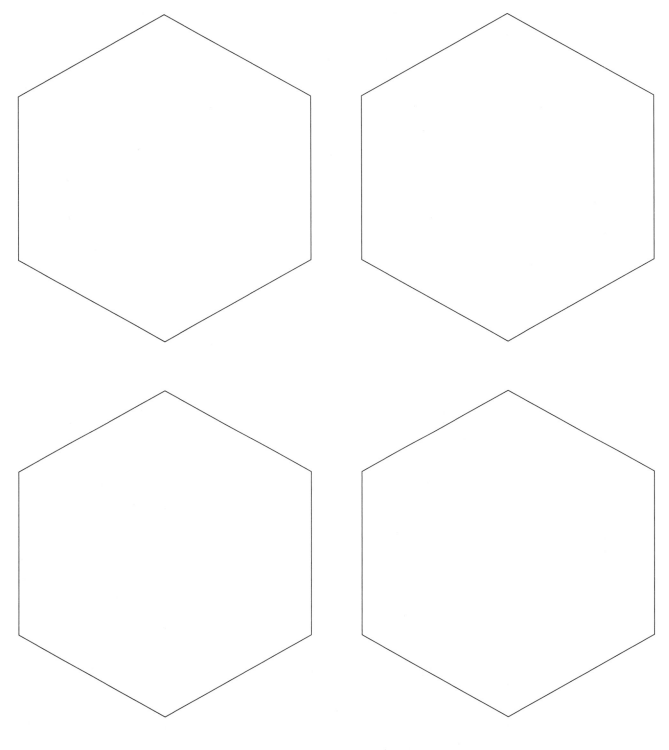

From *About Teaching Mathematics: A K–8 Resource, 3d ed.* by Marilyn Burns. © 2007 Math Solutions Publications.

Pattern Block Triangle Paper

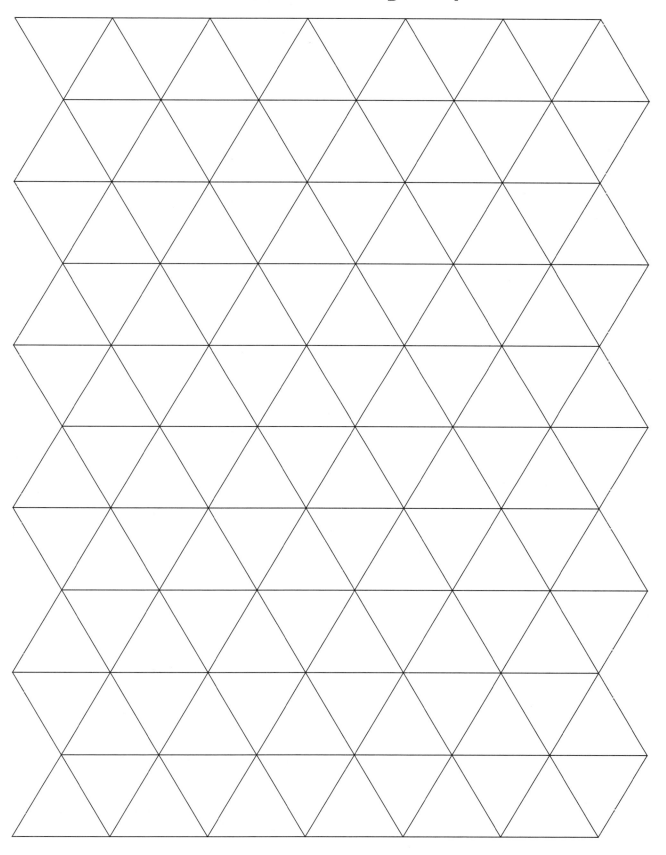

Toothpick Dot Paper

Isometric Dot Paper

Large Geoboard Dot Paper

Medium Geoboard Dot Paper

Small Geoboard Dot Paper

Area on the Geoboard

You Need: a geoboard
            rubber bands

Find the area of each shape.

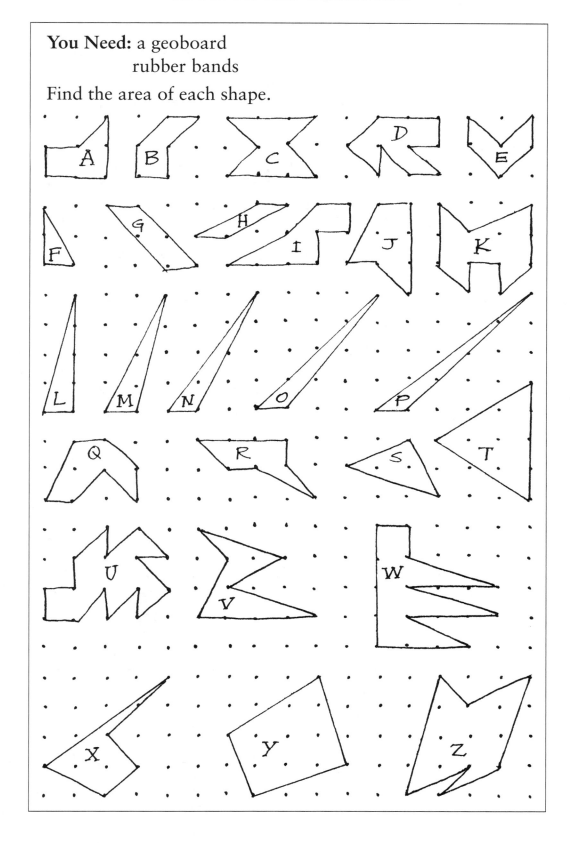

Inch Grid Paper

Large 0—99 Chart

0	1	2	3	4	5	6	7	8	9
10	11	12	13	14	15	16	17	18	19
20	21	22	23	24	25	26	27	28	29
30	31	32	33	34	35	36	37	38	39
40	41	42	43	44	45	46	47	48	49
50	51	52	53	54	55	56	57	58	59
60	61	62	63	64	65	66	67	68	69
70	71	72	73	74	75	76	77	78	79
80	81	82	83	84	85	86	87	88	89
90	91	92	93	94	95	96	97	98	99

Palindrome Recording Sheet

No.	Steps	Palindromes	No.	Steps	Palindromes	No.	Steps	Palindromes
10			40			70		
11			41			71		
12			42			72		
13			43			73		
14			44			74		
15			45			75		
16			46			76		
17			47			77		
18			48			78		
19			49			79		
20			50			80		
21			51			81		
22			52			82		
23			53			83		
24			54			84		
25			55			85		
26			56			86		
27			57			87		
28			58			88		
29			59			89		
30			60			90		
31			61			91		
32			62			92		
33			63			93		
34			64			94		
35			65			95		
36			66			96		
37			67			97		
38			68			98		
39			69			99		

From *About Teaching Mathematics: A K–8 Resource, 3d ed.* by Marilyn Burns. © 2007 Math Solutions Publications.

Small 0—99 Charts

0	1	2	3	4	5	6	7	8	9
10	11	12	13	14	15	16	17	18	19
20	21	22	23	24	25	26	27	28	29
30	31	32	33	34	35	36	37	38	39
40	41	42	43	44	45	46	47	48	49
50	51	52	53	54	55	56	57	58	59
60	61	62	63	64	65	66	67	68	69
70	71	72	73	74	75	76	77	78	79
80	81	82	83	84	85	86	87	88	89
90	91	92	93	94	95	96	97	98	99

0	1	2	3	4	5	6	7	8	9
10	11	12	13	14	15	16	17	18	19
20	21	22	23	24	25	26	27	28	29
30	31	32	33	34	35	36	37	38	39
40	41	42	43	44	45	46	47	48	49
50	51	52	53	54	55	56	57	58	59
60	61	62	63	64	65	66	67	68	69
70	71	72	73	74	75	76	77	78	79
80	81	82	83	84	85	86	87	88	89
90	91	92	93	94	95	96	97	98	99

0	1	2	3	4	5	6	7	8	9
10	11	12	13	14	15	16	17	18	19
20	21	22	23	24	25	26	27	28	29
30	31	32	33	34	35	36	37	38	39
40	41	42	43	44	45	46	47	48	49
50	51	52	53	54	55	56	57	58	59
60	61	62	63	64	65	66	67	68	69
70	71	72	73	74	75	76	77	78	79
80	81	82	83	84	85	86	87	88	89
90	91	92	93	94	95	96	97	98	99

0	1	2	3	4	5	6	7	8	9
10	11	12	13	14	15	16	17	18	19
20	21	22	23	24	25	26	27	28	29
30	31	32	33	34	35	36	37	38	39
40	41	42	43	44	45	46	47	48	49
50	51	52	53	54	55	56	57	58	59
60	61	62	63	64	65	66	67	68	69
70	71	72	73	74	75	76	77	78	79
80	81	82	83	84	85	86	87	88	89
90	91	92	93	94	95	96	97	98	99

0	1	2	3	4	5	6	7	8	9
10	11	12	13	14	15	16	17	18	19
20	21	22	23	24	25	26	27	28	29
30	31	32	33	34	35	36	37	38	39
40	41	42	43	44	45	46	47	48	49
50	51	52	53	54	55	56	57	58	59
60	61	62	63	64	65	66	67	68	69
70	71	72	73	74	75	76	77	78	79
80	81	82	83	84	85	86	87	88	89
90	91	92	93	94	95	96	97	98	99

0	1	2	3	4	5	6	7	8	9
10	11	12	13	14	15	16	17	18	19
20	21	22	23	24	25	26	27	28	29
30	31	32	33	34	35	36	37	38	39
40	41	42	43	44	45	46	47	48	49
50	51	52	53	54	55	56	57	58	59
60	61	62	63	64	65	66	67	68	69
70	71	72	73	74	75	76	77	78	79
80	81	82	83	84	85	86	87	88	89
90	91	92	93	94	95	96	97	98	99

Addition Chart

+	1	2	3	4	5	6	7	8	9	10
1	2	3	4	5	6	7	8	9	10	11
2	3	4	5	6	7	8	9	10	11	12
3	4	5	6	7	8	9	10	11	12	13
4	5	6	7	8	9	10	11	12	13	14
5	6	7	8	9	10	11	12	13	14	15
6	7	8	9	10	11	12	13	14	15	16
7	8	9	10	11	12	13	14	15	16	17
8	9	10	11	12	13	14	15	16	17	18
9	10	11	12	13	14	15	16	17	18	19
10	11	12	13	14	15	16	17	18	19	20

From *About Teaching Mathematics: A K–8 Resource, 3d ed.* by Marilyn Burns. © 2007 Math Solutions Publications.

Ten-Frames Recording Sheet

Large 1—100 Chart

1	2	3	4	5	6	7	8	9	10
11	12	13	14	15	16	17	18	19	20
21	22	23	24	25	26	27	28	29	30
31	32	33	34	35	36	37	38	39	40
41	42	43	44	45	46	47	48	49	50
51	52	53	54	55	56	57	58	59	60
61	62	63	64	65	66	67	68	69	70
71	72	73	74	75	76	77	78	79	80
81	82	83	84	85	86	87	88	89	90
91	92	93	94	95	96	97	98	99	100

From *About Teaching Mathematics: A K–8 Resource, 3d ed.* by Marilyn Burns. © 2007 Math Solutions Publications.

Small 1—100 Charts

1	2	3	4	5	6	7	8	9	10
11	12	13	14	15	16	17	18	19	20
21	22	23	24	25	26	27	28	29	30
31	32	33	34	35	36	37	38	39	40
41	42	43	44	45	46	47	48	49	50
51	52	53	54	55	56	57	58	59	60
61	62	63	64	65	66	67	68	69	70
71	72	73	74	75	76	77	78	79	80
81	82	83	84	85	86	87	88	89	90
91	92	93	94	95	96	97	98	99	100

1	2	3	4	5	6	7	8	9	10
11	12	13	14	15	16	17	18	19	20
21	22	23	24	25	26	27	28	29	30
31	32	33	34	35	36	37	38	39	40
41	42	43	44	45	46	47	48	49	50
51	52	53	54	55	56	57	58	59	60
61	62	63	64	65	66	67	68	69	70
71	72	73	74	75	76	77	78	79	80
81	82	83	84	85	86	87	88	89	90
91	92	93	94	95	96	97	98	99	100

1	2	3	4	5	6	7	8	9	10
11	12	13	14	15	16	17	18	19	20
21	22	23	24	25	26	27	28	29	30
31	32	33	34	35	36	37	38	39	40
41	42	43	44	45	46	47	48	49	50
51	52	53	54	55	56	57	58	59	60
61	62	63	64	65	66	67	68	69	70
71	72	73	74	75	76	77	78	79	80
81	82	83	84	85	86	87	88	89	90
91	92	93	94	95	96	97	98	99	100

1	2	3	4	5	6	7	8	9	10
11	12	13	14	15	16	17	18	19	20
21	22	23	24	25	26	27	28	29	30
31	32	33	34	35	36	37	38	39	40
41	42	43	44	45	46	47	48	49	50
51	52	53	54	55	56	57	58	59	60
61	62	63	64	65	66	67	68	69	70
71	72	73	74	75	76	77	78	79	80
81	82	83	84	85	86	87	88	89	90
91	92	93	94	95	96	97	98	99	100

1	2	3	4	5	6	7	8	9	10
11	12	13	14	15	16	17	18	19	20
21	22	23	24	25	26	27	28	29	30
31	32	33	34	35	36	37	38	39	40
41	42	43	44	45	46	47	48	49	50
51	52	53	54	55	56	57	58	59	60
61	62	63	64	65	66	67	68	69	70
71	72	73	74	75	76	77	78	79	80
81	82	83	84	85	86	87	88	89	90
91	92	93	94	95	96	97	98	99	100

1	2	3	4	5	6	7	8	9	10
11	12	13	14	15	16	17	18	19	20
21	22	23	24	25	26	27	28	29	30
31	32	33	34	35	36	37	38	39	40
41	42	43	44	45	46	47	48	49	50
51	52	53	54	55	56	57	58	59	60
61	62	63	64	65	66	67	68	69	70
71	72	73	74	75	76	77	78	79	80
81	82	83	84	85	86	87	88	89	90
91	92	93	94	95	96	97	98	99	100

Multiplication Table

1	2	3	4	5	6	7	8	9	10	11	12
2	4	6	8	10	12	14	16	18	20	22	24
3	6	9	12	15	18	21	24	27	30	33	36
4	8	12	16	20	24	28	32	36	40	44	48
5	10	15	20	25	30	35	40	45	50	55	60
6	12	18	24	30	36	42	48	54	60	66	72
7	14	21	28	35	42	49	56	63	70	77	84
8	16	24	32	40	48	56	64	72	80	88	96
9	18	27	36	45	54	63	72	81	90	99	108
10	20	30	40	50	60	70	80	90	100	110	120
11	22	33	44	55	66	77	88	99	110	121	132
12	24	36	48	60	72	84	96	108	120	132	144

Fractions with Cookies

Fractions with Bars

Fractions on Grids (4-by-4 Squares)

Fractions on Grids (6-by-4 Rectangles)

10-by-10 Grids

Shake and Spill

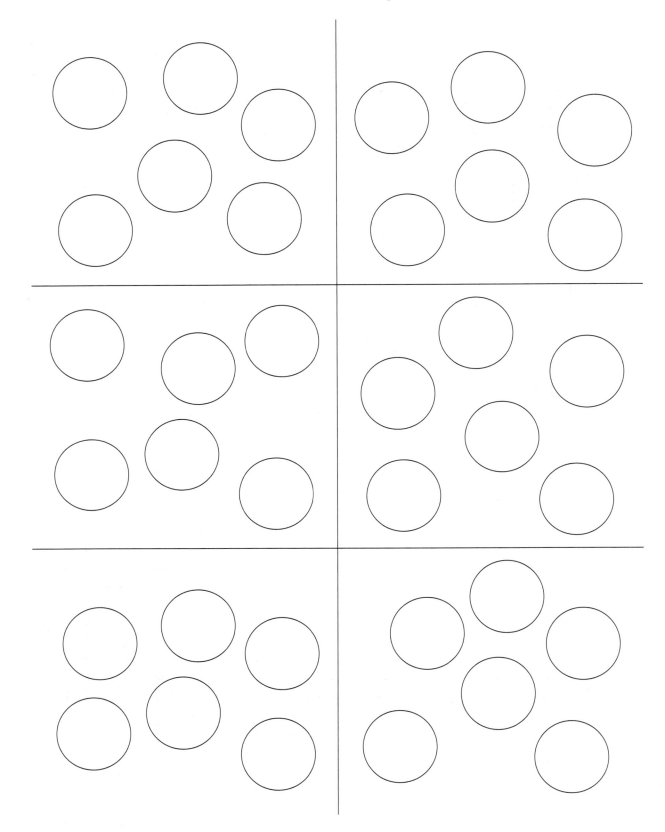

From *About Teaching Mathematics: A K–8 Resource, 3d ed.* by Marilyn Burns. © 2007 Math Solutions Publications.

2-Centimeter Grid Paper

Professional References

Baratta-Lorton, Mary. 1976. *Mathematics Their Way: An Activity Center Mathematics Program for Early Childhood Education*. Menlo Park, CA: Addison-Wesley.

Bay-Williams, Jennifer M., and Sherri L. Martinie. 2004. *Math and Literature, Grades 6–8*. Sausalito, CA: Math Solutions Publications.

Brannan, Richard, and Oscar Schaaf. 1983. *Problem Solving in Mathematics: In-Service Guide*. (Lane County Mathematics Project). Palo Alto, CA: Dale Seymour.

Bresser, Rusty. 2004. *Math and Literature, Grades 4–6*. 2d ed. Sausalito, CA: Math Solutions Publications.

Bresser, Rusty, and Caren Holtzman. 1999. *Developing Number Sense, Grades 3–6*. Sausalito, CA: Math Solutions Publications.

Burns, Marilyn. 1989. *Mathematics: For Middle School (Grades 6–8), Part 3*. Videotape. Vernon Hills, IL: Cuisenaire.

———. 1993. *Mathematics: Assessing Understanding, Part 1*. Videotape. Vernon Hills, IL: Cuisenaire.

———. 1995. *Writing in Math Class: A Resource for Grades 2–8*. Sausalito, CA: Math Solutions Publications.

———. 1996. *50 Problem-Solving Lessons: The Best from 10 Years of Math Solutions Newsletters, Grades 1–6*. Sausalito, CA: Math Solutions Publications.

Burns, Marilyn, and Cathy Humphreys. 1990. *A Collection of Math Lessons: From Grades 6 Through 8*. Sausalito, CA: Math Solutions Publications.

Burns, Marilyn, and Stephanie Sheffield. 2004a. *Math and Literature, Grades K–1*. Sausalito, CA: Math Solutions Publications.

———. 2004b. *Math and Literature, Grades 2–3*. Sausalito, CA: Math Solutions Publications.

Burns, Marilyn, and Bonnie Tank. 1988. *A Collection of Math Lessons: From Grades 1 Through 3*. Sausalito, CA: Math Solutions Publications.

Caldwell, Janet H. 1995. "Communicating About Fractions with Pattern Blocks." *Teaching Children Mathematics* 2 (3): 156–61.

California State Department of Education. 1987. *Mathematics Model Curriculum Guide: Kindergarten Through Grade Eight*. Sacramento, CA: Author.

Chapin, Suzanne H., and Arthur Johnson. 2006. *Math Matters: Understanding the Math You Teach, Grades K–6*. 2d ed. Sausalito, CA: Math Solutions Publications.

Chapin, Suzanne H., Catherine O'Connor, and Nancy Canavan Anderson. 2003. *Classroom Discussions: Using Math Talk to Help Students Learn, Grades 1–6*. Sausalito, CA: Math Solutions Publications.

Feinsilber, Mike, and William B. Mead. 1980. *American Averages: Amazing Facts of Everyday Life*. Garden City, NY: Dolphin.

Hawkins, David. 1983. "Nature Closely Observed." *Daedalus* 112 (2): 65–89.

Jacobs, Harold R. 1994. *Mathematics: A Human Endeavor: A Book for Those Who Think They Don't Like the Subject*. 3d ed. New York: W. H. Freeman.

Lappan, Glenda. No date. "Knowing What We Teach and Teaching What We Know." Accessed at *http://nctm.org/news/pastpresident/1999-11president.htm*.

Lappan, Glenda, James T. Fey, William M. Fitzgerald, Susan N. Friel, and Elizabeth D. Phillips. 1998. *Prime Time: Factors and Multiples. Connected Mathematics Project.* Palo Alto, CA: Dale Seymour Publications.

Mason, John, with Leone Burton and Kaye Stacey. 1982. *Thinking Mathematically.* Reading, MA: Addison-Wesley.

Meyer, Carol, and Tom Sallee. 1983. *Make It Simpler: A Practical Guide to Problem Solving in Mathematics.* London: Addison-Wesley.

National Council of Teachers of Mathematics (NCTM). 2000. *Principles and Standards for School Mathematics.* Reston, VA: NCTM.

———. 2006. *Curriculum Focal Points for Prekindergarten Through Grade 8 Mathematics: A Quest for Coherence.* Reston, VA: NCTM.

O'Brien, Thomas C., and Shirley A. Casey. 1983. "Children Learning Multiplication Part I." *School Science and Mathematics* 83 (3): 246–51.

Raphel, Annette. 2000. *Math Homework That Counts, Grades 4–6.* Sausalito, CA: Math Solutions Publications.

Rectanus, Cheryl. 1994. *Math By All Means: Geometry, Grades 3–4.* Sausalito, CA: Math Solutions Publications.

———. 1997. *Math By All Means: Area and Perimeter, Grades 5–6.* Sausalito, CA: Math Solutions Publications.

Tank, Bonnie, and Lynne Zolli. 2001. *Teaching Arithmetic: Lessons for Addition and Subtraction, Grades 2–3.* Sausalito, CA: Math Solutions Publications.

Wickett, Maryann, and Marilyn Burns. 2003. *Teaching Arithmetic: Lessons for Extending Division, Grades 4–5.* Sausalito, CA: Math Solutions Publications.

Zinsser, William. 1988. *Writing to Learn.* New York: Harper and Row.

Children's Books

Burns, Marilyn. 1982. *Math for Smarty Pants.* Boston: Little, Brown.

———. 1997. *Spaghetti and Meatball for All! A Mathematical Story.* New York: Scholastic.

———. 1990. *The $1.00 Word Riddle Book.* Sausalito, CA: Math Solutions Publications.

Carle, Eric. 1991. *Rooster's Off to See the World.* New York: Simon and Schuster Books for Young Readers.

Cleary, Beverly. 1968. *Ramona the Pest.* New York: William Morrow.

Crews, Donald. 1986. *Ten Black Dots.* New York: Greenwillow.

Hutchins, Pat. 1982. *1 Hunter.* New York: Greenwillow.

———. 1986. *The Doorbell Rang.* New York: Greenwillow.

Lindbergh, Reeve. 1987. *The Midnight Farm.* New York: Dial Books for Young Readers.

Mahy, Margaret. 1987. *17 Kings and 42 Elephants.* New York: Dial Books for Young Readers.

Morozumi, Atsuko. 1996. *One Gorilla.* New York: Mirasol.

Neuschwander, Cindy. 1998. *Amanda Bean's Amazing Dream.* New York: Scholastic.

Pinczes, Elinor J. 1995. *A Remainder of One.* Boston: Houghton Mifflin.

———. 1999. *One Hundred Hungry Ants.* Boston: Houghton Mifflin.

The activities marked with an asterisk (*) are discussed in Part 4.

Acting Out Addition and Subtraction
Stories,   199
Adding to 1,   290
Addition and Subtraction Stories with
Cubes,   200
Addition Table Explorations,   164
Alphabetical Probability,   94–95
Angles with Pattern Blocks and Hinged
Mirrors,   120
Area and Perimeter,   115
*Area on the Geoboard,   127, 333–34
Areas of Four on the Geoboard,   127
*Area Stays the Same, The,   84, 309
*Arrow Arithmetic,   167, 360–61

*Banquet Table Problem, The,   117, 331–32
Billy Goes Shopping,   228
Billy Wins a Shopping Spree,   240
Birthday Twins, The,   97
Block Letters,   299
Body Ratios,   72–74
Book Measuring,   79
Border Problem, The,   165
*Box Measuring,   81, 305–6
Build a Stack,   204
Building Rectangles,   280
Build the Yellow Hexagon,   282

Calculator Patterns,   240
Candy Boxes,   236–37
Candy Box Research (Version 1),   238
Candy Box Research (Version 2),   239
Candy Box Sales Guides,   250
Card Problem, The,   140
*Change from a $10.00 Bill,   163, 356
Chocolate Bars,   253

Chopstick Problem, The,   233–34
Circles and Stars,   235–36
Closest to 0, 0.5, or 1?,   288
Closest to 0, $\frac{1}{2}$, or 1?,   278
Coin Riddles,   162
Color In,   143
Coloring 0–99 Patterns,   218
Comparing Advertisements,   298
Comparing Hands,   226
Consecutive Sums Problem, The,   57–60
Covering Covers,   228
Cross Out Singles,   230

Dealing in Horses,   13, 14
Decimals in Contexts,   288
Decimals in the Newspaper,   289
Decimals on Grids,   286–88
Decision Making,   136
Design Your Own Spinner,   91
Diagonal Problem, The,   150
Difference Puzzle,   134
Difference Trains,   134
Digit Place,   142, 212–13, 215
Discount Coupon, The,   299
Division Stories,   252
Doorbell Rang, The,   246–47
Doorbell Rings Again, The,   253
Dot Connecting,   149
*Double the Circumference,   83, 307–9

Empty the Bowl,   198–99, 207
Estimate and Measure,   227
Explorations Using the Geoboard,   124
Explorations with Four Toothpicks,   121

Factor Fiddling,   266
Factor Game, The,   242

Factory Box Problem, The,   110
*Fair Game 1,   102, 319–20
*Fair Game 2,   102, 321
Figuring Tips in Restaurants,   298
Fill the Cube (Version 1),   215
Fill the Cube (Version 2),   229
Five Tower Game,   216
Fold-and-Cut Investigation, The,   116
Foot Area and Perimeter,   78
Foot Cutout,   77
Foot Figuring,   78
Four in a Row,   143
*Four-Triangle Problem, The,   122, 332
Fraction Kit, The,   271–73
Fraction Riddles,   281
Fractions Close to $\frac{1}{2}$,   280
Fractions in Contexts,   278–79
Fractions with Two-Color Counters,   270

Game of Pig, The,   99, 225
Game of Poison, The,   131–32
*Geoboard Line Segments,   127, 332–33
Geoboard Square Search,   128
Geoboard Triangle Search,   128
Geometry Building,   113
*Got a Match?,   97, 314–15
Grab-Bag Subtraction,   206
Grow and Shrink,   204
Guess My Word,   140

*Handshake Problem, The,   156, 343–47
Harper's Index Problem, The,   293–94
Hexagon Fill-In Puzzle,   119, 407
Hexiamonds,   119
Hit the Target (Version 1),   261
Hit the Target (Version 2),   265
How Big Is Your Hand?,   224
How Long? How Many?,   242
How Long Is a Minute?,   82
How Many Beans?,   259–60
How Many Fingers?,   210
How Many Pockets?,   210–11
How Many Reds?,   197–98

How Many Rolls to Get a 1?,   98
*How Many Sums?,   163, 354–56
*How Many Throws?,   100, 317–19
*How Many Ways?,   101, 317–19
How Many Were Eaten?,   241
How Much Ribbon?,   223–24
How Old Is Ramona the Pest?,   227
How Thick Is Paper?,   80

Ice-Cream-Cone Problem, The,   151
In 1 Minute,   227
*Interior Regions,   112, 328
Interlocking Trains,   155
Introducing the Metric System,   74–77
Introductory Explorations with Pattern
   Blocks,   118
Investigations with Raisins,   161

Junk Sorting,   133

*King Arthur's Problem,   132, 335–38
Kings-and-Elephants Problem, The,   253

Larger Leftovers,   264
Largest Product, The,   263
Last Names,   226
Latin Squares,   138
Left-Handed Experiment, The,   95
Leftovers,   250–51
Leftovers from 100,   261–63
Leftovers with 20,   251
Logical Breakfast,   140
Long Division, A,   259

Make a Shape,   217
*Making Change,   162, 350–53
Mathematical Tug-of-War,   142
Milk Carton Geometry,   110
Mirror Cards,   116
More Candy Box Research,   252
More Circles and Stars,   239
More Explorations Using the Geoboard,   125
*More No-Lift Letters,   113, 329

More Painting Towers, 149
More Rod Stamping, 153
More Squares from Squares, 152
*Multiplication Possibilities, 164, 356–59
Multiplication Puzzlers, 289
Multiplication Stories, 241

Name Graphs, The, 221–22
Necklace Lesson, The, 200–202
*No-Lift Letters, 113, 329
Number Bracelets, 162
Number Puzzle, 216
Number Sorting, 138
*Number Sums, 158–59, 348–50

Odd Number Wins, 143
101 and Out, 229
1-2-3-4 Activity, The, 93
On Which Day of the Week Were You
   Born?, 166
*Orange Juice–and-Water Problem, The,
   139, 341

Painting Towers, 148
Palindromes, 159–60
Paper Folding, 148–49
Paper Tearing, 150
Pascal's Triangle, 163
Patterns in Multiples, 238
Patterns on the 0–99 Chart, 213–14
Penticubes, 123
Pentominoes, 108–10
Pentomino Game, 110
Pentomino One-Difference Loop, 110
Percents in the Newspaper, 297
Percent Stories, 300
Perimeter Stays the Same, The, 80
Perimeter with Cuisenaire Rods, 83
Photocopy Problem, The, 298
Pick's Theorem, 129
Pinch a 10, 217
Place-Value Game, The, 290
Points Dividing a Line, 150

Pool Hall Math, 114
Popcorn Problem, The, 103
*Postage Stamp Problem, The, 167, 359–60
*Prison Problem, The, 135, 338–40
Put In Order, 277

Race for $1.00, 212–13, 214
Race for 20, 141
Ratio with Cuisenaire Rods, 82
Relating Fractional Remainders as
   Decimals, 285
Remainders of Zero, 264
*Riddles with Color Tiles, 141, 341–42
Rod Relationships, 281
Rod Stamping, 152
Roll 15, 224–25
*Round Things, 81, 306
Row of Hexagons, A, 154–55
Row of Pentagons, A, 154
Row of Squares, A, 154
Row of Triangles, A, 153

Sally and the Peanuts, 137
Sampling Bean Populations, 92
Sense of Nonsense, 292–93
Shake and Peek, 98
*Shake and Spill, 101, 310, 312–14
Shape Construction on the Geoboard, 128
Sharing Brownies, 276
Sharing Cookies, 275–76
Snap It, 206
Sorting Shapes on the Geoboard, 126
Spill and Compare, 205
Spinner Experiments, 87–89
*Square Partitioning, 117, 330–31
Squares from Squares, 151
Square Up, 126
*Squaring Up, 79, 304–5
Stars, 214
*Straight or Curved?, 112, 328–29

*Tangram Puzzle, The, 111, 322–27
*That's Just Half the Story, 112, 327

Things That Come in Groups,   234
*Three-Sacks Problem, The,   136, 340–41
Tiles in the Bag (Version 1),   90
Tiles in the Bag (Version 2),   91
Tile Trading,   96
Times Table Plaids,   241
Too Short,   226
Toothpick Building,   155
Trace and Compare,   205
*Two-Coin Toss,   97, 311
*Two-Color Problem, The,   139, 341
Two-Dice Sum Game, The,   96

Using Division Problems to Introduce
   Decimals,   284–85
Using Graphs to Build Understanding
   of Fractions,   273–75

Using Graphs to Build Understanding
   of Percents,   295–96

Warehouse Problem, The,   300
What Percent Is Shaded?,   294–95
What's the Record?,   99
Where Does 100 Land?,   165
Who Ate More?,   277–78
Wipeout,   282
*Wraparound,   81, 307

*X-O Problem, The,   99, 315–17

Yarn Shapes,   82, 205
Your Choice Tic-Tac-Toe,   137
Your Height in Money,   80

0–99 Chart,   163, 213–14

Above-grade-level students, challenging, 388–90
Acting Out Addition and Subtraction Stories lesson, 199
Activities
  instructional (*see* Instructional activities)
  menu (*see* Menu activities)
Adding to 1 (Menu Activity), 290
Addition and subtraction, 221–32
  assessment, 231–32
  benefits of instruction, 221
  counting up to subtract, 374–75
  independent activities (Menu), 225–30
  in measurement activities, 223–24
  patterns and addition, 368–70
  probability activities, 224–25
  regrouping with addition, 374
  repeated addition, 234–35
  statistics lesson, 221–22
  using word problems to introduce, 199–200
  whole-class lessons, 221–25
Addition and Subtraction Stories with Cubes lesson, 200
Addition Table Explorations (Activity), 164
Additive identity, 147
Algebra. *See also* Patterns, functions, and algebra
  value of, 144
  variables, uses of, 147–48
Algorithms
  definition of, 187
  risk of emphasizing in instruction, 187
  role of, in arithmetic, 187
  rules, limits of learning, 181–83
  teaching standard algorithms, value of, 190–91
  in traditional mathematics instruction, 11–12
Alphabetical Probability (Activity), 94–95
Amanda Bean's Amazing Dream (Neuschwander), 384
American Averages (Feinsilber & Mead), 295
Anderson, Nancy Canavan (*Classroom Discussions: Using Math Talk to Help Students Learn)*, 37

Angles with Pattern Blocks and Hinged Mirrors (Activity), 120
Area and Perimeter (Activity), 115
Area on the Geoboard (Activity), 127, 333–34
Areas of Four on the Geoboard (Activity), 127
Area Stays the Same, The (Activity), 84, 309
Arithmetic, 171–95
  basics in, 174–75
  changing view of, 7, 171
  computation in, 171–72
  drill and practice, appropriateness of, 192
  errors, examining common, 10–12
  essential aspects of instruction, 171
  goals of instruction, 7, 171, 192
  how children learn (*see* Learning math)
  motivation in learning, 175
  number sense in, 173
  parents expectations for, 22–23
  problem solving in, 172–73
  questions from teachers, 190–95
  in real-life situations, 174
  real-life situations, relating arithmetic to, 7–9, 192–95
  research, classroom, 175–81
  rules, limits of learning, 181–83
  strategies for computing, 187–90
  teaching what to do versus teaching what to and why, 183–86
  thinking processes about, children's, 10–11
  traditional instruction, 7
  understanding, developing, 195
  value of, 16–17, 171
  word problems (*see* Word problems)
Arrow Arithmetic (Activity), 167, 360–61
Assessment
  addition and subtraction, 231–32
  decimals, 290–91
  division, 253–54
  fractions, 283
  goals for, 47
  instruction and, linking, 47–50
  multiplication, 243–44
  number concepts, 207–8
  percents, 300

place value, 218–20
portfolios, math, 386–87
questions as tool for, 47–48
strategies, 383–84
test prep, 391–93
through class discussions, 49–50
through written work, 48–49
in units of instruction, 65
the "why" of arithmetic, difficulty of assessing, 184
Assignments, allowing students to set parameters of, 389–90
Attendance graphs lesson, 104–6
Axes, on graphs, 147

Banquet Table Problem, The (Activity), 117, 331–32
Basic facts
  learning multiplication and division, 384–85
  timed tests with, value of, 191–92
  value of learning, 191
Bay-Williams, Jennifer M. (*Math and Literature, Grades 6–8)*, 202
Billy Goes Shopping (Menu Activity), 228
Billy Wins a Shopping Spree (Menu Activity), 240
Birthday Twins, The (Activity), 97
Blackline Masters, 403–31
  Addition Chart, 420
  Area and Perimeter Shapes, 406
  Area on the Geoboard, 415
  Centimeter Grid Paper, 405
  Fractions on Grids (4-by-4 Squares), 427
  Fractions on Grids (6-by-4 Rectangles), 428
  Fractions with Bars, 426
  Fractions with Cookies, 425
  Half Inch Grid Paper, 407
  Hexagon Fill-In Puzzle, 408
  Inch Grid Paper, 416
  Isometric Dot Paper, 411
  Large 0–99 Chart, 417
  Large 1–100 Chart, 422
  Large Geoboard Dot Paper, 412
  Medium Geoboard Dot Paper, 413
  Multiplication Table, 424
  Palindrome Recording Sheet, 418
  Pattern Block Triangle Paper, 409
  Shake and Spill, 430

Blackline Masters (*continued*)
    Small 0–99 Charts, 419
    Small 1–100 Charts, 423
    Small Geoboard Dot Paper, 414
    10-by-10 grids, 429
    Ten-Frames Recording Sheet, 421
    Toothpick Dot Paper, 410
    2-Centimeter Grid Paper, 431
Block Letters (Menu Activity), 299
Body Ratios (Sample Activity), 72–74
Book Measuring (Activity), 79
Border Problem, The (Activity), 165
Box Measuring (Activity), 81, 305–6
Bresser, Rusty
    Developing Number Sense, Grades 3–6, 261
    Math and Literature, Grades 4–6, 202
Build a Stack (Menu Activity), 204
Building Rectangles (Menu Activity), 280
Build the Yellow Hexagon (Menu Activity), 282
Burns, Marilyn
    Collection of Math Lessons, A: From Grades 6 through 8, 189
    50 Problem-Solving Lessons, 259, 260
    Math and Literature, Grades 2–3, 202
    Math and Literature, Grades K–1, 202
    The $1.00 Word Riddle Book, 17
    Writing in Math Class, 48

Calculator Patterns (Menu Activity), 240
Calculators, using with decimals, 284–85
Candy Boxes lesson, 236–37
Candy Box Research (Version 1) (Menu Activity), 238
Candy Box Research (Version 2) (Menu Activity), 239
Candy Box Sales Guides lesson, 250
Card Problem, The (Activity), 140
Carle, Eric (*Rooster's Off to See the World*), 202
Casey, Shirley A. (*School Science and Mathematics*), 178–79
Change from a $10.00 Bill (Activity), 163, 356
Chapin, Suzanne H.
    Classroom Discussions: Using Math Talk to Help Students Learn, 37
    Math Matters, 187

Children's literature
    book choices as critical, 45
    counting books, number concept activities initiated from, 202–4
    sample lesson, 45–46
Chocolate Bars (Menu Activity), 253
Choices for students, importance of, 388
Chopstick Problem, The, lesson, 233–34
Circles and Stars lesson, 235–36
Class discussions
    alternate views on solutions, presenting, 52
    assessment through, 49–50
    building number sense with, 25, 26
    following small-group work, 402
    importance of, 36–37
    participation as student responsibility, 37
    supportive atmosphere, establishing, 36–37
    talk moves, 37
    think, pair, share, 37
    turn and talk, 37
    in units of instruction, 65
    whole class, 402
Class inventories
    assessment through, 49
    using student writing to create, 41
Classroom Discussions: Using Math Talk to Help Students Learn (Chapin, O'Connor, Anderson), 37
Classroom instruction, managing, 51–66
    classroom management plans, sample, 62–63
    independent work, structuring (*see* Menu)
    lessons, structuring, 54–57
    organizing instructional program (*see* Units of instruction)
    sample lesson: The Consecutive Sums Problem, 57–60
    small-group work, organizing for, 52–54
    starting instruction, 65–66
Classrooms
    number concepts, use of classroom situations to teach, 196–97
    organizing for small-group work, 52–54
Closest to 0, 0.5, or 1? lesson, 288
Closest to 0, $\frac{1}{2}$, or 1? lesson, 278
Coin Riddles (Activity), 162

Collection of Math Lessons, A: From Grades 6 through 8 (Burns & Humphreys), 189
Color In (Activity), 143
Coloring 0–99 Patterns (Menu Activity), 218
Comparing Advertisements (Menu Activity), 298
Comparing Hands (Menu Activity), 226
Computation, 171–72
    fingers for computing, use of, 366
    inappropriateness of focusing on, 9
    strategies for, 25, 187–90
Consecutive Sums Problem, The, 57–60
Content knowledge of teachers, importance of, 5–6
Content Standards (NCTM), 3–4
Contexts, introducing percents in, 292–94
Counting large quantities, lessons, 209–11
Covering Covers (Menu Activity), 228
Crews, Donald (*Ten Black Dots*), 203–4
Cross Out Singles (Menu Activity), 230
Curriculum, mathematical targets (NCTM), 3–4
Curriculum Focal Points for Prekindergarten Through Grade 8 Mathematics: A Quest for Coherence (National Council of Teachers of Mathematics), 3, 4

Data. *See also* Probability and statistics
    collecting, as concept to be taught, 86
    inferences, making, 86
    interpreting, as concept to be taught, 86, 87
    organizing and representing, as concepts to be taught, 86
    sampling, 86
Dealing in Horses problem, 13, 14
Decimals, 284–91
    assessment, 290–91
    calculators, investigations with, 284–85
    concept of, 375–77
    connecting fractions and, 393–95
    geometric perspective on, 286–88
    grids, lesson on use of, 286–88
    independent activities (Menu), 289–90

mental calculation with, lessons, 288–89
reading, 284
value of, 284
whole-class lessons, 284–89
Decimals in Contexts lesson, 288
Decimals in the Newspaper (Menu Activity), 289
Decimals on Grids lesson, 286–88
Decision Making (Activity), 136
Deductive reasoning, 130
Design Your Own Spinner (Activity), 91
Developing Number Sense, Grades 3–6 (Bresser & Holtzman), 261
Diagonal Problem, The (Activity), 150
Difference Puzzle (Activity), 134
Difference Trains (Activity), 134
Difficulty, of problem solving, 23
Digit Place
    activity, 142
    lesson, 212–13
Digit Place (Menu Activity), 215
Discount Coupon, The (Menu Activity), 299
Discussions, class. *See* Class discussions
Discussions of problems
    geometry and spatial sense, 322–34
    logical reasoning, 335–42
    measurement, 304–9
    patterns, functions, and algebra, 343–47
    probability and statistics, 310–21
Disequilibrium/equilibrium, 28–30
Distributive property, 257–58
Division, 245–54, 255–66
    assessment, 253–54, 266
    distributive property, using the, 257–58
    division grouping problems lesson, 247–49
    division sharing problems lesson, 245–46
    extending, 255–66
    game, 250–51
    independent activities (Menu), 251–53, 263–66
    investigations with raisins, 249
    with large numbers, 255–66
    long division, 390–91
    and multiplication, relating, 258–60
    objectives, 255
    problem situations, introducing division through, 245–49
    relating division to multiplication, 249–50

through real-world problems, 260
traditional instruction, 255
types, 245
using games, 260–63
whole-class lessons, 245–51, 256–63
word problems, 378–79
Division Stories (Menu Activity), 252
Doorbell Rang, The, lesson, 246–47
Doorbell Rang, The (Hutchins), 246
Doorbell Rings Again, The (Menu Activity), 253
Dot Connecting (Activity), 149
Double the Circumference (Activity), 83, 307–9

Empty the Bowl
    lesson, 198–99
    menu activity, 207
Equilibration, 29
Equilibrium/disequilibrium, 28–30
Errors
    common errors, examining, 10–12
    as opportunities for learning, 51
Estimate and Measure (Menu Activity), 227
Estimation, in building number sense, 25
Explorations Using the Geoboard (Activity), 124
Explorations with Four Toothpicks (Activity), 121
Exploring, part of lessons, 55–56

Factor Fiddling (Menu Activity), 266
Factor Game, The (Menu Activity), 242
Factory Box Problem, The (Activity), 110
Fair Game 1 (Activity), 102, 319–20
Fair Game 2 (Activity), 102, 321
Feinsilber, Mike *(American Averages)*, 295
50 Problem-Solving Lessons (Burns), 259, 260
Figuring Tips in Restaurants (Menu Activity), 298
Fill the Cube (Version 1) (Menu Activity), 215
Fill the Cube (Version 2) (Menu Activity), 229
Fingers for computing, use of, 366
Five Tower Game (Menu Activity), 216
Fold-and-Cut Investigation, The (Activity), 116

Foot Area and Perimeter (Activity), 78
Foot Cutout (Activity), 77
Foot Figuring (Activity), 78
Four in a Row (Activity), 143
Four-Triangle Problem, The (Activity), 122, 332
Fraction Kit, The
    menu activity, 271–73
    reasoning behind, 48
Fraction Riddles (Menu Activity), 281
Fractions, 267–83
    assessment, 283
    children's informal learning of, 267
    comparing and ordering, 277–78
    connecting decimals and, 393–95
    independent activities (Menu), 279–82
    introductory lessons, 268–73
    mental calculations with, 278–79
    as parts of sets, introducing fractions, 269–70
    sharing problems, exploring fractions through, 275–76
    strategies, instructional, 267–68
    strategies for operations, 279
    topics for instruction, 267–68
    using graphs with, 273–75
    whole-class lessons, 268–79
Fractions Close to $\frac{1}{2}$ (Menu Activity), 280
Fractions in Contexts lesson, 278–79
Fractions with Two-Color Counters lesson, 270
Friendly numbers, 381–82
Functions. *See also* Patterns, functions, and algebra
    defined, 145
    understanding of, developing, 145–47
    use of formulas with, 146
    use of graphs with, 147
    use of tables with, 146
    value of knowing, 144

Game of Pig, The (Activity), 99, 225
Game of Poison, The (Sample Activity), 131–32
Games
    addition games, 99, 102, 224–25, 230
    division, 250–51, 260–63
    factor, 242
    with money, 371
    multiplication as combining equal groups game, 235–36, 260–63
    number, 197–99

Games (continued)
  for number concepts, 197–99, 206
  Pentomino, 110
  place value, 212–13, 214
  probability game with addition,
    96, 99
  reasoning game, 131–32
  teaching, 388–89
Geoboard Line Segments (Activity),
  127, 332–33
Geoboard Square Search
  (Activity), 128
Geoboard Triangle Search
  (Activity), 128
Geometry and spatial sense, 107–29
  decimals, geometric perspective on,
    286–88
  discussions of problems, 322–34
  instructional activities, 108–29
  percents, geometric perspective on,
    294–95
  sample activity, 108–10
  value of teaching, 107–8
Geometry Building (Activity), 113
Goals
  of arithmetic instruction, 7, 171, 192
  for assessment, 47
  classroom discussions, goals for, 36
  division, 255
  learning to reason as, 186
  multiplication, 255
  NCTM, 3–4
  parents, explaining goals to, 22–23
  with percents, 292
  for writing in math class, 38
Got a Match? (Activity), 97, 314–15
Grab-Bag Subtraction (Menu
  Activity), 206
Graphing
  attendance graphs, 104–6
  fractions, using graphs with,
    273–75
  functions, 147
  introducing, 103–4
  percents, using graphs with, 295–96
  types of graphs, 104
Greeks (Ancient), difference between
  arithmetic and logistics, 186
Grids
  Centimeter Grid Paper (Blackline
    Master), 405
  Half-Inch Grid Paper (Blackline
    Master), 407
  Inch Grid Paper (Blackline
    Master), 416
  10-by-10 Grids (Blackline
    Master), 429
  2-Centimeter Grid Paper (Blackline
    Master), 431

used with decimals, lesson, 286–88
Grow and Shrink (Menu Activity),
  204
Guess My Word (Activity), 140

Handshake Problem, The (Activity),
  156, 343–47
Hands-on-the-table math, 25, 26,
  391–93
Harper's Index Problem, The, lesson,
  293–94
Harper's Magazine, 293
Hawkins, David ("Nature Closely
  Observed"), 186
Height/Circumference (Exercise), 28
Hexagon Fill-In Puzzle (Activity),
  119, 408
Hexiamonds (Activity), 119
Hit the Target (Version 1) lesson, 261
Hit the Target (Version 2) (Menu
  Activity), 265
Holtzman, Caren (Developing
  Number Sense, Grades 3–6), 261
Homework, 398–99
How Big Is Your Hand? lesson, 224
How Long? How Many? (Menu
  Activity), 242
How Long Is a Minute? (Activity), 82
How Many Beans? lesson, 259–60
How Many Fingers? lesson, 210
How Many Pockets? lesson, 210–11
How Many Reds? lesson, 197–98
How Many Rolls to Get a 1?
  (Activity), 98
How Many Sums? (Activity), 163,
  354–56
How Many Throws? (Activity), 100,
  317–19
How Many Ways? (Activity), 101,
  317–19
How Many Were Eaten? (Menu
  Activity), 241
How Much Ribbon? lesson, 223–24
How Old Is Ramona the Pest? (Menu
  Activity), 227
How Thick Is Paper? (Activity), 80
Humphreys, Cathy, 189–90
Hutchins, Pat
  The Doorbell Rang, 246
  1 Hunter, 203

Ice-Cream-Cone Problem, The
  (Activity), 151
Independent activities
  for decimals, 289–90
  structuring, 60–62
  in units of instruction, 64–65

Inductive reasoning, 130, 131
Inferences, making, as concept to be
  taught, 87
In 1 Minute (Menu Activity), 227
Instruction, managing classroom. See
  Classroom instruction, managing
Instructional activities. See also Menu
  activities
  for geometry, 108–29
  for logical reasoning, 131–43
  for measurement, 72–84
  for number and operations,
    158–67
  organization, 69
  for patterns, functions and algebra,
    148–56
  for probability and statistics,
    87–106
Interior Regions (Activity), 112, 328
Interlocking Trains (Activity), 155
Introducing Fractions as Parts of Sets,
  lessons, 269–73
Introducing the Metric System
  (Sample Activity), 74–77
Introductions, to lessons, 54–55
Introductory Explorations with
  Pattern Blocks (Activity), 118
Introductory lessons, 64
Investigations with Raisins
  (Activity), 161

Johnson, Arthur (Math Matters), 187
Journals, math class, 39
Junk Sorting (Activity), 133

King Arthur's Problem (Activity),
  132, 335–38
Kings-and-Elephants Problem, The
  (Menu Activity), 253
"Knowing What We Teach and
  Teaching What We Know"
  (Lappan), 5–6
Knowledge
  logical, 31
  social, 31–32

Language of math, 372–74, 383
Lappan, Glenda ("Knowing What
  We Teach and Teaching What
  We Know"), 5–6
Larger Leftovers (Menu
  Activity), 264
Largest Product, The (Menu
  Activity), 263
Last Names (Menu Activity), 226
Latin Squares (Activity), 138

Learners, characteristics of successful, 51
Learning math, 27–32
  conditions for learning, 31–32
  direct and concrete interaction with math ideas, need for, 27
  disequilibrium/equilibrium, 28–29
  perceptions in, 27–29
  problem recognition in, 29–30
Learning processes, writing about, 40
Left-Handed Experiment, The (Activity), 95
Leftovers from 100 lesson, 261–63
Leftovers lesson, 250–51
Leftovers with 20 (Menu Activity), 251
Lessons, structuring, 54–57
"Let's try" attitude, 51
Lindbergh, Reeve (The Midnight Farm), 203
Literature, using children's. See Children's literature
Logical Breakfast (Activity), 140
Logical knowledge, 31, 32. See also Reasoning
Logical reasoning, 130–43
  benefits of teaching, 130
  concepts to be taught, 130–31
  discussions of problems, 335–42
  instructional activities, 131–43
  sample activity, 131–32
Logistic, 186
Logs, math class, 39
Long Division, A, lesson, 259

Make a Shape (Menu Activity), 217
Making Change (Activity), 162, 350–53
Manipulative materials
  classroom use of, 34–35
  reasons for using, 33–34
  role of, 33–35
Martinie, Sherrie L. (Math and Literature, Grades 6–8), 202
Math, language of, 372–74
Math, Literature, and Nonfiction series, 46
Math and Literature, Grades 6–8 (Bay-Williams & Martinie), 202
Math and Literature, Grades 4–6 (Bresser), 202
Math and Literature, Grades 2–3 (Burns & Sheffield), 202
Math and Literature, Grades K–1 (Burns & Sheffield), 202
Math centers, 366–67
Mathematical ideas, as type of math writing, 39–40
Mathematical targets, 3–4

Mathematical Tug-of-War (Activity), 142
Math Homework That Counts, Grades 4–6 (Raphel), 399
Math instruction
  changes to instruction, making, 395–97
  equilibrium/disequilibrium in, 28
  errors, examining common, 10–12
  how children learn (see Learning math)
  incorporating writing into (see Writing)
  instructional program, organizing (see Units of instruction)
  menu use, 60–62
  in real-life situations, 7–9, 27–31
  teaching the "why," 5–6
Math Matters (Chapin & Johnson), 187
"Math Words" chart, 44
Maturity, as condition of learning, 31
Mead, William B. (American Averages), 295
Meaning in arithmetic procedures, learning the, 185–86
Measurement, 70–84
  in addition and subtraction lesson, 223–24
  concepts to be taught, 70–72
  definition of, 70
  discussions of problems, 304–9
  instructional activities for, 72–84
  reasons for teaching, 70
  sample activities, 72–77
Memorization, in computation, 172
Mental calculations, in building number sense, 25
Menu, 60–62
  benefits of, 61–62
  classroom management plans, sample, 62–63
  definition of, 61
  independent work, structuring, 60–62
  tasks, posting list of, 61
Menu activities. See also Instructional activities
  addition and subtraction, 225–30
  for decimals, 289–90
  division, 251–53
  fractions, 279–82
  multiplication, 237–43
  number concepts, 204–7
  with percents, 297–300
  place value, 214–18
Metric system, introductory activity for, 74–77

Midnight Farm, The (Lindbergh), 203
Milk Carton Geometry (Activity), 110
Mirror Cards (Activity), 116
Mistakes
  common errors, examining, 10–12
  as opportunities for learning, 51
Mode, 222
Modeling
  different methods for computing, 24–25
  a "let's try" attitude, 51
  a "we can" attitude, 51
Money
  games with, 371
  place value lesson, using money with, 211–12
  value of coins and counting activity, 370–71
More Candy Box Research (Menu Activity), 252
More Circles and Stars (Menu Activity), 239
More Explorations Using the Geoboard (Activity), 125
More No-Lift Letters (Activity), 113, 329
More Painting Towers (Activity), 149
More Rod Stamping (Activity), 153
More Squares from Squares (Activity), 152
Morozumi, Atsuko (One Gorilla), 203, 207
Multiplication, 233–44, 255–66
  assessment, 243–44, 266
  broader view of teaching, 233
  as combining equal groups, 234–36
  distributive property, using the, 257–58
  and division, relating, 258–60
  extending, 255–66
  geometric model for, 236–37
  independent activities (Menu), 237–43, 263–66
  interpreting, 377–78
  with large numbers, 255–66
  multidigit, 379–81
  multiples, patterns in, 378
  multiplying by 10 and powers of, 256–57
  objectives, 255
  in real-world contexts, 233–34
  through real-world problems, 260
  traditional instruction, 233, 255
  using games, 260–63
  whole-class lessons, 233–37, 256–63
  word problems, 378–79

Multiplication Possibilities (Activity), 164, 356–59
Multiplication Puzzlers (Menu Activity), 289
Multiplication Stories (Menu Activity), 241
Multiplicative identity, 147
My Metric Length Book, 74

Name Graphs, The, lesson, 221–22
National Assessment of Educational Progress (NAEP), 283
National Council of Teachers of Mathematics (NCTM)
    Curriculum Focal Points for Prekindergarten Through Grade 8 Mathematics: A Quest for Coherence, 3, 4
    Principles and Standards for School Mathematics (See Principles and Standards for School Mathematics (National Council of Teachers of Mathematics))
"Nature Closely Observed" (Hawkins), 186
Necklace Lesson, The, 200–202
Neuschwander, Cindy *(Amanda Bean's Amazing Dream),* 384
New York Times Best Illustrated Children's Book Award, 203
No-Lift Letters (Activity), 113, 329
Nonroutine problems, teaching number concepts with, 200–202
Number and operations, 157–67
    concepts to be taught, 157
    discussions of problems, 348–61
    instructional activities, 158–67
    sample activities, 158–60
Number Bracelets (Activity), 162
Number concepts, 196–208
    assessment, 207–8
    benefits of instruction, 196
    classroom situations, using, 196–97
    games, number, 197–99
    independent activities (Menu), 204–7
    nonroutine problems, 200–202
    whole-class lessons, 196–204
    word problems, 199–200
Number Puzzle (Menu Activity), 216
Numbers
    friendly, 381–82
    value of knowing about, 157
Number sense, 173. *See also* Number and operations
    building, 24–26, 157

value of, 24, 157
Number Sorting (Activity), 138
Number Sums (Sample Activity), 158–59, 348–50
Nye, Sandra, 175–79

Objectives. *See* Goals
O'Brien, Thomas C. *(School Science and Mathematics),* 178–79
Observing children
    with addition and subtraction lessons, 231
    with decimal lessons, 290
    with division lessons, 253, 266
    with fractions lessons, 283
    with multiplication lessons, 243–44, 266
    with number concepts lessons, 207
    with percents lessons, 300
    with place value lessons, 218–19
O'Connor, Catherine *(Classroom Discussions: Using Math Talk to Help Students Learn),* 37
Odd Number Wins (Activity), 143
One Gorilla (Morozumi), 203, 207
One Hundred Hungry Ants (Pinczes), 384
101 and Out (Menu Activity), 229
1 Hunter (Hutchins), 203
1–100 Chart, versus the 0–99 Chart, uses of, 372
1-2-3-4 Activity, The (Activity), 93
On Which Day of the Week Were You Born? (Activity), 166
Orange Juice–and-Water Problem, The (Activity), 139, 341
Order of operations, 397–98
Origins, on graphs, 147

Painting Towers (Sample Activity), 148
Palindromes (Sample Activity), 159–60
Paper Folding (Activity), 148–49
Paper Tearing (Activity), 150
Parents, explaining instructional goals to, 22–23
Partners in small groups, working with, 401–402
Pascal's Triangle (Activity), 163
Patterns. *See also* Patterns, functions, and algebra
    and addition, 368–70
    introducing, 144–45
    in place value activity, 213–14
    repeating and growing patterns, use of, 367–68
    value of teaching, 144

Patterns, functions, and algebra
    discussions of problems, 343–47
    functions, developing understanding of, 145–47
    instructional activities, 148–56
    patterns, introducing, 144–45
    sample activity, 148
    use of formulas with, 146
    use of graphs with, 147
    use of tables with functions, 146
    value of knowing, 144
    variables, uses of, 147–48
Patterns in Multiples (Menu Activity), 238
Patterns on the 0–99 Chart lesson, 213–14
Penticubes (Activity), 123
Pentominoes (Sample Activity), 108–10
Pentomino Game (Activity), 110
Pentomino One-Difference Loop (Activity), 110
Percents, 292–300
    assessment, 300
    in contexts, introducing, 292–94
    geometric perspective on, 294–95
    goal for instruction, 292
    independent activities (Menu), 297–300
    informal exposure to, 292
    mental calculations, 296–97
    using graphs with, 295–96
    whole-class lessons, 292–97
Percents in the Newspaper (Menu Activity), 297
Percent Stories (Menu Activity), 300
Perimeter Stays the Same, The (Activity), 80
Perimeter with Cuisenaire Rods (Activity), 83
Photocopy Problem, The (Menu Activity), 298
Physical experience, as condition of learning, 31
Piaget, Jean, equilibrium/disequilibrium, 28
Pick's Theorem (Activity), 129
Picture graphs, 104
Pinch a 10 (Menu Activity), 217
Pinczes, Elinor J.
    One Hundred Hungry Ants, 384
    Remainder of One, A, 384
Place value, 209–20
    assessment, 218–20
    benefits of instruction, 209
    counting large quantities, lessons, 209–11
    independent activities (Menu), 214–18

logic game, 212–13
patterns, looking for, 213–14
strategies, teaching, 209
using money with, lesson for, 211–12
whole-class lessons, 209–14
Place-Value Game, The (Menu Activity), 290
Points Dividing a Line (Activity), 150
Pool Hall Math (Activity), 114
Popcorn Problem, The (Activity), 103
Portfolios, math, 386–87
Postage Stamp Problem, The (Activity), 167, 359–60
Principles and Standards for School Mathematics (National Council of Teachers of Mathematics), 3–4, 5, 7
on assessment, 50
classroom discussions, goals for, 36
writing in math class, goals for, 38
Prison Problem, The (Activity), 135, 338–40
Probability and statistics
addition and subtraction lesson, 221–22
assigning probabilities, as concept to be taught, 87
concepts to be taught, 86–87
data (*see* Data)
definition of probability, 85
discussions of problems, 310–21
instructional activities, 87–106
mental addition in games of chance activities, 224–25
sample activity, 87–89
statistics, definition of, 85
value of teaching, 85–86
Problems
criteria for math problems, 18–19
definition of, 17–19
with more than one answer, developing number sense with, 26
Problem solving, 172–73
with manipulative materials, value of, 34–35
parents expectations for, 22–23
pros and cons of, 22–23
real-life, 16–17
requiring thinking beyond traditional, 16–17
strategies, 19–21
teachers uncomfortable with, 23
time for, lack of, 22
as too demanding or unrealistic, 22–23
as too hard, 23
as type of math writing, 39
Procedural understanding, 179

Procedures and reasoning, difference between teaching, 184
Process Standards (NCTM), 3–4
Proficiency, definition of, 175
Prompts, starting writing assignments with, 41
Put In Order lesson, 277

Questions
as assessment tool, 47–48
questions teachers ask, 366–402

Race for $1.00
lesson, 212–13
menu activity, 214
Race for 20 (Activity), 141
Range, 222
Raphel, Annette (*Math Homework That Counts, Grades 4–6),* 399
Ratio of Your Height to Your Head, The (Exercise), 27–28
Ratio with Cuisenaire Rods (Activity), 82
Real graphs, 104
Reasoning. *See also* Logical reasoning
deductive, 130
incorporating students', into assessment, 48
inductive, 130, 131
learning to reason as goal, 186
numerical, discussing, 26
procedures and, difference between teaching, 184
Relating Fractional Remainders as Decimals lesson, 285–86
Remainder of One, A (Pinczes), 384
Remainders of Zero (Menu Activity), 264
Riddles with Color Tiles (Activity), 141, 341–42
Rod Relationships (Menu Activity), 281
Rod Stamping (Activity), 152
Roll 15 lesson, 224–25
Rooster's Off to See the World (Carle, Eric), 202, 203
Rounding, 381–83
friendly numbers, 381–82
language of, 382–83
mental math problems, 382–83
Round Things (Activity), 81, 306
Row of Hexagons, A (Activity), 154–55
Row of Pentagons, A (Activity), 154
Row of Squares, A (Activity), 154
Row of Triangles, A (Activity), 153
Rules, limits of learning, 181–83

Sally and the Peanuts (Activity), 137
Sampling, as concept to be taught, 86
Sampling Bean Populations (Activity), 92
School Science and Mathematics (O'Brien & Casey), 178–79
Sense of Nonsense lesson, 292–93
Shake and Peek (Activity), 98
Shake and Spill (Activity), 101, 310, 312–14
Shape Construction on the Geoboard (Activity), 128
Sharing Brownies lesson, 276
Sharing Cookies lesson, 275–76
Sheffield, Stephanie
Math and Literature, Grades 2–3, 202
Math and Literature, Grades K–1, 202
Small groups
assessment through, 50
benefits of, 54
extensions, 402
first experiences, carefully choosing, 402
guidelines for, 52–54
making the rules clear, 401
partner work, 401
procedure for changing, establishing a, 401
strategies for, 399–402
whole-class discussions, leading, 402
work, organizing for small-group, 52–54
Snap It (Menu Activity), 206
Social interaction, as condition of learning, 31
Social knowledge
in mathematics, 31–32
math vocabulary as, 43
Solutions
alternate views on solutions, presenting, 52
generalizing, 57
Sorting Shapes on the Geoboard (Activity), 126
Spill and Compare (Menu Activity), 205
Spinner Experiments (Sample Activity), 87–89
Square Partitioning (Activity), 117, 330–31
Squares from Squares (Activity), 151
Square Up (Activity), 126
Squaring Up (Activity), 79, 304–5
Standardized testing, 184, 391–93
Standards, of National Council of Teachers of Mathematics, 3–4, 7

Stars (Menu Activity), 214
Statistics. *See* Probability and statistics
Stories
    division, 252
    percent, 300
Straight or Curved? (Activity), 112, 328–29
Strategies for Operations lesson, 288–89
Students
    above-grade-level, challenging, 388–90
    characteristics of successful learners, 51
Summarizing, lessons, 56–57
Symbolic graphs, 104

Tables, use of, with functions, 146
Talk moves, 37
Tangram Puzzle, The (Activity), 111, 322–27
Teacher knowledge, importance of, 5–6
Teachers
    importance of content knowledge, 5–6
    questions teachers ask, 366–402
Teaching, improving mathematics teaching, 50
Ten (10), multiplying by 10 and powers of, 256–57
Ten Black Dots (Crews) number-concept activity with, 203–4
Test prep, 391–93
Textbooks, emphasis on procedures, 183–84
That's Just Half the Story (Activity), 112, 327
Things That Come in Groups lesson, 234
Think, pair, share, 37
Three-Sacks Problem, The (Activity), 136, 340–41
Tiles in the Bag (Version 1) (Activity), 90
Tiles in the Bag (Version 2) (Activity), 91
Tile Trading (Activity), 96
Time for problem solving, lack of, 22
Times Table Plaids (Menu Activity), 241

Too Short (Menu Activity), 226
Toothpick Building (Activity), 155
Trace and Compare (Menu Activity), 205
Turn and talk, 37
Two-Coin Toss (Activity), 97, 311
Two-Color Problem, The (Activity), 139, 341
Two-Dice Sum Game, The (Activity), 96

Units of instruction
    assessment, 65
    components of units, 64
    independent explorations (Menu), 64–65
    introductory lessons, 64
    organizing curriculum into, 63–65
Using Division Problems to Introduce Decimals lesson, 284–85
Using Graphs to Build Understanding of Fractions lesson, 273–75
Using Graphs to Build Understanding of Percents lesson, 295–96
Uyeda, Dee, 187–89

Variables, uses of, 147–48
Vocabulary, math
    mathematical, as differing from common meanings, 42–43
    posting math, 40–41
    purpose of teaching, 43
    strategies for teaching, 43–44
    teaching, 42–44

Warehouse Problem, The (Menu Activity), 300
"We can" attitude, 51
What Percent Is Shaded? lesson, 294–95
What's the Record? (Activity), 99
Where Does 100 Land? (Activity), 165
Who Ate More? lesson, 277–78
"Why" of arithmetic
    applying to new tasks, 185
    difficulty of assessing, 184
Wipeout (Menu Activity), 282

Word cues, 14–15
Word problems
    introducing addition and subtraction with, 199–200
    multiplication and division, 378–79
    real-life, 16–17
    requiring thinking beyond traditional problems, 16–17
    routine, 200
    teaching computation skills with, 13–15
    value of, 199
$1.00 Word Riddle Book, The (Burns), 17
Wraparound (Activity), 81, 307
Writing
    assessment through written work, 48–49
    assignments, categories of, 38–40
    assistance, giving, 41
    goals of writing in math class, 38
    incorporating writing into instruction, 38–41
    prompts, starting writing assignments with, 41
    sharing, 41
    strategies for incorporating, 40–41
    variety of assignments, 38–40
Writing in Math Class (Burns), 48
Writing to Learn (Zinsser), 38

X-O Problem, The (Activity), 99, 315–17

Yarn Shapes (Activity), 82
Yarn Shapes (Menu Activity), 205
Your Choice Tic-Tac-Toe (Activity), 137
Your Height in Money (Activity), 80

0–99 Chart
    activity, 163
    versus the 1–100 Chart, use of, 371
    patterns lesson, 213–14
Zinsser, William *(Writing to Learn)*, 38

Continued from copyright page.

The publisher would like to acknowledge the following resources for adapted material:

Page 114: *Pool Hall Math* lesson adapted from *Mathematics: A Human Endeavor* (Jacobs 1994).

Page 142: *A Mathematical Tug-of-War* lesson adapted from *Math for Smarty Pants* (Burns 1982).

Page 142: *Digit Place* lesson adapted from *Make It Simpler* (Meyer and Sallee 1983).

Page 208: Assessment adapted from *Mathematics Their Way* (Baratta-Lorton 1976).

Page 243: *The Factor Game* appears in *Prime Time: Factors and Multiples* (Lappan, Fey, Fitzgerald, Friel, and Phillips 1998).

Page 259: *A Long-Division Activity* appears in *50 Problem-Solving Lessons* (Burns 1996).

Page 259: Another version of *How Many Beans?* appears in *Developing Number Sense, Grades 3–6* (Bresser and Holtzman 1999).

Page 261: *Hit the Target (Version 1)* appears in *Developing Number Sense, Grades 3–6* (Bresser and Holtzman 1999).

Page 283: Assessment 4 appears in "Communicating About Fractions with Pattern Blocks" (Caldwell 1995).

Page 292: *Sense or Nonsense* lesson appears in *Problem Solving in Mathematics: In-Service Guide* (Brannan and Schaaf 1983) and is shown being taught in the video *Mathematics: For Middle School, Part 3* (Burns 1989).

Pages 294–295: *What Percent Is Shaded?* lesson adapted from *Problem Solving in Mathematics: In-Service Guide* (Brannan and Schaaf 1983).

Pages 295–296: Statistics taken from *American Averages* (Feinsilber and Mead 1980).

Page 300: The *Warehouse* problem appears in *Thinking Mathematically* (Mason, Burton, and Stacey 1982).

Pages 397–398: *Four Strikes and You're Out* lesson adapted from *Teaching Arithmetic: Addition and Subtraction, Grades 2–3* (Tank and Zolli 2001).